The Shaping of a City

ERRATA   November 19, 1976

Location   **Correction**

p. (ix), para. 2, line 3   Change "short sighted" to "shortsighted"

p. 23, ***   Oregon Iron Works, not Iron & Steel

p. 28, photo caption   Change "Couch...playground" to "Park"

p. 52, next to bottom line   Change "English" to "Scottish"

p. 73, line 11   Delete ⑩ before....It was an idle

p. 82, para. 2, line 8   Change "team" to "teamed"

p. 104, ••   **Delete**

p. 128, UPRR box, Albina Chart   Change lease date to 1887

p. 129, SS&T box, Albina Chart   Change "Wills" to "Mills"

p. 160, PRL&P box   Add merger date, 12/31/07

p. 199, para. 4, line 5   Change "taget" to "target"

p. 202, *   Change "Fannie" to Mattie" Mitchell

p. 209, last para., line 2   Change "recalls" to "recalled"

p. 251, para. 2, last line   Change "Portand" to "Portland"

p. 280, bottom line ⟩
                                  Change "Word" to "Ward"
p. 281, line 2

p. 292, para. 3, between lines   Insert "friend and St. Paul neighbor
9 and 10   would own almost one hundred billion
                                  feet"

p. 444, vote count   Change East Side "No" vote to 10,228
                                  Change total "No" vote to 16,342

p. 466, line 1   Change "lane" to "Lane"

p. 469, line 4   Change "Ainswroth" to "Ainsworth"

Index

If further errors are noted (excluding punctuation and capitalization)
please inform the publisher.

The Shaping of a City

Business and Politics in Portland, Oregon
1885 - 1915

E. Kimbark MacColl

The Georgian Press Company, Portland, Oregon
1976

Published by The Georgian Press Company
2620 S. W. Georgian Place
Portland, Oregon 97201

Cover and Title Page designed by Corinna Campbell Cioeta

Cover design based on a cartoon from the *Oregonian* of April 19, 1906

LC 76-49334

Manufactured in the United States of America

Typography and Layout by Encore Publishing Inc., Portland, Oregon

Printed by Durham & Downey, Inc., Portland, Oregon

Published November, 1976

To Leeanne,
my enthusiastic and supportive partner
and Sam,
my everpresent companion and watchdog

Contents

Introduction

Some years ago I swore that I would never attempt to write a history of Portland, but a number of subsequent events caused me to change my mind. Over the past decade I have developed an intense interest in the physical shaping of cities. After an extensive amount of reading and research, reinforced by travel and personal experience as a citizen advisor involved in some downtown planning projects, I came to the unoriginal conclusion that the political process, incorporating various inputs and pressures, has usually been the crucial factor in determining the shape of a city. For much of our history, at least, the political process has served the requirements of the free enterprise system.

In this year of the Bicentennial many Americans have increasingly come to realize the extent to which most of the serious problems facing urban America are the costly consequences of short sighted past decisions and weak political leadership. Our inability, as political units, to resolve many of these issues in behalf of the public interest stems from the fact that we are prisoners of traditional habits of mind and action that today appear neither legitimate nor relevant.

In an attempt to provide some insight into the nature of these problems I decided to undertake an examination of the historical background of four topics of growing current interest: (1) the requirements of effective political leadership, (2) the sources of corporate economic and political power, (3) the business-political ethic, and (4) the need for land use planning. My particular focus is upon the relationships existing between many of Portland's business and political personalities who were active at the turn of this century. Politics and business were closely intertwined activities, with most of the important public affairs conducted on a personal level. Of special concern is the extent to which these relationships produced decisions of lasting effect — decisions which, for better or for worse, shaped the basic physical structure of the city.

I chose the period 1885-1915 because it was the time in Portland's history that witnessed the city's most explosive growth: 154 percent in physical size and 300 percent in population. It was also the era in which the reins of power were tightly held by the businessman-politician. During this 30 year period the old family control peaked and then gradually declined, giving way to an emerging new class of merchants, larger and more diverse than the old group but just as eager and hungry for political power, commercial profit and personal gain. This development accompanied a radical alteration in the established business market structure. Local owners of corporate property sold out to giant, absentee owned conglomerates that assumed the sacred rights of traditional individual property ownership. The new corporate and bank managers entered the political arena with an even greater passion than their predecessors.

In a narrow sense, this book is a story of how "the system" operated. In a broader vein, it is an examination of the values and symbols that guided and dominated business-political relationships in 1900 and that continue to dominate many of these relationships even today. Attention will be directed to the social structure of Portland; to the network of relationships existing between the business leaders themselves, and between the business leadership and those political leaders who were part of the same social strata. Not all districts of the city have been equally covered by any means. Time and source restrictions have limited the scope of the study. Downtown Portland and the west side of the Willamette River have received more detailed treatment because most of the decision makers lived and worked in that area.

The organization of a massive amount of material within narrowly defined historical periods posed a number of problems. The end result is a story that is largely episodic. The narrative action does not really develop momentum until chapter IV. The first chapter presents a general sweep of the whole period with some attention given to later consequences of earlier decisions. Chapter II introduces the major personalities who were in firm control by 1885, and chapter III describes the sources of their wealth and power. The Appendix contains a variety of organizational charts and economic data; law firms, corporate and bank officers; and the corporate family tree of the intermarried Corbett, Failing and Ladd relatives.

I wish to thank those members of my family who have aided and assisted me during the past two years, especially my wife Leeanne and my son Kim who gave me the benefit of his legal training. I owe a great debt to my manuscript readers who provided invaluable criticism and helpful suggestions: Terrence O'Donnell, Sabine Wild and Mrs. John C. Watson. Of course these good people cannot be blamed for the final product, but I did incorporate a number of their recommendations. I want to thank Jan Henry, the former City Archivist, for her time and valuable aid. My deepest appreciation is extended to the staffs of the Portland City Club, the University of Oregon Special Collections Library and the Oregon Historical Society for their gracious hospitality and assistance. To many venerable Portlanders, too numerous to mention here but whose names are listed in the bibliography, I express my sincere gratitude for giving me their valuable time for personal interviews. Finally I wish to acknowledge the skill and dedication of both my typesetter and layout director Eleanor Malin of Encore Publishing Co. and my manuscript typist Joyce Chambers, two energetic professionals whose enthusiasm for the subject matter sustained a weary spirit.

—E. Kimbark MacColl

October 1976

Lownsdale's Map.

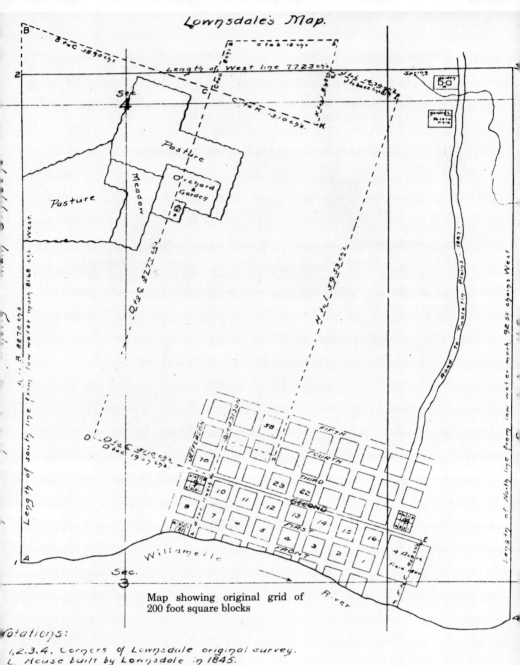

Map showing original grid of
200 foot square blocks

Notations:

1,2,3,4. Corners of Lownsdale original survey.
L. House built by Lownsdale in 1845.
M Houses built by Lownsdale in 1846 and 1847.
O Lownsdale's residence 1854.
Blocks colored red on map (being Blocks bet Washington St. & Jefferson St & 2nd St. & River) laid out by Pettigrove in 1845.
Blocks colored yellow on map (being Blocks bet. Stark St. & Madison St. & 2nd St & 3rd St.) laid out by Pettigrove in 1846.
Blocks colored brown on map (being Block 70 & Blocks bet. Jefferson St. & Stark St. & bet 3rd & 5th Sts.) laid out Feb. 1850.
18. Residence of Coffin from Aug. 20, 1850 to Feb 1851.
22. Coffin's residence from 4th of March to 16 April, 1852.
Block 9, Lot 3, Residence of Coffin from April 1852 to May 1856.
58. Chapman's residence from Fall of 1850 to Sept 1853.
A B C D E F. Boundaries of Coffin's Claim as filed by him, Aug. 19, 1852. Coffins other claim filed same day, the same as above except line from river up Madison St to 2nds
D.a.b.J.I H.G.c Corners of Chapman's Claim, filed. Aug 20, 1852.

TITLE and TRUST COMPANY

Chapter I

A Wide Angle View

From the time of its incorporation in 1851, Portland was a cumulative growth city. Although the founding fathers did lay out an initial grid of 200 foot square blocks, thus setting the pattern for future downtown development, much of the growth was by chance rather than by design. As with the majority of Western American cities, Portland grew by means of the gradual accretion of individual entrepreneurs and by the rapid and often disorderly accumulations of speculators.

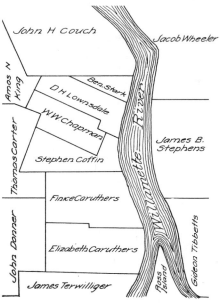

PLAT OF LAND CLAIMS COVERED BY THE CITY

By the mid-1870's Portland had achieved an enviable reputation as a handsome city, but mostly because of its unique natural setting. Recalling his first day in Portland during July of 1874, railroad magnate Henry Villard* was later to write:

"I had heard much praise . . . of Portland, but its attractiveness went beyond my anticipations. [From Marquam Hill] The grand panorama I saw spread out before me from that height with the three snow-clad giants of Mt. Hood, Mt. St. Helens, and Mt. Adams clearly visible in their mighty splendor, seemed to me one of the finest sights I had ever enjoyed. The city . . . appeared to con-

*Villard will be introduced and discussed in chapter 3.

2

tain . . . an unusual number of large and solid business buildings and handsome private residences. There was also a great deal of activity in the streets and on the river, indicating thriving business; altogether, Portland was surpassed in few respects by any other city in the United States that I knew."[1]

Historian John Fiske likened Portland to a New England town and its residents comparable to "New England folks."[2] One visitor after another commented about the quality and comfort of the homes.[3] The public facilities, however, left much to be desired. The *Oregonian* in 1889 bemoaned the unsanitary conditions in the sewers and gutters, "the most filthy city in the Northern States." [4] The city's extensive "home-made" wooden sidewalks provoked the *West Shore* to report: "The new sidewalks put down this year are a disgrace to a Russian village."[5]

In 1891, Portland was observed by *Oregonian* editor Harvey Scott to be a "well balanced, civic and social organism"[6] with few of the problems faced by the large Eastern cities: minimum geographic social segregation, no dirty industry, little permanent unemployment, and few unassimilated immigrants except for the Chinese colony.* As a visitor from New Orleans had written in 1888: "The muddy current of common immigration flowing across the Atlantic

---

*Oregon had the second largest Chinese colony in the United States in 1880 (9,515). California had the largest (75,000). The year of 1886 was rough for Portland's Chinese, especially in March, 1886. Raids, beatings, arson fires were common. Labor was the main culprit. Public animosity was inflamed by politicians such as Sylvester Pennoyer who ran for Governor, and won, on an anti-Chinese plank. Oregon's U.S. Senator John H. Mitchell gave demagogic speeches on the Senate floor.

Front Street, 1876

from Europe drops its silt on the Atlantic slope and in the valley of the Mississippi. This raw, un-American material is too heavy with poverty and ignorance to reach Oregon."[7] Practically no slum type dwellings existed outside of the North End — the "White Chapel" district — that was viewed primarily as a transient area where vice and gambling, although illegal, were accepted as normal activities as long as they were not too openly disreputable.

On the West side of the river the city was compact except for the wealthier neighborhoods developing in the hills and on the fringes of downtown. Even after the merger of 1891, when the built-up areas on the East side were consolidated with old Portland on the West side, the city of 62,000 encompassed only 26 square miles, (about 32 percent of its 1976 size) with a low population density of 2100 per square mile. Writing in 1893, the Rev. H. K. Hines commented that Portland was "so new, and yet so old."

"Approaching it by the river but little can be seen of it but a long, low range of docks and wharves by the side of which are lying scores of steamers, or before them are anchored many ships of the sea. The impression is disappointing. The steep hills to the west seem almost to impend over the city, which appears to rest on a narrow shelf of land at their base, but a little elevated above the tide. As one steps ashore and rises into the streets, and looks up and down and out, between the long rows of stores and hotels, rising for six or ten stories, of massive form and splendid architecture, and sees the ceaseless stream of comers and goers, the flashing by of hundreds of electric cars, and listens to the ceaseless roar of business, the illusion of the first impression vanishes, and he awakens to find himself in the heart of a great commercial emporium."[8]

4

Morrison Street, East of Second — 1889.

Portland prided itself on its unique character, molded in part by this thriving commercial life. It was a city of broad based wealth (one national study claimed it to be the third richest in the world in proportion to population),[9] a development due largely to the character and background of its pioneers.* The influence of the small town in New England, Pennsylvania, New Jersey, New York, and Ohio; the particular personal traits of the German-Jewish, Scottish and English immigrants; the conservative financial practices which eschewed credit for cash; the pursuit of sound investment instead of risky speculation; a commitment to public education; a concern for cultural matters; a dislike of ostentation; all blended together to give Portland a special quality of affluence, tempered by civility and good taste.**

---

*Rated as wealthiest, Frankfurt, Germany; second, Hartford, Connecticut.

**According to ex-Governor Oswald West, the birthplaces of Oregon's pioneers were as follows: 6% New England and Mid-Atlantic; 50% Mid-west; 33% South; 11% foreign.[10] As for Portland, of the 18 wealthiest families who were to remain after 1891, four came from New England; five from New York, New Jersey, Pennsylvania; three from Ohio; two from Scotland; one each from Iowa, Maryland, Germany, Switzerland. Nine came from small towns, none out of poverty and one from an upper income family. The sources of earned wealth were, in rank: shipping and transportation, banking, merchandising, real estate.

5

What was not unique about Portland was the fact that it was a corrupt city, corrupted in part by the very success and power of its wealthiest pioneer families and some of their newly arrived associates. Below the veneer of respectability was a system of dirty politics in which the "plutocrats" would not deign to soil their hands, at least directly. Vice, gambling and liquor were profitable enterprises, especially to those members of Portland's establishment who owned the property but who did not feel any personal responsibility for its use. As the late New York Rabbi Stephen Wise was to comment in his *Challenging Years*, reflecting back on his early rabbinate in Portland:

> "I came into closer touch with the things out of which grew lawless power of civic corruption. It was the union of gambling and liquor interests plus organized prostitution, which, in collusion with city officials and above all with the police department, poisoned and corroded the life of the city. The hold of these forces upon the city's life was fully known to the acquiescent and rather cynical population, which seemed to take it for granted that organized vice was entitled to no small part in managing the city and its affairs."[11]

The major corruption afflicting both Portland and Oregon stemmed from the inability or unwillingness of the business-political leadership to distinguish between two antagonistic interests — the public and the private. The granting of undue privileges to any person, group, or corporation was a corrupt practice, warned the renowned United States Prosecutor Francis Heney in 1905 when he told some of Portland's eminent lawyers and business leaders: "You men corrupt all you touch."[12] Heney cited the activities of the vice interests and the railroads as the major sources of corruption. The system was the demon. It could corrupt any individual, no matter how sincere, distinguished, or personally honest. One could become corrupted by association, by pressure, or by indifference to the ethical distinction between means and ends in human behavior. The protection of private interests and access to power and influence were strong motives. Henry Reed, an acute observer of the Portland scene for over 50 years, spoke to the same issue raised by Heney when he said: "Business in this world is not done according to the Golden Rule . . . Businessmen . . . (in general) . . . adopt that course which offers them the greatest profits or the greatest satisfaction."[13]

6

To most citizens, the purpose of city government, apart from the customary attempts to preserve a modicum of law, order, and health, was to serve economic development. This was a legitimate tradition in keeping with the American credo. It was only natural, therefore, that those men who achieved material success through the free enterprise system would receive public acclaim and be given community — especially political — leadership roles.

In the 30 year period under review, most of the public decisions reached by the Portland City council were in reality compromises between competing private economic interests. Although the city was over 80 percent Republican in registration, few of the decisions were determined on the basis of party affiliation alone; most were arrived at by personal agreement among friends regardless of party. Portland, as with the rest of Oregon, had long experienced a tradition of personalized politics. The decisions reached were based more on the personal relationships involved than on the intrinsic merits of the issues.

The introduction of the statewide direct primary in 1904 and the preferential voting system of the new city charter in 1913* tended to diminish the strength of party discipline. The Initiative, which together with the Referendum had been approved in 1902, was instrumental in the passage in 1908 of a law that required all candidates for the state legislature to commit themselves formally in advance of the general election as to whether or not they would be bound to support the U.S. Senate candidate receiving the largest number of votes in that election. This change in traditional political procedure weakened party loyalty even further. Thus, the power of the local political machines was greatly diminished by 1915. How else can one explain the election of Democrats Harry Lane as Mayor (1905-1909), and as U.S. Senator (1913); George Chamberlain as Governor (1903-1909), and as U.S. Senator (1909), and Oswald West as Governor (1911-1915)? All three played important roles in Portland's political life while they held office. They were rare public leaders who clearly saw the distinction between public and private interests. They were products as well as initiators of the reform reaction associated with the Progressive Era.

---

*The direct primary replaced the party convention as the method of selecting candidates, the election being held in May or June. In the preferential system, those candidates receiving the largest number of votes won election to the City Commission, on a non-partisan basis.

Lane, West, and Chamberlain were genuine public servants — leaders who told the people the truth as they saw it. The city councils and legislatures on the other hand were composed of middle to upper middle class citizens with narrow geographic and economic concerns. They could be expected to follow the paths of least resistance, normally taking their cues from special interests. The nature and composition of the city council did change over the 30 year period. The direct influence and participation of the city's elite in political life diminished, but until 1913 the votes were assured by pressure, favor and sometimes bribery. The reforms of the Progressive Era were primarily technical in nature. Although they did clean up the city council chambers they produced no fundamental changes in the business-political power relationship.

With the exception of Mayor Harry Lane, none of Portland's leaders during the period 1885-1915 foresaw the long-term consequences of many of the political and business decisions that led subsequently to much of today's urban disorder and physical blight. As with most of America's urban development, Portland's growth was — and still is — dominated by the concept of the sanctity of private land ownership. Private property, including that held by corporations, has been considered a civil liberty, not a public or social resource. The prevailing maxim of American city growth has been "life, liberty and the pursuit of the dollar," or, as the late international city planner Constantine Doxiades put it, "human greed."[14]

Early in this century, J.P. Morgan associate George F. Baer, President of the Reading Railroad, made the classic remark about how "God, in his infinite wisdom", had "given the control of property interests of the country" to "Christian men" who proceeded to manage them. In 1910, *Oregonian* Editor Harvey Scott, an active investor in his own right, wrote on a parallel theme when he editorialized: "Every city should leave to private enterprise the active industries, on which development depends" otherwise the city will "advance to a socialistic system."[15] Also in 1910, railroad lawyer and Oregon historian Joseph Gaston accurately expressed the prevailing attitude of Portland's business leadership when he wrote: "The growth of a city does not depend so much upon its machinery of government or even upon the men who fill the public offices as upon those who foster the trade relations and promote commercial activity."[16] In retrospect, the then widely accepted truth of Gaston's statement has been borne out by historical events. Sixty-five years ago, few questioned the notion that growth and progress were synonymous.

Lewis Mumford was given scant attention when he spoke to the

Portland City Club in 1938. He admonished Oregonians for having been asleep in failing to protect their natural resources. "The Columbia land that needed to be controlled most vigorously has already been grabbed up. Certain persons are licking their chops and counting their gold,"[17] he declared, pointing to landowners who were busy making eyes at industrial leaders. Only in recent times has enlightened business leadership begun to see that a system of unrestricted economic growth might not result in progress; that it might contain the seeds of its own destruction.

No less an authority than the widely respected Victor Gruen, designer of many urban centers around the world, has written: "If one considers the magnitude of the problems we are facing and of the opportunities which a rational use of land could bring about, the question arises of whether our feudal concepts of the holiness of private land ownership can be maintained."[18] Gruen is acutely aware of the difficulties facing urban land use planning efforts today, in seeking to alter not only traditional values which are firmly held, but methods of doing business, accepted as standard practice for hundreds of years.

In a similar vein, Professor George Cabot Lodge of the Harvard Business School has recently challenged American businessmen to confront reality. The traditional ideology of the free enterprise system to which most American businessmen have long adhered is disintegrating. By their failure to recognize this change, declares Lodge, business leaders are undermining the legitimacy of their own corporations.[19] No longer should a property owner be able to do as he wishes with his own land. The purchase of property must include the purchase of obligation and responsibility to broader community needs and public purposes. Traditionally business leaders have pled for free enterprise while insisting that the government come to their defense or rescue when threatened with the pain of excessive competition or business failure. "It is interesting to note," writes Gruen, "that the stoutest fighters for completely free enterprise are charac-. teristically the ones most eager to take fullest advantage of opportunities triggered off by governmental planning or public subsidies."[20]

Americans tend to forget that private enterprise in the post Civil War era was subsidized by millions of dollars of public funds — if one equates public land grants with dollars. In addition to such benefits accorded, especially to the major western railroads, franchises were awarded by states and cities as part of an overall promotional policy to street railway and local utility companies, in many cases free of any compensation to the public. In the period from 1887-1914 for example, Portland granted 191 franchises, 50 percent of which went to the major railroads and to the Northern Pacific Terminal Company with no compensation to the city. By 1910, the Portland Railway Light and Power Company, a recipient of 43 separate franchises through various mergers, and the grandfather of the current Portland General Electric Company, was cited by the *American Banker* as a $15 million holding company, a monopoly, which was "liable to anti-trust action under the Sherman Act."[21] This public service giant was sold in 1906 to eastern investors by Portland financiers with the assistance of the state legislature and the city council. The company's history clearly reveals some contradictions inherent in the American free enterprise system. There was little public service involved *per se,* at least as a high priority goal. Although millions of dollars were invested in the company's equipment, thereby increasing its assets and enhancing its financial stature, the public interest usually followed that of the stockholders and their invested capital.

In fairness to the Portland Railway Light & Power Co. it should be noted that Portland was one of the first cities in the United States to develop a true criss-cross interurban-suburban system that was recognized as one of the most complete railway networks in the country. But the street railway division was continually cited (as were the predecessor companies) by public authorities for inadequate service and maintenance of equipment, tracks and street right-of-ways. Safety devices, such as bumpers to protect pedestrians, were installed only under extreme public pressure. The public interest was well served, however, by the excellent street lighting system of the light and power division, even though the city council complained on numerous occasions about the excessive rates charged to municipal operations.

The historical record proves that it is a mistake to accept the notion that what benefits the electric or railway company automatically confers benefits on society at large. The alleged self-corrective mechanism of the free enterprise system has not always worked. People buy goods and services — and municipal government must be included as a purchaser — with injurious consequences for them and for society as well. The price has been high at the public's expense and many permanent scars have resulted. Hundreds of acres of Portland's streets were vacated free to transportation and associated corporations. Tracks were laid indiscriminately to suit the corporate interests, and disorder, inefficiency and physical blight resulted. As one public report stated in 1912: "The present conditions in the center of the City are the result of rapid growth uncontrolled by considerations of public obligation."[22]

In the 12 year period up to 1885, 24 separate wharf permits on the levee* along the southwest bank of the Willamette River had been awarded to private interests by council action. In 1885, the legislature granted to the Portland & Willamette Valley R.R. the last strip of the public levee which the Southern Pacific R.R. acquired in 1887. By 1910, over 50 percent of the city's waterfront on both sides of the river, including most of the larger docks, was owned by the railroads and the Northern Pacific Terminal Company. There was no public dock. Voter reaction to this condition resulted in the creation of the Portland Commission of Public Docks by charter amendment in 1910. The commission was given bonding authority and the power of condemnation.** By the end of World War I, many of the remain-

*Public rights to the levee were ruled invalid by court decision on March 30, 1862.
**The city was granted the authority by the voters to buy back the levee, but legal entanglements and costs precluded any action for some years to follow.

ing private dock facilities were in a state of advanced decay, thus presenting an ugly barrier to public use and enjoyment of a natural resource which today is in the second stage of recapture at enormous public expense. Also by the war's end, private shipyards had been built south of the main dock area, to be converted in subsequent years to ship junk yards which today constitute one of the worst blights on the city landscape. By 1915, the lowland to the northwest of the docks and adjacent to the river was almost entirely filled in and carved up by the railroads and the oil companies. This was the Guild's Lake area, the site of the world renowned 1905 Lewis and Clark Exposition.

During the first decade of this century, Portland grew rapidly. Its population increased by 129 percent to over 207,200; the geographical boundaries were enlarged by 33 percent to almost 50 square miles, while the population density, although expanding, remained at a low figure of 4300 people per square mile, about 40 percent of the national average for cities reaching inception in 1891.* The city was spreading out into the suburbs where the land was less expensive. Peripheral populations were captured by annexation. Mass transit made it possible for wage workers to buy and build for a few thousand dollars, and live comfortably "under their own vine and fig tree."[23] Close-in land was much more costly. For example, a one-quarter block on the edge of downtown Portland that was bought for $13,000 in 1898 was sold for $125,000 eight years later.[24] Many of the owners of the innumerable street railway franchises, at least in the earlier years, were themselves the owners, platters and promoters of the larger suburban tracts that became annexed to the city.

Unfortunately for the future, there was no official (public) planning and zoning to guide this expansion. Attention in planning was given only to the private advantage to be gained by conforming to a plan that had little, if any, reference to future city needs. On the East side of Portland little regard was shown for the sites. They were merely an assemblage of multiple units, platted on the typical grid. Most of the homes that were constructed had a similar appear-

*The date of inception was the year in which the central city first reached 50,000 inhabitants. Throughout all of its history Portland has maintained a low population density. Its current p.d. of 4600 is only 300 more than the 1910 figure, about 75% of the national (1970) average for cities of the same inception date.

N.E. Hollywood District

ance. The suburban tracts, or railway communities, encouraged a process of decentralization by promoting the development of neighborhood shopping areas. The old balance of land uses and mixes, characteristic of West and East Portland before 1890, broke down. The city became separated into clearly defined lower and upper class neighborhoods with excessive congestion in the former, a condition produced by crowding multiple and single-family dwellings into limited areas without regard for yard space or adequate ventilation. The new neighborhoods further encouraged a type of residential segregation that led to another form of mixed land use. The areas around the neighborhood shopping centers, and the arterials connecting them, became increasingly commercial. Industry, on the other hand, tended to place itself close to the railroads and the riverbanks where easy access to transportation was available. But there was no public plan to guide this development; it just happened.

Throughout this period of expansion, little concern was shown for parks or recreational facilities. Twice as much money was being spent on private investment in saloon properties* as was being in-

*Liquor license income from over 500 saloons produced one-half of the general city revenue fund in 1900.

vested by the public in parks for which Portland was literally starved until well after World War I. In the late 1840's the five founding fathers* had shown amazing foresight when they agreed to establish a green strip across the entire length of the young city, from south to north. Unfortunately, the Park Blocks, as they were to be known, never came to full realization. The failure of Daniel Lownsdale's widow to sign a deed, an adverse court decision, the timidity of the city council, and the recalcitrance of Benjamin Stark, all combined to keep eight blocks in private hands and out of the public domain.

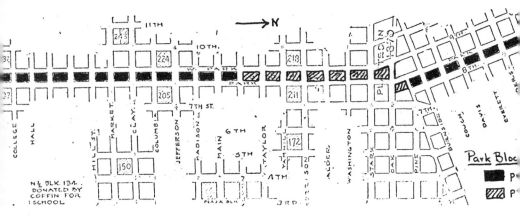

In 1871, the city had purchased 40 acres of wooded hillside in west Portland from wealthy pioneer Amos King for $800 an acre. Commenting upon this event with unusual prescience, Harvey Scott wrote: "It may be suggested that forty acres is very small for anything really fine. Let six hundred be added to it. A good piece of land along the river, or perhaps Ross Island; and a square mile or two on the East side should also be secured before values become too exorbitant."[25] City Park did become the foundation for a later and much larger development known today as Washington Park. In1897, Scotsman Donald MacLeay, successful businessman and banker, donated 107 acres in Northwest Portland in commemoration of Queen Victoria's 60th year of reign. By 1900 the city owned less than 200 acres of park property, placing it well behind Seattle, Tacoma and the major cities of California. Most of the park land was located in one area of the city, nearest to the wealthiest homeowners. One

*See the plat of original land claims on page 1.

critical public report noted that "it's a long climb from the working quarters . . . . Only those who have trees, lawns and roses of their own are within easy walking distance . . . . It is easy to forget the North End and the Eastside in planning a city park."[26] For the very poor, the cost of a roundtrip streetcar ride for a whole family to enjoy City Park was prohibitive. Few members of the business-political establishment seemed to recognize the social truth that the poor much more than the rich needed to have the countryside brought to their doors.*

By 1915 geographical social segregation had become a fact of life, with the wealthier families escaping from in-town to secluded enclaves on the fringes of the city. Over 60 percent of Portland's population was now living on the East side of the river, although the West side remained the heart of the city, with "the highest land value, most intense land use, and most productive pedestrian traffic." The opening in 1913 of the Broadway Bridge, Portland's fourth, "caused the greatest shifting of land values and business ever seen in a city of Portland's size in a short time."[27] The core of the retail trade moved west from Third Street to Broadway (Seventh) and the north-south boundary widened from Stark to Morrison. The West side was to remain the administrative, financial and professional center of the city, with the core, less than one-half mile from the city's point of origin, containing the spots of highest land values in the city.

Six thousand automobiles were already in use, the major traffic arteries were already paved, and traffic jams were already common on the bridges and at the main intersections. Street railway use had diminished by 12 percent.** The local City Beautiful Movement attempted to gain public support for the Greater Portland Plan of 1912 — the Bennett Plan — which incorporated wide park-like boulevards with a more open, publicly owned waterfront, but the real estate and business interests successfully emasculated it.***

------

*In his gift to the city MacLeay stipulated that the proceeds from the sale of any cut timber were to go to St. Vincent and Good Samaritan Hospitals. Also, in constructing any improvements, the city was to provide "a conveyance for carrying patients from the hospitals through the park during the summer."

**It would rise again during W.W. I, peaking in 1919.

***A public referendum in November, 1912 approved the plan in principle, by a meager vote of 16,202 to 7,996, but no action was forthcoming for lack of appropriated funds and an equal lack of legal enforcement power. The Bennett Plan recommended doubling the existing park acreage.

Thus, by 1915, the basic shape of the city was set. Over 80 percent of the 1975 city boundary limit was reached. The consequences of automobile idolization, with its attendant frustrations and strip development ugliness, were not apparent as yet. And the freeways would not make their appearance until the late 1950's.*

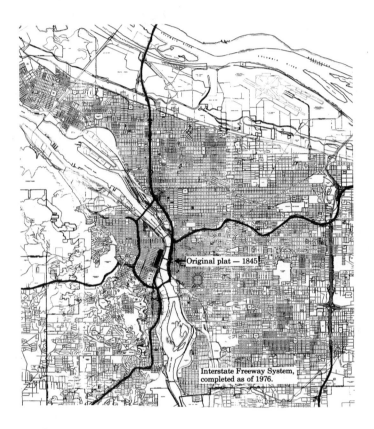

Original plat — 1845

Interstate Freeway System, completed as of 1976.

*See Appendix L.

Chapter II

The Early Investors

1.

Portland's initial fortunes were made in river transportation, banking and merchandising. The city's location at the confluence of the Willamette and Columbia Rivers in the very heart of a region enormously rich in natural resources preordained its future growth and wealth. Being at the head of deep-sea navigation it could take full advantage of an ancient maxim, that commerce seeks its most inland point of distribution.

The source of Portland's earliest fortunes was the Oregon Steam Navigation Company,* organized in 1860** by a group of rugged ship captains, owners, and engineers who wanted to merge their competing river transportation interests into a monopoly. The company cashed in on the rich placer gold mines discovered in the Territories of Idaho, Eastern Washington and Western Montana, widely scattered areas that were all hooked together by navigable tributary water routes that flowed into the lower Columbia River Basin. "The Oregon Steam Navigation Company was the financial wonder of its day and age," noted one of the original owners, 87 year old Jacob Kamm, in 1910.[1] The Oregon correspondent to the San Francisco *Post* reported in the late 1870's: "If there is a better thing in the United States, I haven't heard of it."[2]

---

*Cited hereafter as the OSN.
**The company was not incorporated in Oregon until 1862.

The OSN brought great wealth to five of the original twenty-two shareholders: Captain John C. Ainsworth, president of the company; Jacob Kamm, chief engineer; R.R. Thompson, shipowner; Simeon G. Reed, merchant and investor; and William S. Ladd, banker and financial advisor. Capitalized originally at $2 million, it was worth over $5 million eight years later.* Starting a trend which became traditional in Portland's history, the local stockholders, wishing to liquidate their investments and bank their profits, sold out to eastern financiers in April 1872. A three-quarter interest in the OSN was peddled to Jay Cooke, the Philadelphia investment banker and underwriter of Northern Pacific Railroad bonds.** But when Cooke went bankrupt in 1873, several of the original group of Portland stockholders bought back from Cooke 55 percent of the stock for $13 a share, thus reacquiring control of the company and still netting about $250,000 apiece in the process.[4] To protect their monopoly over all the water traffic on the lower Columbia River, the owners purchased land right-of-ways along the south shore of the river and these would prove to be invaluable in later transcontinental railroad construction.

Six years after reassuming direction of the OSN, the owners sold out to Henry Villard with the largest shareholders each receiving about $800,000 from the sale. Villard merged the OSN into a newly formed corporation, the Oregon Railway and Navigation Company,*** with some of the Portland investors acquiring large blocks of stock in the new venture. This story will be recounted in greater detail in Chapter 3.

2.

Of the group of Portlanders who had been the heaviest investors[5] in the OSN and who had been paid off handsomely Captain John C.

---

*In October, 1871, Ainsworth, Ladd, Thompson and Reed were sued in U.S. Court for fraud, the famous "Oregonian" case. Settled out of court, the facts were established that the big four, by duplicity, defrauded a number of original OSN stockholders by purchasing their shares through a blind at a depreciated value. The recently constructed ship, "Oregonian," was not recorded as an OSN asset. When it was later sold to the Ben Holladay interests, the proceeds went directly to the big four who by that point owned a large portion of the OSN stock between them.[3]

**The OSN investors received $1.5 million, one-half in Northern Pacific Railroad bonds.

***Cited hereafter as the OR&N.

Ainsworth, the former president, took his profits and started the Ainsworth Bank in 1881.* Within two years he left for Oakland, California where he was to increase his fortune and live out his life, relinquishing management of his Oregon properties to agents and later to his son, John C. Ainsworth. Another early investor, Robert R. Thompson** soon retired to San Francisco, leaving behind sizeable real estate holdings.

Simeon G. Reed, John C. Ainsworth and Robert R. Thompson

Simeon G. Reed*** remained in Portland until late 1891, associated with William Ladd in numerous enterprises, investing in mining stocks, cattle and horse breeding operations and real estate. Sometime before his death in 1895 at Pasadena, California, Reed had apparently discussed the founding of some sort of educational institute in Portland with his wife and his former minister, Dr. Thomas Lamb Eliot of the First Unitarian Church, but no provision was actually made in his will for such a bequest.

---

*The Ainsworth Bank became the Ainsworth National Bank in 1885; it was merged with the United States National Bank in 1902, and son John C. Ainsworth became President of the USNB. Capt. Ainsworth (1822-1893) was born in Springboro, Ohio; an orphan, he went to work at thirteen.

**(1820-1908). Born in Pennsylvania. He owned most of the property on Jefferson Street between 11th and 13th Avenues, and the block that later housed the Multnomah Hotel.

***(1830-1895). Born in East Abbington, Massachusetts.

Simeon G. Reed Mansion — S.W. First between Montgomery & Harrison.

"When Mrs. Reed died in 1904, some nine years after her husband, it was found that she had in her will provided for establishing an institution of learning having for its object the increase and diffusion of practical knowledge among the citizens of Portland . . . to be named and known as the Reed Institute."[6] Dr. Eliot's dream was eventually fulfilled in 1911 with the opening of Reed College.*

Jacob Kamm** and William Ladd were to remain in Portland for the rest of their lives. Kamm, the Swiss born former chief engineer of the OSN, was to outlive all of his associates, spending his remaining years supervising his banking and real estate investments. He purchased 14 acres outside of the then western city limits in the late 1860's and in 1872 built one of Portland's handsomest homes. Today, though in a state of disrepair, it is considered the finest mansard roofed residence still standing.***

---

*Upon Mrs. Reed's death in 1904, the Reed Estate was valued at $1,884,966.[7] Dr. Eliot, a distant cousin of President Charles W. Eliot of Harvard, was the son of the founder of Washington University in St. Louis, William Greenleaf Eliot.

**(1823-1912). Kamm designed the first steamship to sail the Willamette River.

***Currently the site of Lincoln High School. The Kamm house, built in the French Second Empire Style, was moved in the early 1950's.[8]

Kamm Mansion — site of Lincoln H.S.

3.

In many respects, William Sargent Ladd* fit the prototype of the successful "self-made man in America" image.[9] He was born into a family of average means and raised in a small Vermont town, became a serious student through public school and was teaching in a village academy at 19. Like many of his associates, he was attracted to California during the Gold Rush but ended up traveling north to Portland in search of wider horizons. "Importers of and dealers in Wines and Liquors" read the advertisement for W.S. Ladd & Co. at 42 Front Street. Ladd grossed over $2,000 in the first four months of trade.[10] The next year he went into silent partnership** with an old Vermont schoolmate, Charles E. Tilton who resided in San Francisco.[11] Also that year he was joined by

---

*(1826-1893). Born in Holland, Vermont.
**Tilton invested $2,839 in cash and goods; Ladd $2,500 in cash.

Simeon Reed who came from similar New England roots and had recently arrived in Portland. Reed acted as clerk, handling customer sales. According to one account: "These two thrifty gentlemen got their start in the liquor business. . . . Ladd, it appears, attended to the wholesale end. . . . Sim was the best dressed bartender in early day Portland."[12]

W.S. Ladd

In 1853, Ladd moved his business to 163 Front Street where he had constructed the first brick building in Portland. For the eighteen months ending in December 1854, Ladd grossed $82,316 in cash.[13] The previous year he had broadened out the line of wares to general personal items and groceries. In 1859 he took Simeon Reed into partnership and formed Ladd, Reed & Company. For some time Ladd had been loaning money to his customers at 1 percent per month, so it was not long before he had sufficient capital to open Portland's first bank, along with his silent San Francisco partner, C.E. Tilton. Ladd & Tilton was a private institution as state banks were thought to be disallowed by the Oregon Constitution. In 1880 the Oregon Supreme Court was to rule that this was not the case; that it had been the intent of the framers to prevent the issuance of paper money banknotes, not to prohibit state banking institutions *per se*. Beginning with an initial capitalization of $50,000, the bank grew rapidly, assisted along the way by the infusion of new capital from his uncle, Stephen Mead of New London, Connecticut.* In 1869, Ladd, Tilton and Mead each invested $200,000 in the bank. By 1875, each share was worth over $1 million.** By 1910, 17 years after William Ladd's death, the assets of the Ladd & Tilton Bank would grow to $14.7 million, making it the second largest bank in Portland.

Ladd & Tilton Bank — S.W. First & Stark.

Besides the store and the OR&N Co., Ladd associated with Reed in other enterprises: The Ladd & Reed Farm Co., the Oregon Iron & Steel Co. (incorporated 1882);*** the Oregon Telegraph Co. (incorporated 1862); and the Auburn Canal Co. (incorporated 1863). Both men invested heavily in real estate. They were noted for being quick to take advantage of their opportunities. In October 1865, Reed wrote to Ladd's brother in California: "Real Estate is changing hands quite lively here and prices are advancing. The purchasers are not newcomers, but in nearly every instance are old residents."[14] Six years later

---

*Ladd was to be trustee of his uncle's estate after his death in 1875. In addition to the bank, Ladd invested over $164,000 from the Mead Estate in various Portland enterprises and real estate.

**Tilton was bought out in 1880, to be succeeded by W.S. Ladd's son, William M. Ladd. W.S. Ladd also organized the Ladd & Bush Bank of Salem in 1868.

***A predecessor company, Oregon Iron & Steel Works, was incorporated by Ladd and Reed in 1862.

Reed noted to a friend that he had purchased over 7,000 acres of the finest improved farming lands in the Willamette Valley for $17.50 an acre and that good timber land was available at $2 to $5 an acre.[15]

William Ladd's character has generated conflicting appraisal: cited as both generous and miserly, he was seen by some to be a cautious and conservative investor, and by others an adventurous and speculative trader. The record is clear that he built his bank on investments in business enterprises over which he gained control — the Portland Flouring Mills and the Oregon Iron & Steel Co. to name just two. He created his vast real estate holdings out of forfeited mortgages and defaulted loans. A notation in Judge Deady's diary of May, 1871 implied that Ladd was a bit of a "Shylock"* on debts owed him. "I wish," wrote Deady, "rich people were always generous, but probably if they were they would not be rich."[17] A few months later, Deady commented: "The Ladds are growing more luxurious and more sumptuous every year."[18] In the long run, much of Ladd's accumulated wealth was the result of wise selection of properties, careful management and patience.** The period just prior to 1885 witnessed rapid growth in real estate values. In a letter to Judge Deady, Ladd wrote: "Business is better this fall [November, 1881] than ever heretofore. Real Estate has been, since Mr. Villard's friendly visit,*** booming, particularly in the Couch Lake [site of the proposed Northern Pacific Terminal — the present Union Station] and river frontage down as far as Swan Island,"[19] which Simeon Reed and two others had just bought. The price of land was running at $500 per front foot on the river. By 1891, Ladd's holdings would be increasing in value by 20 percent per month. Over 400 acres of property in the current Laurelhurst tract which he had

---

*The case of Colburn Barrell is illustrative. Barrell had given Ladd his first drink and a new pair of shoes when he walked down the gangplank into Barrell's saloon in 1851. Barrell was too generous, however, and found himself short of cash in 1877. Ladd loaned him $3850, with Barrell putting up his last 13 acres as collateral. Barrell assumed it to be a mortgage. Ladd recorded it as a demand note which was called one year later. After 15 years of litigation, Barrell and his crippled wife were tossed out of their home onto the sidewalk and the house was burned to the ground. Thus ended the career of a Mayflower descendant and the founder of Portland's historic Lone Fir Cemetery. Barrell's grandfather, Joseph, a wealthy Charlestown, Mass. merchant, was one of three sponsors of Capt. Gray's voyage to the Northwest in 1792.[16]

**Stories were legend about Ladd's eccentric habits of thrift. He would reply to a letter sent to him by writing in between the lines of the letter and then mail it back. He would also slice open envelopes and use the opened inner side for letter paper.

***To be discussed in chapter 3.

acquired in 1874 for $20 an acre were to be sold in 1909 for almost $5,000 an acre.

W.S. Ladd Mansion — site of the Oregonian Building.

William Ladd's ambitions transcended business. At the age of only 28 he was elected mayor. Although he was occasionally mentioned as a possible gubernatorial candidate he never again involved himself directly in political office. His presence was, however, keenly felt by many an officeholder in subsequent years. During the last decade of his life, his physical activity was curtailed by a growing paralysis in his legs. Mentally he was as alert as ever. A vigorous and imaginative man of austere mien, with an air of dominance, he was a difficult person to oppose. More than one friend was to note that William Ladd could be haughty; that he had a weakness for his own judgment. In business matters his financial acumen proved sound. When he died in 1893, he left an estate estimated in excess of $10 million,* almost half of which was in 4,000 acres of undeveloped real estate in the Portland** and Tacoma, Washington regions. His influence

---

*The estimate was probably undervalued as 1893 was a depression year in which real estate values tumbled.

**Major Ladd (Mead) properties included: *Laurelhurst* (Hazel Farm, 462 acres); *Eastmoreland* (Crystal Springs Farm, almost 500 acres — 150 to City Park and Golf Course, 40 to Reed College, 275 for 127 lots); *Ladd's Addition; Westmoreland; Brooklyn District; Lake Oswego* (Golf Course, Tryon Creek Park, Dunthorpe Hts., all part of Oregon Iron & Steel property except for Dunthorpe); *Burlingame* (Terwilliger Blvd.); *Highlands* (Canyon Rd.); south of *Guild's Lake* (about 10 acres sold to American Can Co.); N.W. Cornell Rd.

was to be long felt, particularly in the Portland area, at least until 1926, when the last of his land was sold for private development.*

View from the Kamm Tower — 1888.

4.

Cicero Hunt Lewis** was born and raised until his thirteenth year in Cranbury, New Jersey.[20] When his family moved to Newburgh, New York, Lewis went to work clerking in a crockery store. Seven years later, he moved to New York City where he clerked for Chambers & Heiser, a drygoods firm. Early in 1850, he formed a partnership in New York with Lucius Allen, for the purpose of engaging in business in Portland. After three months in San Francisco, he arrived in June of 1850 and opened his grocery store on Front and West "B" (Burnside) Streets. Before the decade was out, Lewis had expanded his business into the largest wholesale grocery house on

---

*Ladd's oldest son, William M., was to remain actively involved in Portland business and cultural affairs for nearly 40 years. His second son, Charles E, was also active in business, especially in mining ventures. William M.'s career will be discussed in chapter 12.
**(1826-1897)

the West Coast and had made a propitious choice in his marriage to Miss Clementine Couch, daughter of Captain John H. Couch.* His pattern of life differed from that of his close friends, Corbett and Failing, in that he was wholly absorbed in his business. His work was his pleasure and his sole recreational exercise was walking both ways to his office. Although he was a charter member of the socially exclusive Arlington Club (incorporated in 1881), he most always returned to his house for lunch. He spent his life at his desk and never went out in the evening for entertainment or the theater. "I could amuse myself no other way,"[21] he once admitted. He was walking back to his office on a Saturday afternoon when he suffered his fatal stroke. He was never known to have taken a pleasure trip, spending what remaining leisure time he had with his wife and 11 children.

C.H. Lewis

Lewis was respected for his shrewd conservatism, utmost integrity, remarkable energy and tireless attention to every detail. He was stern in his office relationships, never said good morning to his em-

---

*Captain Couch (1811-1870), the pioneer ship captain from Newburyport, Massachusetts, whose original land donation claim occupied most all of what was then North Portland (Northwest Portland today), produced 4 daughters, 22 grandchildren, and 33 great-grandchildren. In terms of size and future influence historically, the Couch clan must be considered the most significant.

ployees, and always wanted things done his way. To any merchant in whom he had confidence he would grant unlimited credit* — "the long credit" was the basis of all business. "Allen & Lewis' sales in 1864 were $800,000 — 'all on credit,' said Mr. Lewis, 'and we cannot tell how it will come out until we get our money.' "[22]

C.H. Lewis Mansion — N.W. 19th, between Glisan & Hoyt Streets. Site of Couch School playground.

Lewis never showed any interest in politics as such although he was a staunch Republican. During the last decade of his life he was to serve by appointment on the Boards of the Port of Portland and the Water Committee,** two of the most prestigious public agencies in the city. By virtue of his marriage into the extended Couch family, Lewis was to become increasingly immersed in complicated family real estate investments, most of this activity occurring during the last third of his life. In 1882, he built one of Portland's finest residences at the west end of the Couch tract which gradually became a Couch compound. C.H. Lewis had immense influence when he was

*Lewis owned one of the few large safes in the city. He stored gold for the miners who came to his store to purchase supplies.
**Also known as the Water Board.

willing to let it be used. He was a quiet man who exhibited a deep sense of loyalty in his friendships and community activities. He gave generously but with little desire for public recognition. For years he was one of the largest supporters of both Good Samaritan Hospital and Trinity Episcopal Church, by 1900 Portland's most socially prominent house of worship.

5.

In contrast to his close friend Lewis, Henry Failing's* interests were broader and more publicized. Although he was born in New York City, his family's social and cultural heritage was in the rural life of the Mohawk Valley in upper New York State.[23] Finishing his formal education at the age of 12, he went to work as an office boy in a New York City counting house, advancing to bookkeeper and accountant in the employ of a large dry goods firm owned by New York millionaire Amos Eno. In later years, Mr. Eno was to bemoan the fact that he did not offer young Failing sufficient inducement to keep him.

Henry Failing

*(1834-1898).

Failing came to Portland at the age of 17 in 1851, accompanied by his father, Josiah and brother, John. Josiah had been employed as a minor official in New York City government, but he apparently needed more income to support his growing family; thus he decided to seek greater fortune in the Oregon country. Within two years after their arrival, J. Failing & Co. was well established on Front Street and Josiah was elected mayor, preceding William Ladd's term of office. Some years later, Josiah retired from active business and devoted himself to the public school system and Baptist Church affairs.

Henry Failing Mansion — site of the Public Service Bldg.

Josiah Failing was obviously a source of emulation to his son, as young Henry quickly became involved in the total life of the small town on the Willamette. In 1858, he married Henry W. Corbett's sister, Emily, and by 1864, he had been elected to his first term as mayor. Five years later, he and his brother-in-law bought control of the First National Bank from the Starr brothers who had organized Oregon's first national banking institution in 1865. In 1871, he and Corbett further cemented their relationship by merging the two family merchandise houses into the Corbett-Failing Company which became the largest hardware supply business in the Northwest. Failing was to remain as president of the bank until his death, with Corbett in the role of vice-president. Corbett in turn ran the hardware business except when he was out of the state serving in the United States Senate, from 1867-1873. With Corbett's return to Portland, Failing was elected by popular acclaim to his second term as mayor, and he was almost immediately faced with the worst disaster to befall the city since its founding: the fire of August, 1873 which destroyed over 20 blocks of the city center, leaving a net loss of $670,000. Failing's organizational talents and tireless efforts did much to restore the city's equilibrium, but because the mayor declined all offers of assistance from outside sources, he received strong criticism — enough to insure his defeat in 1875.*

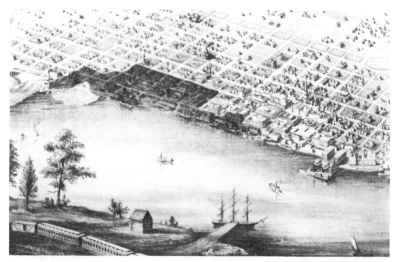

1873 Fire Zone.

By 1885, Failing was not only president of the First National Bank and the Northern Pacific Terminal Company, but a director of the OR & N, the Corbett-Failing Co., the Oregon Improvement Co., and a street paving concern. What kind of a person was Henry Failing? The evidence indicates that he possessed an orderly, methodical mind with uncanny powers of exact calculation. The counting house had been his schoolroom. During his years as president of the Water Committee, beginning with its establishment in 1885, his estimates of annual revenues and expenses would always turn out to be absolutely accurate. Judgment, thoroughness, honesty, industry and patience were his hallmarks. He was also a generous supporter of cultural and religious activities. In contrast to some of his close friends, Henry Failing continued his education throughout his

---

*Failing's defeat by 6 votes must also be blamed on the opposition of Ben Holladay whose personal candidate Dr. J.A. Chapman won.

life. He was widely read in literature, science and the arts. He was a believer in a strong classical education which had been denied him in his early schooling. For many years he was to be president of the Portland Art Museum, Public Library Association and the University of Oregon Board of Regents.

Because of his enormous prestige, family relationships, and extensive business interests, Henry Failing was a power in Portland politics in 1885 even though he did not seek further elective office. He was to become increasingly active in the routine of daily city life and government, not only through his presidencies of the Port of Portland and the Water Committee, but through his involvement with the railroad and terminal interests and the burgeoning suburban streetcar and power companies all of which were enfranchised by city government. Upon his death in 1898, his estate listed 38 lots of prime downtown property, valued at nearly half a million dollars. His total worth was less than $1.5 million, but the estate was to more than double in value by 1915.

6.

Henry Winslow Corbett* emerges as the most significant — and most complex — of the frontier merchants who laid the business-political foundations of late 19th century Portland.[24] As with many of his fellow pioneers who found success in the Northwest, Henry Corbett was born in a small New England town. At the age of 4, his family moved just over the New York state line to Cambridge, another small rural town, where he lived until he was 16, working in a local store for three years after graduating from school. He then left home for employment in a New York City wholesale dry goods house where he made friends with C.H. Lewis.

At the age of 24 the opportunity presented itself for him to go West to Portland, carrying general merchandise on consignment from wholesale houses in New York. H.W. Corbett Co. was opened on Front and Oak Streets in 1851 and prospered from the first day of sale, despite his being the first Front Street store to close on Sundays. Over the next few years, Corbett would make occasional trips back to New York to establish new contacts in order to increase and diversify his supply of merchandise. He purchased directly from New York, always buying quality goods as cheaply as possible and al-

---

*(1827-1903). Born in Westboro, Massachusetts.

ways paying cash for his purchases. At the end of 1857, his net worth was $50,763, all made in seven years of legitimate business.[25]

The depression of that year proved to Corbett and his merchant friends the advantage of not having any banks in the Pacific Northwest. They had no bank debts and no deposits to be lost through closures. All wholesale merchandise had been bought with gold coin, with transactions proceeding through the San Francisco banks to New York. This conservative financial practice, which prohibited purchasing supplies on credit, established a tradition which guided Corbett, Failing and Ladd when they set up their own banks and expanded their business interests in subsequent years. In the early days, at least, they scrupulously avoided speculative ventures. Although Corbett and the other frontier merchants would extend credit, make loans, receive deposits and in general function as bankers to their own customers, they themselves did not believe in borrowing on credit lest they be caught short during a periodic recession.

In the 1860's Corbett branched into transportation, iron manufacturing and of course banking, all the while continuing to collect profits from the Corbett-Failing hardware supply business. An additional source of income came from his holding of the United States Mail contract between San Francisco and Portland which he carried for four years.

A handbill for the stage line ran the following advertisement:[26]

"Overland mail route to Oregon
Through in six days to Portland
Avoid risk of ocean travel
Most beautiful and attractive as well
As bold grand and picturesque scenery
Stages stop one night at
Ureka and Jacksonville for passengers to rest
Lay over at any point and continue journey within one month

July 20, 1866   H.W. Corbett & Co.
$50   Proprietors, Oregon Stage Lines

A term on the city council in 1858 whetted Corbett's appetite for politics.* Several years later he was encouraged to seek the choicest

---

*Corbett also ran unsuccessfully for mayor in 1857 and 1862.

political plum of all, one of the United States Senate seats, which he won in the election of 1866 after having secured the Republican nomination from John H. Mitchell, who was to be his political enemy for 40 years.* By 1870, at the age of 43, Henry Corbett had reached the pinnacle of success in business and politics, and he was to continue to fulfill the attendant responsibilities to the point of near exhaustion. In addition, he took a controlling interest in the *Oregonian* for the period 1872-1877, during a time when owner Henry Pittock was short of cash. Also by 1870, Corbett had become the largest non-corporate investor in downtown real estate, with 12 major parcels of land, including at least 9 buildings, under his ownership.

Henry W. Corbett

Henry Corbett embodied many seemingly contradictory qualities. He could be kind and generous, and yet tough and unscrupulous. "No one ever said 'No' to Mr. Corbett."[27] Perhaps the key to his behavior was disclosed by Henry Reed, writing about Ben Holladay: "Once he [Holladay] set his mind to a purpose he pressed on to his objective, swerving neither to the right nor left. In many respects, he and Henry W. Corbett resembled each other. Both expected their wills to prevail, but Corbett was the more persuasive and the calmer in his discussion with men."[28] It was Corbett's demeanor — his calm, smiling expression, like an understanding father — which disarmed his listeners. As the story of Corbett's later life unfolds, the record

*With Ben Holladay's backing, Mitchell defeated Corbett's bid for renomination in 1872. Corbett never forgave Mitchell.

reveals a "Dr. Jekyll and Mr. Hyde" syndrome: he could be ruthless in politics and benevolent in community projects, supporting all of the worthy causes to the best of his financial ability.

Corbett Mansion — site of the Greyhound Bus Terminal and Pacific Bldg.

Henry Corbett's life provides a fascinating study in the use of economic and political power, as well as in the exercise of human discipline. Moments of deep sadness cut through his personal life. His first wife died after 13 years of marriage. One son died before reaching manhood and his other son, Henry J., husband of Helen Ladd, the one on whom the father placed so much hope for the future continuance of the family fame and fortune, died of tuberculosis at 35. Upon Henry W. Corbett's death in 1903 at the age of 76, his estate was valued in excess of $5 million. His oldest grandson, Henry Ladd Corbett*, was summoned to take up the family reins at the age of 22, just prior to his graduation from Harvard. He was to play an active role in Portland business and political affairs during the decade prior to 1915, and for a long time thereafter.

---

*(1881-1957).

7.

In retrospect, it would appear that Oregon's ample resources were available for exploitation by those who arrived early and filed their claims. The purpose of government was to service and protect these claims which were invested with the sacred rights of private property. The self-made man — the "individualist" — deserved such rewards that were the result not so much of genius as talent; of diligence, hard work, frugality, thoroughness, personal sacrifice, common sense and sobriety. The late 19th century was awash with books extolling the art of money-getting and the virtuous examples set by millionaires such as Thomas Mellon, George Peabody and Andrew Carnegie, just to mention three. Many of the leading proponents of salvation through wealth were Protestant clergymen like Henry Ward Beecher, who spoke on occasion in Portland, and Massachusetts Episcopal Bishop William Lawrence*, scion of the wealthy industrial family which founded the city of Lawrence. The Reverend Russell Conwell made a small fortune out of his all-time classic, *Acres of Diamonds,* which he delivered on the lecture circuit more than six thousand times.[29] The eulogies spoken by Portland Protestant ministers at the funerals of successful pioneer sons rang with praises of "a job well done."

To upper class America in 1885, it was the character of the self-made man and not the abundance of natural resources that determined success.** U.S. Senator Joseph N. Dolph,*** Portland's leading corporate lawyer, ascribed his success and that of his late senatorial colleague Leland Stanford of California to their early experiences on a New York farm. Eulogizing Stanford in 1893, Dolph wrote: "In labor upon a farm, he laid the foundation of bodily vigor, acquired

---

*Bishop Lawrence's daughter married one of C.H. Lewis' grandsons.
**Sixty-five years later, similar feelings were expressed by James H. Polhemus, President of the Portland General Electric Co., before a meeting of the Newcomen Society, June 6, 1951 at the Arlington Club.
> "It has always seemed to this writer that, in the development of a new country, the heredity of people rather than physical environment in the way of natural resources initially plays the greater role in determining the manner of existence .... Unlike the immigration of the pioneers, . . . [the new immigration] has been marked by the *common* rather than the *uncommon*."[30]

***(1836-1897) Dolph and his brother Cyrus A. (1840-1914) were born near Watkins, New York. They were distant cousins of Commodore Vanderbilt. Dolph dropped all business connections upon entering the U.S. Senate. He favored women's suffrage and civil service reform.

habits of industry and learned the value of money; and in the district
school he laid the foundation of an education." Citing his own experience which parallelled that of many wealthy capitalists such as
Stanford and Ladd, Dolph declared that "teaching in a country
school was the stepping stone to success."[31]

In the mind of the successful business and professional leader such
as Joseph N. Dolph, wealth and character were directly related. A
wealthy man could be trusted; his judgment was obviously sound.
In a letter to Judge Matthew P. Deady in July 1886, brother Cyrus A.
Dolph wrote: "I welcome every influence which tends to hasten the
time when the policy of municipal government relating to the amount
of expenditure and taxation will be controlled alone by those having
a pecuniary interest therein."[32] In the years following 1886, these
hopes would be largely realized.

Riverview Cemetery, final resting place for prominent families.

Chapter III

The Organization and Financing of Rail Transportation

The history of Oregon railroad financing and construction[1] is lengthy and complicated. At one stage or another, most of Portland's leading merchants and bankers were involved. Also to be involved were some of the largest German banking houses which were discovered by American entrepreneurs to be flush with funds, following the Franco-Prussian War. Initial interest was directed to the construction of a rail connection between Portland and the California border. Sizeable federal land grant subsidies awaited the most nimble footed. California investors vied with Oregon investors for the lucrative rewards that appeared — on the surface at least — to be readily available to those who arrived first with the most capital. The Californians chose the East side of the Willamette River and the Portlanders, led by Joseph Gaston and William S. Ladd, the West side.

The key figure on the Oregon railroad scene in the late '60's and early '70's was Ben Holladay, of Kentucky birth, who came to Oregon in August 1868 at the age of 49, fresh out of San Francisco where he had organized the country's largest stage coach business which he subsequently sold to Wells Fargo for $1.5 million.[2] Within two years Holladay was to create a vast empire. In short order, he gained control of the illegally incorporated, and California financed, Oregon Central Railroad Company of Salem, transferred the assets to a new legally incorporated enterprise, the Oregon & California Railroad Company, and in 1870 bought out his West side competitors, the Oregon Central Railroad Company of Portland.

Both Oregon Central Railroad Companies had broken ground in April 1868, four months before Holladay arrived on the local scene. A year later Congress authorized the awarding of the land grant to whichever company first completed 20 miles of operational railroad track. The race was on and Holladay used every trick known to man. By his own admission he spent $35,000 to bribe the Oregon Legislature to endorse his company in October 1868. It was suspected that he also bribed several United States Senators including George H. Williams of Oregon. The other Oregon Senator, Henry W. Corbett, was of course supporting the West side company. By mid-1870 Holladay had won. The newly incorporated Oregon & California Railroad Company secured the Congressional land grant and the Portland group decided to liquidate its investment and sell out. The canny banker, W.S. Ladd, correctly predicted the outcome: Holladay would eventually hang himself financially.

Before that happy day was to arrive, however, Holladay was to enjoy enormous power and success. He inveigled Germany's leading bankers into financing his ventures by purchasing $6.4 million of his bonds.* In the 1872 Republican Party state nominating convention he spent $20,000 in bribes to defeat Henry W. Corbett and thus assure the nomination of his man, John H. Mitchell.[3] In addition to his railroads, he organized four separate corporations: the Portland Dock and Warehouse Company, owning the docks and warehouses on both sides of the river; the Oregon Transfer Company, with a monopoly of the local transportation of passengers and freight, two real estate companies,[4] and the Oregon Steamship Company.

Oregon history has produced probably no more colorful a figure than Ben Holladay, and certainly no one as controversial. At first appearance he seemed a gentleman, dressed in the latest fashions and bejewelled in diamond rings and studs, wearing a "flashy" heavy gold linked watch chain and sporting a cane with a long handle "of the richest polished quartz." By his speech and manners, however, he showed himself to be a "vulgar," or "low fellow," as Henry Villard described him.[5] Holladay "possessed many of the characteristics of Napoleon," according to his former attorney John Doniphan.[6] He was "haughty . . . dictatorial . . . anxious to get the best of every bargain." He could be most generous to those he liked. Because he loved show, he was considered a "nabob" by some. He had the "bearing of one born to command," for whom "the end justified the means." He was clever, shrewd, cunning, illiterate,

---

*Holladay's total bonded debt was $10,950,000.

coarse, and completely unscrupulous. Joseph Gaston, his severest critic, charged him with being "wholly destitute of fixed principles of honesty, morality, or common decency."[7] When he bought one of Portland's largest homes from the city's most prominent physician, Dr. Rodney Glisan, he remodelled it and immediately installed a harem of high class prostitutes.[8] Portland's sedate pioneer merchants found themselves in a quandary: they could not abide the man and yet they feared to alienate him.* The panic brought on by Jay Cooke in 1873 came at a propitious time for them. Holladay found himself overextended and was eventually forced to relinquish control of his railroad and other business enterprises.

Ben Holladay

Henry Reed, a student of Oregon railroad history, wrote years ago that Holladay deserved more credit than he received because he "was the first man to do anything in a large way for Oregon."[10] He and his associate George Weidler built the first horsedrawn car line in 1872, from N.W. Glisan Street to S.W. Sherman Street along

---

*Reed and Ladd put up a good front. Judge Deady reported that at one four hour dinner party, they appeared on friendly terms with Holladay, (entry dated April 19, 1872). Holladay had proved useful to Ladd, Reed and their OSN colleagues at the time of the S.S. "Oregonian" episode. In June 1873, Deady wrote that Holladay was running a "Whorehouse" in his own home, on the word of Ben Holladay, Jr.[9]

First Avenue. He built two hotels in Portland and one in Seaside.* He also acquired what became known as Holladay's addition, in East Portland,** the current site of Lloyd's Shopping Center, one of the largest in America. Perhaps more important for Portland's future, he literally "grabbed"[11] 10 blocks of prime real estate along the riverfront in north Portland and gave them to the Oregon Central Railroad. The surviving transportation corporations have owned them ever since with no compensation to the city.

Henry Villard

Henry Villard*** arrived in Portland in mid-summer of 1874. He was dispatched to Oregon by the German bondholders, for whom he had been appointed financial agent, to investigate the condition of Holladay's railroad construction venture which was in default on its bond interest payments in the amount of $452,760.****

*Clarendon Hotel and Holladay Hotel in Portland; Holladay House in Seaside, later known as Sea Side House.

**Upon arrival in Portland in the late summer of 1868, Holladay bought his large plot of land on the east side of the river where he thought that the city of the future would be built.

***(1835-1900) Born in Bavaria, a Civil War correspondent for European newspapers, Villard married the daughter of abolitionist William Lloyd Garrison. When he returned to Germany in the early '70's for his health, he established contact with the German bankers.

****Richard Koehler accompanied Villard and was to remain in Oregon as Villard's personal agent. In later years Koehler became identified with the management of the Southern Pacific Railroad properties in Oregon.

Villard drafted a legal contract containing strict operational guidelines designed to protect his employers' investments. Holladay
signed it with great reluctance. After two years, when it became apparent to Villard that Holladay was not fulfilling his obligations,
Holladay was bought out and the German bondholders' investments
were refinanced. In the process of conducting these negotiations
Villard extended his personal control, as majority investor, over
all of Holladay's major enterprises, using additional funds provided
by eastern and Portland financiers. Villard had substantial New
York banking contacts which he used to underwrite his own interests
and ambitions.

One of these ambitions — a vision of grandeur, some thought — was
to make Portland the western terminus for a transcontinental railroad. His ultimate goal was to gain independent access to San Francisco. He received encouragement from the OSN stockholders who in
1879 were ready to sell out once and for all.* Thus, Villard arranged
to buy 80 percent of the stock of the existing OSN for $100 per share
— or $4 million — and to merge the OSN into a newly formed corpora-
tion to be called the Oregon Railway and Navigation Company,
with himself as president. His plan called for the construction of a
railroad line to Portland on the old OSN right-of-way along the
south bank of the Columbia River, and he would tie this into the
Oregon and California Railroad line which he was currently extending into southern Oregon. The initial purchase of the OSN only cost
him $2 million, the money being loaned him by his New York bank-
ers, The Farmers Loan & Trust Co. For each $100 share, the OSN
stockholders received $50 in cash, $20 in bonds and $30 of the newly
issued OR&N stock.[12] Shareholders Ainsworth, Reed, Thompson,
and Ladd each netted about $800,000 from the sale. Jacob Kamm,
George Weidler — pioneer steamboat owner and merchant — and
other local stockholders received less in varying amounts.

Initially, Villard succeeded in selling $6 million of OR&N stock.
Additional stock of equal amount was issued and sold each year
until the total outstanding was $24 million in 1882. The original $6
million of issued stock was to be worth $50 million in 1910. Ladd and
Reed invested heavily in the first issue and Ladd became the second
largest stockholder after Villard. The next three largest stockholders

---

*The OSN directors had little choice. The future profits of river trans-
portation were threatened by the advent of the transcontinental railroad.
Villard offered them a way to protect their interests while at the same time
giving them a financial stake in the railroad development.

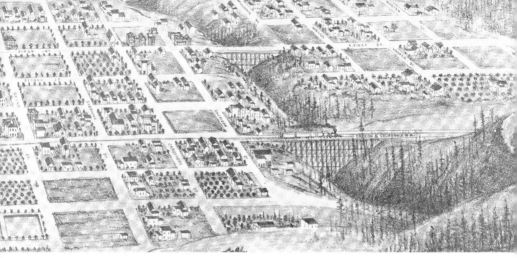

Oregon & California R.R., 1881 — West Side line — S.W. 4th Ave. — Marquam Gulch (Barbur Blvd. today).

in the new group of investors were: Henry W. Corbett, Henry Failing and Cicero H. Lewis of Portland. The company prospered. By 1881, according to Villard: "Our net earnings showed the wonderful increase in two years from $750,000 to $2,500,000, making over 41 percent on the original capital of $6,000,000, and over 20 percent on $12,000,000."[13]

In late December, 1880, Villard became worried about the activities of the Northern Pacific Railroad. "The Northern Pacific had in its power seriously to affect the value in the market of our securities," worth at the time nearly $200 per share,* "by a simple threat to build at once on the north bank of the Columbia . . . . I determined to form a new corporation, which was named the Oregon & Transcontinental Company, to acquire a controlling interest in the Northern Pacific and the Oregon Railway & Navigation companies."[14] It was not so much the fear of Northern Pacific competition at Portland that motivated Villard. "It was, rather, the obstinate persistence with which the Northern Pacific clung to plans to build to the Sound which forced Villard to his policy of complete domination."[15] The N.P. planned to make Tacoma its main terminus, with a branch line to Portland. Villard had failed in his effort to interest the Union Pacific in a joint venture two years previously.

---

*By August 1882, however, the OR&N stock would slide to $154; by January 30, 1885, to $61.5. Northern Pacific Stock was to slide from 51-1/4 to 15-1/8 in the same period. The investors lost money until the mid-1890's; by 1910, huge profits would be realized for those who did not sell out.

Moving quickly and secretly,* using his own money and securities, together with funds provided by an eastern purchasing syndicate which he had formed, Villard gained majority control of the Northern Pacific Railroad by mid-1881. In two years he had put together a $60 million empire and Portland's business leaders had been intimately involved in all of the negotiations. Villard was treated like a hero when he spoke before the Portland Board of Trade on October 22, 1881. "It is no extravagance to say," eulogized the *Oregonian,* "that Mr. Villard has organized and combined interests which . . . form the most stupendous scheme yet undertaken on the American continent."[16]

Although Henry Villard was clearly the one most responsible for advancing Oregon's transportation interests, a question remains as to his motives for doing so. There is evidence that he was "motivated more by the publicity potential for speculations, deals, and manipulations in securities markets, than by the true economic character of the venture.[17]** At least Villard must be credited with being the first to make practical use of the water level route of the Columbia River for railroad transportation. When the first transcontinental train steamed into East Portland on September 11, 1883, a virtual holiday was declared. "The greatest display ever witnessed in this city," headlined the *Oregonian.*[20] A gigantic commercial pageant lasted well into the night. " 'We are now incorporated with the rest of the world,' wrote Donald MacLeay, president of the Board of Trade. 'The day of long credits is past.' "[21]

In the course of his Board of Trade speech in 1881, Villard also announced plans for the construction of freight terminal and shop facilities in Albina on the east side of the Willamette River (the land was already under purchase option), and the building of a passenger

---

*Villard formed a "blind pool." Villard put up $900,000 of his own money, George Pullman $500,000 and William Endicott Jr., of the Boston office of Kidder, Peabody, $500,000.

**Commenting on Villard in April 1883, Judge Deady wrote: "He is evidently a strong, deep man and I think an upright one — at least compared with other Railway Kings and speculators of the U.S."[18] Five months later, Deady noted that he was "sorry" to hear some of Villard's financial operations characterized as "criminal" by John H. Hall, a Villard associate and director of both the OR&N and NPRR.[19] Such comments as Hall's need to be examined in broad perspective. The value of Hall's stockholdings had obviously suffered greatly and he blamed Villard whose massive issuance of bonds had lowered stock values. Excessive construction costs put the N.P. $5.5 million in the red, eliminated dividends and were ultimately to bankrupt Villard. He had promised N.P. stockholders 11% dividends when he was purchasing their stock in 1881.

terminal and hotel in Portland. It would be another decade* before either of the latter facilities was completed, but at least the foundations had been laid for an expansive physical growth of greater Portland. Early in 1882, the Northern Pacific Terminal Company** was

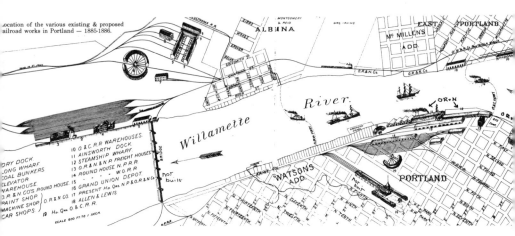

Location of the various existing & proposed railroad works in Portland — 1885-1886.

DRY DOCK
LONG WHARF
COAL BUNKERS
ELEVATOR
WAREHOUSE
O.R. & N CO'S. ROUND HOUSE
PAINT SHOP
MACHINE SHOP
CAR SHOPS

10 O.&.C.R.R WAREHOUSES.
11 AINSWORTH DOCK.
12 STEAMSHIP WHARF.
13 O.R.& N.P. FREIGHT HOUSES.
14 ROUND HOUSE N.P.R.R.
15 " . . W O.R.R
16 GRAND UNION DEPOT
17 PRESENT Ha. Q'ws. N.P.&O.R.&N.Co.
18 ALLEN & LEWIS
19 Ha. Q'ws. O.&.C.R.R.

*Financial reverses in late 1883 forced Villard to relinquish his presidencies of the OR&N, the Oregon & Transcontinental and Northern Pacific on January 4, 1884. On April 11, 1887 (retroactive to January 1, 1887) the OR&N leased most of its North Portland and Columbia River Division trackage and railroad real estate, including the Albina yards, to the Union Pacific Railroad. In July, 1887, after much negotiation, the OR&N's Oregon and California and Oregon Central properties were leased to the Southern Pacific Co. The OR&N still survived as a corporation. Its stock took a precipitous dive, and the directors became concerned about the leasing arrangements with the U.P. When Villard reassumed the presidency of the N.P. in September 1887, it was learned that he favored a joint leasing of the OR&N properties to both the U.P. and the N.P. The U.P. favored a new contract because it was unhapy with the 6% rental it was paying the OR&N. The Boston and Portland OR&N directors bitterly opposed such an arrangement if for no other reason than they felt that competition between the U.P. and N.P. would grant Portland more favorable shipping rates which they demanded. In March of 1888, a delegation of prominent Portlanders, including C.H. Lewis, Henry Failing, and *Oregonian* Editor Harvey Scott went to New York to see Villard about the matter.[22] Ultimately the U.P. backed off on the joint lease arrangement and in 1892 bought control of its leased OR&N properties through purchase of Villard's Oregon & Transcontinental railroad holdings. The OR&N name was changed in 1911 to the Oregon, Washington Railway and Navigation Co. The Oregon & Transcontinental Co., divorced from the railroad business, was reorganized into the North American Co., which later grew into the second largest public utility holding company in the United States.
**Cited hereafter as the NPT.

incorporated and capitalized at $5 million. The OR&N held 40 percent of the stock, with the rest being bought by a number of Portland business leaders including William Ladd, Henry Corbett, and Henry Failing who became the president.

By 1885, the Oregon Railway & Navigation Company had become the most powerful corporation affecting the life of the City of Portland. In real estate alone, it owned over 10,000 feet of waterfront property, including all of the former Holladay holdings and much of lower Albina*. Its total real property holdings in Portland were assessed at nearly $1 million.** The second largest corporate property holder was the N P T , with real estate on both sides of the river assessed at over half a million dollars.** In North Portland*** alone, both companies controlled 39 block-streets for the use of their track and terminal operations. Private corporate interests, especially those of the railroads, had achieved virtual control over the public life of the city and state. In Henry Reed's words: "Railroad influence dominated politics."[23]

Railroad influence also dominated the thinking of the members of the federal judiciary, including Judge Deady.**** By 1885 the U.S. Supreme Court had fairly well accepted the notion, long advocated by Associate Justice Stephen J. Field, that corporations were *persons* entitled to all the protections of the Fourteenth Amendment. Due process of law constituted a guarantee of vested rights against state action.***** The rights of private property were sacred to Field who was responsible for the Ninth Circuit Court which included Oregon. Deady did not always agree with the more conservative Field with whom he sat on the Circuit Bench several times a year, but it is doubtful that he would have accepted the severity of railroad rate

---

*The growth of Albina, from an attractive residential community to a shabby commercial, industrial, lower income residential area within a span of 40 years — the black ghetto following World War II — was largely shaped by decisions made in downtown Portland. The town became the vassal of the OR&N, the NPT, and the Union Pacific Railroad. It was incorporated into the City of Portland in 1891. (See Chapter VI.)

**Actual market value was perhaps three to four times greater.

***Northwest Portland today.

****Deady and Field regularly accepted free passes for rail travel.

*****See *Stone v. Farmers Loan & Trust Co.,* 1886; *Chicago, Milwaukee & St. Paul Railway Co. v. Minnesota,* 1890.

regulation and taxation enacted by Minnesota, Illinois and even California in the decade prior to 1885. Judge Deady was very close to Portland's ruling elite, especially to Henry Failing for whose judgment he had infinite respect.* However, there was no reason for

Matthew P. Deady

concern in Oregon. The legislature was too dominated by special interests to threaten the railroads with any form of regulation.

By 1885, the railroad had become the preeminent form of corporation in America. Profits were to be made primarily through the manipulation of securities, not through transportation. The same could be said for the establishment and promotion of the street railways and public utilities in the decades following 1885. The banks would become increasingly involved, and bonds and stocks would be issued as "self-awarded bonuses"[24] to the organizers, with little concern shown to the public domain or public interest.

The future consequences for Portland and for other Western towns and cities that were subjected to railroad exploitation were clearly spelled out by urban historian John Reps when he wrote:

---

*Matthew P. Deady was born in Maryland in 1824. He arrived in Oregon in 1849, taught and practiced law and served on the Territorial Supreme Court. He was appointed U.S. District Judge in 1859. His wife's sister was married to Henry Failing's brother, Edward. Deady was a founder of the Public Library, on the vestry of Trinity Church and President of the Board of Regents of the University of Oregon. He died in 1893.

"The philosophy of speculation, of treating land like a commodity to be put in handy packages for quick sale . . . of making the physical layout of towns subservient to the railroad line and its requirements — these were the dominant attitudes. . . . The country was settled — yes, and quickly — but at a price which generations since and those yet to come will be paying for in discomfort, danger, monotony and sterility."[25]

A Crack River Boat

R. R. Thompson, Largest Sternwheel Boat in

Station in Eastern Oregon

O R & N

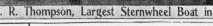

Palatial Steamships of the Portland San Fr

RAIL,
RIVER
AND
OCEAN
STEAMSHIP
LINES

n O. R. & N. Transcontinental Passenger Train.

Hauling Wheat to Puget Sound Over
the Heavy Grades of the Cascade
Mountains.

One Engine Can Haul 40 Loaded Cars from Lewiston, Idaho, Down Through the Tide-
Pass of the Columbia River, via the O. R. & N. to Portland.

WHY PORTLAND IS THE NATURAL GREAT WHEAT-SHIPPING PORT OF THE NORTHWEST

O. R. & N. Train Entering Gorge of Columbia River at Rooster Rock

THE OREGON RAILROAD AND NAVIGATION COMPANY;

THE ONE ROAD WITH WHOSE INTERESTS THOSE OF PORTLAND ARE SO CLOSELY ALLIED

Chapter IV

The Business-Political
Power Structure,
1885-1890

1.

Portland in 1885 was recovering slowly from a recession which had set in sixty days after the historic arrival of Henry Villard's transcontinental train in September, 1883. When Villard was forced to step down as president of the Northern Pacific Railroad in December, 1883, it was reported in the press that six of Portland's richest men, who had invested in Villard's Oregon & Transcontinental holding company, had lost $3 million.[1] The Railroad money had vanished, reported Board of Trade President Donald MacLeay in 1884. By 1885, however, Macleay noted some improvement, as evidenced by increased construction and retail activity.[2] The new city high school had just been opened. Meier & Frank, soon to become the city's largest general store, moved into its first two story building on First Street. The center of the retail trade was moving west, away from the river.* Henry Corbett's Cambridge block, costing $65,000, was completed and Jacob Kamm was almost ready to move into his four story

---

*The first center of the city's retail trade was at Front and Washington. After the fire of 1873 it moved to First Street. After 1894 it was to jump Second (largely occupied by the Chinese colony) and move to Third. The increasing severity of the floods, especially that of 1894, was a major cause of the shift.

51

block which was to cost him $94,000. Three new major projects were underway, totalling $165,000: the four story Portland Savings Bank, and the Mulkey and Kearney blocks. Late in the year, the public eagerly awaited the opening of the new Turkish & Russian Bath at Second and Ash Streets, cited by the *Oregonian* as "a step nearest to Godliness."[3]

Twelve major businesses were incorporated during the year, including three involving sizeable investments by W.S. Ladd: The Oregon Artificial Stone Co., The Oregon Pottery Co., and The Oregon Paving & Contracting Co.* All three companies were to be major recipients of street paving and waterpipe contracts awarded by the city. The secretary of all three was James Steel,** Ladd's brother-in-law, who was to play an increasingly important role in Portland's business and politics over the next 20 years.

Portland Savings Bank

Grain export became one of the most profitable enterprises in 1885 with $7,394,000 worth of wheat and flour shipped out of the state, an increase of $2,000,000 from the previous year. Playing an important role in this development was the English owned Balfour-Guthrie Co. which had established a Portland office in 1877, to be managed

---

*Actually organized late in 1884.
**Born in Ohio, 1834. Died in 1913.

52

Balfour Guthrie's 800 foot Oceanic Dock, Albina, north of the OR&N shops, circa 1900.

successfully for many years by Walter J. Burns.* Wheat production had boomed following the opening of the transcontinental railroad and William S. Ladd was the first local investor to benefit. In 1883 he had incorporated the Portland Flouring Mills which was to become the largest milling operation in the Northwest, guided and directed in later years by his protege, Theodore B. Wilcox.

Also in 1885, expanded Scottish investment in Northwest farm, commercial and residential property added new stimulus to Portland's economic growth. With the arrival of lawyer Robert Livingstone, the Edinburgh capitalists acquired an able and dedicated director who replaced William Reid in the management of the Oregon Mortgage Co. which Reid had organized to promote investment in

---

*The story is told that after Walter Burns arrived in Portland he inquired of George Weidler about what steps he should take to assure his future happiness and success in his new home. The advice given: join Trinity Episcopal Church and marry a Couch. He did both and prospered accordingly.

improved farm property. Reid* had been the initiator of Scottish investment in Oregon; he brought in over $6,000,000 in 11 years. His original backing came from Dundee capitalists headed by the Earl of Airlie, who provided $2,500,000 for Reid's major railroad venture, the construction of the narrow gauge Oregonian Line down the west side of the Willamette Valley. Reid also founded, with Scottish support, several banks and mortgage companies, including the first savings bank of deposit in Oregon. The formation in 1883 of the Oregon Mortgage Co. introduced the Edinburgh capitalists to the Oregon market and they were to expand their interests appreciably during the decade following Robert Livingstone's arrival.

Mortgage banking was hurt by a special tax passed by the Oregon Legislature in 1882,** so Scottish money was directed increasingly into the investment trust areas. The investment trust institution was, after all, founded in Scotland and became the forerunner of the present day mutual fund. Between 1874 and 1890, over ten major Scottish financial companies were doing business in Oregon.***

William Reid severed relationships with his Dundee backers in 1882 for reasons that will be discussed later in this chapter. In 1883 management of the Dundee interests was placed in the hands of Board of Trade President Donald MacLeay and his fellow Scots William MacMaster and A.H. Birrell. After Reid was forced out of the Oregon Mortgage Co. in 1885 by the Edinburgh investors, he went on to found the Portland & Willamette Valley Railroad and the Port-

---

*(1844-1914). Born in Glasgow, Reid practiced law in Dundee and served as U.S. Vice-consul there, 1869-1874. He was a founder of the Portland Board of Trade (1874); Oregon, Washington Savings Bank (1876); organizer of the Salem Mills Co. (1881); City of Salem Co. (1882); First National Bank of Salem (1882); Oregonian Railroad Co. Ltd. (1880); Portland & Willamette Valley R.R. (1885); Portland National Bank (1885); Astoria & South Coast Railway; and co-purchaser with J.B. Montgomery of the original Albina tract, the lower part of which was sold to the NPT and OR&N for railroad and shop development.[4]

**Repealed in 1885.

***Oregon, Washington Trust Investment Co. 1873 (Reid); Oregon, Washington Savings Bank 1876 (Reid), became the Oregon, Washington Mortgage Savings Bank 1880; Dundee Mortgage Co. 1876 (Reid) merged with OWT&I, 1880 (Reid replaced in 1883 by MacLeay, MacMaster, Birrell) to become Dundee Mortgage & Trust Inv. Co.; Scotch Bank 1879 (Reid); Oregon Mortgage Co. 1883 (Reid, replaced in 1885 by Livingstone); American Mortgage Co. Ltd. of Scotland 1886 (Livingstone); Alliance Trust Co. Ltd. 1890 (MacMaster & Birrell). Three other investment companies (not listed in the City Directory) are known to have loaned money in Oregon, especially the Scottish American Inv. Trust Co. Ltd. of Edinburgh (Livingstone). Others included the East of Scotland Inv. Co. and the Scottish American Inv. Trust Co. Ltd., both of Dundee.

land National Bank. He kept majority control of the Oregon, Washington Mortgage Savings Bank — a decision that was to lead him into bankruptcy in 1893.

West Park Blocks & Montgomery St. — 1882.

2.

The residential section, along with the business core, was spreading westward. In the late 1870's, West Park 'Avenue on the Park Blocks,* near Montgomery Street, had become a "Boulevard" of formal mansions built in the "Italianate" style.[5] Development in the '80's extended beyond Jacob Kamm's property northwest to the exclusive "Nineteenth Street" compound of the Couch-Lewis clan.

> "For ten blocks back — 16th to 26th streets — or even further, and from about N street southward to Jefferson, or some twenty streets, the region is, by popular consent — and still more by prevailing prices — forever dedicated to dwellings of wealth and beauty. The streets here are, for the most part, well paved and delightfully ornamented, but not overshadowed by trees. The houses are projected

---

*The current site of the expanded campus of Portland State University.

and their accompanying grounds are laid out on such an
ample scale, and there is so little crowding, the sun and
sky have such complete access that one is much impressed
with the general air of elegance and taste. There is, of
course, none of the marble and stony grandeur of New
York or Chicago, of the splendor of Euclid Ave., in Cleveland, or the lavish adornment of Jackson street in Oakland, California, or the pre-eminent extravagance of the
palaces of the money kings of Nob Hill, in San Francisco;
but for substantial comfort and tasteful display the west
end of Portland has few rivals. It is, moreover, devoid of
superfineness, or niceness, but is wholesome and neat.
The general spirit of this portion of town might be distinguished from the streets or avenues of other cities, in
that the separate houses appear to be built independently
and with reference only to their own needs and entirety,
while the others referred to are more often constructed as
complete streets, each edifice being planned and laid out
with reference to the rest, and as but a part in one continuous whole. The characteristic of Portland in its residential quarters will probably prevail even when the city
attains its largest population, since the irregularities of
ground and peculiarities of situation will necessarily mod-

ify the architecture, and, to quite an extent, at least, make each dwelling a complete whole in itself."[6]

Adjacent to City Park, at the top of "B" (Burnside) Street, Henry Green, a founder of the Water and Gas Companies, had built his plush Cedar Hill estate, known as "the gayest home in Portland." On a tract of five acres the house was almost "submerged in a wealth of beautiful trees." Mrs. Green* maintained large hot-houses, filled with the finest of exotics."[7] Daily, she could be seen "driving out in her Victoria, behind her cockaded coachman and bobtailed horses, silver jingling on the bridles and a carriage robe made from the peacock green neck feathers of mallard ducks, bound with seal skin spread over the back of the seat."[8]

Despite the fact that the value of OR&N stock had tumbled by over 70 percent in four years, the way of life for most of the propertied rich did not seem to have suffered appreciably. An article in *The Northwest* for November 1885 cited twenty-one millionaires as living in Portland. "In all the essentials of a high civilization the city is as

---

*Mrs. Green was the grandmother of John Reed, Portland born writer and "revolutionist," the only American buried in the Kremlin. Reed's godfather was Judge Matthew P. Deady.

far advanced as the old cities of New England and New York of like size that have enjoyed more than a century of growth."[9] Portland was considered unique, especially in the matter of private residences. "In this respect," commented the *West Shore* in 1888:

> "Portland leads all the cities of the coast in the number of elegant and costly dwellings as compared to her total population. . . . In the matter of perennially green grass and ever blooming flowers, the people of Portland possess an advantage over their friends in the east. The services of the lawn mower are in constant demand, for the rains of winter and the ever-ready garden hose of summer keep the lawns fresh and beautiful the entire year. . . . The beautiful lawns and profusion of choice and carefully cultivated flowers speak more loudly of the culture and refinement of the people than do palatial residences. Flowers are the property of rich and poor alike."[10]

3.

Economic power was gradually being dispersed in 1885 as evidenced by the growth of new banks and other commercial enterprises. And yet the center of power still lay with those who controlled the operations of the OR&N which continued to be the dominant force in the business and political life of the city. Excluding Henry Villard's interests which were rapidly diminishing, the OR&N affairs were in the hands of Messrs. Ladd, Corbett, Failing, Lewis, Weidler and the Dolph brothers. As the leading corporate lawyers in Portland, the Dolphs represented a new type of "captive professional — lawyers at big business' elbow." In addition to corporation matters, they also handled the personal affairs of their director associates on the OR&N board. In 1885, Joseph Dolph was serving in the U.S. Senate (having defeated John H. Mitchell for the nomination in 1882). His brother Cyrus replaced him on the OR&N board and also served as vice president of the NPT, of which Henry Failing was the president. The fortunes of both companies were obviously tied very closely to those of the Ladd & Tilton and First National Banks, the total assets of which were more than four times the combined assets of the other seven Portland banks.

POSTOFFICE

COURT HOUSE PARK.

Politically, the lines of authority were more complex. "The Boss," as he was called by his detractors, was Joseph Simon,* Republican State Chairman, member of the state senate, and law partner of the Dolph brothers.[11] Simon, among his numerous activities, also acted as corporate secretary for both the OR&N and the NPT. The German born and American educated lawyer was accused of carrying a "stiletto" in each hand. "He ruled with a rod of iron . . . without mercy," reported the *Oregon Journal* some years later.[12] Although these statements appear extreme, having been uttered in the heat of a fierce mayoralty campaign in 1909, there is no question that Simon was singly the most powerful political force in Oregon politics from 1880-1910. Over the years he was to be accused of performing innumerable "dirty tricks." Declared the *Oregonian* in 1886: "Simony in Oregon politics is sale of the party."[13] Within two years, however, the paper would be supporting Mr. Simon who had become one of owner Henry Pittock's partners in the Fulton Park real estate development and the secretary of the NPT. The "Boss" was an intense, ambitious "wheeler-dealer" of great personal charm who dedicated his life to business, law and politics. He never attempted to separate his private and public affairs.**

Despite Simon's control of the state and county political machinery, the Republican party was to be splintered into various factions until 1905. "Probably no state in the union (excluding perhaps Delaware), ever witnessed party strife so malignant or so deadly."[14] Aside from personal competition, the party was divided between the big city Republican and the rural or downstate members. There was also a growing animosity between the Republicans on the city council and those in the legislature. The councilmen jealously guarded their prerogatives in the face of legislative inroads into what the council considered to be strictly municipal matters. Through the smoke of political battle, however, no matter how many skirmishes were fought, the major transportation corporations and banks, somewhat aloofly, maintained their dominance over the economic life of the city.

---

*(1851-1935.)
**Simon's political career included: Portland City Council, 1877-80; acting mayor, March 16, 1877; Republican State Chairman, 1880-1886; State Senate, 1880-1891, 1895-1898; Senate President, 1889-1891, 1895-1898; U.S. Senate, 1898-1903; Mayor of Portland, 1909-1911.

Joseph Simon

The most bitter struggle in Portland municipal politics throughout this period involved the Mitchell and Simon factions. John H. Mitchell eagerly sought return to the U.S. Senate in 1885, but the regular winter session adjourned after 69 ballots without electing anyone. Simon had promoted the candidacy of an eminent German-Jewish Portland merchant named Solomon Hirsch.* When this effort failed, Simon proposed his close friend and political ally, former Senator Henry W. Corbett. The downstate Republicans would not accept Corbett, citing his corporate and national banking interests and his known attachment to the Simon "Ring."** When the legislature was called into special session in the fall of 1885, Mitchell won his return to the Senate by one vote.*** He was now back in office and, therefore, presented an obvious threat to the Corbett-Simon Portland interests.

_____

*Hirsch served as U.S. Minister to Turkey, 1889-1892.
**Corbett proceeded to get himself elected as Multnomah County Commissioner for the term 1885-1886.
***With the help of over half of the Democrats.

Locally, the Simon forces appeared to control the offices of district attorney and mayor. The former was held by John Gearin,* an honest Democrat who respected Simon's ability and would soon become his law partner. The mayor was John Gates, a kindly, hardworking, religious man, and a successful inventor and steamboat designer. He was also the chief of engineering for the River & Sound division of the OR&N, a relationship maintained throughout his term of office. In December of 1885, Gates made what would appear to be an unlikely appointment when he named Ralph Dement, a Mitchell law partner and Arlington Club member, as the Police Judge.** The other office controlled by the Mitchell forces was that of city attorney, held by A.H. Tanner, the third partner in the senator's law firm. Along with Mitchell, he would be convicted in the land fraud trials of 1905.

The nine member city council was unpredictable. It could usually be counted upon to support the Simon-Corbett economic interests, but it was jealous of Simon's political power in the legislature. Elected from three wards, the council included: Sylvester Farrell, a wealthy pioneer fish canner and grain merchant; Jacob Fliedner, a prosperous German born realtor; C.M. Forbes, a downtown real estate investor and furniture store owner; A.F. Sears, Jr., a prominent young lawyer who was to become an assistant district attorney the following year; Frank Hacheny, a German born grocer who was to become a professional politician and city treasurer for 10 years; a hotel owner; a wholesale liquor dealer; a ship carpenter and a shipsmith, both of whom were affiliated with OR&N related enterprises. The latter three represented the North End.

In an attempt to isolate Mitchell's power and simultaneously to gain tighter control over a municipal government that Simon and his friends did not trust, Simon succeeded in securing the passage of two major pieces of legislation during the special fall session of 1885. One created the Board of Police Commissioners, and the other, The Portland Water Committee, also known as the Water Board.

The Board of Police Commissioners was given total authority over the direction of Portland's Police Department. To be appointed by the governor, it was to be composed of three civic minded patriots

---

*Gearin was to be appointed U.S. Senator by Governor Chamberlain in 1905-1907, succeeding the deceased Senator Mitchell.

**Five years previously Dement had been convicted in Federal Court for vote fraud — giving an altered voting ticket to a man to vote for Mitchell who was Dement's law partner. Judge Deady fined him $250.[15]

who would donate their valuable time to serve one, two and three year terms, their successors to be elected by the voters of Portland. Upon the passage and signing of the charter amendment, Governor Zenas Moody, a Simon-Corbett man, appointed three prominent Republicans to the Commission:* Joe Simon, Jonathan Bourne, Jr., and Byron P. Cardwell, recently retired from 21 years of service as the local collector of internal revenue.[17]

Jonathan Bourne, Jr.

Bourne**, a wealthy Harvard drop-out and son of a prosperous New Bedford, Massachusetts textile manufacturer, was climbing the business-political ladder rapidly in 1885 after only seven years' residence in Oregon. As a key House member of the 1885 session he had worked closely*** with Simon to ensure the passage of the police amendment. By 1887, he would be president of the Portland Stock Exchange and Mining Board and owner of mining properties capitalized at over $8.5 million. His partner in many of these ventures was Charles E. Ladd, second son of William S. Ladd. Bourne represented a new breed of businessman-politician beginning to emerge — more aggressive, more speculative financially and more impatient. He was

*Moody had been a member of the famous packed Grand Jury in 1873 that had refused to indict known bribers in the 1872 election "won" by Senator John H. Mitchell. In 1882, Judge Deady noted that Moody "can be relied on to do anything which the exigencies of party politics may demand.[16]
**(1855-1940.)
***Bourne introduced the bill, H.B. 87.

63

later to work secretly with Henry W. Corbett* in several political skirmishes. He proved that he could be ruthless in both business and politics. Early in the 1900's, he was to undergo an amazing "metamorphosis" and be elected to the U.S. Senate as a reform Republican.**

Bourne and Simon turned the police board into one of the most influential public agencies in the city — an instrument of their personal political ambitions. But before the decade was out, the police department would be in shambles.***

4.

The decision to create a special Water Committee with the power to acquire and operate a municipal water system was probably the most constructive political move in Joe Simon's long career.[18] It was to result in Portland developing one of the purest water systems in the United States. Initially, however, there was much local opposition to its establishment. The bill, as drafted, listed the names of fifteen of the most prominent businessmen in Portland, to serve as members of the committee. Among those included were C.H. Lewis, W.S. Ladd, Henry Failing, H.W. Corbett, Simeon Reed, Frank Dekum and W.K. Smith. The city council reacted negatively to the proposal, especially to those individuals named as committee members. By a 6-1 vote, the council labeled the committee an "Oligarchy of 15." The committee had no responsibility to the people who bore the burden of taxation; there was no limit on the terms to be served; and the primary qualification for service was "simply to be moneyed." By a further vote of 7-0, the council sent a resolution to the county's legislative delegation, requesting that the waterworks be restored as a function of city government.[19] Turning a deaf ear under Simon's prodding, the legislature enacted the charter amendment the following week, on November 25, 1885.

The Water Committee held its first meeting on December 8, 1885 and elected Henry Failing, president and C.H. Lewis, treasurer. Although Failing would be the official leader for 12 years, William S.

---

*In 1885, Bourne did not support Corbett for the U.S. Senate. He absented himself when the quorum vote was called. Bourne was strongly pro-silver and supported John Mitchell whose silver position, he thought, was closer to his own. In 1896 Mitchell equivocated; Bourne felt double-crossed and switched his allegiance to Corbett.
**1907-1913.
***To be described in Chapter VIII.

Ladd was the dominant spirit until the time of his death in 1893. The meetings were always held in his office at the Ladd & Tilton Bank. The committee approved a Ladd & Tilton advance of $20,000 to "get the program going." Ladd had long been interested in the development of a municipal water system. In March of 1862 the City Council had voted 5-2 to grant Ladd and his associates a 30 year exclusive franchise to lay waterpipes through the city streets, with the fire department to receive free service.[20] Not much came of these efforts. Seven months later, John and Henry Green, together with H.C. Leonard, bought Ladd's water interests along with the water rights of Balch Creek and the properties of the Pioneer Water Works* which at that time included only one mile of wooden pipe leading to a small stream in Caruther's Canyon.**

The Water Committee was authorized initially to sell $700,000 in bonds to finance the cost of an expanded municipal system. Except for the purchase of the Crystal Springs Water Co. for $150,000 in February 1886,*** the committee took no additional action until December 8, 1886 when it made its final offer to purchase the Portland Water Company for $464,551.[21] The company claimed that it had invested $800,000 in the water works and was requesting $700,000. The engineer's evaluation came to $478,000. The inventory included 30 miles of iron water mains, three reservoirs and one pumping station at Palatine Hill with a 12 million gallon daily output. After the offer was accepted, the Water Committee agreed to assume control of the company on February 1, 1887 and to proceed immediately to arrange the financing. As might be expected, William S. Ladd was high bidder and purchased $200,000 of the bonds. The First National Bank bought $170,000 worth and the Portland Water Company was issued the remaining $108,000 as part of its payment.

Early in January 1887 the committee began consideration of the

─────────────────────

*The Pioneer Water Works had been organized in 1857 by Stephen Coffin.

**Incorporated in September 1862, the Portland Water Co. was capitalized at $50,000, later increased to $500,000. The first pumping station was at the foot of S.W. Market St., adjacent to a well, with the reservoir at Fourth and Market. In 1868, a new pumping station was built at the foot of S.W. Lincoln St. In 1883, the Palatine Hill pumping station was constructed, for river water.

***There was little formal discussion of this purchase according to the minutes of the Water Committee. The Ladd family had an interest in the company; to this degree, at least, one could surmise that some conflict of interest was involved.

Bull Run Lake.

long term water needs of the city. For the first time, Bull Run* water
became the major subject for discussion: was this a desirable main
source for the future water supply? How could it best be brought to
Portland? Was a gravity or pump system the most feasible? And
what would be the total expense? At the January 11th meeting, the
cost of a Bull Run pipe line plus pumping station was estimated at
more than $500,000. The committee voted 12-1 to develop a Bull Run
water supply and to seek legislative authority for $500,000 in addi-
tional bonding capacity; only $100,000 remained of the initial author-
ization. Simeon Reed was the sole member to oppose this action. He
felt that the existing system would be adequate for at least five years
and there was nothing wrong with Willamette River water anyway;
it was just as good as Bull Run water. Furthermore, Reed favored
cheap water rates and did not wish to saddle the rate payers with increased costs. The bond interest would have to be met by either a

---

*Bull Run was (and is) the name given to a pristine mountain lake and
river flowing out of it through a virgin forest northwest of Mt. Hood. Federal
action in 1892, 1897, 1904, and 1913 preserved much of the area for the Portland City water supply. Because it serves over one-third of the state's population, it must be counted as the most important body of water in Oregon. In later years, 2 additional pipe lines and 2 dams would be built. On occasion permission has been granted to harvest some of the timber and there has even
been talk of power generation. The U. S. District Court has recently ruled that
timber cutting and extended recreational practices in the reserve are danger-
ous and illegal. The issue is still under court review.

special tax on all residents or a combination of tax and increased rates.[22]

Ladd reminded Reed that a recent newspaper poll showed nine out of ten Portlanders favoring Bull Run water. At the February 5th meeting, Ladd read an engineer's report to the effect that Bull Run water would provide Portland with the purest water of any city in the world except for one in Scotland. Then Ladd played his little joke. He reached up on top of his desk and produced a small bottle of water which had been drawn from the Willamette River at high stage on February 5, 1886. After one year, the bottle was absolutely clear; not a speck of sediment was visible. Ladd's experiment verified Reed's contention of river purity, but this point was of secondary importance to the banker. He envisioned the future with more accuracy than his friend Reed and was not about to weaken his position by revealing the pure quality of the Willamette River water until after the Bull Run decision had been reached.[23] In 1888, the Water Committee purchased approximately four square miles of property within the Bull Run watershed. Most of the remainder of the land within the watershed was owned by the federal government.

Unfortunately for the Water Committee in February 1889, Governor Sylvester Pennoyer vetoed a legislative bill that would have granted the extended bonding capacity. Inasmuch as Judge Deady had drafted the bill on behalf of Henry Failing and the committee he was a bit miffed to say the least. "In view of his impracticable, cranky nature and conduct he ought to be called Sylpester Annoyer."[24] It would be four years before the desired bonding capacity would be approved. Although Pennoyer based his veto on his opposition to tax free bonds, he apparently never did accept the value of Bull Run water as worth the expense involved. Six years later, at a celebration honoring the arrival* of the first Bull Run water in the city, Pennoyer was asked to give a toast. After tasting his glass of Bull Run water he commented that it had neither body nor flavor; he much preferred the old Willamette.

From its inception, the Water Committee was continually embroiled in discussions over residential water rates which had been set at $1.50 per month per family of six persons or less. Except for Reed, the strongest protest came from H.C. Leonard, an associate of the Greens in the gas company and the old water company. Appearing before the committee, Leonard told Ladd that he, Ladd, could well afford $5 a month but a poor man could not afford $1.50 a month

*January, 1895.

when his take home pay was only $2 a day. Ladd wanted to wait before consideration of a reduction. The committee should base its action on its own experience, not on that of the old company, which he apparently did not trust. On March 2nd, however, the committee gave in to public pressure and set the rate at 75¢ per month. Each family resident in excess of six would be charged 10¢ a month.[25] Simeon Reed was satisfied. For years Portland's rates were to remain the second lowest in the nation, slightly above those of Niagara Falls, New York.

The Water Committee provided efficient and economic service. It was given a freedom to operate, in a way that might not have been possible had it been prey to the whims and fancies of a council system long criticized by the press and others for not taking the long view. Although the board was clearly an oligarchy — the elite of the business establishment — most of the members had a farsighted perspective about urban water needs not held by the average citizen. Henry Failing, the first and only president for 12 years, was a student of the classics. Undoubtedly he had read about the Ancient Roman aqueducts and knew how vital an ample and clean water system was to the health and growth of a city.

In this case, at least, it was probably propitious for Portland's future that the local democratic process was partially circumvented. Although questions would be raised subsequently about conflicts of interest in the awarding of construction and equipment contracts, the benefits to the public were substantial.*

5.

During the regular legislative session of February, 1885, the legislature enacted a bitterly fought measure that was decidedly not propitious for Portland's future. Inasmuch as Joe Simon was the major opponent as a state senator and William Reid the major proponent as an organizer and investor, it seems appropriate at this point in the story to examine closely Reid's previous railroad activities[26] which led to this confrontation and which were, ultimately, to have a determ-

---

*Major contracts in 1887 were let to the Oregon Paving and Contracting Company. James Steel, banker, street railway promoter and W.S. Ladd's brother-in-law, was the vice president, secretary and controlling investor. Additional conflicts of interest would be cited in the period 1898-1907.

ining effect on the physical shaping of Portland, epecially in the southwest section of the city.

In February 1880, Reid, Donald MacLeay and Ellis Hughes, Portland lawyer, formed the Oregon Railway Co. (of Oregon) to take over the properties of the Willamette Valley R.R. which in turn had succeeded to Joseph Gaston's old Dayton, Sheridan and Grand Ronde narrow gauge line in 1879. Gaston had been offered $10,000 by Henry Villard's attorney, Joseph Dolph, to sell the railroad to the OR&N, but Gaston had refused. With the support of the Earl of Airlie and the Scotch Bank of Dundee, the Oregonian Railway Co. Ltd. was incorporated in Dundee in April 1880, as the parent company of Reid's construction enterprise. Reid had plans to extend Gaston's line by tying it in to a new Eugene to Portland connection. He needed a Portland depot site.

For over ten years the City of Portland had considered itself the owner of a 400 foot (three acre) strip of the river levee immediately south of Jefferson Street, the only remaining portion not privately owned. Pioneer Stephen Coffin had dedicated the levee to the city for public use,* but the city fathers had not improved the land. To Reid, the former Coffin property seemed the most suitable spot for his depot. With the support of Eugene and Willamette Valley legislators he was successful in pressuring the legislature into granting the public levee to his railroad in October of 1880, several months after construction of the line had actually begun downstate.

Governor Thayer vetoed the bill but the legislature promptly overrode it. The city filed suit and five months later the Oregon Supreme Court declared the "seizure" of the levee unconstitutional. In the early summer of 1881 Henry Villard sent emissaries** to Dundee and convinced the Scottish bankers who controlled the Oregonian Railway Co. Ltd. that they should lease their properties to the OR&N at 7 percent per annum. Reid was instructed to terminate all further building; no more Dundee money would be forthcoming. Reid should not have been too surprised at this turn of events. A cash shortage had been developing in Scottish financial circles ever since the failure of the City of Glasgow Bank in 1878. Furthermore, the Dundee

---

*In January, 1865, Coffin and his wife, after receipt of patent, deeded the tract to the city of Portland, in trust, for a public levee or landing — reserving ferry privileges. In July, 1871, Coffin and others, in consideration of $2500, undertook to convey to the city an absolute fee simple title.

**Including James B. Montgomery, Reid's fellow Scot and former associate in the early real estate development of Albina. Montgomery's mission must have placed a severe strain on his friendship with Reid.

bankers had problems with Reid. There was too much bickering in their relationship. Reid was considered not sufficiently conservative.[27]

William Reid

Reid was angry. He had completed over 163 miles of road and was only 28 1/2 miles from Portland. Late in 1881 he severed his ties with the Dundee financial community.* Villard had played "a thieving game" and there was nothing he could do about it. Reid warned his former colleagues that Villard had no intention of completing the line; that he would remove the iron rails and use them on his main road to California. All Villard was interested in was suppressing competition, he said. As it later turned out, Reid was right. When Villard suffered financial reverses in December 1883, the OR&N defaulted on its interest payments and cancelled its lease in November 1884.** The Scots were forced to sue the OR&N. They lost the case on an appeal to the U.S. Supreme Court in 1889, and the Oregonian Company entered into bankruptcy proceedings in the Dundee courts.

---

*The OR&N signed the lease on August 1, 1881. The Earl of Airlie died in Denver in late September, 1881. (His son showed no interest in Oregon and proceeded to spend his fortune lavishly in Colorado.) These two events terminated Reid's relationship with Dundee, Scotland.

**Villard's railroad construction ended for good on May 4, 1884. His Oregon & California line had reached Ashland, less than 15 miles from the California border. The Oregonian Company properties, however, had been "sadly neglected" and, when abandoned by the OR&N in 1884, were "in a frightful condition."[28]

In January 1885 Reid was a free agent, no longer associated with either of the major Scottish banking interests. At the urging, supposedly, of the downstate farmers, he reincorporated his old rail line as the Portland & Willamette Valley Railroad. He had a new depot site bill introduced into the legislature, containing essentially the same grant provisions as the 1880 law. After a stiff fight, he won, and this time he was not thwarted by court action. The climate of opinion had changed in Portland. The local directors of the railroad included the city's leading businessmen: W.S. Ladd, C.H. Lewis, S.G. Reed,* V.B. DeLashmutt, and Aaron Meier. When suit was brought subsequently, in an attempt to preserve Portland's only remaining public levee, it was too late. Reversing a position taken five years earlier, the courts held that the grant to the railroad was not inconsistent with the land's use as a public levee, on the ground that the dedication having been made in favor of the public, the state rather than the city was the actual beneficiary. The Dundee to Portland connection was completed in July, 1887 and the depot opened in July 1888.**

At the foot of S.W. Jefferson St.

---

*The P&WVRR would service the Oregon Iron & Steel Works near Lake Oswego (incorporated 1882) owned by W.S. Ladd, Simeon Reed and Henry Villard. The company was the largest metal working plant in the Northwest in 1889.
**The city council granted a right-of-way franchise in South Portland on June 17, 1887.

In retrospect, the whole episode now seems to have been one gigantic sleight of hand trick. Unbeknown to the public, but certainly not to Reid, Ladd and the rest of their local cohorts, most of the funding for the Portland & Willamette Valley R.R. was provided by Collis P. Huntington, President of the Southern Pacific R.R.* It is hard to believe that the OR&N hierarchy could have been fooled; it is more likely the case that they gave tacit support. In late 1885, the OR&N had apparently begun some preliminary negotiation with the S.P. for the leasing of all of its southbound trackage and right-of-ways, including that of the Oregon Central Railroad. The OR&N had suffered a 40 percent drop in net earnings in 1885.[29] The Southern Pacific knew that the OR&N was badly in need of increased revenues. It was now anxious to gain a foothold in western Oregon. Meeting Reid's financial exigencies would provide just the opportunity. The S.P. would also be given added leverage in its negotiations with the OR&N.

Senator Joseph Simon deserves credit for trying every possible parliamentary maneuver in his attempt to defeat the 1885 law. Only he and Senator H.B. Miller from Josephine County in southern Oregon voted against it. Apparently Miller smelled something "fishy" because he publicly stated that the Portland & Willamette Valley R.R. was "not a bona fide enterprise." It is difficult to figure out Simon's motives; his past record would indicate that he was not concerned about giving away the public levee *per se*. Most of his colleagues on the OR&N board were in favor of the action; even Solomon Hirsch, his U.S. Senate candidate, voted for the depot grant. Basic to Simon's opposition was probably the influence within the legislature of John H. Mitchell who was on the payroll of the S.P. He had, after all, spent most of the session fighting Mitchell's renomination. It was not until 20 years later that Mitchell's long-standing financial relation with the S.P. would become a matter of public record. Simon must have been aware of it in 1885.

In May of 1887, the S.P.'s control of the Portland & Willamette Valley R.R. was revealed by the announcement that the Pacific Improvement Company was the real owner. The officers of this latter enterprise were the "big four" of the Southern Pacific Co.: Huntington, Crocker, Stanford and Hopkins.** At about the same time, the OR&N

---

*$550,000 in securities were sold; $150,000 in stocks and $400,000 in bonds. Reid put in some of his own money along with Huntington.

**In the words of *Fortune Magazine* (1937):

"The simple theme that the quartet evolved was that riches should be distributed to all, though not necessarily in equal mea-

completed its lease arrangements with the S.P. which formally assumed operating control of the P&WVRR in 1890. Many years later, the depot site was closed, the building torn down and the property sold to private industry, but the tracks and rail right-of-way have been maintained in the possession of the S.P. to the present day.* Harvey Scott noted in 1890 that the property was no longer listed as belonging to the public, let alone to the city, even though the city was meant to have received back the property once it was no longer used for the purpose served by the legislative grant of authority. "The whole river front is in private possession, and the city or the public makes claim to no adverse rights. . . . "It was an idle thought," concluded Scott, "to place any . . . trust in the hands of men chosen at municipal elections. Special trustees, apart from all political interests and persuasions, should have been appointed and the property managed much as are the City Water Works at present."[31] If nothing else, this episode proves how necessary it is that the public properties requisite to a city's development be "nailed down." Portland's history clearly reveals that public properties have not been guarded as zealously as private properties.

In one other important way the Portland & Willamette Valley line exercised a decided influence upon the city. It opened up the southwest suburban districts to increased residential development by providing 14 trips daily between Portland and Oswego, with stops at half a dozen intermediate stations. With accurate prophecy, the *West Shore* predicted that "in a few years this route will be the main reliance of thousands of suburban residents employed or doing business in the city of Portland."[32]

In a two year period, the Southern Pacific Railroad had become a powerful force in Portland economic and political life, and the process had been initiated by William Reid in his quest for funding of the Portland & Willamette Valley R.R. There is no way to prove that Reid was not, in fact, secretly induced to reactivate his dormant rail

---

sure. The legislators should make a profit for passing laws, and the state . . . should make a profit for having a railroad, and the town should make a profit for the same reason, and the railroad should make a profit (in the form of subsidies as well as traffic) from the state and the towns. Provided with a formula like this, a hardware man [Huntington] who could find no profit for himself certainly would never make a profit by selling hardware."[30]

*The depot site was bought before 1900 by F.W. Leadbetter, Henry Pittock's son-in-law. The S.P. also acquired 800 ft. (8 acres) of PWVRR river frontage, 2 miles south of the depot site on the west bank of the Willamette River.

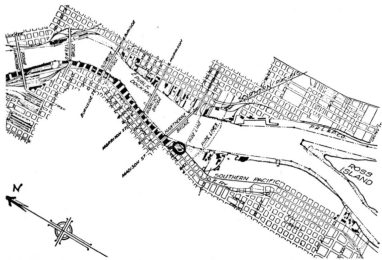

1913 Map. The site of the Southern pacific depot (originally granted to the P.W.V.R.R. in 1885) is circled.

project by Huntington to whom he had made overtures back in 1880. Furthermore, knowing what the S.P. did in later years, it is not inconceivable to suggest that some of the legislators might have been "unduly influenced" by the S.P. to support the 1885 law. Whether Reid was used as a tool, willingly or not, is of little historical significance. What became important to Portland's future was that by 1887 the Southern Pacific had virtual ownership of railroad tracks and river frontage on both sides of the Willamette River. It inherited franchises that went back 20 years, awarded originally by the legislature to other companies;* franchises that would be invested with the sacred rights of private property. The Southern Pacific profited enormously at the expense of the Portland public treasury. Furthermore, the existence of the Southern Pacific tracks and right-of-ways encouraged the mutilation of both river banks, especially the one running along the southwest edge of the city, a close-in area that was soon to become a major industrial site.**

*One franchise, so inherited, belonged to the OCRR (the old west-side Oregon Central). It provided the SP with direct access into the center of the city by way of Fourth St. It was to cause the city government and the residents much anguish before it was finally terminated some twenty years later.

**Excerpts from former Governor Oswald West's account of the episode are worth noting:

"The legislature, wishing to see determined what rights, if any, the city of Portland had in and to the levee, imposed upon the company the duty of acquiring any such rights through condemnation proceedings. In August, 1885, proceedings were initiated and, in March, 1888, brought to a conclusion. The city was awarded $8750, which the railway company paid.

Later all rights of the Portland and Willamette Valley Railway Company in and to the levee were acquired by the Oregon and California Railroad Company, and thus passed to the Southern Pacific Company.

While serving as a member of the Oregon Railroad Commission, I had occasion to look into the Southern Pacific Company's title or claim to the levee, and reached the conclusion that, when the tract was dedicated to "public use," the State of Oregon and not the city of Portland, became trustee; that the legislature might regulate its use or permit improvements, but could not subject it to use, inconsistent with the terms of the dedication; that neither the state nor the city of Portland had an interest in the property which could be disposed of.

Upon becoming governor of Oregon I deemed it in the public interest that the grant act of 1885 be repealed; and that the state or city undertake the administration of the trust. So, to that end, and through the cooperation of the Portland city attorney's office, a measure was prepared and introduced at the 1911 legislative session, by Senator Dan Kellaher.

The legislature refused to pass the bill but, by resolution, authorized the governor to further investigate the matter and report his findings to the 1913 session of the legislature.

My report to the legislature follows:

1. That the property had been dedicated to the use of the public.

2. That the legislature has power to regulate that use, but without power to permit its being diverted to uses inconsistent with the terms of the dedication.

3. The legislature could have made the railroad company its agent and authorized a use of the premises in keeping with the conditions of the dedication, but could go no further.

4. That the Southern Pacific Company holds under no other right than as licensee of the state, and the legislature may revoke such license at any time.

5. That the act through which it was attempted to grant the property to the railroad should be repealed.

6. That the property should be transferred to the city of Portland, trustee, to be devoted to the uses intended by the donors.

A bill repealing the grant act of 1885 was introduced by Senator Dan Kellaher at the 1913 session and approved, but with an amendment providing for the payment of $50,000 to the Southern Pacific Company.

Negotiations with the company resulted in the city of Portland receiving a quitclaim deed to the levee — the company receiving from the city a lease to such ground as was needed for right of way purposes. The $50,000 appropriated by the legislature was retained by the state."[33]

MT. SHASTA.
Portland-San Francisco
Line of the
Southern Pacific.

SOUTHERN PACIFIC COMPANY

SUNSET
OGDEN & SHASTA
ROUTES.

Midwinter Scene Near Sisson.

The Picturesque Ride Over the Siskiyous on the Oregon Slope.

The Great Scenic Attractions of the Siskiyous.
Southern Pacific's Portland-San Francisco Line

The Famous Shasta
Headwaters Sacramento

Crossing the Willamette River at Portland.

First Glimpse of Portland's Water Front From Southern
Pacific's Train Entering Oregon's Metropolis

PASSING THROUGH THE GREAT WHEAT FIELDS OF THE WILLAMETTE VALLEY, THE GARDEN SPOT OF OREGON

THE MATCHLESS SOUTHERN PACIFIC COMPANY'S SYSTEM.
PORTLAND IS THE TERMINUS OF THIS GREAT RAILROAD IN THE PACIFIC NORTHWEST.

Chapter V

Bankers, Politicians
and Street Railways

1.

"Wealth may be a powerful factor in building up an industrial and commercial community, or it may be a mere hindrance and obstruction. There is plenty of proof that obstructive rich men are more in the way of the development of a country than poverty itself."[1]

So editorialized the *Oregonian* in April 1887 in a surprisingly harsh blast at Portland's financial establishment.* The paper accused Portland's financial leaders of being anti-development; of discouraging "investments in productive industry;" of a "narrow and absurd fear of competition" from the East and California; of a "dread of the introduction of new and unknown forces."

What was the reason for this state of mind? Was it fear of losing local control, of sharing profits with outsiders? In attacking what it called "this chronic and all-pervading pessimism," the *Oregonian* blamed Portlanders' "provincial narrowness of character, . . . fostered . . . by extremely slow progress and long isolation. . . . Men come

---

*If one were to remove the references to "rich men" and "wealth" the editorial might sound like the current wails of organized labor and the Chamber of Commerce which are bemoaning attempts by environmentalists and others to impose a "no-growth" policy on the State of Oregon.

from the East to Portland looking for opportunities to make investments." They would "build suburban railways and bridges, . . . erect lumber and flour mills" and "set up a variety of manufacturing establishments." From Portland's leaders "there is seldom anything but an effort to discourage and dissuade."

The editorial is puzzling. One has to assume that it was written by the perennial "booster," Editor Harvey Scott, while also reflecting the feelings of majority owner Henry L. Pittock.* There is much irony in the episode as the year 1887 witnessed a boom such as Portland had never before experienced, one that was to accelerate in velocity until the depression of 1893. In 1887, furthermore, Pittock was an organizer of the Portland Trust Co. and a founding partner of the Southwest Portland Real Estate Co., developers of Fulton Park.** It is true that most of the new growth was locally owned and operated.*** The local bankers had kept pretty tight control over Portland's economic development for some years. Conceivably Messrs. Ladd, Failing and Corbett held second thoughts about the wisdom of having sold out their transportation interests to Henry Villard, and for this reason were reticent about encouraging further outside capital investment.

The Lombard Investment Company, a national investors service, published a glowing but greatly exaggerated statement of Portland's economic health, using 1887 figures.[3] It cited a total of one hundred millionaires and invested capital of $50 million. It also reported that several million dollars of Portland money had been invested in eastern Oregon and Idaho mines within the past three years, a development that led to the organization of the Portland Stock Exchange in 1887 under the leadership of Jonathan Bourne, Jr. Primarily a mining exchange, it listed 25 of Portland's leading businessmen as charter members. Two of this group, Van B. DeLashmutt and Tyler

---

*Scott owned one-third of the *Oregonian* stock.
**For a description of the Fulton Park Development, see Appendix D.

***Locally owned industry in 1887[2]

Industry	# Workers Employed	Value of Product
Saw Mills	500	$1,596,000
Foundries, Metal Works	583	1,176,000
Planing Mills	204	550,000
Furniture Mfg.	301	750,000
Woolen Mfg.	335	750,000
Breweries	72	500,000
Meat Packing	95	435,000

FULTON PARK!

PROPERTY OF THE SOUTHWEST PORTLAND REAL ESTATE COMPANY.

The Largest, Best Located and Most Desirable Tract Ever Placed upon the Portland Market.

SALE COMMENCED JUNE 20TH, 1888.

FULTON PARK is located one mile south of the present corporate boundary, and in the rapidly growing direction of the city.

FULTON PARK consists of fifteen hundred choice residence lots, 50 x 100 feet each, with full width streets and improved boulevards.

FULTON PARK is convenient to public schools and churches, and enjoys telephone and telegraph communication with the city of Portland.

FULTON PARK affords a charming view of Mount Hood, Mount St. Helens, Mount Jefferson and the rugged Cascade range.

FULTON PARK enjoys a perfect system of natural drainage, and is absolutely free from the baneful effects of malaria.

FULTON PARK is reached by the Narrow Gauge railway. Trains passing every fifteen minutes. Fare five cents.

FULTON PARK is also reached by the Oregon & California railway, only ten minutes' ride from the Portland post office.

FULTON PARK is supplied with an abundance of the purest of spring water, as clear as crystal and as cold as ice.

FULTON PARK is located on Riverside avenue (White House road), conceded by everybody to be the most beautiful drive on the Pacific coast.

FULTON PARK affords a splendid view of the cities of Portland and East Portland and the beautiful Willamette river.

FULTON PARK is the future great residence site of the city of Portland, and affords a splendid field for investment.

FULTON PARK property, by reason of its convenient location to the city, will quadruple in value within two years.

FULTON PARK will be fully and correctly illustrated in the August number of THE WEST SHORE. Don't fail to secure a copy.

PRICE, TERMS, ETC.

Prices of lots in FULTON PARK range from $50 to $500 each, according to location. No deviation will be made from the printed price list, except on cash purchases, when a discount of five per cent. will be allowed. TERMS—One-fourth cash, balance in quarterly payments of twenty-five per cent. each, with interest on deferred payments at eight per cent. per annum. An advance of five per cent. will be made on the printed price list on the first day of each month for a period of twelve months, commencing September 1, 1888, thus insuring first purchasers an absolute profit of sixty per cent. per annum. Parties at a distance purchasing by mail or otherwise, in order to determine the amount of first payment, must add five per cent. to printed list after September 1, otherwise remittance will be returned at expense of sender. The title to FULTON PARK property is guaranteed to be absolutely perfect. Abstracts, bonds and deeds will be furnished without additional charge.

For lithographic maps, printed price lists or other information, call on or address

PACIFIC LAND AND INVESTMENT CO., Agents,

No. 46 Washington St., Portland, Or.   J. T. FLYNN, Manager

Site of Johns Landing Development

Woodward, along with banker George B. Markle Jr. also a mine investor, were to play crucial roles in Portland's business and political affairs during the years following 1885.

PORTLAND, OR.-WILLAMETTE STEAM MILL, LUMBERING AND MANUFACTURING COMPANY.

West side of the river, across from the Albina Union Pacific Car Shops just south of current Terminal 1 site.

A brief review of Portland economic activity covering the period 1885-1891 would tend to belie the *Oregonian's* charges. Ten banks and two insurance companies were incorporated. The Portland Hotel was completed and the municipal water system expanded. Twenty-four separate street railway franchises were awarded to ten companies. Two electrical utility and street paving concerns were organized. The first three Willamette River bridges were completed, owned and operated privately.* Over $54 million were invested in new residential and commercial construction in 1889. And the Port of Portland Commission was established in 1891, thus officially launching Portland as a major world seaport.**

Only two years after the *Oregonian's* pessimistic appraisal of Portland's business climate, the *West Shore* declared that "Portland is waking up." New, active forces were discerned to be at work and there was the "push, energy and practical business sense to manage

---

*(1) Morrison Bridge, April 1887, the largest bridge west of the Mississippi; (2) Railroad Bridge (Steel Br.), July 1888, the first steel bridge on the West Coast, built by the OR&N and UPRR; (3) Madison Street Bridge (Hawthorne Br.), July 1891.
**See Appendix E. for 1888 statistical table of manufacturers.

them."[4] The subject of this article was George B. Markle Jr. from Hazelton, Pennsylvania. Within three years of his arrival at the age of 30, Markle had been instrumental in organizing the following companies: Portland Hotel, Oregon National Bank, Northwest Loan and Trust, Vancouver & Ellensburg R.R., Portland Mining and the Sunset Mines, Ellensburg National Bank, Commercial Bank of Vancouver, Portland Traction, Columbia Fire & Marine Insurance, Portland Tanning, and the North Pacific Industrial Association. "A long and promising career is ahead of him" predicted the *West Shore*. "He has the prescience to perceive and the talent to improve."[5]

Markle came from a wealthy coal mining family in the Scranton area. His father had founded the Jeddo-Highland Coal Co., one of the largest independent anthracite mining operations in the East. George B. Sr. was also an early associate of Thomas Edison in the building of the first two central station coal fired electric power plants in the United States. After eight years with his family's coal and banking enterprises, following his graduation from Lafayette College, George Jr. traveled through seven western states and selected Portland as the place to settle permanently. Here, he felt, was offered the best inducement for bettering his fortunes by investing his money, of which "he had plenty."[6] He first needed to make the proper friends. A man of enthusiastic temperament, he found just the vehicle: a campaign to resurrect the construction of the Portland Hotel, the foundations of which had lain exposed for over two years,*

"Villard's Ruins", painting by Francesca Grothjean, mid-1880's.

---

*"Villard's ruins" as they were called, into which the railroad magnate had pumped $125,000, were an "eyesore and a public nuisance."[7]

ever since the time of Henry Villard's financial collapse. Within months, Markle was successful in persuading 150 of Portland's leading citizens to subscribe a total of $525,000. William S. Ladd invested $100,000; Henry W. Corbett, $80,000; Henry Failing, $50,000; C.H. Lewis, $25,000; Simeon Reed, $20,000; and Van B. DeLashmutt, $20,000. Corbett was elected president of the Portland Hotel Co., lawyer C.A. Dolph, vice president and Henry Failing, treasurer.

Markle was now in with the right crowd and he had proven his ability. Just how much he invested himself is not recorded, but his efforts resulted in the creation of a close friendship with Van B. De-Lashmutt, prominent banker, mine investor, horse breeder and long time associate of Simeon Reed. DeLashmutt was also a local power politically and his wife's first cousin was Penumbra Kelly,* U.S. Marshal and Sheriff of Multnomah County from 1888 to 1894. In short order, Markle and DeLashmutt team up to buy control of the Multnomah Street Railway Company and merge it into the newly incorporated Portland Traction Company (1887). In 1888, they organized the Oregon National Bank,** with DeLashmutt as president, and the Northwest Loan & Trust Company with Markle at the helm. For anyone starting a bank, the readiest source of large deposits was public tax revenues, so it was not surprising when Sheriff Kelly elected to deposit the school tax funds with the Markle banks. The public funds attracted private deposits. Soon the banks had sufficient assets to launch an aggressive campaign to promote commercial loans for investment in real estate and traction properties.

In the spring of 1888, Markle was admitted to the prestigious Arlington Club;*** he also became a local celebrity. His mother and two sisters were visiting him in Portland when word was received that his father was desperately ill back home in Hazelton. He hired a two car special train and headed east with his family at breakneck speed. "Tables and chairs were piled in a heap as the cars swayed and bounced over the rails."[8] In 63 hours the Markles were in Chicago, the fastest trip ever recorded to that time and only five hours slower than the streamliner schedule 60 years later. Costing him $2,000, the

---

*Kelly had married a daughter of wealthy pioneer Philip Marquam, judge, legislator, owner of the Marquam Theater. Marquam Hill commemorates his name.

**The Oregon National Bank absorbed the Metropolitan Savings Bank which had been incorporated in 1882 by DeLashmutt and Harvey Scott.

***Members of Arlington Club were drawn largely from the socially prominent business and professional male community most of whom lived on the West side of the river.

venture enhanced his reputation as a colorful man of action. Not long after his famous trip back east, Markle's father died and the son's already substantial wealth was increased by an inheritance. Markle used this money to build up his banks and street railway properties, and to purchase several hundred acres of Portland real estate.

His eyes lit upon a handsome brick mansion which was being constructed in early 1889 on Hawthorne Terrace, on the heights above Portland. It belonged to lawyer-realtor J. Carroll McCaffrey,* who, along with Preston Smith, was largely responsible for promoting both the new Cable Railway and the early residential development

---

*McCaffrey, a transplanted Philadelphian, was Secretary and Manager of the Portland Building and Loan Association in 1889.

of Portland Heights, regarded as the playground and "toy of the wealthy." Markle purchased the house, along with several acres,* finished the interior and readied the home for occupancy in late May 1889.[9] One month later he married a considerably younger lady, Miss Kate Goodwin, daughter of an army colonel stationed in

The Markle home.

Summit of Portland Heights

Cable Ascent to Portland Heights.

Looking North From Portland Heights.
City of Portland 600 Feet Below.

---

*The purchase price is open to question. McCaffrey was reported to have put $18,000 into the house in 1888. The abstract of title reveals that Markle paid McCaffrey $12,334 in cash and assumed an $8,000 mortgage in February 1889. Markle also paid $2700 for additional acreage. Portland Heights real estate was going for $250 an acre in 1888 but would increase to $5,000 an acre by 1910. An *Oregonian* article of May 29, 1904, reporting a $70,000 sale price, would appear to be grossly in error. A similar report that McCaffrey had spent $50,000 on the house would appear to be erroneous.

Vancouver. He began to live in the grand style to which he felt he was suited, experiencing a way of life that he had sought when he first decided to settle in Portland. Mr. & Mrs. Markle were now occupying the largest and most prominent home on the Portland skyline.*

Markle's star was beginning to shine ever brighter in 1890. He was appointed to the Public Improvement Standing Commitee of the Board of Trade which was merged into the newly incorporated Portland Chamber of Commerce on April 7th. On that same day, the Portland Hotel opened its eight floors, 326 bedrooms and extensive dining facilities to an eager public. Well over a million dollars had been spent on construction and furnishings and its imposing and lively presence boosted civic pride and confidence in Portland's future growth. The architects were W.M. Whidden, formerly of the Boston office of the Stanford White firm, and Ion Lewis, also of Boston. In terms of architecture, the Portland Hotel introduced to Oregon "a new sense of breadth of form."[10] For three decades it was to play a leading role in the social and business life of the city.

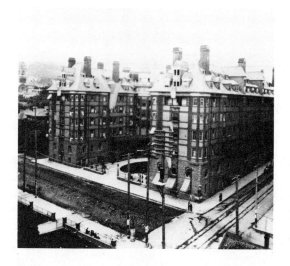

Hotel Portland. Site of present Meier & Frank parking lot and future downtown park.

---

*Known for 60 years as the Pittock House, not to be confused with the later built Pittock Mansion.

NORTH PACIFIC INDUSTRIAL EXPOSITION BUILDING.
PORTLAND, OREGON.

Interior of the Industrial Exposition Building.

Markle was already involved in several other projects which reflected *his* confidence in the future. Along with Frank Dekum, he had been responsible in 1888 for promoting the construction of the North Pacific Industrial Association Exposition Building on the site of what is now the Civic Stadium Apartments at S.W. Burnside and 18th Avenue. In fact he had bought the land and taken out a $62,000 personal mortgage with the Scottish American Investment Trust Co. Ltd. of Edinburgh. Erected at a cost of $150,000 it opened in September 1889 and was an immediate success, with "people coming in for attendance from all parts of the Northwest." It was a "mammoth structure of brick, iron, glass and fir . . . certainly the largest edifice on the Pacific Coast."[11] Covering two full blocks, 400 feet long by 200 feet deep, three stories in height, the building could accommodate 250 exhibits with 200 square feet each.* On the night of May 5, 1891, over 15,000 Oregonians squeezed within its portals to give President Benjamin Harrison one of the heartiest welcomes he had ever received.[12]

George Markle was also instrumental in persuading the Chamber of Commerce membership to undertake the construction of a new headquarters building, on the north side of Stark Street, a half block running between Third and Fourth Avenues. As ground was broken on September 2, 1890, he committed the support of both of his banks which would be moved and headquartered in prime space at street level. He negotiated the mortgage with the New York Life Insurance Co., and when the construction costs began to mount up to considerably more than what was budgeted, almost $170,000 worth, Markle personally secured signed notes covering the overrun. When the building opened three years to the month later, it was advertised as the outstanding office structure in the Pacific Northwest. To be known in later years as the Commerce Building, it was the major meeting place of business and political figures, its eight floors containing everything from banks, offices, saloons, bowling alley, billiard room and auditorium, to the prestigious Commercial Club.**

---

*The building burned to the ground in 1910.

**Before it was wrecked in January 1934 by its owners, the SP&S Railroad, which considered the building a "white elephant," The *Oregon Journal* commented:

"The forward course of progress pays no heed to values of a sentimental nature. The fact the building is rich in history is of no consequence. That the building has tenanted a great many of our state leaders who have gained national prominence is of no import. Nor are we concerned with the almost human personality of the building. Were it standing in a European city, it would probably be kept and used for

Chamber of Commerce Building. S.W. Stark, between
3rd & 4th Streets.

fifty or one hundred more years; but, to impatient America, it is merely
a symbol of a former era and is standing in the path of the jugger-
naut, Progress."

For 40 years, that half-block has stood vacant, the site of an ugly surface
parking lot. This case is a good example of what absentee ownership does
to destroy local pride. The railroad had bought the building in 1906, several
years after the New York Life Insurance Co. foreclosed on the mortgage, following the depression of 1893. The SP&S R.R. decided to move its local office
to the American Bank Building. The company considered the Commerce
Building to be too old fashioned. In the immediate post depression years of
the 1930's, the company said that it could not maintain tax and upkeep costs.
To put the building into what the company called operational shape to meet
its then current needs, the building would have had to have been gutted and
this endeavor was considered "too expensive and impractical."[13]

By the age of 34, George B. Markle, Jr. was well along the road to a successful career that would carry him to the top of Portland business life and see him elected president of the Chamber of Commerce within three years. He fulfilled the *Oregonian's* wildest dreams and became Harvey Scott's hero. Eulogizing him in 1890, Scott wrote:

George B. Markle, Jr.

"At an age when most men are only beginning to see their way clear toward the substantial things of life, Mr. Markle has already achieved a well earned success. He not only has the ability to project great schemes, but what is more essential the nerve and energy, the courage and financial skill to carry them to a successful issue. Young in years, strong in intellect, in the full vigor of life, and buoyant in hope and aspiration there can be but a career of usefulness and prosperity before this gentleman, especially in a region where the greatest scope is open to one possessing the prescience to perceive, and the talent to improve the great opportunities the future so abundantly promises.

Mr. Markle is of ordinary height, heavy built with a full ruddy face indicative of good health, and a hearty, robust constitution. He is mature in appearance and gives the impression of being older than his years. He is cool and deliberate in manner, and under the most exciting circumstances would not be apt to lose his equilibrium. He is a man of positive convictions and is not easily turned aside from an undertaking his judgment approves, no matter how difficult the consummation of his scheme may at times appear. It is this quality of persistence, added to the ability of being able to promptly provide means to meet emergencies, which is the strongest element in his character, and to which more than all else is due his success in life."[14]

While Markle was in the east, his associate, Van B. DeLashmutt, was elected mayor by the city council to succeed John Gates who had died in April 1888. One wonders how he could find time to perform the necessary duties associated with the office, although it was not a full time job, paying only $1200 a year. One would like to hope, furthermore, that it was the honor which attracted him but the record would indicate that more than honor was involved.

Van B. DeLashmutt

Van DeLashmutt's* career[15] was even more varied and colorful than Markle's. In the 46 years since his birth in a small Iowa town, DeLashmutt had enjoyed extraordinary financial success. He was a man of "unusual personal attractiveness which led to wide acquaintances and great popularity."[16] Originally a printer by trade, he entered the grocery business not long after his arrival in Portland. In 1882, he organized and became president of the Metropolitan Savings Bank. Two of his closest associates in this enterprise were *Oregonian* Editor Harvey W. Scott and William W. Thayer, outgoing governor and future chief justice of the state supreme court. He also entered the real estate market by purchasing and platting some of the acreage on which was to be built part of the future town of Beaverton. Near Hillsboro he developed his Witch Hazel Farm and horse track which became the "sporting center" of the state. In the Woodstock district he netted over $40,000 from the sale of 194 acres in 1889 while he was Mayor.** He also founded the Columbia Street Bridge Co., the Oregon Lumber Co., and three mining companies,*** in addition to entering into partnership with George Markle. In 1892 he was to be the first president of the Bank of Albina.

DeLashmutt home, S. W. 12th and Columbia

---

*(1842-1921.) DeLashmutt died in Spokane where he had lived for over twenty years.

**Bought from his wife's cousin for $17 an acre in 1880 and sold for $250 an acre.

***Sierra Nevada Consolidated, Stem Winder, and Granite. Capitalized at over $2 million, the mines generated dividends of $100,000 in 1890 while he was mayor.

DeLashmutt lived with his family in a large home at S.W. 12th and Columbia Streets although his heart was really in the country. He would have preferred to spend all of his time with his horses, but he needed to make money to underwrite what became an increasingly expensive hobby. Horse breeding was also a consuming passion of Simeon G. Reed's and the two men spent much time dickering over sale prices. After Reed left for California, his nephew Martin Winch carried on the same pattern of negotiations and on one occasion wrote his uncle that DeLashmutt "is queer. You can't tell from one day to another what he will do."[17]

The city council over which Mayor DeLashmutt presided in the summer of 1888 had several different faces but structurally it had changed little in three years. The most important newcomer and the man who was to dominate the council during his six year term of office was Tyler Woodward. At the time of his first election in 1886, Woodward was president and general manager of the Transcontinental Street Railway Company, founded in 1882 by Woodward and Elijah Corbett, brother of Henry W., and in 1888 by far the largest streetcar operation in the city. Seven years later, Woodward would be elected president of the U.S. National Bank.

Born in Hartland, Vermont in 1835, Woodward had been reared on a farm, attended Kimball Union Academy, taught school and emigrated to California in 1860. For ten years he lived in frontier gold mining communities in California, Idaho and Montana, doing everything from mining to running a trading post. After a brief stint in Portland real estate, he put in another 10 years in the Walla Walla country supervising railroad construction. Elijah Corbett persuaded him to return to Portland in 1882 to take charge of building the Transcontinental system, an endeavor which he performed brilliantly. As was to be noted in a later account of his career, Woodward experienced "no failures." All he undertook was "crowned with success."[18]

From the record one must assume that Tyler Woodward served on the council for one reason only, to enhance and protect his private business interests. No governmental function in the 1880's and '90's was more susceptible to interest conflict than the awarding of corporate franchises.[19] Just to cite one year, for example, from December 1888 to December 1889, the council awarded four separate franchises to the Transcontinental system. In each case, Woodward voted in favor of the ordinance and on two occasions he actually signed the ordinances while serving as acting mayor by virtue of his role as the elected council president. The 30 year franchises called for no payment to the city for use of streets, only for car license fees of $50 per year for a two horse model, and $25 for a one horse rig. It should be added that these were standard fees for all Portland streetcar operations. Conflict of interest was made even more obvious when Woodward voted against the awarding of franchises to competing lines, such as the Mt. Tabor Street Railway and the Multnomah Street Railway companies. The latter of course belonged to Markle and DeLashmutt and the mayor could and did play the same game. In the two year period from 1889-1890, DeLashmutt voted in favor of and signed four franchises awarded to the Multnomah Street operation, all with the same fee schedule.

From 1888 to December 1891, ten different traction companies spread their tracks over Portland's streets. The city council approved every franchise application. The financing of much of this activity was provided by some of the newer trust and savings banks which were investing in real estate developments served by the street railways that were gradually becoming electrified in the early 1890's. The Metropolitan Railway Company* was a prime example. Founded in 1889 by George A. and James Steel, W.S. Ladd's brother-in-law, it ran through south Portland, on the West side, to the Fulton Park

*Known as the Fulton Park line, it was the second electric line on the Pacific Coast.

development and Riverview Cemetery. It was financed largely by the Merchants National Bank of which James Steel was president, and to a lesser degree by the Portland Trust Co. and Henry Pittock. Some Ladd money was funneled into this and other Steel enterprises, but by and large William S. Ladd did not implicate himself deeply in these more speculative ventures. The same held true for Henry W. Corbett* whose personal investment in traction properties was limited. The First National Bank, however, did become involved in 1891 when it became apparent to Henry Failing and Corbett that order needed to be brought out of potential chaos. There were too many traction companies, too much competition, growing inefficiencies in service and increasing financial burdens created by the cost and physical requirements of electrification.

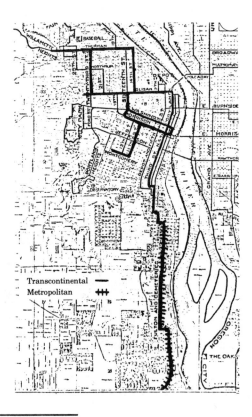

Transcontinental ━
Metropolitan ┿┿┿

---

*Corbett would be vice president of the City & Suburban Railway Co. after 1898, representing primarily the First National Bank's interests rather than his own.

The immediate impetus for reorganization, however, was provided by the voters of Portland, East Portland and Albina who accepted a new charter of consolidation in June 1891, combining the east and west sides of the river into one unified municipality. Henry Failing and Tyler Woodward were responsible for incorporating the City & Suburban Railway Co. one week after the vote of consolidation. Combining the Transcontinental with three other companies,* the City & Suburban was enfranchised in December 1891 with Woodward guiding the ordinance through the council.

More was involved in this reorganization than the mere combination of three street railway companies. For the first time, the city's largest bank became a partner in what was to become, 13 years later, a gigantic enterprise: the amalgamation of all of the street railways into a monopoly, financed by the two largest banks. Henry Failing, representing the First National assumed the presidency of the City & Suburban initially. Within a few months, however, Tyler Woodward was named president and held the post for 13 years,** while also serving as president of the U.S. National Bank from 1895-1902.

The young man who actually was to run the company as general manager during this span of time was a relative newcomer to Portland, 29 year old Charles F. Swigert.*** A self-educated construction engineer, Swigert was to become a major promoter of electrified railroads, the leading constructor of bridges, and the president of both the Port of Portland and the Chamber of Commerce, all before reaching the age of 46. By 1887, at the age of 25, he had helped design and supervise the construction of the city's first bridge across the Willamette River.[20] In the same year he was instrumental in promoting the construction of the Willamette Bridge Railway Company, to connect the new Morrison Street span with East Portland, Albina and Mount Tabor. Two years later he built the city's first electrified line from Northwest Third and Glisan across the new Steel Railroad Bridge to

---

*Willamette Bridge Railway Co., Portland & Fairview Railway Co. and Waverly-Woodstock Electric Railway Co.; merged in September 1891.

**Failing became vice-president when Woodward formally took over. When Failing died in 1898, Henry W. Corbett became vice-president.

***(1862-1935.) Born in Bowling Green, Ohio, Swigert was sent to Portland in late 1880, to help establish and manage an office for the Pacific Bridge Co. of San Francisco, owned by his uncle Charles Gorrill. Pacific Bridge had a contract to begin work on the first bridge over the Willamette (Morrison) in October 1880. The project was enjoined by U.S. District Judge Matthew P. Deady in March 1881. The U.S. Supreme Court overturned Deady's decision and the Willamette Iron Bridge Co. was reincorporated in early 1886.

Albina. With Henry Failing and the First National Bank, he organized the Union Power Co. in 1891 as a major power source for his extended electrified services. Shortly thereafter he built the Waverly-Woodstock and Portland & Fairview electrified railways. All of these lines were merged into the new City & Suburban system in September 1891. Swigert was to link most of his construction and electrified

Charles F. Swigert

railroad enterprises together, receiving, in the process, a full line of credit from the First National Bank. Like Reid and Markle, Swigert was an inexhaustible builder with great self-confidence, whose influence was to be strongly felt as Portland expanded rapidly in the early years of this century. But, unlike Reid and Markle, he enjoyed the support of Henry Corbett and Henry Failing.

George B. Markle was supremely confident about both his own future and that of the city, especially following Portland's consolidation in July 1891. He spent months of effort in laying plans to merge three operating traction companies* into one giant electric railway conglomerate that he hoped would equal the City & Suburban in size. Increasing the assets of his banks was a necessary first step. To this end, his friend and colleague, Mayor DeLashmutt, had provided invaluable assistance during his three year term of office. As mayor, DeLashmutt not only had promoted and signed franchise ordinances in behalf of the traction company which he and Markle owned, but had been responsible for the county and the city depositing public

---

*Multnomah Street Railway Co. (Portland Traction); Metropolitan Railway; and the Portland & Vancouver Railway, owned by Frank Dekum, R.L. Durham and the Dekum Banks.

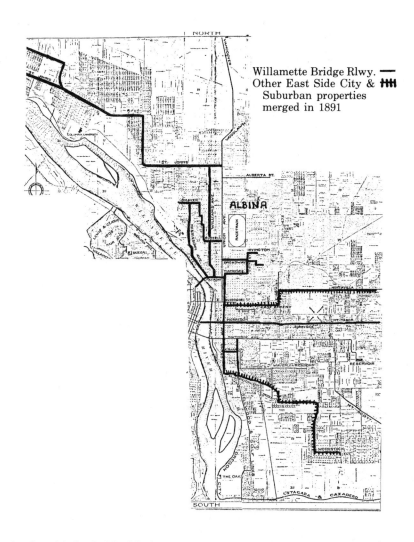

Willamette Bridge Rlwy. ——
Other East Side City & ┼┼┼
Suburban properties
merged in 1891

funds with both Markle banks, one of which, the Oregon National, he himself presided over as president until 1892. It had been no coincidence that the city treasurer from 1886-1890 was H.C. Monnastes, a long time mining investor associate of the mayor. Furthermore, the new city treasurer in 1890, Frank Hacheny,* was also a close friend of the mayor. In fact, DeLashmutt had sold him his wholesale grocery business eight years earlier.

---

*Born in Germany, Hacheny was to be city treasurer for ten years.

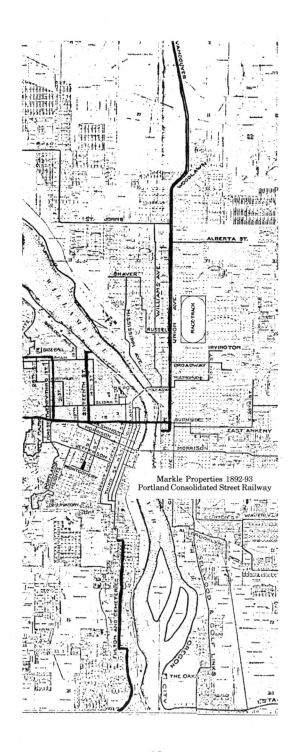

Markle Properties 1892-93
Portland Consolidated Street Railway

In the spring of 1892, at about the time that Markle was appointed to the Port of Portland Commission, he incorporated the Portland Consolidated Street Railway Company in association with W.S. Ladd's brother-in-law, James Steel, and lawyer-banker Richard L. Durham,* a comer in Portland business, society and politics in the early nineties. Durham was vice-president of the Commercial National Bank which was to become financially involved with the new corporation. To finance his scheme, Markle planned to do three things: (1) Use as seed money deposits already on hand in his banks, plus whatever other bank money he could raise. These funds would be loaned to the Consolidated line to get it functioning and make it attractive to potential investors. (2) Float a million dollar bond issue, the proceeds of which would be used to repay the bank loans; and (3) seek the financial backing of property owners who would benefit from improved service to their businesses and homes. In December 1892, Martin Winch wrote to his uncle, Simeon Reed in California, that there was a movement afoot among First Street property owners to try and hold business on the street. To this end, Markle was offering to lay double track and "put on a first class service" if the property owners would agree to be assessed a share of the costs. In Reed's case the amount would be about $1500 and Winch advised him to accept the terms.[21]

Everything went according to schedule. On February 16, 1893, Markle's Consolidated Street Railway Company was awarded a franchise by the city council, an action that was sponsored by Councilman Woodson A. Scoggin who just happened to be a director of the railway. At about the same time, Markle readied his campaign to sell a million dollars in railway bonds to finance the new company.

2.

The year 1893 had opened with a flourish, especially within the Portland business community. President Markle told the Chamber of Commerce membership at its annual dinner in January that "this is the most remarkable period in the history of Portland."[22] The city was experiencing its "highest level of prosperity" and its "lowest level of financial depression." Citing the role and responsiblity of

---

*Durham, son of the founder of Lake Oswego, was initiated into Republican politics as a deputy county clerk and a deputy city auditor. An early investor in Albina real estate, he was at the time of his death in 1914 the president of the Merchants National Bank.

banks, Markle made the interesting comment — in the light of what was to follow a few months hence — that "public monies need to be protected."

In what proved to be one of the most accurate appraisals on record, the *Pacific Banker & Investor* reported two months later that "Oregon is singularly deficient in laws pertaining to banking institutions. In fact it may be said without fear of contradiction that it has no laws at all upon this subject."[23] It should be noted, parenthetically, that it would be 14 years before Oregon would be blessed with its first bank examiner who would be none other than Markle's old associate, the inveterate railway promoter and banker, James Steel.

Ill winds were beginning to blow in from the East Coast where banking institutions were feeling the effects of the Reading Railroad bankruptcy in February. The stock market had been falling for three years, from the time that the esteemed London banking house of Baring Brothers had been saved from collapse by the Bank of England. Gold had been rising in value while the general level of prices had been declining. England, which had enormous investments in America, especially in Western lands and railroads, began withdrawing capital from the American market. The structure of speculative credit cracked, and banks and railroads, including street railways, were seriously affected. Throughout the country, a general tightening of credit was already at hand in the early spring of 1893. Worried depositors were withdrawing funds and banks were calling loans.* Unbeknown to the Portland financial community at large, on April 17, 1893, George Markle took out a home mortgage loan of $120,000 with Robert Livingstone's Scottish American Investment Trust Co. Ltd. of Edinburgh.** The mortgage carried an annual interest rate of 7 percent and was payable at the end of five years in gold coin.[25] The roof was about to collapse, literally, on George Markle's head as financial conditions deteriorated rapidly during the spring and early summer.

---

*Even Markle's brother-in-law, Henry W. Rustin, "became somewhat uneasy about all that was going on and quietly withdrew his personal funds from George's bank before the real trouble began."[24] Rustin was GBM's closest associate and chief engineer for his electrified street railway operation. He was married to Kate Markle's sister.

**This seems an excessively large mortgage, to be secured by house and property not worth over $50,000 at the most. It would appear that Livingstone got bamboozled.

100

"Finances were improving here a little but today are worse than ever," reported Martin Winch to Simeon Reed on July 27, 1893. "The Northwest Loan & Trust Co. and the Oregon National Bank here failed to open this morning. These are controlled by George B. Markle. It of course has created a very uneasy feeling again."[26] The following day the *Oregonian* reported that deposits were being withdrawn faster than the banks could call in their notes. George Markle declared that "all depositors will be paid dollar for dollar. . . . Our paper is good. . . . Our capital and assets are in good shape."[27] The word was already out that Sheriff Kelly had at least $100,000 of county tax funds on deposit with the Oregon National Bank. City Treasurer Hacheny had an undisclosed sum on deposit with the same bank. Police Judge Charles H. Carey, one of U.S. Senator John H. Mitchell's chief political lieutenants, also had an undisclosed amount of Municipal Court funds on deposit with the Northwest Loan & Trust Co. The Port of Portland, of which George Markle was a commissioner, had $5,000 on deposit with the Oregon National.

In short order the Oregon-Washington Mortgage Savings, First of East Portland, Union, Commercial National, and Portland Savings Banks all closed. The Ainsworth National Bank closed briefly but was to reopen within a month.*

The First National Bank had a close call. The story is told that in the early morning hours of July 28th, Sigmund Frank and young Max Hirsch [31] secretly wheeled bags of gold coin from the Meier & Frank safe in through the back door of the First National Bank. The following morning found a smiling Henry W. Corbett gladly redeeming deposits with personal assurances to the fretful that there was no need to worry; all deposits were safe. In the weeks to follow the First National Bank performed yeoman public service by distributing over two million dollars throughout the Northwest to help stabilize the banking community.[32]

Writing to Simeon Reed on August 1st Martin Winch reported: "Friday and Saturday last week were the gloomiest days this place

---

*The Commercial National and Portland Savings Banks (which invested in Markle's Consolidated line) had the same officers. Frank Dekum was president of both. David P. Thompson, former mayor and wealthy investor, was the second largest stockholder in both. He had just returned from being American Minister to Turkey, and was appointed receiver for the Portland Savings Bank. In later years, Jay Bowerman[28] was to charge Dekum, Thompson and Jonathan Bourne Jr. with fraud. The bank had been looted, he said, and hundreds made destitute. As an example, Bowerman cited a $5,000 note, signed by Bourne, which was known to be worthless as far back as 1886 and yet had been carried on the books as a fully valued asset. The PSB, like Markle's banks, had conducted a commercial loan business with savings

ever saw, and we will feel the effects of it for sometime to come. . . . DeLashmutt I guess is in a very bad way financially. Common report has it he is busted, and from the worried hang dog look he has I judge it isn't far out of the way."*[33] Two days later George Markle quietly took out a second mortgage** on his home and property for $60,000.[34] Markle then let it be known to the Portland Community that he had $46,000 of his own money on deposit in his banks and that this should breed confidence. Given time, he would redeem all deposits as requested.[35]

What had happened?[36] George Markle had used his depositors' money to purchase two additional street railways in order to combine them into his new electrified Consolidated system.*** When the panic threatened, he began to use the public tax funds to pay off some of his depositors. And when Sheriff Kelly tried to withdraw the school tax funds he was told, "No. . . . The banks would close." Kelly then did a foolish thing. He deposited additional tax funds with

---

deposits. It was not a commercial bank and yet it had incurred heavy risks in large commercial loans. Furthermore, it had paid too high interest rates on its savings accounts.[29] Five thousand of the seven thousand depositors had $500 or less on deposit. The Port of Portland had $11,500 on deposit. The PSB did reopen in May 1894 but it closed in October 1894 after the death of Frank Dekum. Bowerman accused Thompson of reopening the bank just long enough for Thompson to bail out his favored creditors. When the PSB liquidation was finally settled in 1901, less than 40 percent of the depositors' money had been refunded. Thompson, owner of the New Market Theater Block, had a long standing reputation for being a shrewd operator. As far back as 1871, Judge Deady had commented that one never knew just how much Thompson was worth because "he would hide his assets."[30] The Commerical National Bank was bought out by Wells Fargo of San Francisco in January 1894 and R.L. Durham went along with the shuffle as vice president. Wells Fargo issued and sold $500,000 in new stock.

*Although DeLashmutt withdrew from the Oregon National Bank in 1892, he was badly hurt by the depression. He was still an investor in the Consolidated Street Railway, unfortunately.

**Underwritten by three friends: Lewis Russell, Percy Blyth, Donald McLeod.

***The Northwest Loan & Trust Co. had loaned the Consolidated Street Railway Co. $160,000, secured by a mortgage on 40 miles of track, property, stock, etc. With the crash, the Consolidated system went bankrupt and on into receivership in 1894.

Markle's banks to the amount of $200,000. When Markle found that he was unable to sell the million dollars worth of railway bonds which had just been negotiated for sale, he was caught short, and the Portland Consolidated Street Railway Co.'s future was sealed. Markle promised Sheriff Kelly that he would get him his money. He was going to make a trip back east and see what he could raise from his friends and relatives. He hoped to come up with $300,000.*

Mikado Building. Restored in 1974.

Early in September Markle apparently wired his associates that he had the money, whereupon the Oregon National Bank reopened on September 9th. By the time Markle returned from his travels, however, he learned to his dismay that the deal had fallen through. The Oregon National closed for good; the Northwest Loan & Trust never did reopen, even briefly. Neither bank ever occupied its new quarters in the Chamber of Commerce Building which opened inauspiciously the same month.

---

*According to his nephew, Henry Wilkins Rustin, "George's family called him the world's greatest optimist."[37]

Markle promised Sheriff Kelly $50,000 for the December school payroll but Kelly only received $5,000. On December 8, 1893, George Markle, his cashier D.F. Sherman and Sheriff Penumbra Kelly were indicted by the Multnomah County Grand Jury and arrested for misuse of $318,000* of public funds. It was revealed for the first time that Markle had been one of Sheriff Kelly's performance bondsmen. Kelly was afraid to draw out the money and thus close the banks. Instead he deposited the additional $200,000, but the banks closed anyway.

Bail bonds of $20,000 were posted for Markle and Kelly and signed by Harvey W. Scott, the esteemed editor of the *Oregonian,* and David P. Thompson.** No further word of this case was ever printed in the local papers. One must assume that the charges were eventually dropped. There is no record of the disposition of the case in the court files of Multnomah County.

Pleading for exoneration, Henry Pittock's evening paper, the *Portland Telegram,* declared: "Portland needs people like George Markle, . . . his progressive and go ahead spirit. . . . He overreached himself in the endeavor to build up important interests associated with Portland's growth and development. He was merely the victim of unfortunate circumstances." He would have "pulled it out if left alone. . . . The city can ill afford to lose the services of a man like Mr. Markle."[38]

Portland did lose his services, a lot of citizens lost their life savings, and Markle lost his wife and house. One day early in 1894, Kate Markle and her young child, George B. 3rd, ran away from their home and fled back to her family in Allegheny City, Pennsylvania where she filed for divorce. Sometime in mid-spring, Markle himself stole quietly out of town, never to be seen or heard from again, owing approximately $140,000 to Robert Livingstone's Scottish American Investment Trust Co. Ltd. of Edinburgh. The Multnomah County Circuit Court issued a summons for his arrest on March 12, 1895, but of course Sheriff G.C. Sears never found him. After years of litigation, Markle's home on Hawthorne Terrace was awarded to Livingstone's SAIT Co. which in turn sold it in December 1904. Other Markle supported ventures experienced a similar fate. The Exposi-

---

*As later recorded, Kelly had $149,000 in the Oregon National Bank and $169,000 in the Northwest Loan & Trust Co.

**Thompson's son Edward L., was to become the real estate partner of J.L. Hartman, close associate of Markle's and treasurer of the N.W. Loan & Trust Co. in 1893. Hartman became Manager of the Portland Clearing House in 1894. They developed the Rose City Park Addition (1906).

tion Building had defaulted on its mortgage and was sold to local investors for $85,000. The Commerce Building was sold ultimately to the SP&S R.R. in March 1906 for $800,000. One month later it suffered a $100,000 fire which destroyed the Commercial Club on the eighth floor.

The depression of 1893 had taken its toll. Everything came to a dead halt. Nationally, over $1 billion in railroad investments went into the hands of receivers. Seventy-four railroad companies, including the Northern and Union Pacific, fell into bankruptcy. Over 600 banks and banking institutions folded. When Joseph Gaston reflected back on the period some years later, he wrote: "There was a large population of unemployed and penniless men. . . . Men walked the streets, idle and hungry. . . . There was no work for them to do."[39] There was no house building, no municipal street repairs and no railroad construction. Banker C.F. Adams, President of the First National in 1932, recalled that the summer of 1893 produced "the hardest days I have ever known. . . . Why, men went about with fringe on the bottom of their pants and no shoes. They didn't have anything to eat or know where the next bite was coming from."[40] *Oregonian* owner, Henry L. Pittock, was not going to starve, but in October 1893 he was in dire need of short term cash. From his close friend, George T. Myers, he requested a loan of $35,000 and offered five real estate lots as collateral. He planned to secure a $125,000 mortgage on the Oregonian Building and borrow $50,000 from the publishing company. He told Myers that Henry W. Corbett would lend him $75,000 when the money picture improved.[41]

Much real estate changed hands as mortgages were defaulted. In a belated effort to help ameliorate matters, especially for the small property holder, the legislature enacted a law that gave debtors a year to redeem their real estate after it was sold at public auction by the sheriff. From 1893 to 1900, the total assessed valuation of all property in Multnomah County dropped by 47 percent. An era of strict governmental economy ensued. And the *Oregonian* blithely assured its readers that "there are no poor in Portland who need to be hungry or cold. Our rich men have always shown beneficence of a large and judicious kind."[42] Yet even the Arlington Club "rich" felt the effects of the depression. Writing to a friend in September 1893, young Scottish grain merchant Peter Kerr noted: "The stringency (banks) is indeed very severe, and many names that would surprise you are upon the delinquent board at the Club."[43]

The two bankers hardest hit, besides Markle and DeLashmutt,

were Frank Dekum* and William (Dundee) Reid. Before he died in 1894, Dekum managed to salvage enough out of the wreckage, with David P. Thompson's help, to leave an estate of over one million dollars, largely in downtown real estate; his railway and banking holdings had collapsed, along with Markle's and DeLashmutt's. William Reid did not fare as well. After his Oregon-Washington Mortgage Savings Bank closed in June 1893, leaving 196 depositors devoid of their savings, Reid skipped town. Five months later he was reported in the vicinity of the Mexican Border, "on account of his health."[44] He returned to Oregon in 1898 a poor man. He was quoted as saying: "I came to Portland with $10,000, made $200,000 and left with $1."[45] People had forgotten his many good deeds because of one failure.**

Frank Dekum.

---

*Frank Dekum, born in Bavaria in 1829, arrived in Portland in 1852 and opened the first bakery. He became a very successful banker, realtor, insurance and railway executive. He is best remembered today by the Dekum Building on S.W. 3rd, a major landmark in Portland's history, built in 1891-92. It is currently in the process of restoration. At one time or another he was president of: Columbia Investment Co., Oregon Land & Investment Co., Columbia Fire & Marine Ins. Co., Portland Savings Bank, Commercial National Bank, Portland & Vancouver Railway, Trinidad Asphalt & Paving Co., Portland Exposition Co. He was also a member of the Portland Water Committee.

**It would appear that Judge Deady had sized up William Reid's weaknesses quite accurately when he noted in March of 1889 that Reid "has a talent for confusing and obscuring everything he puts his hands to or in..."[46] Perhaps the Dundee bankers saw the same qualities appearing in their agent in whom they had gradually lost faith eight years earlier.

THIRD AND WASHINGTON STREETS, PORTLAND—The lower
stories of the corner building are occupied by the great department store of Lipman, Wolfe & Company.

Except for a year as a U.S. Vice-Consul in New Zealand, Reid
spent the remaining 16 years of his life eking out a meagre income from the practice of law and an occasional job as a consultant
on minor railroad construction projects. According to Henry Reed,
he "spent his last business days in a cheap inside office,"[47] in Henry
Corbett's Worcester Building. Reid's spirits were not daunted, however. In an interview granted to the *Oregonian* in 1902, Reid voiced
the same concerns and criticisms expressed by Harvey Scott back in
April of 1887. Portland's greatest need, he declared, "is the investment on a large scale of corporate outside capital." When the capitalists come to Portland, we must see that "no technical objections, obstructions or delays are placed in their path."[48] Reid bemoaned the
fact that Oregon was still considered a slow-going state back east;
outside investment was discouraged. In truth, however, Oregon had
actually awarded more legislative rights and franchise privileges

to outside or foreign corporations than any other state in the Union.*
The Scottish investors had benefited from these enactments. Reid's
memory was short. A number of outside investors had been burned
in 1893. It would take time to rebuild confidence, and old Portlanders
were in no hurry.

3.

At the young age of only 38, George Markle slipped home to Hazelton, but not a defeated man. Over the years he involved himself in a
number of family related enterprises and drew his dividends from
the immensely profitable coal business.** Markle apparently made
no attempt to repay his Portland debts, nor did he ever remarry. He
lived what must have been a lonely life and allowed his weight to
exceed 300 pounds. He died a wealthy man in July 1914, at 58, of
post-operative complications resulting from his overweight condition. Thus ended the career of a most unusual man who, in a short
span of seven years, made a lasting imprint on the physical shape
of Portland.

---

*By legislative action in 1878 and 1887.
**Markle had two brothers. Alvan was president of the Markle Bank and
Trust Co. John was president of the family coal company. In 1930 John was
reputed to be worth over $76 million. He was the second largest stockholder
in General Motors, after Coleman DePont. George ran the Hazelton Manufacturing Co., which produced, among other things, coffins for the miners who
died in the family coal mines. He also ran the company stores and company
housing; Hazleton was a company town. The story is told that some ten or so
years later, while on a trip to Pittsburgh, Markle kidnapped his son, George
3rd. The boy was sent off to boarding school in England and Germany and
developed what became a lifelong interest in theater and music. In the 1930's
George B. Markle 3rd established a record, unbroken even today. He produced a consecutive string of eight losing Broadway shows.

Portland, circa 1893.

Chapter VI

Growth and
Decentralization,
1890-1892

"Decentralization is growth away from a center. In
every city all growth is away from the point of origin."[1]

These words were spoken by historian and former County Assessor
Henry Reed in November 1926 when he addressed the Friday Break-
fast Club on the reasons for Portland's growth. Reed noted that since
the advent of the automobile much had been written about its impact,
often cited as the major cause of decentralization, and that most com-
mentators were erroneously equating the term decentralization with
dissolution or destruction. Decentralization might result in decay to
the old sections of a city, as it did in Portland and most other American cities, but there was no natural law predetermining this outcome,
other than the free working of the profit motive. Growth was by
chance, and there was no pressure to preserve the old buildings if
such efforts were deemed unprofitable to the private interests that
owned them. Reed's point was well taken: decentralization was a consequence of growth and there could be no growth without decentralization occurring. The City of Portland's consolidation in 1891 greatly increased the trend toward decentralization because it launched
Portland into a period of phenomenal growth, promoted and directed
by the street railways. Within a span of nine years the population
would increase by 50 percent and the geographic area by 40 percent,

all of this despite the ill-effects of the depression of 1893.

Within the 24 year period, from 1891 to 1915, Portland's population would increase by 300 percent and its land area by 150 percent. Fifteen annexations would expand Portland to within 82 percent of its 1976 boundary limits.

In the months preceding the consolidation of July 6, 1891, many West Portlanders felt that their city stood at the beginning of a career of greatness. For several years previously, consolidation of the three cities had been increasingly advocated. When Mayor Van B. DeLashmutt and a citizen's committee he headed discovered that the first 1890 census was in error by 11,000 and that Portland's West side actually contained nearly 46,000 people, the move for consolidation was practically irresistible. With a land area of only 7.38 square miles, the population density had reached 6230, an alarmingly high figure for people not accustomed to being crowded together.

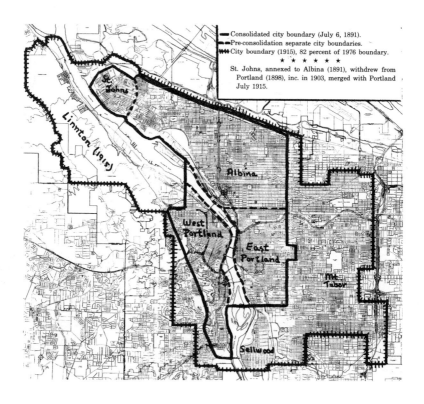

Consolidated city boundary (July 6, 1891).
Pre-consolidation separate city boundaries.
City boundary (1915), 82 percent of 1976 boundary.
★ ★ ★ ★ ★ ★
St. Johns, annexed to Albina (1891), withdrew from Portland (1898), inc. in 1903, merged with Portland July 1915.

While the population had been growing rapidly since 1885, fed by and in turn feeding an economic boom, over 20 major buildings had been constructed within the corridor between First and Third Streets. Many of them were "unified architecturally by colonnaded and arched cast iron facades. The column design, produced locally, ranged from a spare, elegant Florentine style to full baroque exuberance — an amazing achievement and display for a four-decade-old city."[2] Less than half of them survive in 1976, in varying stages of decay. Many were wrecked in the mid-fifties concurrent with the construction of the new Morrison Bridge ramps. Few cries of alarm were heard. One survivor, the New Market Annex (1889) at Second and Ash, is a good example of the Richardsonian influence. Boston architect H.H. Richardson was noted for his Romanesque style which featured massive forms of stone and brick. For a short time it appeared that the area between First and Second, near Ash Street, might remain as the core of the city.

Corner of S.W. 3rd & Alder Streets. Site of the J.K. Gill Co. (1911), Hamilton and Dekum buildings.

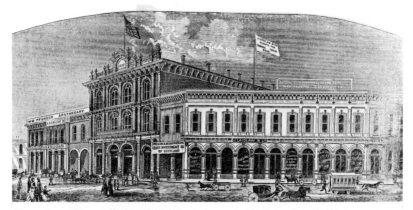

Note the office of William Reid's Oregon & Washington Trust Investment Co. of Scotland. The New Market Theater (flying the American Flag) still survives, but as a parking garage.

Skidmore Fountain.

On September 22nd of the previous year, the Skidmore Fountain*
had begun to flow amid great fanfare with thousands in attendance.[3]
Erected at the intersection of First and Ankeny with funds bequeathed by the late druggist and City Councilman Stephen G. Skidmore,
the fountain was expected to be of sufficient attraction to keep the

First Street, North of Morrison.

FIRST STREET, NORTH OF MORRISON,

*When Skidmore died in 1883 he bequeathed $5000 to the city for the
construction of a fountain. Nationally prominent New York Sculptor Olin
Warner was chosen to execute the work. The actual cost was more than
$25,000, with the additional funds raised by a committee headed by Henry
Failing. Brewer Henry Weinhard had offered to pipe free beer into the fountain to replace the water for the opening ceremony but Henry Failing declined the offer as undignified. The water valve was turned on by Council
President Tyler Woodward. In later years, the square surrounding the fountain fell into a state of decay. Warehouses, garages and finally parking lots
took over. In 1962 the process of restoration was begun with the council formally adopting a design zone for the area. It is now the center of the Skidmore
Old Town Historic District.

Current site of the American Bank Building, S.W. Morrison between Broadway & 6th.

Oregonian Building, 6th & Alder Streets.

area alive as a retail center. But by 1891, the core was moving to Morrison Street which seemed more attractive from a business point of view. A new core was arising at Sixth where the Post Office, the recently opened Portland Hotel and Marquam Grand Opera House formed a conspicuous cluster. One block away, on Alder at Sixth, construction had begun on the new Oregonian Building, the largest of the Richardsonian type designs ever attempted in Portland. In the late spring of 1891, West Portland's atmosphere was indeed a curious blend of the cosmopolitan and the frontier.

For a number of years it had been a matter of wonder to many Portland area residents that this core district on the West side of the river was actually the financial downtown for three cities rather than one. When Portland was laid out in 1845 no one thought that it would reach its 1891 proportions. The possibility of there being two flourishing East side cities was never dreamed of.

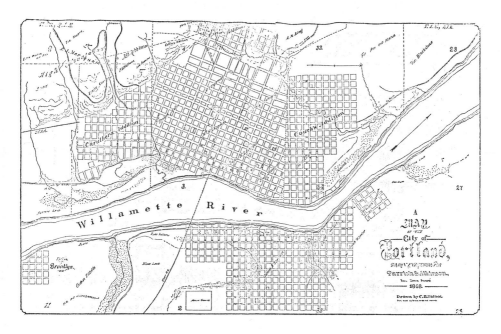

An article in 1873 described East Portland (incorporated in 1870) as "a picturesquely located city, being surrounded by some striking rustic scenery."[4] With an estimated population of 1500, the city contained four churches (two Methodist, one Episcopal and one Lutheran), four schools (three public and one private), a sawmill and a grist-

117

East Portland, Oregon & California R.R. tracks — 1881.

mill, a car and a machinery shop. "It is well adapted," reported the article, "to be the suburb of the metropolis, as it contains good locations for private residences."[5] The article noted that the city was served by two ferries that ran continually and transported over 300 people daily.

The major impetus for East side development came from the Oregon & California Railroad Co. which began construction in April 1868 as the Oregon Central R.R. Co. of Salem. In succeeding years the O&C was to be controlled by Ben Holladay, Henry Villard and the OR&N and finally by the Southern Pacific Co. It built its tracks along the East river bank, purchasing the property for practically nothing. The townsite developed back from the river, but when the town expanded toward the river and platted East First Street, the O&C received a perpetual franchise which has been maintained to the present day, with no compensation to the public.*

The first city fathers (and the legislature) showed some vision in 1870 when they incorporated an area of approximately 4.5 square miles, with a population density of only 200. Although the city's population would increase tenfold over the next two decades, the boundaries would expand by barely half a square mile, official legislative action being taken just four months before consolidation. The East side showed a steady growth and an increasing percentage of the greater metropolitan population, from 9 percent in 1870 to 25 percent in 1891. A definite trend had been established. Within less than 20 years, over 50 percent of the metropolitan population would

---

*On June 17, 1876.

118

be residing on the East side. The awareness of this trend strongly influenced the thinking of the downtown establishment. Although many of them, such as Ladd,* Bourne, Pittock and James Steel were partially responsible for this expansion through their various real estate developments, they were fearful of losing control of an area which some day might become more powerful economically and politically than the downtown.

The opening of the Morrison Bridge in 1887 and the rapid extension of the street railways beginning in 1888 were the two major causes of explosive East side population growth. The promotional campaigns of the real estate developers who had bought up thousands of acres of cheap land** were also a prime force in behalf of consolidation, because many of the developers and the street railway companies had financial interconnections, and most of the wires led to downtown Portland.

East 4th Street — 1881.

*Ladd had recently completed two large buildings on East 4th Street.
**Land in the current Rose City Park area, just north of Laurelhurst, East of 45th Street, sold for $6 an acre in 1876 and $400 an acre in 1907.

119

A case in point was the narrow gauge Portland & Vancouver Railway built by downtown businessmen and bankers Frank Dekum and Richard L. Durham. Beginning at the Stark Street Ferry landing in East Portland and running north through Albina to the Columbia River opposite Vancouver, with which it was connected by ferry, the road offered "cheap and quick communication between its terminal points," passing through "some of the most desirable suburban property in East Portland and Albina."[6] Another illustration was the

Portland Railway Co.'s Ferry — connecting Vancouver, Washington with the Oregon Shore.

case of the Willamette Bridge Railway Co. Organized in 1887 by William Beck and Rufus Mallory, a partner in the Simon-Dolph firm, (C.F. Swigert became heavily involved in 1888), it began to operate in East Portland in the spring of 1889 on East "N" (Morrison) Street with a 50 year franchise. The street had been extended to East 20th, to the Lone Fir Cemetery, a development that many considered foolish. Who would ever move that far out? "There was great opposition to the placing of a steam motor" railway by the Willamette Bridge Co. on East Morrison, "and there were rumors of an injunction" to prevent it. "Those who predicted that it would kill the street

MAP OF
SUNNYSIDE
SCALE 200 FT TO 1 INCH.

J. FRED CLARK AND SONS
GENERAL AGENTS
FOR THE
SUNNYSIDE LAND & IMPROVEMENT CO.
OFFICES:
13 STARK ST. PORTLAND.
AND AT SUNNYSIDE.

were disappointed, for [Morrison St.] . . . quickly became the most important thoroughfare on the East Side. Some of the finest residences were erected along it."[7]

The railway was also responsible for opening up the Sunnyside tract,* between East 33rd and 44th Avenues, this being the one-half square mile area added in 1891 to the original incorporation of 1870. Just north and east of Sunnyside and the city boundary was Ladd's 462 acre Hazel Farm (Laurelhurst) that would be sold in 1909 for $2 million. In 1905 the Mount Tabor region would be annexed; and four years later East 92nd Avenue would be reached, the general eastern boundary line of the city today. The Willamette Bridge Railway Co. was merged into the City & Suburban two months after consolidation was approved. Failing, Woodward, Corbett, Swigert and Mallory had seen it coming and they were not only prepared, they

---

*Led to the development of the first neighborhood shopping center in East Portland.

gave it a good push. Economic consolidation would accompany political consolidation and the established business leadership would keep control.

Several major East side landmarks were to remain out of the city until 1893. The village of Sellwood, at the south end, was developed by the Sellwood Real Estate Co. founded in 1883, with *Oregonian* owner Henry Pittock as majority stockholder. It was incorporated in 1887. Just to the north, in the area known today as Westmoreland, was located the City View Park race track, one of the most famous

Ladd's Addition, circa 1918.

Description of the future plan of development, from *The Oregonian Souvenir, 1892:*

"Mr. Ladd has had the addition all platted and laid out and it is perhaps not going too far to assert that this is the most attractive addition ever put on the Portland market. The property is reached by three different lines of electric cars and is in every sense strictly inside city property.

In no addition ever before put on the Portland market has such attention been paid to beautifying the property as Mr. Ladd is able to guarantee in the new Ladd's Addition. He has not only made every preparation to pave all the streets of the addition with asphaltum, at his own expense, but he has provided for supplying the residents of this tract with gas and electric lights, he has arranged for a splendid system of sewerage and drainage, a system perfected in the most modern lines of scientific research; he will lay sidewalks fronting on every block and he will have a perfect water system that will insure residents an ample supply of the purest water for domestic purposes. Mr. Ladd's well-known aversion to the liquor traffic has led him to make provisions for excluding saloons from this tract for all time. He will allow no liquor to be sold on the property, a reservation which insures residents here the freedom from a great annoyance which has baffled the efforts of many of the residents of Portland to remedy, more especially where the saloon was located within the immediate vicinity of their homes."

courses on the Pacific Coast. Much of this area was developed by two prominent Republican businessmen-politicians, Jonathan Bourne Jr. and Julius Caesar Moreland. "J.C.," as he was better known, was *the* Multnomah County Judge at the same time that he headed the Portland Real Estate Co. and was secretary of the Willamette Falls Electric Co., the major power operation in the Portland area. To the north and east of the race track was a little community built around the Southern Pacific shops, known variously as "Car Shops" and "Brooklyn." Much of this land had been owned by William S. Ladd who still controlled several hundred acres of land east of the S.P. tracks and south of Holgate Street. Known as Crystal Springs Farm, this tract was to become the center of the Reed College campus and the Eastmoreland community 20 years later. A mile northwards, well inside the southern boundary of East Portland, Ladd owned an eight block square that would be called Ladd's Addition when developed 20 years later as a model community for railroad workers.* To the west of this tract, along the riverfront, was the Inman-Poulson sawmill. Within ten years it would become the largest lumber operation in Oregon, covering 37-1/2 acres, some of which was landfill.**

---

*In 1939, the Realty Board was to consider Ladd's Addition to be: "one of the few better districts for Orientals."[8]

**From 1954-1959, the mill and property were sold to nine diversified light manufacturing and warehouse operations, including Georgia-Pacific Co. and Portland General Electric Co. A ready-mix concrete co. bought a portion of the dock area. No effort was made to prevent this emasculation of the waterfront.

East Portland business and political leadership strongly supported consolidation largely for economic reasons. The city was in a bad way financially. It had already issued $100,000 in sewer and water bonds and was not generating enough tax revenue to retire them let alone pay the interest. The city's most serious financial problems stemmed from the construction of elevated roadways and streets. The near East side, just back from the river, was dotted with creek beds and marshy swamps, necessitating either land fills or elevated, bridge-like roadways. Many of these early thoroughfares were hastily and poorly designed.

> "The greatest loss entailed on the city was in the construction of the bridge over Sullivan's Gulch . . . now known as Grand Avenue. A flimsy structure was built there, which the contractors were afraid would fall down before they could get it finished. Property owners declined to pay for it, and the city, after long and expensive litigation, was compelled to pay for the whole structure, the cost being over $6000."[9]

The city later experienced a similar fate with an elevated section of East Morrison Street.

East side, Sullivan's Gulch, 4th St. Bridge — 1884.

An examination of East Portland council minutes and ordinances[10] reveals that the city fathers approved practically every franchise request that was presented them. They appear to have been almost desperate for services. Two or more companies were often enfranchised for the same type of activity. Downtown interests receiving favorable consideration were companies such as the OR&N and the O&C Railroad, and business leaders such as Portland Gas Co.'s Henry Reed and H.C. Leonard, Board of Trade president Donald MacLeay, James Steel, W.S. Ladd, Richard Durham, Frank Dekum and the Hogue brothers who finally installed an electric plant that worked and supplied part of the city with its first incandescent lighting. Several franchises were granted in the closing days that witnessed the frantic passage of much hastily drawn legislation.

Portland Reduction Works, East Portland (a Ladd property).

Many amusing things occurred in the history of the old East Portland city government. Two in particular are worthy of note. For many years there had been an ordinance in force that required saloons to be closed on Sundays. But by a peculiar wording of the enactment, only the front doors had to be locked while the back doors could and did remain open. "The battle of nearly every election was fought out on this question" which apparently "cut quite a figure in the vote for consolidation." After July 6, 1891 the saloons were thrown wide open on Sunday, and, as the *Oregonian* reported two years later, there was no more drunkenness on the East side than before consolidation. The other humorous issue related to the Salvation Army which was heartily disliked on the East side, so much so that nowhere on the Pacific Coast was an organization so well entrenched as in East Portland. Quoting again from the *Oregonian's* account:

> "It is said that nothing causes anything to flourish better than persecution. . . . Whenever the city council was in session the army made it an object to march to the council chamber and serenade that body, much to its annoyance."

The council finally passed an ordinance prohibiting all bands from playing in the streets, and the first night following its passage the entire band was marched off to jail.

> "The army flourished, and finally secured permanent quarters, said to be the best on the coast. The night after consolidation went into effect the army was out in force with a well-equipped band, and the event was celebrated with great enthusiasm. It was regarded as a great victory over the devil. The army never became a fixture in Albina."[11]

To the north of East Portland in the small township of Albina the Salvation Army may not have been given much of a chance but the devil was surely given his due. Few cities in American history, excluding strictly company owned and planned communities such as Pullman, Illinois or Hazleton, Pennsylvania, were as dominated by private business interests as was Albina. Until the time of its incorporation in 1887, it was almost a privately owned community, a sort of medieval fiefdom presided over by the lords of the corporate manor, except that manor headquarters was in downtown West Portland. An examination of the accompanying chart indicates the general lines of authority that kept control of Albina. Many familiar names are evident; also some new ones including that of George W. Bates whose career will be discussed later in this chapter.

Albina was located on a donation claim owned by J.L. Loring and Joseph Delay. There was a dispute as to ownership, and Delay won the claim, which he sold to attorney William Winter Page.* Page in

---

*Page was born in Virginia in 1838; died in Portland, 1897.

turn sold the land in 1872 to the Englishman Edwin Russell, manager of the Portland branch of the Bank of British Columbia, and George H. Williams,* who was just leaving the U.S. Senate after representing Oregon for one term. Russell and Williams named the town for Page's wife and daughter, Albina (which the family pronounced Al-BEAN-ah).** Russell had controlling interest in the venture but Williams laid out the general dimensions of the community. The original town site was platted close to the waterfront on the bend in the Willamette River. In 1872 it was merely a pastoral wilderness without any graded streets. Beyond it, to the east and north, the land was heavily forested.

Russell plunged into his new enterprise with gusto; he also invested all of his savings and borrowed heavily. He dreamed of Albina swallowing up Portland, particularly after the devastating fire of August 1873. Within a period of two years he constructed a sawmill to process his timber and a shipbuilding plant, both on the waterfront directly across the river from George Weidler's mammoth mill. He organized machine and engine shops and built a palatial home. By the end of 1874, however, he was wiped out and left town mysteriously for San Francisco.*** After his departure, his controlling interest in the form of foreclosed mortgages was sold to William (Dundee) Reid and James B. Montgomery who proceeded to lay plans for additional development. The early homes were built on the flat ground back from the water and on the gently sloping hillside which led up to Russell's former mansion on the bluff. Scarcely a trace of any of these structures is left today.

Few, if any, towns in Oregon grew more rapidly than did Albina. In 1880 the population was counted at 143. By 1888, the year after

---

*Williams was born in N.Y. in 1823 and died in Portland, 1910. He was to serve as U.S. Attorney General during President Grant's second administration (1873-77); be nominated as Chief Justice of the U.S. Supreme Court (and in turn be rejected by the Senate Judiciary Committee); and return to Portland to practice law, serving as Mayor from 1902-05. His career was plagued by continual controversy.

**Miss Page described the dinner at which the town received its name at a meeting of the Albina Pioneer Society[12] in March, 1934. She died in 1957, at 92, and left a fortune of nearly $1 million which was placed in an educational trust fund.

***Russell suffered from the effects of the bank panic of 1873; the bankruptcy of the Oregon Iron Works the following year sealed his financial collapse. He was unable to pay interest or principal on his real estate mortgages which were foreclosed.

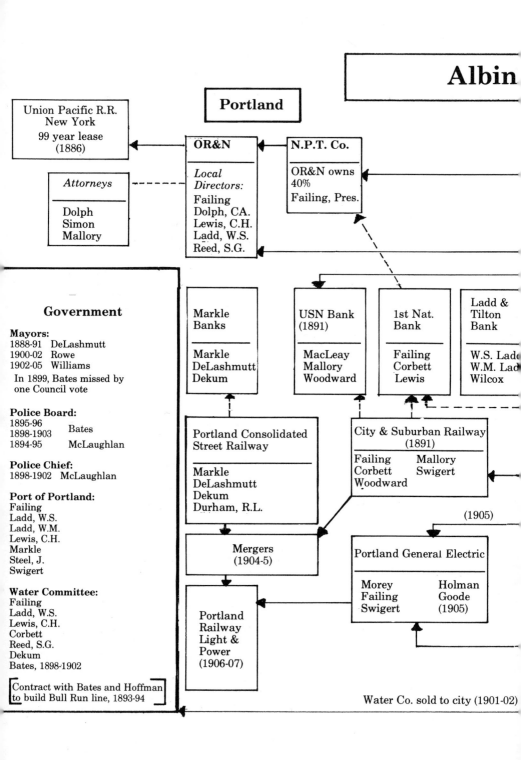

Albin

Portland

Union Pacific R.R.
New York
99 year lease
(1886)

OR&N

Local Directors:
Failing
Dolph, C.A.
Lewis, C.H.
Ladd, W.S.
Reed, S.G.

Attorneys
Dolph
Simon
Mallory

N.P.T. Co.
OR&N owns 40%
Failing, Pres.

Government

Mayors:
1888-91 DeLashmutt
1900-02 Rowe
1902-05 Williams
In 1899, Bates missed by one Council vote

Police Board:
1895-96
1898-1903   Bates
1894-95   McLaughlan

Police Chief:
1898-1902   McLaughlan

Port of Portland:
Failing
Ladd, W.S.
Ladd, W.M.
Lewis, C.H.
Markle
Steel, J.
Swigert

Water Committee:
Failing
Ladd, W.S.
Lewis, C.H.
Corbett
Reed, S.G.
Dekum
Bates, 1898-1902

Contract with Bates and Hoffman to build Bull Run line, 1893-94

Markle Banks

Markle
DeLashmutt
Dekum

USN Bank
(1891)
MacLeay
Mallory
Woodward

1st Nat.
Bank
Failing
Corbett
Lewis

Ladd &
Tilton
Bank
W.S. Ladd
W.M. Ladd
Wilcox

Portland Consolidated
Street Railway

Markle
DeLashmutt
Dekum
Durham, R.L.

City & Suburban Railway
(1891)
Failing   Mallory
Corbett   Swigert
Woodward

Mergers
(1904-5)

(1905)

Portland General Electric
Morey   Holman
Failing   Goode
Swigert   (1905)

Portland
Railway
Light &
Power
(1906-07)

Water Co. sold to city (1901-02)

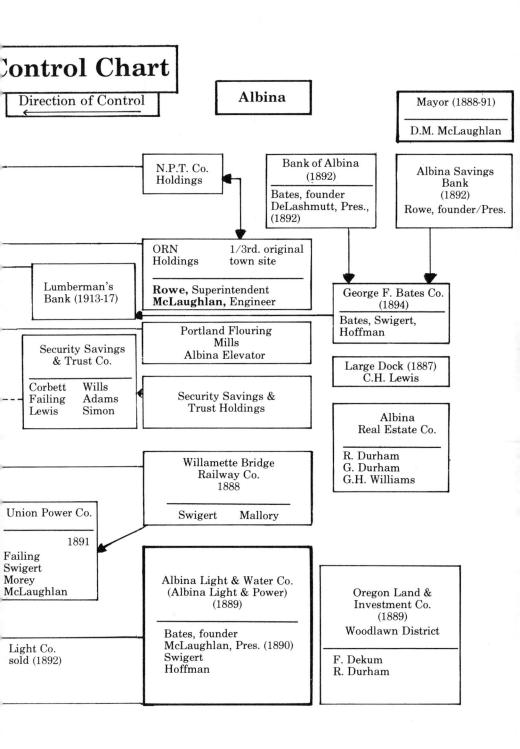

Control Chart

Direction of Control

Albina

Mayor (1888-91)

D.M. McLaughlan

N.P.T. Co.
Holdings

Bank of Albina
(1892)

Bates, founder
DeLashmutt, Pres.,
(1892)

Albina Savings
Bank
(1892)
Rowe, founder/Pres.

ORN   1/3rd. original
Holdings   town site

Rowe, Superintendent
McLaughlan, Engineer

Lumberman's
Bank (1913-17)

George F. Bates Co.
(1894)

Bates, Swigert,
Hoffman

Portland Flouring
Mills
Albina Elevator

Security Savings
& Trust Co.

Corbett   Wills
Failing   Adams
Lewis   Simon

Security Savings &
Trust Holdings

Large Dock (1887)
C.H. Lewis

Albina
Real Estate Co.

R. Durham
G. Durham
G.H. Williams

Willamette Bridge
Railway Co.
1888

Swigert   Mallory

Union Power Co.

1891
Failing
Swigert
Morey
McLaughlan

Albina Light & Water Co.
(Albina Light & Power)
(1889)

Bates, founder
McLaughlan, Pres. (1890)
Swigert
Hoffman

Oregon Land &
Investment Co.
(1889)
Woodlawn District

F. Dekum
R. Durham

Light Co.
sold (1892)

incorporation, the total would reach 3000; it would more than double by the time of consolidation in 1891. As with East Portland, the impetus for growth came from the railroads. Shortly after Henry Villard's Portland speech in 1881, he exercised options to purchase initially from Reid and Montgomery 320 acres of flat land along the waterfront, north of the Albina Saw Mill. The purchase was made in the name of the Northern Pacific Terminal Co., of which Henry Failing was president, but the actual owner was the Oregon Railway & Navigation Co. Within five years the OR&N would own 7900 feet of waterfront on both sides of the river. But also, within five years, the OR&N would be controlled by the Union Pacific Railroad which spent over $1.5 million on the construction of a massive rail center. In April 1887, the *Oregonian* observed that Albina was growing rapidly. The town was scattered over a large area but there was an "air of thrift, neatness and comfort" about the place. The town's main industry was the railroad yard which could count as many as 900 cars on sidings in a given afternoon.[13]

In March 1888, the *Oregonian* carried a revealing interview with William N. Killingsworth, a major real estate investor in Albina. Said Mr. Killingsworth: "Albina has been selected as the place to build these industrial enterprises;" selected of course by the power establishment in downtown Portland. This was a major private decision that was to have a long term impact on the public life of greater Portland. Of course, Mr. Killingsworth was ecstatic over all of this activity from which he and his friends were benefiting immensely. He had good reason to be "bullish on Albina's future."[14] He noted that lots which had sold for $250 in 1882 were now going for between $2500 and $4500.[15]

The local realtors put pressure on the legislature in 1889 and 1891 to permit Albina to annex territory that was nine times larger than its original incorporation, much of it being a vacant, partially timbered wilderness. Prominent property owner James B. Montgomery served in the 1891 House session primarily for this reason. Serving in the 1891 Senate session was P.L. Willis* who was to be an associate of C.F. Swigert in electric railway development and in the future promotion of the University Park tract, to be located east of St. Johns in the expansive northern Albina annexation of 1891, later known as the Peninsula section of Portland.

---

*Willis was with the Electric Land Co., a Swigert concern. He was also an associate of G.W. Bates and served on the Portland Police Commission with Bates in 1895-96.

At the time of consolidation, Albina covered more land area than East and West Portland combined: 13.5 square miles with a population density of 450. It augured well for the future metropolis that the land became city property early in its growth period, but, as so often happened in Portland's history, the right decision was made for the wrong reasons. For over 30 years there would be no public planning agency to guide the various private developments that were assembled in random fashion throughout much of northern Albina. It was the placement of the street railway tracks and the promotional schemes of the private developers and utilities that would set the pattern of future growth. In Albina, all of these economic activities were interlocked.

A description of Albina, written by Harvey Scott early in 1890, is illuminating:

> "Two great buildings at Albina demand first attention, and show upon what a great scale the city is now working. These are the Portland Flour Mills and the Pacific Coast Elevator. The flour mills occupy two immense buildings of seven stories in height, and turn out a product that not only feeds our own people, but goes the world over. Trains of cars run immediately to their walls. They are the property of W.S. Ladd & Co.
>
> The Elevator is a new enterprise, and a building has been erected this summer at a cost of about $1,000,000. It was established by a capitalist of Minneapolis, F.H. Peavey, who is the principal owner. . . .
>
> Albina itself strikes one with the general weight and importance of its operations. It lies — so far as the business portion is concerned — upon a low tract of land about the level of high water, but twenty-five feet above the low stage. It is most admirably adapted to railroad work, and is the terminal of the O.R. & N. line. Here is seen upon the plat a labyrinth of tracks, long trains of cars, the immense brick roundhouse with twenty-two stalls; the car shops of brick, the largest more than 400 feet in length, and 60 feet to the peak, with arched doors and roofs furnished with windows for admission of light. A brick chimney of 156 feet in height, an engine of 500 horse power, and two other shops of large dimensions, afford means of repair and of manufacture.
>
> Almost the whole river front of Albina is occupied by

Looking south, Albina is at the bottom, left. Note the U.P.R.R. car shops and W.S. Ladd's Portland Flouring Mills Albina elevator. East Portland is south of Albina.

wharf buildings as much as 200 feet deep, with arching roofs as much as fifty feet above the water. They rest on piling set systematically and of selected smooth, uniform logs. The business part of the town, aside from its great works, is of rather mean appearance, of cheap temporary structures, small sized and of inferior architecture. The residence portion is built well back on the face of the bluff or on the plain beyond, and has attractive school houses and churches and many pretty cottages. On the river bank is the saw mill of John Parker & Co., with a capacity of about 30,000 feet per day."[16]

Albina's history provides a first rate example of what can happen to an urbanized community that grows without long term planning and historical perspective; or of what can happen to a human settlement that is controlled by private economic interests concerned solely with immediate profits. Until the turn of the century Albina actually consisted of two almost separate communities: (1) the low-lying riverside land and the adjacent hilltop plateau developed as industrial, and (2) the adjoining residential hinterland. Wealth was present in the latter area, as evidenced by the fact that three of the seven mansions illustrating the border of the now famous Clohessy & Strengles isometric Portland map of 1890* were located in Albina.

The construction of the rail shops in 1885 produced a change in the population mix; increasing numbers of working class Irish and Germans moved in and occupied the "cheap temporary structures" hastily slapped together along the railroad tracks. "Stringtown," it was called. When the Union Pacific closed The Dalles shops in 1893, several hundred more employees were dispatched. Within a few years Albina was to become primarily a working class community, living in small cheap homes. The railroad yards and the adjacent industry would expand, with consequent pressure on the commercial district to invade the residential area of more expensive homes. A helter-skelter conglomerate of residential, industrial, commercial and institutional activity resulted. By World War I a commercial strip would develop along Williams Avenue, one of the major thoroughfares for the Willamette Bridge Railway streetcars, and along Union Avenue as well.

Following a common pattern in American history, the gradual expansion of non-residential uses of land produced mixtures of use,

*Should be dated 1893.

133

OREGON— THE RAILWAY WORKS AT ALBINA.

often to the detriment of each, and every new non-residential use decreased the residential population. This development tended to drive out the more affluent white and in turn attract the poor white and the black. Over the years Albina was often characterized as a "tough" town, a place of "booze and battle." Author Stewart Holbrook's research led him to conclude that Albina was divided between "the old settlers, decent, kindly and quiet and the hard working folks."[17]

Heart of Albina business district, circa 1913. (Willamette Bridge Railway Co.)

"The Portland Development Commission has taken preliminary steps to preserve a landmark in the Albina neighborhood. An onion-shaped dome (cupola) and certain other architectural elements have been salvaged from the Hill Building, a two-story structure built in 1890 and recently razed as part of the Emanuel Hospital Urban Renewal Project. (Removal of the building was necessary in order to widen Russell Steet.)

Charles H. Hill, Albina's first mayor, was the owner and builder of the Hill Block. Located at the intersection of Russell and Williams Avenues, the building stood in the heart of the business district of the old city of Albina, which later was incorporated into the city of Portland.

Mr. Hill took great pride in the fact that the building afforded him a prominent place to display the American Flag and, according to old newspaper accounts, when the Oregon Volunteers went to the Philippines during the Spanish-American War, he declared that he would leave the flag there until the regiment could return "in victory and glory." And he did, although the flag became battered and torn. On the day the Oregon troops returned he took down the old banner and raised a new flag.

Several businesses were housed in the building, the most prominent one being the drugstore beneath the cupola which was first owned by Francis A. Watts and Edward B. Holmes.

Stephen A. Matthieu bought an interest in the drugstore from Watts and Holmes in 1893 and acquired control of the business around 1905."—*Portland Profile,* Portland Dev. Com.

The influx of blacks into the Albina region began slowly before World War I. By 1906, most of Oregon's 1200 blacks were living in Portland and spread throughout every ward. "Blacks voted and served as jurors. Their children shared classrooms with white children. They sat side by side with whites in restaurants and theaters. . . . Almost any person who had a job was a member of the black elite, but waiters, cooks, government workers (janitors in federal buildings), ministers and businessmen held the most enviable positions."[18] But as waves of European immigrants came into the area, the labor unions refused to admit blacks and the ugly process of discrimination became a reality. As early as 1902 blacks were barred from attending the Republican party conventions in both Portland and Multnomah County. This was the work of party chairman W.F. (Jack) Matthews, the notorious boss who succeeded Joe Simon and worked closely with Senator John Mitchell and Judge Charles Carey. It was now difficult for blacks to rent houses. Increasingly they were forced by unpublicized realtor pressure into less desirable "districts," beginning with the old North End, and culminating with Albina by the time of World War II.* In 1960, approximately 80 percent of Portland's 15,637 black population would be confined to Albina, clustered around the Williams Avenue corridor.[20]

Albina's founding fathers never envisioned a growth pattern of this sort. The 1887 charter of incorporation contemplated boulevards and magnificent parks. As late as 1903 John Olmsted was proposing a river bluff park for the North Albina district.[21] Little ever resulted from these dreams, however, because from the very first, the city of Albina's appetite outran its resources. More was promised than was possible to be achieved, and the controlling corporate interests were not willing to assume the necessary tax burdens.

A review of Albina's city ordinances for the period 1887-1891 reveals both hunger for private economic development and fiscal irresponsibility in municipal management. Charles F. Swigert's Willamette Bridge Railway Co. was awarded four franchises, three of them

---

*A comment made in 1939 by prominent Portland realtor, Chester A. Moores of Commonwealth Inc. supports this statement:

"We were discussing at the Realty Board recently the advisability of setting up certain districts for negroes and orientals. We talked about the possibility of creating desirable districts which would actually cater to those groups and make life more pleasant for them. After all, they have to live too, the same as youngsters."[19]

within two months of consolidation. The last one on June 30, 1891 was to extend for 50 years and was so loosely drafted that it constituted a carte blanche for the company.

> "... thence north along and upon "C" street in Peninsular addition No. 2, as it may be extended north and south to the city limits; also along and upon either "I", "J" or "K" streets in said ... addition ... as the same may be extended north and south to the city limits. . . . "22

All designated routes were to be extended as the city limits themselves were extended. This franchise should go down in history as a classic give-away.

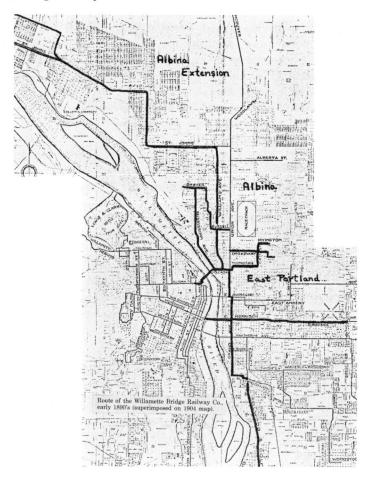

Route of the Willamette Bridge Railway Co., early 1890's (superimposed on 1904 map).

The Albina Water Co. was organized in 1888 by C.F. Swigert and George W. Bates. It was granted a franchise to lay water pipes and the following year it signed a contract with the city to provide fire hydrants and cisterns. In 1890 the company was reincorporated as the Albina Light & Water Co. and it was immediately granted a franchise to erect poles and wires for the transmission of electricity once the power plant was completed. The president of the company in 1890 was D.M. McLaughlan who had been serving as mayor since 1888 and who, of course, signed each of the franchise ordinances. McLaughlan had been a long time employee of the OR&N as a field engineer and master mechanic and he was to maintain a close relationship with the company during his public service. The Light & Water Co. also generated the power needed for the Willamette Bridge Railway operation in the Albina area.

The 1891 legislature which had authorized Albina to annex territory all the way north and west to and including the village of St. Johns also authorized the city to issue $150,000 of improvement bonds. In an act of irresponsibility, the city council, under McLaughlan's prodding, passed three ordinances one month before consolidation that authorized: (1) $40,000 to pay the floating indebtedness and meet the current expenses of the city; (2) $50,000 for paving streets and boulevards; and (3) $50,000 for street paving and parks. Such actions perpetrated a fraud on the taxpayers of consolidated Portland who inherited the obligations with no visible means of meeting them. For years the Portland taxpayers had to carry the added financial burdens loaded on them at the last minute by the very developers who stood to gain by such public expenditures that serviced their own private enterprises.

In its final act of public service, the Albina city council authorized an exclusive contract with Edward Quackenbush's Investment Company to provide lighting for the recently developed Piedmont District in North Albina adjacent to Dekum and Durham's Portland & Vancouver Street Railway line that would become part of George Markle's ill-fated Consolidated Street Railway Co. in 1892.* The City of Portland had to assume this obligation also.** The franchise

---

*Frank Dekum and Richard Durham, downtown bankers, developed the Woodlawn District, directly east of Piedmont, through their Oregon Land & Development Co.

**All franchises and contracts in effect before consolidation were kept in force after consolidation, with the consolidated city government assuming full obligation.

was awarded and signed on July 6, 1891, the very day that Albina joined consolidated Portland.[23]

Mayor McLaughlan was personally opposed to the timing of consolidation in 1891 because he was afraid that Albina property values would decline. What he most likely feared was a loss in value of some property in which he had an interest; that with consolidation he would not have the freedom to wheel and deal that he had enjoyed under the old regime. In reality there was no alternative for Albina. It could not carry the financial load for which it had obligated itself. In an attempt to keep corporate taxes low, the county had way under-assessed Albina's property, at the low amount of only $557,000.[24] Furthermore, without free ferry service and without free Bull Run water that would be flowing within four years, the city could not hope to survive.

George W. Bates,[25] organizer of the enfranchised Albina Light & Water Co., disagreed with his friend McLaughlan. Along with C.F. Swigert he became a leading advocate of consolidation; his West side ties were close. Because Bates was a preeminent example of the new type of businessman-politician — the power jobber — who was emerging in the 1890's and whose leadership exerted strong impact on the physical shaping of Portland, a close look at his career is in order.

George W. Bates.

Born in Iowa in 1851 of German parentage, Bates joined a California & Oregon Railroad construction crew at 17. Six years later he was employed by C.F. Swigert's uncle in the San Francisco office of the Pacific Bridge Co. In 1880 Bates and Swigert were sent to Portland to open an office for the supervision of local construction projects, including the building of a large dock for William (Dundee) Reid and fellow Scot James B. Montgomery on the Albina waterfront. Bates was immediately introduced to the opportunities awaiting him, especially in Albina. Shortly thereafter he became proprietor of the Portland Box Factory and in 1883 teamed up with Lee Hoffman, forming a company that specialized in the construction of covered bridges and bridge piers throughout the Northwest. The record is unclear as to what, if any, official connection Hoffman & Bates Co. maintained with Pacific Bridge, but there is an account of Hoffman being involved as a superintendent in the Morrison Bridge project with Swigert, in 1885-1887. Be that as it may, for over 20 years Bates, Swigert and Hoffman* enjoyed a close personal and financial association, much of it centered in Albina.

As the chart on page 128 reveals, Bates and his friends organized the Albina Water Co. in 1889 by purchasing the existing little water plant in the center of Albina. In 1890 the Albina Light & Water Co. was organized, resulting in the first electric lighting system for the Albina region. Concurrent with these efforts, Bates' associate Swigert was constructing the first electrified street railway line in the Portland area, the St. Johns division of the Willamette Bridge Railway Co., which ran from Third and Glisan in Northwest Portland, across the new Steel OR&N Railroad Bridge, into the western and northern reaches of Albina. In January of 1892 Bates sold the lighting division of Albina Light & Water to the Portland General Electric Co. for $200,000 most of which he used to organize and support three banks founded in 1892-1893: The Bank of Albina, the Albina Savings Bank and the Multnomah County Bank. The president of the Savings Bank was H.S. Rowe, a superintendent for the OR&N and future mayor of Portland (1900-1902). Bates had sufficient funds to ride out the panic of 1893, and the following year he merged all three banks into the George W. Bates Co., with Swigert, Hoffman, and Rowe as stockholders and directors. In 1893, he and Hoffman received a $467,000 contract to build the first Bull Run pipe line for the Portland Water Committee. In succeeding years he organized the Union Laundry Co. (one of the largest in the Northwest) bought control of two sawmills, and was president of the Diamond Vitrified Brick Co. of Vancouver.

---

*Lee Hoffman's son was to found the L.H. Hoffman Construction Co. in 1922 and to marry Walter Burns' daughter, the great-niece of C.H. Lewis. The Hoffman Construction Co. has become one of the largest general contracting firms in the United States.

Bates' political career was inaugurated officially with his appointment to the Portland Board of Police Commissioners in 1895. His first experience proved shorter than expected, due to political intrigue. He went on to serve in one session of the Oregon State Senate (1897-1898) which appointed him to the Committee on Insurance and Banking. In July of 1898 he began a five year term on the Police Board, and missed, by one vote, being elected mayor of Portland in May of 1899 when the council was required to select a successor to the deceased Mayor William S. Mason. He held office for four years as a member of the Water Committee (1898-1902) concurrent with his service on the Police Board. Thus for that period of four years George Bates was a member of two of the three most powerful and prestigious public commissions in the city of Portland. While sitting on the Water Committee, he peddled his Albina Water Co. to the city for $200,000, an action that was roundly criticized in some circles. There was obvious conflict of interest here, although Bates did not attend the one meeting in December 1901 at which the purchase was officially approved. Some questions were subsequently raised as to whether or not the city received full value for the amount paid, but that matter will be examined later in the story.

Bates was also a member of the Lewis & Clark Centennial Exposition Association Board (1902-1905), an experience that brought him in close touch with the leading establishment figures of Portland business and society. He lived in a fashionable district on Northwest Flanders Street in a large and commodious home designed by Whidden and Lewis. In 1910 he moved his bank headquarters from Albina to downtown Portland and sold his company to the Lumberman's Bank in 1913. He was president of Lumberman's until his death in 1916, and the following year Lumberman's was acquired by the U.S. National Bank.

At the time of his death, George Bates was cited for his energy, personal force, steadfastness, and his quiet, genial personality. A former associate who was much younger than the old banker has characterized Bates as "a rugged, smart man who thought everything out. He knew exactly what he was doing."[26] Bates had appeared on the local scene at the right time and he had the talent to make maximum use of his opportunities, following a type of game plan that was generally accepted as the path to financial success in 1900. But he and his friend Swigert did more than just take advantage of opportunities; they created them and in the process assumed a number of risks. For such an "intrepid promoter of western enterprises,"[27] politics and business were not two separate human activities, never to be mingled. On the contrary, politics provided the means — and often the power — for achieving business success. In June 1891, political consolidation of Portland was viewed in exactly this light by Portland's business establishment.

The vote for consolidation produced overwhelming approval. In Portland and Albina, the voter response was three to one in favor; in East Portland it was six to one.[28] Elected to his first term as Mayor was William Spencer Mason,* a prominent business man not aligned with the traditional wing of the Republican party which ran former Congressman M.C. George as Mason's opponent. "Mason was swept into office by a larger majority than had ever been polled in a Portland mayoralty contest. The election result was hailed as 'the end of municipal misrule and the defeat of bossism, the sack, insolent policemen and hoodlum firemen.' "[29]

W.S. Mason

Unfortunately for Portland, bossism and misrule did not depart, for long, from City Hall although Mason was an honest and generally effective mayor during his three year term. Mason was described as a "man of positive, well founded convictions. . . . A progressive businessman . . . with conscience and common sense." He was tall and portly, with "a commanding presence." A quiet, thoughtful and determined man, he usually made "haste slowly."[30] Mason presented a marked contrast to his predecessor, Van B. DeLashmutt. None of his official actions was ever tainted with conflict of interest even though he was the president of the Mason-Ehrman Grocery Co., vice president of the Chamber of Commerce, and would be named

*Born in Virginia in 1832, Mason was entirely self-made. He started from nothing.

president of the Portland National Bank in 1892. He derived no personal benefit, except publicity, from any of his public duties.

The new charter increased the city council from nine to sixteen members, representing eight wards. In keeping with the mayor's background, this was a chamber of commerce type council, a true cross section of the economic life of the city. Included were three manufacturers and realtors, two merchants and bankers and street railway investors, one lawyer and contractor, a travel agent and a carpenter. Albina sent two prominent residents: realtor John Pittenger and sawmill owner John Parker, both good friends of Bates and Swigert. The upper social tier was represented by two members of the Arlington Club, banker-manufacturer J.F. Watson and furniture merchant C.M. Forbes, Council President in 1892-1893. Elected officers, City Attorney William T. Muir and Police Judge Charles H. Carey, both members of the Mitchell machine, would seek and receive Arlington Club membership subsequently, in keeping with their eagerness to climb the political-social ladder as quickly as possible.

S. E. corner, Burnside & First

The charter provided explicit limitations on municipal debt and expenditures, but not before the city was already committed to assuming inherited obligations from the three previously separate municipalities which had issued a number of bonds but had retired none. "The City of Portland was required to take over these obligations, many of which were for running expenses and floating debts and not for improvements."[31]

According to former Mayor Earl Riley,* the city built bridges and provided no sinking funds. For instance, "the first Morrison Street Bridge (1887) was torn down in 1904, and yet the bonds issued for its construction were not retired until April of 1925. . . . All the bonds were term bonds, and yet there had been no provision for a sinking fund,"[32] and there would be none until 1910.

Six months before consolidation, the *Oregonian* had run the headline: "City Funds at a low Ebb."[33] The fire department had not been able to pay salaries the previous month. The police force was far too small to perform an adequate job. Ironically, Portland — one of the wealthiest cities per capita in the country — had the smallest police force of any major city in proportion to its size. Extensive private resources did not find their way into public expenditures, even for necessities. Until well after 1900, Multnomah County's ratio of property assessment to true cash value would remain at 25 percent. Thus 35 officers on day duty were expected to patrol 23 square miles of streets and dry land as well as to police the bridgeheads and monitor the busy street crossings. For these efforts they, along with the firemen, received only $1080 per year, to be cut back to $780 after the depression of 1893.[34] Portland's banks, real estate, street railway and railroad corporations had to share much of the blame for these conditions. For 12 of the 20 year period from 1885 to 1905, Portland mayors had direct affiliation with one of these interests. The other mayors were merely subservient to them.

The new debt limit was not to exceed $150,000 except for: $500,000 for the new city hall; $2,500,000 for the water works, already authorized; $250,000 for parks; and $500,000 for free bridges. A two year limit was placed on all non-bonded debts. The charter also stipulated that water bonds "shall be taxable."[35]

Mayor Mason had his work cut out for him. He was to face three difficult years. He was a man of simple tastes who made himself totally accessible to the public. Even when he moved into the new City Hall in early 1894 he refused to closet himself from citizen contact, locating his desk in public view. The panic of 1893, decreasing city revenues, the vice probe of 1892-93, and police department morale and discipline presented him with a full time challenge although he was only receiving a half-time pay, which he returned to the city.

---

*Riley was Commissioner of Finance, 1933-1941 and Mayor, 1941-1949.

Portland's City Hall, completed 1894.*

*Portland paid $100,000 in 1890 for the improved block, bounded by S.W. 4th and 5th, Madison and Jefferson Streets, on which was located the St. Helens Hall for girls. The building cost $575,000 ($175,000 had already been authorized before the 1891 charter was approved). In December 1889 the initial authorization was for a building that was started and never completed. The council had engaged architect Henry Hefty who had come up with a plan for a huge ostentatious structure that appeared to be modeled on the Kremlin. After the new charter was approved, smouldering dissatisfaction erupted. The new City Hall Commission cancelled the contract and spent almost $125,000 tearing out the foundation and much of the first floor.[36] The City Hall Commission, charged with the construction of the facility, included: Henry Failing, Henry J. Corbett, William M. Ladd, Donald MacLeay and others — a blue ribbon group. Designed by architects Ion Lewis and W.H. Whidden, recently arrived from Boston to work on the Portland Hotel project, the City Hall successfully incorporated "many 15th century details of the type now termed Mannerist." Whidden had been employed by the nationally prominent firm of McKim, Mead and White. They tended to work in the Renaissance style, although with the City Hall, Whidden came up with a design that was less derivative.[37]

OREGON—IN THE COTTONWOODS NEAR PORTLAND.

Chapter VII

A Community
of Many Interests,
1891-1895

1.

Mayor Mason opened the first meeting of the new council on
July 23, 1891 with a stinging criticism of the "hasty" legislation
passed by the former councils of East Portland and Albina during the
last month before consolidation was to take effect on July 6th.[1] He
underscored the fact that the city was faced with serious financial
difficulties, resulting largely from the recently assumed obligations
and the long term bonded debt that had not been retired. The previously cited Morrison Bridge bonds provided one example. Another
was the still outstanding issue of $56,000 worth of 10 year, 10 per-
cent general fund bonds sold in May 1871. Of this amount raised,
$20,000 had been used to retire river improvement bonds issued for
12 percent in May 1866. The general fund bonded indebtedness had
to be refinanced in 1881 and 1891, except that in the latter instance
the issue was extended to 25 years at 4 percent. It was to be 57 years
from date of initial sale before these bonds were finally paid off, on
May 1, 1928.[2]

As the council convened in the old City Hall at Second and Ash
Streets, the first order of major business was a discussion of the need

to redeem a campaign pledge made by the supporters of consolidation: to provide free bridges within the City of Portland.* Through a series of ordinances over the next two months, the council authorized the mayor to appoint a Free Bridge Committee which was instructed to determine the purchase prices of two of the three existing private spans, the Morrison and the Madison Street; the Steel (railroad) bridge was excluded from consideration. The committee was instructed to make recommendation to the council and was authorized to sell $500,000 in bonds to provide the necessary funding for eventual purchase. It was also authorized to conduct the necessary negotiations.

The Morrison Street Bridge had been opened in April, 1887. Built by the Pacific Bridge Co. under the supervision of C.F. Swigert and Lee Hoffman, it attracted wide attention as the largest bridge west of the Mississippi. Costing $175,000, it consisted of three Pratt wooden truss combination spans, each 260 feet long, a steel draw span of 310 feet and one Howe wooden truss span 160 feet long.[3] For the privilege of crossing the bridge on foot one paid a toll of five cents, the same amount charged by the Albina, Stark Street and Jefferson Street ferries. During the first months many paid and walked cheerfully just to satisfy their curiosity. The ferries went right on operating, but with increasingly reduced traffic, their days were numbered.

> "The opening of the draw was always an event and it happened many times each day. A clanging bell stopped traffic and pedestrians scurried. Drays, express wagons, one-horse deliveries, farm wagons, buggies and surreys with fringe on top formed in long lines at each end to give right of way to the river boats.
>
> There was a law on the statute books that no horse could proceed faster than a walk, but the bridge tenders allowed something of a dog-trot to clear the bridge."[4]

The Steel Bridge, owned by the OR&N and Union Pacific Railway, was completed in July 1888. The first steel bridge on the West Coast,** it was 1245 feet long, including approaches. The lower of the two decks was for exclusive use by both the U.P. and S.P. Railroads as a means of entry to the yards of the Northern Pacific Terminal Co.

---

*Free to all users but street railways.
**Manufactured by the Union Bridge Co. of Utica, N.Y.

Steel Bridge at Portland — Train entering the great double-deck structure.

The upper deck, opened in 1889, had a roadway 19 feet wide for pedestrian and street car traffic.[5] This was the bridge over which C.F. Swigert built Portland's first electric street railway, running from N.W. Glisan Street to Albina. For a time tolls were charged but when Multnomah County agreed to pay a monthly rental of $350 the toll system was abolished.

An average day's traffic between the east and west sides in 1889, on the two bridges and the three ferries, was 4747 pedestrians, 1967 street car passengers, 1061 teams and 37 horsemen.* More than half of all the pedestrians used the Stark Street ferry,[6] and it was just as well that they did, especially after dark. Walking across the bridges at night posed some danger. The story was told by H.G. Colton, a Massachusetts Mutual Life Insurance Co. agent, about an experience with his first customer after reaching Portland in October 1889. The customer, Johan Poulson, had himself just recently arrived in town. The co-owner of what was to become the large Inman-Poulson Lumber Co. on the East Side of the river was persuaded by Colton to purchase a small policy.

---

*Tolls were charged as follows: 20 cents for two horses and a driver, 10 cents for a horse and rider, 10 cents for loose horses and cattle, and 5 cents for sheep, hogs and footmen.

"Mr. Poulson wasn't exactly sold, to use a current phrase, and he might never have reached the doctor for the usual examination, except for an accident. . . . 'That night, after I had obtained his check for the policy,' said Colton, 'Mr. Poulson was walking across the steel bridge on Glisan Street . . . It was dark and the draw was open. Mr. Poulson didn't know the draw was open and he walked into the river. Mr. Poulson was pretty mad about it. He swam ashore, all right, but the next day he came in and doubled the size of his policy.' "[7]

The Madison Street Bridge, connecting Madison Street on the West Side with Hawthorne Street on the East, was opened on January 11, 1891. Built by Pacific Bridge, it was a Pratt wooden truss structure 1470 feet long, exclusive of approaches, and 40 feet wide.[8] For some unexplained reason, the Free Bridge Committee recommended that the city purchase this bridge first, rather than the older Morrison Street span. From its earliest days of operation, it had developed a much deserved reputation for being a poorly designed structure, incapable of withstanding the heavy jolts produced by the Mount Tabor Street Railway traffic. Perhaps its owners who were well connected politically, and who included Sheriff Penumbra Kelly, wanted to get out as fast as they could and recover their investment at minimum risk. By a vote of 12-3,[9] the council authorized the purchase of the bridge for $142,500, eleven months after it was completed. A public outcry ensued. The city had paid at least 10 percent too much, it was charged. The papers were quoting an erroneous cost of $140,000, whereas the actual cost was $145,000. Eleven years later the county would have to expend $22,500 to reconstruct the rickety structure following a fire that destroyed one section. In 1910-11 the city would replace the wooden span with the current steel Hawthorne Bridge at a cost of over $500,000. The ordinance authorizing purchase in 1891 also granted a franchise to the Steel brothers'* Mt. Tabor Street Railway Co. for 30 years of use at only $1200 per year,[10] an action that was to be roundly assailed for decades. "The City got the worst of the bargain," claimed the *Oregonian* in 1926.[11]

---

*The Steels bought the Mt. Tabor Railway Co. from George Brown on the very day the franchise was awarded. James' nephew, William M. Ladd, was Treasurer of the Free Bridge Committee. George was the politically powerful Portland Postmaster from 1890 to 1894.

Portland and Mount Tabor via Madison Street Bridge.

In November 1892, the city began construction of the first Burnside Bridge, designed to serve Markle, Dekum and Durham's Consolidated Street Railway Co.'s Portland-Vancouver line. By the time the bridge opened on July 4, 1894, however, Markle had vanished and his rail line had gone through receivership and reincorportion as the Portland, Vancouver and Northern Railway Co., with Richard L. Durham as one of the new owners.

On April 1st of the preceding year, during the onset of the panic, the bridge committee had purchased the Albina Ferry and abolished the toll. Seven months later, the much disparaged Madison Street Bridge suffered more adverse criticism when a fatal accident occurred on November 1, 1893. It was a cold foggy morning when the East Side Railway* car "Inez" neared the bridge. As the car reached the approach ramp the span went up to permit a ship to pass through.

> "When the motorman saw the red signal, he applied his brakes but they failed to hold on the icy track. As the street car skidded along the rails, the conductor, motorman and most of the passengers leaped to safety. Then with a horrible crash, the car plunged through the gate, hung for a moment on the edge of the span and plunged into the black, icy waters of the Willamette River below carrying 5 passengers to their death."[12]

---

*The Steel brothers had incorporated their Mt. Tabor Street Railway into the new East Side line earlier that year.

The second of the private bridges available for purchase, the Morrison Street, was bought by the city in July of 1895 for $150,000. An interesting story is related to this episode, particularly as to the reasons for the lengthy delay in consummating the transaction.

It was well known throughout Portland that the major opponent of city purchase was James Lotan,[13] a maverick businessman-politician who happened to own one half interest in the Stark Street ferry. He had fought a futile battle against city consolidation. Lotan got his start in the business world as a shop foreman with the Willamette Iron Works which was controlled by a branch of the Corbett family. He was to be an officer of the concern for many years thereafter. Early in his career Lotan had become a protege of Joseph Simon, performing a number of minor but distasteful tasks for the political boss. The payoff came in the mid-eighties when he was appointed to a series of federal positions: local inspector of shipping and machinery, inspector of boilers, and finally, in 1892, customs collector, a real political plum.

Half-way up the ladder of his rapid political ascent, Lotan broke with Simon, most likely over the question of providing support to Senator John H. Mitchell, Simon's deadly enemy. By 1887 both Mitchell and Lotan were fellow Arlington Club members and close political allies. Lotan wrested control of the state Republican leadership from Simon in 1890, one of the few occasions in his long career that such a mishap ever befell Joe Simon. For three years Lotan was a power in state Republican circles and he enjoyed extensive influence within the legislature. Because Portland had already exhausted 80 percent of its authorized bonding capacity for free bridge and ferry acquisition the city was forced to return to the legislature for a further authorization of $200,000. Lotan made sure that the bill remained buried throughout the 1893 session, the one term Joe Simon did not seek office. Lotan was demanding that he and his partner receive $50,000 for their ferry as the price of legislative approval of the extended authorization.

In early December 1893, Lotan's power base was damaged when he was indicted in federal court for smuggling in 4190 pounds of opium during the last six months of 1892 while he was serving as U.S. customs collector.[14] Indicted along with him was Seid Back, the wealthiest and most prominent Chinese merchant in the Northwest, and a dozen lesser known figures. The much publicized trial saw future U.S. Senator Charles W. Fulton defend Lotan, and future U.S. Senators Joe Simon and John Gearin defend others of the accused. The judge was Simon's and Gearin's ex-law partner, C.B. Bellinger, and the jury foreman was Charles E. Ladd, son of William S., fellow Arlington Club associate of Lotan's and business colleague of Jonathan Bourne, a close friend of Lotan's. The jury convicted 10 of the group but could not agree on Lotan or Back.[15] A retrial was not sought by the government due to the unexplained disappearance of the leading witness, a disreputable character named Nat Blum. Lotan thus survived, with his reputation more or less intact, supported loyally throughout the ordeal by his fellow Arlington Club comrades.

During the 1895 session of the legislature, Joe Simon managed to push through the required authorization. As Senate president he exercised considerable power; his absence in 1893 had created a vacuum which Lotan had used to good advantage. Included in the authorization was the provision to purchase the Stark Street ferry for $40,000. The price of the bridge was to be $150,000. When these figures were released public reaction was immediate. Although the bridge had cost $175,000, it had deteriorated badly during its eight years of heavy use by the street railway cars. It would be replaced within 10 years at a cost of $385,383. Seven months later, in the heat of a vicious political campaign, District Attorney W.T. Hume charged "fraud and a steal" in denouncing the Morrison Bridge "deal" before a public audience.[16] Hume was not referring to the Lotan pay-off but only to the amount paid for the bridge itself. He was a member of the Lotan-Mitchell Republican faction and was aiming his barbs at the Simon-Corbett faction.

The press reported some years subsequently that Henry W. Corbett had a sizeable amount of money tied up in the old Morrison span.[17] If he did, it would have been through First National Bank loans to C.F. Swigert* and his associates who controlled both the bridge and the City & Suburban Railway that was enfranchised to use it. It was similarly reported that Lotan had amassed heavy bank debts, but the bank was not named; its identity can only be surmised. Simon was certainly not doing Lotan a favor. But he wanted the bridge bill approved, and if there were outstanding First National Bank loans to either the bridge company or Lotan it was worth it to him, as Henry Corbett's lawyer, to seek approval of the total package. In any case, within seven months, the Stark Street ferry was abandoned. Although its passenger payload had diminished markedly, the ferry boat itself proved to be mechanically inoperative and generally unseaworthy. It was a piece of junk.

---

*Swigert's loans are a matter of record.[18]

2.

One of the more pressing orders of business that faced Mayor Mason and the council during the summer of 1891 was another obligation assumed through consolidation: the construction of an East Portland electric light power house. Knowing the financial plight of the city at the time, one could logically assume that the mayor did not relish having to expend public funds on such a project even though the bonds had already been sold. Ultimately the public would have to pay for them. In a hasty and ill-conceived action, the East Portland Council had authorized the sale of $50,000 of bonds for a city light works less than a month before consolidation was to take effect — four days in fact after the affirmative plebiscite. Through a series of ordinances passed over a period of four months,[19] the council authorized the expenditure of $40,342 to build and equip the power plant.

Within 15 months of the plant's completion, the council voted 12-4[20] to sell the Light Works to the Portland General Electric Co. for $27,000. Although the company agreed to some reduction of charges for municipal power use, the transaction constituted a generous gift to a private company at the expense of future taxpayers. The ordinance was drafted and promoted by Councilman Scoggin, a director of George Markle's Consolidated Street Railway Co. which held a contract with PGE to supply electricity for this recently enfranchised conglomerate. The mayor signed the ordinance on March 3rd because he did not want the city in the power business, particularly in the spring of 1893.

The generation of electric power in the Portland region had begun unobtrusively in September 1880 when George Weidler, Ben Holladay's former agent and early investor in the OSN Co., erected a dynamo in his sawmill on the Willamette River across from Albina. He was the first person to sell electric lighting in Portland when he ran a primitive transmission line to the nearby Ainsworth Dock in 1881. Within three years he was instrumental in organizing the U.S. Electric Lighting and Power Co. which operated off of steam generated dynamos. His three associates were to be the prime movers

157

in the early development of the Portland electric utility industry:
L.L. Hawkins, P.F. Morey and F.V. Holman.[21]

Leander Hawkins was one of the most colorful personalities in
Portland's history. As a young man he had managed the local personal affairs of Capt. J.C. Ainsworth and R.R.Thompson. He was the
first president of U.S. Electric, the organizer and first president of
the Ainsworth National Bank, the president of the Portland Hydraulic Elevator Co., an organizer of the Portland Cable Railway Co., and
the first Portland resident to conceive a comprehensive plan of skyline trails and parks for the outlying hill sections of the city. Fred
Holman was a brilliant and scholarly attorney who mastered the
legal technicalities of utility organization and was to become the
leading utility lawyer in Portland for over 20 years. One of the few
Democratic members of the Arlington Club, he was a recognized historian and rose fancier; in fact, "he originated and caused to be
adopted 'The Rose City' as the popular name for Portland."[22]

The key man in the development of Portland electric power from
1888 until his retirement in 1902 was P.F. Morey. He was responsible
for organizing the Willamette Falls Electric Co. in November 1888
with a capitalization of $1 million. The assets of U.S. Electric were
transferred to the new company which received a city franchise in
April 1889. On June 3rd, Willamette Falls Electric introduced to
the United States the first long distance (13 miles) commercial transmission of direct current hydro-electric power. Henry Villard, who
was to become actively involved in electric utility organization
nationally during the early '90's* had contributed to Oregon's unique
accomplishment when, six years previously, he had paid for a survey of water power potential at the Willamette Falls in Oregon City.
The company's first generating station was at this spot on the east
side of the river. A second station would be built on the west side
in 1892.

---

*Villard had organized the North American Co., an outgrowth of his old
Oregon and Transcontinental Co., to gain control of the Detroit Edison Co.
and other utilities in Milwaukee and St. Louis. He also became president of
the Edison General Electric Co. which was merged with the Thomson-Houston Electric Co. of Lynn, Massachusetts in 1892 to form the General Electric
Co. of Boston. Charles A. Coffin was president with J.P. Morgan as the
underwriter. From 1890-91, the Thomson-Houston Co. built and operated a
single car track in the Woodstock area. It was merged into the Waverly-
Woodstock line in 1891.

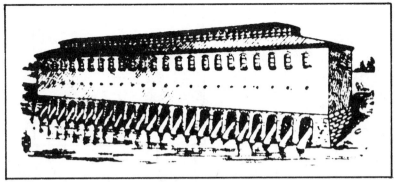

Exterior of the power station, electric long-distance transmission plant, at Willamette Falls, Oregon City, 1895.

In March 1890, the company bought two lots on the river at the foot of Montgomery Street for the site of its first Portland substation. Within a year, Willamette Falls Electric found itself growing rapidly but without sufficient local capital to replace equipment that became obsolete quickly in those days. Morey had many plans in the works. He also felt it necessary to get himself elected to the 1891 session of the legislature for the obvious purpose of protecting and advancing the interests of his burgeoning industry. The most important immediate step to be taken was to work for the approval of consolidation.

On August 6, 1892, Morey, Holman and Henry Failing formed the new Portland General Electric Co. which bought all of the assets of the Willamette Falls operation. Capitalized at $4.25 million, the company received its major outside financing from the Old Colony Trust Co. of Boston.* The General Electric Co. of Boston also invested in PGE, following a practice it would pursue throughout the country: invest in the operating companies which would be strongly "encouraged" to purchase their electrical equipment from General Electric, the manufacturing company. Not wishing to limit itself in a fast growing market that promised large profits, G.E. proceeded to form a series of holding companies for the purpose of acquiring a controlling interest in a number of operating electric utilities, of which PGE was not one, at least directly. PGE would eventually be controlled by

---

*Old Colony was Boston's famous "old guard" bank. It was bought by the First National of Boston in 1929 and the investment division was spun off in the mid-1930's to form the First Boston Corp. of New York. The city of Boston was the financial center for investment in railroads, copper, textiles and utilities such as G.E. and AT&T.

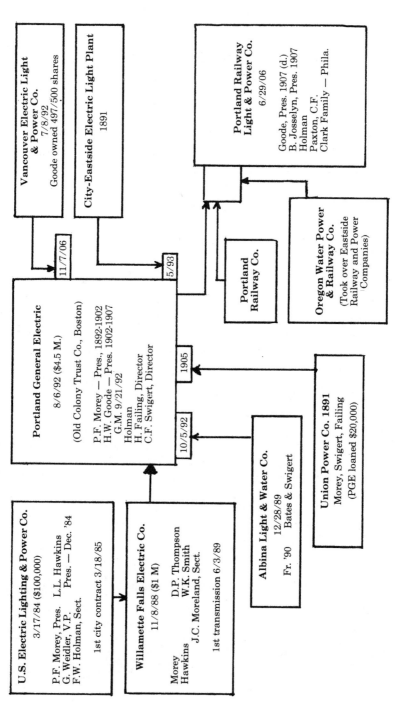

Electric Utility Mergers

eastern capital, but not until 1906 when it was combined with all of the region's electrified street railways to form the gigantic Portland Railway Light and Power Co., Portland's first bona fide monopoly.

In the intervening years, Portland General Electric would gradually expand its operations by acquiring additional local power companies such as the city's Eastside Light Works, the Union Power Co., the lighting division of the Albina Light and Water Co. and the Vancouver Electric Light and Power Co. which was organized in 1892 by PGE's General Manager, H.W. Goode. When Morey retired in 1902, he was to be succeeded by Goode who would dominate the Portland electric utility industry until his untimely death five years later.

By 1892, the electric power companies had found their place in the local and national scene. Writing recently in *Environment,* Sheldon Novick noted that:

> "The axioms of electric power — that electricity could not be stored and that power plants must be large and expensive — quite naturally went unchallenged. . . . They allowed and even dictated, a power system that could be run only by huge regional monopolies."[23]

The utility companies welcomed franchises in the same way that the railroads did, as long as they were not deemed too restrictive or "confiscatory." A franchise established a legal base for their operations. It guaranteed the continuance of exclusive or monopolistic practices without the threat of competition. The franchising power became the source of large new fortunes. In the mid 1890's franchises were loosely drafted documents; it was, after all, a period in which the private interest was deemed paramount to public policy. It was also the period when many of the great modern American corporations were formed, an era referred to in United States History as the "merger movement." More than 3000 industrial firms disappeared into merger, resulting in a number of corporations that are still the largest companies in their respective fields. The General Electric Company is one of them.

Although the two electric utility companies which currently serve the Portland area — Portland General Electric and Pacific Power & Light — are not operating under existing franchise authority as such,* they can claim a degree of legal sanction by virtue of franch-

---

*The power companies are licensed by the city and pay a 3 percent gross revenue tax.

ises awarded as far back as 1882 to predecessor companies, with which they are linked. With the exception of the East Portland Lighting Works, the city has never operated a municipal lighting plant. On several occasions around the turn of the century the subject was discussed, most notably during the lengthy deliberations of the Charter Commission in 1901. In the "Papers of Henry W. Corbett"[24] reference is made to a letter that Corbett, as chairman of the Water Committee, wrote in January 1899 proposing that the city consider developing its own lighting project to light its streets, for an initial term of 10 years. A recent charter amendment had given the Water Committee the authority to erect and maintain an electric lighting plant. A report was actually prepared by a consulting engineering firm, showing that a plant could be built for $175,000 and that annual cost of operation would amount to approximately $54,000. "The taxes lost to the city would be practically nothing."[25] There is no record of any further consideration of this proposal.*

The Northwest Natural Gas Co. has a history[26] similar to that of Portland's electric utilities. Except for water, gas was the first recognized public utility in Oregon. The company dates its origin from January 7, 1859 when it received a non-compensatory franchise from the territorial legislature which acted favorably upon a petition approved by the Portland City Council on December 17, 1858. According to the company today: "This franchise is perpetual, and was exclusive for the period of 15 years from January 10, 1859,"[27] the date the act was signed by the governor. "We are still operating under that franchise."[28]**

The company's founders, H.C. Leonard and Henry D. Green, were colorful pioneers who had known each other in New York and remet

---

*The 1902 charter, put into effect on January 23, 1903, authorized the city to acquire or build a municipal lighting plant, expending a maximum of $300,000, if the council submitted the proposal to public vote for approval. Subsequent charters have included a similar authorization and requirement but no such action has ever been taken. It is interesting to wonder what the current residential charges would be had Portland developed a full service municipal lighting system. The present charge for 1,000 kw hrs. is $19.76 for PGE and $18.67 for PP&L. For PUD customers in Salem, it is $10.60; Vancouver, Washington, $10.20; McMinnville, $10.20.

**The State Constitution, approved in February 1859, would have prohibited a perpetual franchise such as that awarded to Leonard and Green. The legal standing of the franchise was thoroughly investigated in 1907 but it has never been successfully challenged in the courts.

again in San Francisco in 1849. As with many of Portland's early residents, they decided that Oregon offered better opportunities than California. They formed a partnership, loaded a small ship with merchandise and sailed for Astoria where they opened a general store in the old Hudson Bay Co. storehouse in 1850. Moving on to Portland in 1851, they opened a shop on Front Street and built the city's first landing dock for vessels. They prospered, became ship agents for the Pacific Mail Co. and opened their own exporting business with the Hawaiian Islands. They also shipped the first cargo of flour from Portland to the Orient.[29]

Leonard and Green's first investment in the gas business amounted to about $50,000. They built a plant with six small retorts on the banks of the Willamette at the foot of Flanders Street in Couch's addition. The foundations of the original structure are now buried under Harbor Drive and the Steel Bridge ramps. The gas was made from coal shipped down from Vancouver Island in their own brig, the *Orbit*. The first gas was turned on in late 1859; the first gas lights on June 1, 1860. Portland thus became the third city on the Pacific Coast, after San Francisco and Sacramento, to provide regular gas service, the capacity of the plant being about 40,000 cubic feet a day.

Concurrent with their incorporation of the Portland Gas Light Co. in 1862, Leonard and Green purchased the franchise of the Portland Water Co. Both companies were kept separate although the gas and water systems were first developed together. Six hundred tons of cast iron pipe, "suitable for gas and water distribution,"[30] were purchased from New York. In 1882, the partners incorporated the East Portland Gas Light Co., building a plant on East Second and Ankeny Streets. Henry Green died in 1885, having resided for some years in his lavish home at Cedar Hill. Brother John and H.C. Leonard sold the Water Co. to the city in December 1886 and carried on the gas business until August 1892 when they received a generous offer to sell the gas works to a newly formed syndicate headed by two recently arrived young bankers: C.F. Adams and Abbot L. Mills. More will be said later in this chapter about these ambitious gentlemen who were to build two of the most successful business careers in Portland's history.

The Gas Light Company was now launched on a familiar course that was to carry it into the main stream of American business consolidation. The sale price for the Leonard and Green properties was supposedly $850,000. The new owners reincorporated their purchase as the Portland Gas Co., and, following the general financing pattern of the times, issued $1 million in bonds and $1 million in common stock. Two months later they acquired the stock of the East Portland

Gas Light Co., and in the process picked up two more franchises. They connected the two systems with a ten inch pipeline, the first transmission main laid under the Willamette River, and then they dismantled the east side plant. The new company had more than its share of troubles, brought on by the depression of 1893 and the devastating flood of 1894, but it managed to grow steadily, to the point that by 1905 its assets totalled $2.2 million. In 1910, Adams, Mills and their associates sold the company for about $3.5 million to the American Power & Light Co. and its name was changed to the Portland Gas and Coke Co. At time of sale, each share of common stock was worth $130, representing a 50 percent increase in value in just seven years.[31]

American Power, the father of the Pacific Power & Light Co. (incorporated in 1909), was itself a subsidiary of the Electric Bond & Share Co. of New York, organized in 1905 to assume control of General Electric's weaker utilities.* With financing provided by American Power, Portland Gas supported the establishment of the St. Johns Gas Co. in 1910 and the Clackamas County Gas Co. in 1913 and formally assumed control of both firms in 1915. As a $3.5 million holding company Portland Gas was cited as a monopoly by the *American Banker,* subject to anti-trust action under the Sherman Act.

By 1915, all of the major public service corporations in the Portland area would be absentee owned; all integrated into national holding corporations that were monopolies in the truest sense.** The utilities, like the railroads, "were joined in a 'community of interest,' a favorite [J.P.] Morgan phrase to indicate the consolidation of businesses competing for the same markets."[32] Total capitalization of American public service corporations ballooned from $200 million in 1890 to almost $20 billion by 1915.[33]

---

*EBASCO already owned the Astoria Lighting System, a Sidney Z. Mitchell property, picked up by EBASCO when Mitchell was made president in 1905.

**James J. Hill of the Great Northern acquired control of the Northern Pacific Railroad in 1894, with J.P. Morgan's help. Edward H. Harriman of the Union Pacific acquired control of the Southern Pacific in 1898 with John D. Rockefeller bank money. Both of these mergers were to have strong impact on the Portland area.

C.F. Adams

3.

Gasco president C.F. Adams was born in Baltimore in 1862, educated at Phillips Exeter Academy and at Yale where he majored in civil engineering. Secretary-treasurer Abbot Low Mills was born in Brooklyn, New York, in 1858, educated at Brooklyn Polytechnic Institute and Harvard. His cousin, Seth Low, was to be elected mayor of Brooklyn, president of Columbia University and mayor of New York City. Both men came west in 1882 in search of new opportunities, Adams to work in a bank at Walla Walla, Washington, and Mills to take up farming near Carlton in Yamhill County in company with a Harvard classmate.* In 1885, both men happened to end up in Colfax, Washington, near the Idaho border, living in the same rooming house. Mills had gone into a banking partnership and Adams had taken a job as cashier with the First National Bank which had been organized by ex-Portlander Levi Ankeny, with C.H. Lewis and Henry Failing as two of the larger stockholders.

Sometime in 1889, Adams and Mills decided to expand their opportunities by founding their own bank. They apparently secured

---

*Mills and his classmate William A. Howe bought 1000 acres of land on the North Fork of the Yamhill River for $8 per acre, later sold for $40 an acre.

Abbot L. Mills

pledges of support from friends and relatives back east to the unbelievable amount of $5 million. Arriving in Portland in late '89 they discussed their plans with Lewis, Failing and Corbett and were told that $5 million of outside money was much too much for two young men to be investing in a new banking venture in Portland.[34] It was agreed that the bank should be locally controlled and capitalized at $500,000, with $250,000 to be raised initially: $112,500 from the east and $137,500 from local sources. It was also agreed that the new bank should concentrate on savings and trust functions as well as offer general banking services. The Security Savings and Trust Co. opened formally on June 10, 1890 with the stated primary purpose of providing trustee services for individuals, families and estates in the management of residential and commercial real estate properties. It was to be closely identified with but separate from the First National Bank until July 27, 1914, even though the headquarters of both institutions were in the same building and the same board of directors presided over both banks. Henry W. Corbett was to be president until his death in 1903. C.F. Adams was secretary until he succeeded Corbett as president. Abbot Mills was second vice-president until he became vice-president of the First National. Upon Corbett's death he became the First National's president.

The historical record from the 1890's is unclear as to how Adams and Mills arranged the financing for the purchase of the Portland

166

Gas Light Co. The pattern was probably similar to that followed in the organization of the Security Savings and Trust Co. which played an important role in the later Gasco reincorporation. Abbot Mills was the key to the financing of both institutions, particularly as far as eastern money was concerned.[35] He had strong connections within Boston and New York financial circles. His uncle, Abiel Abbot Low, had come from Salem, Massachusetts, settled in Brooklyn and made a fortune in the China trade. He had also shared in the financing of the first Atlantic cable, and in the building of the Chesapeake and Ohio Railroad. The White brothers of New York, William Augustus and Alfred M.,* were married to Low cousins and were wealthy Wall Street investment financiers. Mills' Harvard class of 1881 contained several well-heeled and well-connected friends who proved to be of invaluable assistance. As for Portland, Mills had established close personal relationships with the first families, especially with Cicero H. Lewis, by virtue of his marriage in 1891 to daughter Evelyn Scott Lewis. In that same year Mills and Adams were admitted to the Arlington Club; both were to play an active part in Portland club and society life.

The Security Savings and Trust Co. issued 2500 shares of stock at par value of $100. The Oregon investors bought 55 percent — 1375 shares — as follows: Asahel Bush, C.H. Lewis, H.W. Corbett, H. Failing and C.A. Dolph purchased 225 shares each; Mills and Adams, 125 shares each, giving the young bankers a 10 percent interest. Of the 18 eastern investors, six were Low relatives. Uncle Abiel contracted for the largest amount, 180 shares worth $18,000. Augustus and Alfred White came in for $5000 apiece. The Boston group purchased one-quarter of the total issue and the list included some very prominent names: Charles A. Foster, John Frothingham, B.W. Crowninshield, Charles J. Paine, Francis Bartlett, George Lyman** and S.E. Huntington. New York sugar heir Theodore A. Havermeyer committed $10,000 to the cause.[36] The lesson to be drawn from this experience was that although talent and industry were important personal qualities for a seeker of venture capital, family, club and old school ties proved even more valuable — the ingredients of a true community of interest.

---

*Mills worked for the Whites for a year after graduating from Harvard.
**The Lymans were distant relatives of the Mills. The Lymans became large investors in the American Telephone & Telegraph Co. and the Paines in the General Electric Co.

The full story of the gas company reorganization and financing in 1892 may never be known. In 1906, lawyer-judge-politician Henry McGinn, who together with the *Oregonian* launched a vitriolic attack against Gasco, charged that Mills and Adams had not paid anything for the company in 1892, "not a solitary dollar."[37] "The organization of the Portland Gas Co.," declared the *Oregonian*, "was the most astounding illustration of high finance in the entire history of Portland."[38] The company was "over capitalized." "The bonds were overvalued and the stocks watered," McGinn claimed.[39] Although the company issued $1 million in bonds and an equal amount in stock, not more than half of this total was actually sold in 1892. The major local investors were Corbett, Failing and Lewis. The nationally prominent investment banking house of Lee, Higginson & Co. of Boston took the major portion of the eastern subscription and shortly thereafter sold $50,000 worth of stock to Augustus and Alfred White.[40] The White brothers not only became a major force in the affairs of the company but they now became increasingly involved in numerous other Northwest ventures. For over 20 years Mills was to work closely with his cousins-by-marriage. The Whites were responsible for the sale of the Portland Railway Co. to the Clark-Seligman interests and the Portland Gas Co. to American Power & Light. They were also to be instrumental in the organization of the Oregon Electric Railway and Willamette Valley Traction Companies. In all of these dealings, Abbot Mills would play a key role.

Putting all of the available gas company pieces together, it is entirely plausible for one to conclude that Adams and Mills could have arranged for the purchase of the company without actually committing any of their own cash. The record indicates that sizeable loans were received from the First National Bank, the Security Savings & Trust Co. and the Brooklyn Trust Co. of New York, in which Abbot Mills' father and the Low family had large interests. In payment for their properties, Green and Leonard most likely received newly issued bonds and possibly some cash raised through one or more of the bank loans. By 1901, however, Adams and Mills had increased their equity capital enough to enable them to invest $250,000 of their own funds, thus reducing the company's bonded indebtedness by that amount.

The only complete service interruption in the history of the gas company occurred during Portland's record flood in early June of

High water in 1894 stopped the gas generators at the plant (left), flooded the office at Second and Stark and knocked out the main to the East Side.

1894 when the Willamette River peaked at 33 1/2 feet* over low water mark.[41] The high water covered 250 square blocks, reaching to N.W. 10th and Glisan and S.W. 6th and Washington. Water on Front Street totally inundated the first floors of all establishments. Not only were the gas works flooded, but the submerged line connecting the East and West sides was washed out and the early records of Leonard and Green were destroyed. Business was virtually at a standstill, all the bridges were open and 1500 boats of all sizes and descriptions were operating in the flooded district. Train service into Portland had been shut off on May 27th.**

Merchants frantically erected platforms on which to place their stocks and some provided free boat transportation to their stores. Prominent businessman and social leader, General Charles F. Beebe, almost drowned when he fell off one of his Front Street store platforms into 7 feet of water. Lumber companies thrived as they were swamped with emergency orders to furnish the necessary building materials for the elevated sidewalks and platforms. "One could step from the elevated sidewalk to a floating saloon and after quenching his thirst he could catch a quick shave on the floating barber shop before entering his favorite retail store by way of the second story."[42]

---

*Henry Reed recorded, in one of his many notebooks, that the flood actually reached 36.2 feet, three feet above the U.S. Corps of Engineers' published figure.

**Previous floods occurred in: 1853, 1854, 1861, 1862, 1871, 1876, and 1880. Each one proved worse than the preceding one.

Dekum Building — S.W. 3rd & Washington.

August Erickson, proprietor of the saloon boasting the longest bar in the world — 684 feet long, horseshoe shaped — "rented a houseboat and stocked it full of booze and other necessities for his thirsty customers. . . . Row boats, homemade crafts, catamarans and canoes brought customers to the floating saloon. . . Some of the customers never left the floating saloon until the waters receded *and* they were broke."[43]

Boys were fishing in the streets and carp were plentiful. Sidewalks and elevated roadways floated everywhere and the flooded sewers were "belching out their filth."[44] The Fire Department went nautical when it mounted engines and hoses on 40 and 60 foot barges which were propelled "at a good rate of speed by two powerful streams of water from the pumps shooting into the water at the rear of the barges."[45]

A hundred or more homes on the east side were destroyed and nearly everything on the Columbia Slough was swept away. The Union Pacific R.R. suffered severely with over 100 miles of track

Union Depot.

washed out and 2 1/2 feet of water in the Albina Shops. Many wharves and warehouses along the riverbank were twisted from their foundations. Shantytown in lower Albina was "literally destroyed," as was the Portland and Vancouver Railway line. George Bates showed "commendable energy in keeping water out of the boiler room of the Albina Water Co. pumping station."[46] With Lee Hoffman's experienced assistance, he built a cofferdam of brick and cement around the machinery and as fast as the water rose the walls were increased. The submerged pumps never stopped.

The aftermath presented a frightful mess. Reported the *Albina Weekly Courier,* "The receding flood is leaving behind it an intolerable stench which will require the wholesale use of disinfectants, to prevent general sickness . . . Dead rats, dead fish and sewer filth" were reported everywhere. Portland had suffered "unbelievable damage,"[47] and Mayor Mason and the city government were in a state of shock. Fortunately for them, the offices of the council and mayor had been moved into the unfinished new City Hall six months earlier. They were now on higher ground; the old City Hall at Second and Ash was sealed off by a wall of water.

The clean-up cost was projected to be excessive, way beyond the city's available funds. Portland was still experiencing ill-effects from the disastrous depression of the previous year. The flood did, however, prove to be a godsend to the unemployed, many of whom were hired, but only on a temporary basis. Mayor Mason had been con-

cerned for some months about the plight of the unemployed. The day before Christmas of 1893 he had donated 400 sacks of flour to the poor. And during the winter of '94 he had strongly recommended to the Water Committee that a low service reservoir be constructed at Mount Tabor and that unemployed married men be given job priority for the project. Unfortunately, a public works project of this nature was not viewed with favor by the city's old guard leadership which did not consider such a rescue operation a proper function for the independently financed municipal water system.

Despite the increased deficit and the strain on municipal services, the city managed to survive without any epidemics, major fires or riots. Even the crime rate, excluding pranks, remained unusually low. The emergency had brought out the best traits in Portland's citizenry which responded to the challenge with amazingly good humor.

Forty years later, recalling this period of time when he was president of the struggling Gas Company,* C.F. Adams declared: "In those days . . . men were men." They had "real verve." No one asked for help; everyone did the job that had to be done. "Men in those days were so keen . . . and so filled with grit." They "battled" and they "succeeded," with crucial outside aid, Adams should have added.

---

*Speaking from the "vantage point" of the 1931-1932 depression.

Adams continued, waxing nostalgic: "When I came to Portland we had ten or a dozen of these keen, virile men and let me tell you they are needed right now. I wish we had them back."[48]

4.

It is interesting to contemplate just what ten or dozen keen, virile men Adams had in mind. One could list at least 50 who might have fit this description. Adams was most likely referring to his close friends and colleagues, including the older generation of Messrs. Ladd, Corbett, Failing, and Lewis. The wealth ranking followed that order. The aggressive pursuit of money seemed to have some direct relationship to the degree of one's maleness. In December 1892, young Scotsman Peter Kerr wrote from his room in the Arlington Club: "There are scores of men who have made large fortunes here and some of them are fabulously wealthy. I wish I could find out the way to do it."[49] He did, and in a big way, largely through the grain business and wise real estate investments. Four years after admission to membership, Kerr was elected President.

From the time of its incorporation in 1881, the* Arlington Club was, and still may be, the supreme bastion of gentile male chauvinism in Portland. The 1894 *Blue Book* called it "the most aristocratic club in the city." The Arlington Club dates its beginning from December 1867 when 35 business and professional men gathered informally to organize a "Social Club." Over the years the members have considered themselves "a company of men," who "cherish the opportunity to fraternize for mutual enjoyment and relaxation, and to discuss destiny pertinent to them and the city."[50] The key words of this quotation from an early chapter in the centennial history are "them" and "the city." In the 1890's at least, what was good for "them" was usually considered good for "the city." Rarely did the members distinguish between the public interest and their own private interests if actions and words have been reported accurately. It would appear that many of the major decisions affecting Portland's business and political life were actually reached during "informal" discussions held within the club's portals.

---

*The author is aware of the fact that Arlington Club members do not use the definite article *the* before the name of the club. He has taken the liberty to insert it for euphonic effect.

Arlington Club built its second home, West Park at Alder Streets. Occupied it from 1892 until present building completed in 1910.

An examination of the club roster during the 1890's would lead one to conclude that there must have been sharp differences of opinion on many issues among some of the members. Transcending such discord, that could only have become intensely personal at times, must have been the sense of male fellowship. "Nowhere else on earth can the fellowship generated in this club be surpassed."[51] If this was the accepted feeling of the club membership in 1967, one can imagine the intensity of feeling 70 years earlier. The Arlington Club's "company of men" and J.P. Morgan's "community of interest" were concepts that rested on a similar philosophic basis, embodying a similar set of values. Lewis Mumford placed the traditional business value relationship into critical focus some years ago when he was discussing the private exploitation of the west by the railroads: " . . . the outright donation of priceless lands to great railway corporations [were] acquisitions which were not called theft, and doles which were not denounced as inimical to manhood and independence, . . . because the sums involved were so huge and the recipients so rich."[52]

The large banks, the utilities, the railroads and Oregon's United States Senators were especially well represented within the Arlington Club membership. During the '90's the club could normally count at least four or five of its members serving in a session of the Oregon State Legislature. The direct political influence of the club reached

Current Arlington Club, S.W. Salmon St. Built in 1910.

its peak around 1900 with two successive mayors* who were members. William S. Mason was not a member, and neither for that matter were Tyler Woodward, the Steel brothers or Lee Hoffman.

During the decade of the '90's three other clubs associated with the same traditions entered upon the Portland scene: The Multnomah Amateur Athletic Club (1891), the Waverly Golf Club (1896), and the University Club (1897). There was overlapping membership among all four, especially among the Waverly and Arlington sets. The Concordia Club, established in 1878, was the Jewish counterpart to the Arlington Club. According to the *Blue Book,* it included "the best Jewish citizens of Portland,"[53] and Joseph Simon was among them.

If the Arlington Club provided the social cement for Portland's gentile elite, Trinity Episcopal Church furnished the religious ties that bound them even more closely together. The First Presbyterian, First Unitarian, First Baptist, First Congregational and Grace Methodist Episcopal Churches followed in order of social import-

---

*H.S. Rowe and G.H. Williams.

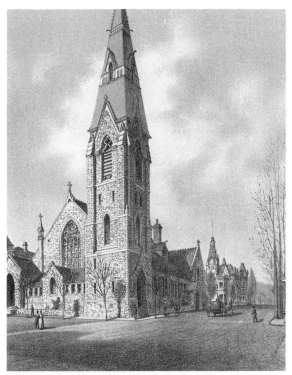

First Presbyterian Church.

First Congregational Church.

177

Dr. Thomas Lamb Eliot.

ance. All were located in "downtown", Southwest Portland, within reasonable access to the homes of the parishoners. Although the Unitarians constituted one of the smallest sects, the First Unitarian's leader, the outspoken Dr. Thomas Lamb Eliot, was clearly the most influential religious figure in Portland during the decade. His voice was often referred to as "the conscience of the community." Among Portland's three Jewish synagogues, all located in the same Southwest section, Temple Beth Israel at Twelfth and Main Streets was first in order of social prominence, drawing its constituents from the upper income strata of the Jewish community. Young Rabbi Stephen Wise launched his national career here by fearlessly attacking many of the social and political ills of contemporary America. Although equally as forthright and courageous as Dr. Eliot, he could not, for obvious reasons, exert the same degree of influence within the business-political power structure.

Portland was well endowed with churches, with approximately one for every 600 residents.* By the end of 1894, the East Side, including North Portland, had taken a commanding lead — 69 church-

---

*The leading denominations in 1894 were:

Methodist — 21	Roman Catholic — 10
Presbyterian — 11	Episcopal — 9
Baptist — 10	Lutheran — 9

Of the 25 missions, the Baptists ran 7, and the Presbyterians, 6. Over half of the missions ministered to the Chinese. The two Methodist-African Churches were on the West side, at S.W. 13th and Main and at N.W. 12th and Glisan.

Representative churches of Portland — 1895.

es to the West side's 37, excluding missions — with a 75 percent increase in church construction in the three year period following consolidation. The Roman Catholic expansion reflected the influx of Southern Irish immigrants who worked for the Union Pacific Railroad in Albina. The Italian community continued to center around its initial settlement in Southwest Portland near the present

Duniway Park, also the initial home of many early Jewish immigrants from Eastern Europe. The expansive East side growth of the Baptist, Evangelical, Methodist and Lutheran Churches reflected an influx of Germans and Finns to the rapidly growing sections of Northeast Portland.

The one prestigious organization that cut across traditional ethnic, religious and social barriers was the Commercial Club of Portland, founded in 1892 and located on the top floor of George Markle's Chamber of Commerce Building. It was essentially a dining club but it undertook various programs and activities similar to those pursued by the present day Chamber of Commerce. Counted among its membership were Mayor Mason, Joseph Simon, General Charles F. Beebe, Richard L. Durham, William M. Ladd, Abbot L. Mills, George W. Bates and Charles F. Swigert.

The cultural life of the city was centered around the library association and the art association, both of which relied heavily on the old families for financial support. The Orchestral Union, organized in the winter of 1881, was popular for a time but received only sporadic support. As a community-type ensemble it presented subscription concerts and experienced several reorganizations during the last two decades of the century.

The first formal organization of the Library Association of Portland was in 1864, with William S. Ladd elected president. Located in a small reading room on the second floor of the Stark Building, it was not a free but a subscription library for its members. "Indeed, the feeling was held by not a few that a free library was not to be desired."[54] Juge Deady and Dr. Eliot worked long and hard to build a strong public library but not until 1902 would such efforts be successful. Deady was president until his death in 1893, and Henry Failing was president until his death in 1898. It took several sizeable bequests of money and books in addition to county support to bring the public institution to realization. When Judge Deady was trying to raise $50,000 for a building fund in 1888 he must have encountered strong resistance, for he wrote on January 28th: "The rich men of Portland will never do much for it until they die, and maybe not then."[55] However, after three more years of labor on Deady's part, the rich men of Portland did apparently come through. When construction was authorized for the new facility to be located at S.W. Seventh and Stark, over $150,000 was on hand. The largest donors were Henry Failing and Simeon Reed who gave $10,000 apiece.

The Portland Art Association was organized in 1888 and formally incorporated in 1892. At about the same time, Henry W. Corbett, who was also active on the Library Board, conceived the idea for an Art Museum as a part of the Art Association. He gave W.B. Ayer $10,000 to take with him on a forthcoming trip to Europe. "Find out how to start a museum," Corbett told Ayer.[56] Ayer was a bit taken back by this request, but, as he later remarked, "nobody ever said 'No' to Henry W. Corbett."[57] Ayer asked the old gentleman where to start, and Corbett replied: "The Greek is the beginning."[58] And so it was. With some additional funds sent by Mrs. William S. Ladd, Ayer ordered a series of reproductions of classical works of sculpture, and the museum opened in 1895 with a modest gallery of plaster casts, located in the new Library Building. When Henry Corbett died in 1903, he bequeathed to the association a quarter block of land at S.W. Fifth and Taylor, and $50,000 for the endowment fund. Mrs. William S. Ladd subsequently gave the building which opened in 1905.*

5.

Looking at the record, one must conclude that the old guard, consisting of Henry W. Corbett, William S. Ladd, Henry Failing, and Simeon G. Reed, together with the young John C. Ainsworth and William M. Ladd, gave willingly and generously to many worthy cultural and social causes. They were the major supporters of the YMCA, the Humane Society, the Ladies Relief Society, the Boys and Girls Aid Society and the Children's Home to which Corbett gave $10,000. Whether or not they should have given more is beyond debate. In proportion to other wealthy famlies in Portland's early history they contributed more than their fair share. Perhaps this was the group of benefactors whom Harvey Scott had in mind when he advised the poor of Portland in 1893 not to worry; the rich would provide. It is doubtful, however, that enough trickled down to furnish more than minimum benefits to those with even the most extreme needs. Could society at large expect any greater beneficence from the rich, or even from the government for that matter? Not in America of 1894. Social welfare was a private responsibility, ex-

---

*Currently the home of the Portland Chamber of Commerce. The building was extensively renovated in the 1960's.

ercised largely by the older and more secure rich. Survival of the fittest was the prevailing code of behavior for most of the affluent who were making money for the first time.

Old Portlanders remained comforted in their optimistic belief that Portland would never mortgage her future. The strength of Portland lay in its close knittedness — its homogeneous character. Portland was obviously a city of civility and refinement, and in its social life had none of the crudity so often found in other active and rapidly growing cities of the West. Portland could not be upset by the transitory problems of the age, such as the poverty, grief or affliction resulting from the depression or the flood; or by the other momentary problems related to civic corruption, vice or indifference. Portland, as a community of many interests, would move on to a greater destiny, combining the "conservatism of the past and the activity of the present with the inspiration of the future."[59]*

---

*These views expressed by Harvey Scott in 1891 remained unchanged until his death in 1910.

Garden — Industrial Exposition Building

Chapter VIII

Corruption, Vice
and the Police Board,
1891-1899

1.

From the earliest days of the Republic, political corruption and
municipal vice seem to have held a certain fascination for most Americans, including the critics. The national record during the 1890's
was replete with the cries of crusaders and the wails of self-proclaimed reformers aimed at the unprincipled political bosses and vice
peddlers who were usually associated with saloon and liquor interests. To the present day, the evidence appears to indicate that
there has been little basic change in citizen behavioral patterns at
least within the realms of business and politics. Finley Peter Dunne's
Mr. Dooley seemed to be expressing an ubiquitous truth when he
said: "Vice . . . [and he might have added bribery] . . . is a creature of
such heejous mien . . . that th' more ye see it th' better ye like it."[1]
During the decade of the 1890's Portland, in company with the rest
of Oregon, had its share of vice and bribery. Although such practices
were usually assailed — to a point — more often they were condoned
and even justified for the simple reason that enough people considered immoral and unethical behavior natural to the human condition,
especially in a society dedicated to personal liberty and the competitive free enterprise system.

The story of Portland's political strife in the decades following
1891 is more than an account of ceaseless struggles among and between bosses and reformers. The conditions and personal relationships involved were far too complicated to be fitted into such a rigid

and simplistic framework. The bosses were not all villains and the reformers not all heroes by any means. But there were some villains as well as heroes, and this chapter will attempt to reconstruct the power struggle between the villains — an epic Republican battle that was fought in stages and that consumed the energies of several of Oregon's leading citizens for over ten years. Even though much of the the warfare took place in Salem, the effects were always keenly felt in Portland.

Portland never came under the exclusive domination of one mighty boss who could wield the degree of power held by some of the eastern bosses like George Washington Plunkitt of New York City and George B. Cox of Cincinnati. Nor did Portland's bosses dispense the services such as were provided by their eastern counterparts. Joseph Simon held sway for over 20 years, primarily as a political tactician, and his authority was continually challenged by others such as the Mitchell Republicans. On one or two occasions he actually lost control, but in each instance he managed to bounce back and regain his power. Simon's major compatriots were banker Henry W. Corbett, Judge Henry McGinn, Senator Joseph N. Dolph, and Jonathan Bourne Jr.* *Oregonian* editor Harvey W. Scott usually supported this wing of the party until around 1902 when his own senatorial ambitions moved him to embrace the Mitchell faction. John H. Mitchell's chief lieutenants were lawyer Charles H. Carey, W.F. (Jack) Matthews, and James Lotan. Jonathan Bourne, Jr., a Bryan silver Republican, was to switch his allegiance abruptly from Mitchell to Simon and Corbett after the McKinley election in 1896 when Mitchell unexpectedly abandoned his pro-silver position to embrace the predominant gold wing of the paty.** Matthews was the only one of this group of party bosses, excluding Mitchell of course, who was a full time professional, although he only held top control for three years from 1902 to 1905. The others were active lawyers, businessmen and

---

*After December, 1896.

**The "Silver—Gold" controversy was to be an active political issue nationally until the 1930's. Those senators from the silver states, or those like Bourne who had personal silver interests, favored the free coinage of silver at a ratio of 16 ounces of silver to 1 ounce of gold. The pro-silver forces wanted a bi-metallic coinage system that would favor the debtor classes and put more money in circulation, thus creating inflationary tendencies. The pro-gold forces wanted a controlled, stable currency which favored the lender who expected repayment in gold. The Democratic party was badly split over

investors. Matthews got his start as a clerk with the Board of Police Commissioners and gradually worked his way up the ranks into a position of power.

The record of changing party loyalties reveals the complex nature of the Republican party strife that engulfed Oregon and Portland until Mitchell's downfall and death in 1905. Personal idiosyncrasies, economic self-interests and individual ambitions all became intertwined, sometimes in harmony but more often in discord. Bribery and fraud were the tools of the trade; the end always justified the means. As one local promoter of good government commented — referring to the bitter Republican infighting of 1896: "If God Almighty should come to this city during the campaign and try to work against the schemes and combinations of practical politicians, he would lose the fight."[2]*

It is appropriate at this point to introduce Lincoln Steffens, the noted reporter for *McClure's Magazine*. Steffens was not to appear on the Portland scene until 1905 but his articles on municipal corruption in the United States depicted accurately the type of business-political relationship that dominated Portland life during the 12 years preceding his arrival. Steffens was often criticized, even by his editor, for biased reporting. "He was convinced that what ailed American politics, from hamlet to national capital, was the American businessman, grasping for profits, corrupt and corrupting; and he spread this conviction as thick as peanut butter over everything he wrote."[3] But it was not too many months after Steffens began his crusade in 1901 that S.S. McClure was obliged to admit that Steffens' bias was rooted in solid fact. "Corruption . . . came not only from those who bribed police to break the laws — the saloonkeepers, say, and the entrepreneurs of organized vice; it came also from those who bribed legislators to rewrite the laws — the supposedly respectable financiers, bankers, merchants, and industrialists."[4]

---

this issue from 1894-1904. Only a few Republicans joined the free silver ranks and remained Republicans; most silver Republicans became silver Democrats.

Jonathan Bourne was not guided so much by principle as by opportunism that related to his own mining interests. During the Alaska Gold Rush fever in 1897-98, he proved equally adept at supporting a single gold standard after he had incorporated three new gold mining companies, capitalized at $5 million.

*C.K. Henry, prominent Portland realtor.

In the introduction to his *The Shame of the Cities;* Steffens wrote:

> "The business man has failed in politics as he has in citizenship. Why? . . . Because politics is business. That's what's the matter with it. . . . Don't try to reform politics with the banker, the lawyer, and the dry-goods merchant, for these are business men and there are two great hindrances to their achievement of reform: one is that they are different from, but no better than, the politicians; the other is that politics is not 'their line.'
>
> The commercial spirit is the spirit of profit, not patriotism; of credit, not honor; of individual gain, not national prosperity; of trade and dickering, not principle. 'My business is sacred,' says the business man in his heart. 'Whatever prospers my business, is good; it must be. Whatever hinders it, is wrong; it must be. A bribe is bad, that is, it is a bad thing to take; but it is not so bad to give one, not if it is necessary to my business.' . . . 'Business is business' is not a political sentiment, but our politician has caught it."[5]

These words have a familiar ring in 1976.*

Bribery was the accepted practice in Oregon politics during the 1890's and early 1900's. "There was never a time that the [U.S.] Senatorship wasn't up for barter or sale,"[7] declared Judge Henry McGinn, a former state senator and long time associate of Henry W. Corbett and Joseph Simon. "The Oregon Assembly is a great big political machine in disguise,"[8] exclaimed Clackamas County leader, ex-senate president and businessman George C. Brownell. Henry Villard and the Northern Pacific Railroad spent $300,000 on Joseph Dolph's unsuccessful reelection bid in 1895; the NP offered $50,000 for two votes.[9] Jonathan Bourne admitted that he spent $10,000 of his own money on George McBride's victory in the same election —

---

*A 45-year-old secretary of the Lockheed corporation was quoted as saying: "Today, everybody in business is immoral. The auto-repair shops overcharge customers, the restaurants give kickbacks, and the television repairmen charge for work they don't do. Lockheed is just a lot bigger, so what they did looks a lot worse." A 25-year-old service engineer agreed: "Managers forget ethics once they leave the classroom. . . . Any big company has to give bribes to stay in business today. Lockheed got caught, so what else is new? Lockheed is just the fall guy."[6]

they were both Republicans. National Republican Committee Chairman Senator Mark Hanna of Ohio, told Bourne that the Commitee had spent $7 million to beat William Jennings Bryan in 1896; $390,000 of that amount in Oregon alone, distributed by Sol Hirsch.[10] There is little doubt that Bryan's loss of Oregon by only 2000 votes was due to a massive vote fraud.

Bourne admitted that he had spent several thousand dollars of his own money to stuff the ballot boxes for John Mitchell's legislative candidates. According to Governor Oswald West: "The prevailing prices [for political bribery] were four and three — four thousand for Republicans and three thousand for Democrats — such prices became common knowledge. As a Democrat I always resented this unjust discrimination and when once I asked a political kale purveyor how they justified the discrimination he said: 'As a rule the Republicans occupied a higher social scale.' "[11] Brownell cited an occasion when $5000 was given to a go-between to purchase a legislator's vote, and another time when a nominee for governor allegedly paid $10,000 to one man and $15,000 to another to quiet an opposing faction.[12] Bourne admitted in later years that the Southern Pacific had put up $225,000 for Mitchell's campaign in 1896. The honorable legislative candidates, 60 in all, had signed and given pledges to Bourne before receiving their money and the SP had the pledges locked in the corporate safe.[13] To Jonathan Bourne an honorable man was one he could buy, who would stay bought, and who would maintain his silence.

In the face of such long-standing activities that constituted nothing more than dirty politics, Oregon leaders like Senator Dolph had the effrontery* to proclaim publicly that, "The Republican Party is wedded to truth, duty and patriotism. . . . The Democratic Party is a negative party."[14] Surveying the previous decade, in 1902, Harvey Scott 'editorialized: "Men come and go, machines rise and fall, but the purposes of the Republican Party . . . must be maintained" with "unwavering support."[15]

Some years later, former police Judge Charles H. Carey** was to express similar feelings with equal temerity. Addressing the Oregon Bar Association in 1908, he decried the growth of "popular democracy. . . . The mouth of the demagogue in these days is full of phrases

---

*Or naivete if one wishes to be charitable. Dolph was a man of great personal integrity but he believed first and foremost in the Republican Party.
**Born in Ohio, 1857, died in Portland, 1941. Portland police judge, 1891-1894. President, Oregon Bar, 1912: president of the Arlington Club, 1917.

about the rights of the common people [which were threatening to demolish traditional party control]. . . . I venture to say that complaints against . . . public officials for partiality or venality are made in every civilized country and in all periods. I believe that the public men of our time are not a whit worse than those of earlier days. . . . Bribery has always been a common charge,"[16] and, he should have added, a common practice in Oregon. Carey was well acquainted with the tactics of political bribery. He had been totally immersed in the Mitchell machine for over 10 years as he ambitiously climbed the ladder to public recognition and social acceptance. In 1896, furthermore, he was chairman of the Mitchell Republican party convention. He was also the major defender of the Northern Pacific Railroad in the timber fraud trials in 1905. His law firm* represented the Hill interests for many.years.

Charles H. Carey.

Carey was to express deep concern in 1908: "It has come to pass in these days that the restraints and limitations of the constitution are no longer respected."[17] And one might ask why they deserved to be. They had been badly abused. Could Carey afford to sermonize about respect for law and order when his own early political life had revealed little respect for established legal and political procedures. Nowhere in Carey's much praised *History of Oregon* was any attention given to this ten year period of political strife in which he was so intimately involved. His coverage was confined to general economic growth and the contributions of the railroads.

---

*Carey and Kerr, predecessor firm to the current Portland giant, Davies, Biggs, Strayer, Stoel and Boley.

Carey was typical of a number of young Portland lawyers at the turn of the century who subsequently rose to civic prominence, who became actively involved in the Oregon Historical Society,* and who were instrumental in fabricating an "Oregon Story" that was heavily laden with mythology, hero worship and pioneer idolization. Carey, Scott, and others, constituted a group of politician-writers who advised: Don't hurt the party. Don't divide up America into classes by denouncing the rich and exciting the "the envy and hatred of the poor." Spare the city's reputation.

To such pleas, which he frequently heard in the course of his travels, Lincoln Steffens' response was brutal:

> "The Fourth of July [type] oration is the 'front' of graft. There is no patriotism in it, but treason. It is part of the game. The grafters call for cheers for the flag, 'prosperity', and 'the party', just as the highway man commands 'hands up,' and while we are waving and shouting, they float the flag from the nation to the party, turn both into graft factories, and prosperity into a speculative boom to make 'weak hands,' as the Wall Street phrase has it, hold the watered stock while the strong hands keep the property. . . . By just such palavering . . . the bosses, political, financial, and industrial, are befuddling and befooling our sovereign American citizenship; and — likewise — they are corrupting it."[18]

In the course of his Bar Association address, Judge Carey was particularly critical of an impending Initiative measure that would enact a "Corrupt Practices" law. The wording of the law was too long and complicated for the average voter to read and understand. It was "Highly penal," — the punishments were too severe. The voters pamphlet scheme was limiting and expensive to a candidate. The regulations governing the keeping and filing of accounts were too elaborate. In conclusion, Carey said: "Many of the law's features trench upon personal rights that have long been cherished; and in seeking to regulate elections the elaborate and paternal supervision of persons and political organizations will seem to many citizens extreme and unnecessary, if not unconstitutional."[19]

---

*With the exception of Scott, all of the presidents of the Oregon Historical Society from its founding through 1936 were lawyers: Scott (1898-1901), C.B. Bellinger (1901-1905), William D. Fenton (1905-1907), Fred V. Holman (1907-1926), Carey (1927-1936).

This type of thinking was all too common among Portland's leading attorneys and political figures at the turn of the century; men who had reached the top after years of fighting their way up through the turmoil of party strife and corruption.* Carey and Scott would never admit that they had made mistakes or that the old system was rotten. At least credit must be given to the battle scarred party warhorses like Judge McGinn, George Brownell and Jonathan Bourne, Jr. who were willing to confess their past sins and admit that the old system had subverted American political ideals. As Brownell declared in 1910,** there had been "too much corporate greed in politics."[21] The Oregon Bar Association would have done better to heed the advice of reform Governor Charles Evans Hughes of New York,*** the future Chief Justice of the U.S. Supreme Court, when he said that the weakest point in American popular government was the inability to find men *worthy* to perform the duties entrusted to them.[22] Fortunately for Oregon, its voters did manage to find several such "worthy" men and elect them to office before 1915.

2.

The Board of Police Commissioners, established by the legislature in 1885 through the efforts of Joseph Simon and Jonathan Bourne, Jr.,**** was at the center of much of the local political corruption and bribery. During the first three years of its existence, police affairs were operating so smoothly in the minds of Simon and Bourne, who were also two of the original commissioners, that they managed to slip through the legislature in February 1889 a charter amendment, which if interpreted literally, provided for life terms for the existing commissioners. Even though the 1891 charter of consolidation subsequently reversed the procedure and restored control to the voters

---

*The prevailing form of corruption was bribery — influence peddling — not looting the public treasury, at least directly. Many businesses received favorable treatment in municipal contracts. Tax assessments were kept low through political influence. There is no record of Portland mayors or other public officials receiving pay-offs as such. Real estate speculation and business investments were the primary sources of wealth for this class.

**Brownell did not tell the whole truth, according to C.B. Moores, one of Oregon's most honorable citizens. In a letter to the press on July 8, 1910, Moores cited Brownell as "the reputed representative on the floor of the State Senate of the Southern Pacific Railroad." He strongly implied that Brownell had long been "open for bribery."[20]

***(1906-1910.)

****Refer to earlier mention of the Board in chapter IV, section 3.

by providing for elective commissioners to serve three year terms, such an independent agency was not, in and of itself, responsive to the needs of the city.

In a message to the city council on November 11, 1891, Mayor William S. Mason declared: "We lack the power to enforce the laws. . . . [We have] . . . no control . . . over the police force of our city. . . . Our police perambulate the streets day and night and we hear of no arrests for the violations," most specifically for gambling and for saloons open illegally on Sundays. The ordinances on gambling, said Mason, "are a dead letter on our statute books." Are the police the "protectors, the sharers in the spoils?" he asked.[23] Railroad builder Joseph Gaston felt they were. In a letter to President Benjamin Harrison on December 8, 1891, Gaston excoriated Simon who was at the time a candidate for judgeship on the U.S. Circuit Court of Appeals.* Gaston accused Simon of ruining the police force by making it a political tool. Enforcement was lax; the officers were receiving bribes and Simon as chairman of the police board was re-

_____

*Judge Deady supported Simon for the position.

sponsible. "Mr. Simon is not a man of honor and integrity in public affairs," declared Gaston.[24]

Simon remained on the board until 1892 when he was succeeded by an ambitious young lawyer named D. Solis Cohen who was to play an increasingly active role in business-political affairs for 20 years. Bourne was succeeded in 1888 by George Frank* who was to be elected mayor in 1894. Frank's public life was to reveal him as a man of few principles and extreme rascality whom even George H. Williams, ex-senator and future mayor, had the temerity to call "an infernal scoundrel."[25] Both commissioners were Simon disciples although Frank was to split away and join the Mitchell ranks along with Bourne before the 1896 election.

By the time that Mayor Mason assumed office in July 1891, police affairs had become highly politicized and the Board of Police Commissioners had become a springboard to future political power. During Frank's last year on the board (1891) he secured the appointment of future boss Jack Matthews as clerk of the department. Matthews proved to be a dedicated professional.** He was shrewd and crafty, smooth and debonair.[26] As more than one news account described him, "he took to machine politics like a duck to water."[27] He avoided all personal publicity and never allowed his picture to be taken. His personal habits were Spartan; he never drank or smoked. His whole life was devoted to the achievement of political power*** and he proved to be Simon's most effective opponent. Matthews and Judge Carey were the linchpins of the Mitchell machine until Matthews was removed from the U.S. Marshal's office in 1905 by order of President Theodore Roosevelt.

---

*Frank was owner of the Frank Implement Co.; no relation to Sigmund Frank of the Meier & Frank store.

**Matthews' early career was fairly typical of that followed by political machine bosses in other parts of the United States. As a protege of James Lotan, he first secured appointment from Mayor DeLashmutt as deputy city clerk, then he moved up to deputy city auditor and finally city auditor before receiving the police job. While Matthews was deputy city auditor in 1889, he also was overseer of street cleaning and he apparently did a very poor job. Portland was "the most filthy city in the Northern states" according to the *Oregonian* of June 19, 1889. Matthews only stayed with the police board one year, but he was a symbol of the system and an omen of things to come. He next went to work for George Frank's Implement Co., before being appointed by Senator Mitchell as assistant postmaster for Portland in 1901 and U.S. Marshal in 1903.

***He also was to accumulate a sizeable estate, worth $125,000 upon his death on July 14, 1915.

With characters like Joe Simon, George Frank and Jack Matthews running the police department or at least setting policy, the job of police chief became increasingly untenable. C.H. Hunt, who was probably as well qualified as any who had previously held that position, complained privately on numerous occasions that he was "constantly hindered in enforcing the laws by political influence." He could not depend on the officers and men of the police force to obey his orders.[28]

Beginning in the fall of 1893, Chief Hunt's administration was beset by a variety of additional problems not the least of which was the retrenchment of police department resources brought about by the depression.* Then, in October, Bunco Kelly and Larry Sullivan, one of Jonathan Bourne's North End agents, were accused of palming off 14 corpses — as drunken sailors — on the skipper of the "Flying Prince." Shortly after the publication of this event — Portland's most famous crimping episode — public criticism of the police department became further inflamed when the Ministerial Association of Portland launched the first of several vice probes in a major attempt to control prostitution. Chief Hunt and Mayor Mason were discouraged. They both gave full support to the vice committee under the chairmanship of the Rev. George R. Wallace of the First Congregational Church, but their hands were tied. They had no control over the police board which was beholden to the proprietors of the vice properties.

Prominent citizens whose property housed vice operations included Cyrus A. Dolph, brother of Senator Joseph Dolph and Joe Simon's law partner. Dolph and John A. Caples, the partner of County Judge J.C. Moreland, owned a building at the Northeast corner of Second and Everett Streets, labelled a "rendezvous of thieves and stolen goods." The vice committee found "young girls of 16 years of age . . . consorting with the Negroes, Italians and the lowest elements of the city."[29] Other eminent property owners included: Henry Weinhard, brewer; W.K. Smith, vice president of the Ainsworth Bank and one of Portland's wealthiest investors; recent mayor and banker Van B. DeLashmutt; L. Therkelsen, president of the North Pacific Lumber Co., and a member of the prestigious water committee; R.R. Thomp-

---

*The budget was cut from $118,000 to $98,000. Patrolmen's annual salaries began to slide backward, reaching $780 in 1895. In the same two year period, the patrol force was cut by 30 officers, to only 8 more than had existed in 1889 when the population was only one-half that of the 1895 total and the city's geographic area one-fifth as large.

Erickson's Saloon, West Burnside St., between 1st and 2nd. The site of the world's longest bar.

son, pioneer transportation magnate; and Joseph Simon. Henry W. Corbett was named as the property owner of the largest wholesale liquor store, on the Southeast corner of Second and Oak Streets.

Of the 245 saloon properties identified, DeLashmutt and R.R. Thompson each owned seven. Owners of at least three properties included Weinhard, Corbett, Ainsworth, MacLeay and J.W. Cook. Of the many gambling locations cited, three were singled out as "the most notorious:" "The Brunswick," on S.W. Third, owned by former mayor David P. Thompson; "The Arion," on SW. Yamhill, half-owned by Henry Corbett; and a dive on N.W. Burnside and Second owned by Frank Dekum's Portland Savings Bank. To the consternation of the local ministers, many of the 50 or more prominent citizens named were active parishioners in their own churches. When queried as to why the *Oregonian* refused to publicize the efforts of the local citizenry to clean up the town and to join in support of such endeavors, editor Harvey W. Scott admitted that "the persons most concerned in the maintenance of these abuses are the principal men of the city — the men of wealth on whose patronage the paper relied. It could not afford to alienate them. It would ruin his paper."[30]

Editor Harvey W. Scott.

Harvey Scott, for all of his authoritative and often reactionary pronouncements, was a voice to be reckoned with, a voice that was highly respected even by his opponents. As several accounts have mentioned, "he knew his Milton and his Burke ... "[31] But he apparently did not take the moral lessons of the great writers to heart. As Edmund Burke once wrote: "The only thing necessary for the triumph of evil is for good men to do nothing."[32] There was the strong possibility, of course, that Scott was not a good man. The esteemed *Oregonian* editor was not about to challenge the establishment which looked upon vice probes as both unpleasant and a nuisance. These matters would pass with time. As a "well balanced civic and social organism," Portland, said Scott, would not be "upset by transitory problems or changes."[33]

One change that was to produce disastrous consequences for Portland resulted from an 1893 legislative enactment. Effective the first Monday in July, 1894, the mayor was authorized to appoint the three police commissioners who would hold office at the mayor's pleasure. On his first day in office Republican Mayor George Frank, Mason's successor, used this new power with a vengeance despite having vowed before his election to divorce the police department from politics. Three new police commissioners* were installed early in July. Three months later the beleaguered Chief Hunt was fired, to be replaced

---

*Commissioners D.M. McLaughlan, former mayor of Albina and employee of the OR&N; A.L. Maxwell, employee of the OR&N and Arlington Club Member; and H. Haussman, wholesale tobacconist.

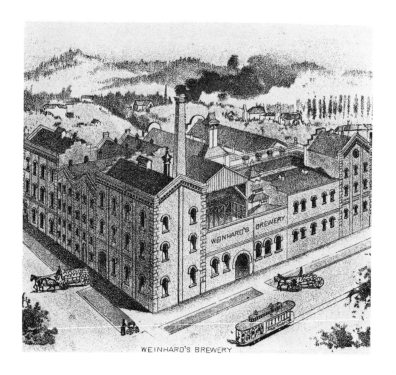

WEINHARD'S BREWERY

by Frank's political crony John Minto who belonged to the anti-
Simon Mitchell faction. Allied to Frank and Minto were District Attorney W.T. Hume and his assistant, Dan J. Malarkey whose political star was to rise in future years.

In spite of the reluctance of the *Oregonian* to grant much space to
the vice probe, word did manage to leak out to the community at large
and public pressure forced Chief Minto to conduct a few raids, initially on the least important places. Liverpool Liz and her Senate
saloon were not touched as she was in the North End where such activities belonged and the police were handsomely paid off. It was
the downtown or Southwest district that finally began to receive
official attention because such "lower pleasures" were not deemed

dignified for a civic center. Madame Fanshaw's "Mansion of Sin," across from the Portland Hotel, was the "ne plus ultra of Portland's parlor houses," reported Stewart Holbrook. There was "nothing more elegant or refined in Portland."[34] Apparently on one occasion, a leading Portland citizen accidentally encountered his son while he was leaving and his son was entering. This sort of mix-up did not happen often, according to Holbrook. Twelve of Madame Fanshaw's girls were arrested but were exonerated due to the lack of absolute proof.[35]

Through the winter and early spring of 1895 scores of prostitutes were picked up but most of them were immediately released. The judges found that lewdness could not seem to be established "beyond a reasonable doubt." On April 10, 1895, the *Oregonian* proclaimed: "The farce is at an end." A trial jury had acquitted the last of the accused. All the top madames had escaped punishment, only the "negresses and other low types were convicted." District Attorney Hume declared that there would be no more indictments although he had profited personally from the vice investigations, because by ordinance he received $17.50 for each indictment regardless of whether conviction was obtained.[35] Hume took in over $20,000 a year in fees.

Mayor Frank's two year term proved to be a stormy one. He not only fired three of his own appointees to the fire board but four of his own police commissioners.* In three years he replaced almost the entire police force. He told prominent businessman and Fire Commissioner Sylvester Farrell: "I am going to control the politics of this town. . . . I have the Police, Street Cleaning, and now the Fire Department in my control. . . . Why ain't you my friend, Mr. Farrell?"[37]

Frank's blustery and crude arrogance stirred up Portland's old guard. Even Joseph Simon now realized that his original support of Frank had proved to be a disastrous mistake. Various reform groups were formed, including the Committee of 100 Taxpayers, headed by Henry W. Corbett. Their main taget, apparently, was organized gambling which was giving the city a poor reputation. Mayor Frank's profligate administration was labeled "the tax eaters." By some peculiar coincidence, the names of many of the Committee of

---

*Frank added: P.L. Willis, associate of C.F. Swigert; A.B. Croasman, active Republican and Arlington Club member; and George W. Bates whom he removed, after a year, for F.C. Barnes. One of Frank's replacements on the fire board was prominent attorney, George H. Durham.

100 were also included on the list of vice and saloon property owners compiled by the ministerial association. Possibly they decided to take the initiative in an attempt to cleanse their own reputations. Six months later, concurrent with the demise of the vice investigations, the Central Municipal Reform League was organized. A disparate group to say the least, it included: W.M. Cake, a Mitchell Republican; James Steel, railroad man and banker and a Simon-Corbett Republican; T.E. Osborne, the first president of the Chamber of Commerce; and E.W. Spencer, the former police chief who was dismissed by Mayor Mason. They all had one interest in common: an intense dislike of Mayor Frank. But little would result from these efforts, for within a year the state's leading Republicans would be slicing each other up and down over "who would control the spoils."[38] The campaign of 1896 was fast approaching.

3.

By March of 1896, the battle lines had hardened. The Republican party was split down the middle between the Simon — or regular Republicans — and the Mitchell Republicans. Each group composed its own slate of candidates for legislative and appointive office. Mayor Frank, choosing not to seek re-election, was supposedly promised the U.S. collector of customs job by Senator Mitchell. To this end he had personally raised a fund of $12,500 by requiring all city officials appointed by him to contribute one-tenth of their salaries over a period of months. Matthews would take the money to Salem after the legislature convened in January 1897. Police Chief Minto was to receive appointment as the U.S. Marshal if Senator Mitchell won re-election.[39]

Joe Simon succeeded in keeping control of the regular party machinery at the local level by virtue of his narrow election as Chairman of the Republican County Central Committee. His slate of state senatorial candidates included George W. Bates, D.M. McLaughlan and Ben Selling, a prominent Portland merchant who was to become one of Oregon's staunchest Republicans over the next 20 years.[40] The Mitchell forces were led by District Attorney Wilson T. Hume who was a candidate for the state Senate. Hume publicly leveled charges of "a fraud" and "a steal" at Simon, Henry Corbett and the Ladd family over the Morrison Bridge "deal" of the previous year.[41] He also attacked the Trinidad Asphalt Paving Co., a Ladd-Simon firm, for monopolizing the lucrative municipal paving business in Portland. The charges were partially true. By requiring high performance bonds, the council had eliminated most other bidders who did not possess the financial resources to meet the bond requirements.

The slate of mayoralty candidates confused the political line-up even more. D. Solis Cohen, the former police commissioner, was Simon's Regular Republican candidate. Prominent merchant, General Charles F. Beebe, was listed as the Independent Republican candidate, drawing some Mitchell support. Former Governor Sylvester Pennoyer was running as the Democratic-Populist candidate, with backing from other Mitchell Republicans and from Jonathan Bourne Jr. who at the time was Secretary of the Republican State Central Committee, an office that he was forced to relinquish under pressure from Simon during the height of the presidential campaign four months later. The odds obviously favored the former governor who handily won the mayor's race in the June election. As a consequence, Simon's local power base was severely damaged, but before much could be done to repair it, Simon had to concentrate his efforts on the forthcoming legislative session that would consider Senator Mitchell's bid for re-election.

4.

No one in Oregon's history has ever aroused more popular enthusiasm or more intense animosity than John Mitchell Hipple, alias John H. Mitchell. Born in Washington County, Pennsylvania, in 1835, Hipple attended the local university, taught school and studied law. In 1857 he was forced to marry a 15 year old girl whom he had seduced and made pregnant. After being admitted to the bar, he deserted his wife and two of his children and headed West to California, accompanied by his first born daughter and a young school teacher with whom he had been having an affair. In July 1860, he abandoned the schoolmarm and arrived in Portland with his daughter, having just changed his last name to Mitchell.[42]

He had the "personal graces that count for everything in a small community — good looks, amiability, personal force, and a certain dash and aggressiveness that passed for intellectual brilliancy."[43] Within weeks after his appearance on the local scene, Mitchell managed to get himself appointed Portland City Attorney; the next year he won a seat on the city council and the year following a term in the state senate. In 1862, he began an 11 year partnership with Joseph N. Dolph, specializing in land litigation and railroad right-

John H. Mitchell.

of-way cases. Dolph & Mitchell soon became the leading railroad law firm in the state. Also in 1862 he entered into a bigamous marriage with a young local lady whom he increasingly came to dislike but who in the process bore him six children. By 1871 he was to fall in love with his wife's sister and carry on an open affair for many years.*

The Dolph-Mitchell relationship revealed signs of strain in 1870 when Mitchell was retained by Ben Holladay as his personal lawyer and adviser. A remark was attributed to Mitchell, to the effect that: " 'Ben Holladay's politics are my politics and what Ben Holladay wants I want.' "[44] Whether or not he actually made the statement, it was an accurate reflection of his political morals. Increasingly Mitchell became personally ambitious and financially greedy, two traits that were to mark his life until his death in 1905.

The law partnership began to dissolve at about the time that it became obvious to Dolph that Mitchell would contest U.S. Senator Henry W. Corbett for the Republican nomination, as Ben Holladay's handpicked candidate. Holladay was prepared to spend upwards of $20,000 to assure Mitchell's election. Judge Deady wrote in his diary, on April 19, 1872: "I told Mitchell that I liked him personally but disliked his political action because he had too much 'business' in his politics."[45] Over one-fourth of the votes in the June legislative

---

*One of Mitchell's daughters, Fannie, later married the Duc de Rochefoucald and lived the rest of her life in Paris.

elections were estimated to be illegal by the *Oregonian* which happened to be controlled by Corbett at the time. Corbett, however, could read the handwriting on the wall. In September he withdrew from the race and Mitchell was elected by 41 votes. Corbett never forgave him; Mitchell had stolen the election. Corbett developed a disdain for Mitchell that bordered on hatred. He was to be supported in subsequent years by the young and ambitious Joseph Simon who had studied law in Mitchell and Dolph's office and who became Dolph's partner in 1873 after Mitchell went to Washington. No issue, whatever its merits, could force either Corbett or Simon to support Mitchell in any future activity — political, business or otherwise.

One final event related to this episode is worth noting. The U.S. Attorney, with Judge Deady's support, proceeded to seek indictments for vote fraud. Senator Mitchell, in Washington, went to see Attorney General George H. Williams, his fellow Portlander, with "the demand" that the U.S. Attorney either be "forced to desist, or be removed."[46] Williams was on the spot. He was awaiting Senate confirmation as Chief Justice of the United States, an appointment that was not popular, and he needed Mitchell's support. To make a long story short, Williams succumbed to the pressure, the U.S. Attorney was replaced and the investigations were terminated.

Mitchell was defeated in 1878 by Democratic ex-Congressman James H. Slater from Eastern Oregon. Holladay was no longer able to bankroll his campaign expenses. He spent much of the next five years building a financial base for a comeback. It was reported in *The Dalles Times-Mountaineer* on January 5, 1884, that Mitchell had already accepted money from Jay Gould.[47] For 20 years stories of similar pay-offs would occasionally reach print but they never seemed to diminish his popularity. As was related earlier, Mitchell managed to squeak back into office by one vote in the 1885 special session of the legislature.

It cost money to be a senator and Mitchell let few opportunities pass him by. In a letter to Simeon Reed on March 24, 1891, Mitchell reminded Reed that he still maintained his law practice in Portland and that Judge Tanner, his partner, was "one of the best lawyers in Oregon."

> "My pay as Senator meets considerably less than one-half of my expenses here [in D.C.]. Hence it is necessary that I should keep up my law business, and my object in writing to you is to know if you and your friends will not take some little interest in throwing your legal business,

or at least a portion of it, in the direction of our firm. Sabe!"[48]

In making this ungrammatical request, Mitchell must have known that Reed and his friends retained Simon and C.A. Dolph for most of their business. Perhaps Mitchell had an ulterior motive but one can only conjecture. Despite his obvious talent for mixing business with politics, and his tarnished record of indiscretions and misdeeds, Mitchell's personal charm, generosity, striking appearance and direct, forceful way of talking made him the favorite son for a majority of Oregonians until the end of his life, even though the legislature would end up not re-electing him in 1897.

The man most responsible for John Mitchell's failure to secure re-election was his fellow Arlington Club mate Jonathan Bourne Jr., whose earlier career has already been described.* No one worked harder for Mitchell in June of 1896 and no one expended more energy against Mitchell in January of 1897. What had happened in that period of seven months to cause such a complete reversal of political loyalty? In the first place, political consistency and loyalty never meant as much to Bourne as personal economic interest and personal ambition. Bourne prized political and economic power as means to gain his ends and he was prepared to use people as instruments in the struggle. Ruthlessness was his trademark.

"All his life, Bourne . . . feasted on excitement and adventure,"[49] wrote Burton J. Hendrick in *McClure's Magazine*. By temperament he was a gambler, subject to sudden bursts of enthusiasm. When he became interested in silver in 1885, he was absolutely impenetrable to other interests. As he wrote to President A.L. Mohler of the Union Pacific Railroad in 1904: "from 1885-93, I invested something over a million dollars in the purchase of mining claims, and the development and the equipment of same."[50] He admitted that he lost much of it subsequently. As Oswald West reported many years later: "Jonathan spent three good sized inherited fortunes. And he had a wonderful time doing it."**

As Mitchell's campaign manager in 1896, Bourne was responsible for the election of the 60 legislative candidates whose pledges were locked in the Southern Pacific corporate safe. He spent over $10,000 of his own money to stuff the ballot boxes. The usual procedure in-

---

*See chapter 4, section 3.
**West added parenthetically that Bourne was also "an avid lover."[51] In this respect, Bourne and Mitchell had much in common.

This cartoon, reproduced from The Oregonian of October 11, 1896, shows **JONATHAN BOURNE, JR.**, while holding a republican office (Representative from Multnomah County) urging workingmen to vote for William Jennings Bryan, Democratic Candidate for President of the United States. Was this not an act of treachery to the Republican Party? Should treachery be rewarded by a seat in the United States Senate?

When asked once why his pockets were full of railroad passes, Bourne replied: "I make the railroads give them to me."

BRYAN-SEWALL MAN.—There ain't no electoral ticket for me to vote, eh? Got to swallow Watson and the Populist Party, have I? Well, I think I'll fool that fusion lay-out. I'm no Populist, I'll vote for McKinley.

volved the hiring of hobos to "work" in the primaries. They would congregate in gangs about the polling places and were never bothered by the police. The day after the June election, a steady stream of such characters was reported standing in long lines, passing by the headquarters office in the Chamber of Commerce Building, clamoring for their pay which they promptly received. In the same election, Bourne himself won a seat in the House and he looked forward to being chosen speaker with Mitchell's backing.

Bourne was also active in behalf of Bryan's November campaign against McKinley and in this endeavor he was joined by a number of silver Republicans. As reported by Cornelia Marvin Pierce, from her diary:

> "Jonathan told me that he sent to California for a notorious criminal who supplied repeaters for elections.... Jonathan agreed to pay transportation and the living costs of repeaters, all of whom should leave the state the day after election. The terms were settled except for the leader. The agreement was fully carried out and the night after the election the leader met Jonathan in the Arlington Club and together they burned in the fireplace the picture of the leader, which had been taken from the police walls by Jonathan.... It seemed that when he asked the leader what his price would be, he said he wanted just one thing — and that was that his picture should be removed from the Rogue's Gallery in Portland. . . . The reason they didn't win was that Corbett employed more men and sent them up and down the river to vote and they voted at outside towns as well as in Portland."[52]

The "notorious" Californian was probably the "Mysterious" Billy Smith referred to by Oswald West in his account of the 1896 election. Smith worked with Larry Sullivan, a pugilist and known political fixer who was Bunco Kelly's partner in the "Flying Prince" crimping episode. Sullivan, known as the "King of the Boarding House Operators,"* was Bourne's Chief North End Lieutenant. Because of Bourne's close relationship with Mayor Pennoyer, and because he knew his way around the police department from his days on the police commission, he assumed a superordinate role in police affairs, to the point that he was accused by the *Oregonian* of exercising sup-

---

*As related to vice activities.

reme dictation over the department. "His word, backed by that of Mayor Pennoyer, is the law."[53] Thus Bourne had little trouble removing the picture from the department's files. Using the Arlington Club for such an undignified activity did not seem to bother Bourne although it may have ruffled a few of his club mates. After all Bourne was secure in his membership, having been one of the club's organizers in 1882 and having served as president in 1888.

Shortly after the election of November 1896, Bourne met Mitchell on the street in Portland and was horrified to learn that the Senator was abandoning his silver friends and planning to embrace the "gold crowd." Bourne warned him on the spot: "You are *not* going to be elected." As Bourne later told Mrs. Pierce:

> "I then hired the best chef in the State of Oregon; sent him to Salem to fix up apartments in the Eldridge Block; things to eat and drink and entertainment. I said to the chef, 'I pay all expenses. I want to take care of all my friends in the lower House who signed pledges with me, the friends of silver."[54]

Bourne immediately hooked up with his former political opponents Simon and Corbett and plans were developed to stall the forthcoming session of the legislature — to prevent it from organizing if need be — in order to deny Mitchell his re-election. As Henry Reed was to note some years later: "Nothing that Holladay ever did approached the extraordinary hold-up of 1897, when the House of Representatives failed to organize and there was no legislation."[55] Simon and Bourne were aided in their efforts by William U'Ren, the future father of the Oregon System's direct legislation and the leader of the state's Populist movement. U'Ren also felt betrayed by Mitchell who apparently refused to honor a pledge he had made to give full support to U'Ren's efforts to enact the Initiative and Referendum amendments to the Oregon Constitution.

George C. Brownell later recounted that the Eldridge Block, called "Bourne's Harem," "was a den of prostitution and evil." Many of the Representatives "were kept drunk and intoxicated for days." The whole episode amounted to "forty days of rotten putridity that will never be forgotten."[56] Although Bourne admitted paying for much of the entertainment,* he denied that his money had actually bribed

---

*$80,000 worth.

THE "PUSH" AND ITS OBSTACLES.

The painful position of an United States senator with more ambition than self respect.

208

anyone. It was enticement, not bribery. He would not, however, reveal the other sources of funding for operation "hold-up."

A supposed copy of a notarized affidavit from the widow of Seth Lewelling, a close friend of William U'Ren's, read as follows:

> "In one or more . . . conversations [with U'Ren] relative
> to matters pertaining to said legislative session [1897]
> . . . U'Ren stated to me that H.W. Corbett, of Portland,
> Oregon, was furnishing the money to pay the expenses
> of the members of said Legislature who were refusing to
> assist in the organization of said Legislature."[57]

U'Ren apparently was the main bag man. He would pick up the money from the First National Bank, take it with him to Lewelling's home and then proceed to Salem to deliver it to Bourne. A year later Corbett denied that he had committed any improprieties. In a letter to the *Oregonian,* Corbett declared: "I had not communicated with or spoken with Mr. Bourne or made any combination with him to hold up the Legislature, and I had no desire to do so. . . . I may have done many things that I should not have done and left many things undone that I should have done, but I have never been accused of being a grafter or levying blackmail." Corbett then went on to say that he did what he could to defeat Mitchell, "legitimately!" He concluded by citing an account of Mitchell going to the late President Billings of the Northern Pacific and demanding $20,000 for his re-election campaign. Billings had repeated this to him personally.[58]

Strictly speaking, Corbett may have been truthful. But there is no question that he and Simon were in close contact, and the "Bourne Papers" are full of notes about Bourne's nightly conferences with Simon in their Salem hotel. It is doubtful that Mrs. Lewelling would have lied, and in any case, former Governor Oswald West later confirmed Mrs. Lewelling's account.[59]

Many other stories were to make the rounds over the years. West recalls handling deposits of some of the "subsistence" money in his capacity as a young teller at the Ladd & Bush Bank in Salem. Joseph Simon's nephew was to inform his friends about the cash that he took from Portland to his uncle in Salem. In addition to his own money, Bourne apparently raised at least $10,000 through blackmail contributions from Chinese gamblers and North End saloonkeepers, easily secured by virture of his control over police activities in the North End.

When the 40 day session ended on March 3rd, absolutely nothing had been accomplished. Governor William P. Lord, a close associate of Corbett and Simon, appointed Henry W. Corbett to the U.S. Senate, to succeed John Mitchell. Corbett's long standing ambition to return to Washington had finally been realized. Unfortunately for Mr. Corbett, the Senate refused to seat him. Stories of the hold-up session were circulating through the Capitol. Mitchell had some well placed friends in Washington, and it must be assumed that the Southern Pacific interests, vigorously promoted by Collis P. Huntington, were not about to let their $250,000 investment disappear without a fight. When the legislature re-assembled in special session in October 1898, Joseph Simon was elected. On October 6th, Corbett had formally withdrawn his name as a candidate in the interests of party harmony. Oregon needs a senator, said Corbett, who is "in accord with the sound financial principles of the party."[60]

5.

A week after the hold-up session had adjourned, Bourne wrote to friend Benjamin Baker that he felt that "he had accomplished a big victory, . . . one of the greatest political battles ever made in American History."[61] For the next year or so Bourne was to occupy his time largely with his new gold mining interests and with family affairs back in New Bedford, Massachusetts. Joe Simon kept in close touch with his former teammate. Simon was disturbed about affairs in Portland. He felt that Mayor Pennoyer was making a mess of things and he wanted to see some good old traditional leadership restored to Portland, through his own efforts of course. In August of 1897, Simon wrote Bourne in New Bedford, "I am anxious to get control of our city government."[62] Two weeks later, he referred to "the plan that we mapped out last winter."[63]

Mayor Sylvester Pennoyer, labeled a "political freak" by former Attorney General George H. Williams, had charged into office in July of 1896 like a myopic bull.* He replaced the entire police force

---

*Pennoyer was born in Groton, New York in 1831 and died in Portland in May 1902. He was educated at Harvard. His independent spirit was revealed in numerous incidents: he snubbed President Harrison during his only Oregon visit; he challenged President Cleveland over governmental policy; and in November 1894 he proclaimed Oregon's Thanksgiving Day holiday one week later than the rest of the nation.

Sylvester Pennoyer.

in one year, appointed four chiefs in two years and involved himself deeply and unpredictably in the daily life and details of police and fire operations. Pennoyer was a successful lumberman and an adroit politician, but he was very independent and easily hurt by personal opposition.* He is best remembered today as the donor of Governor's Park, a narrow six acre overgrown tract that runs up the hill from S.W. Broadway Drive. Perhaps the best that could be said about Pennoyer's two year term of office was Harvey Scott's strong disapproval.

In December of 1897, Simon and Bourne were making plans for the June 1898 elections. In a letter to Bourne in Massachusetts, Simon referred to the previous support for Mitchell "from the railroad companies." It was necessary to enlist Henry Corbett's services;[64] his money was needed.** Two weeks later, Simon again wrote Bourne: "It is absolutely impossible to carry this county in opposition to the *Oregonian,* and without Multnomah County we could not possibly succeed in our plans.*** Simon predicted that the Mitchell Republic-

---

*After only four months of service, Pennoyer removed prominent business leader, brewer Paul Wessinger, from the Board of Fire Commissioners.

**Corbett had written Bourne two months earlier that he had been left with considerable expenses after his son's death. "I took upon myself quite an amount of his obligations which are not yet liquidated."[65]

***The "plans" were never spelled out in the Simon-Bourne correspondence. One can only conjecture that they related to Mitchell who was determined to regain his Senate seat. The 1898 mayoralty election must also have been a concern. Henry Corbett, furthermore, was still on the East Coast waiting hopefully to be seated by the Senate.

ans would join hands with "the Pennoyer outfit." There was need to arouse public sentiment through the *Oregonian*. Continued Simon: "I would have no influence without the *Oregonian's* support. . . . The friends I have and who usually cooperate with me are largely embraced among the business element of the community." Their support would be lost if the *Oregonian* became antagonized. Simon ended his long letter with the advice that they get rid of the Mitchell Republicans "adroitly." But in all that they did, "they must follow the Republican Party."[66] In other words, Jonathan was not to consider breaking party ranks again, as he had done in 1896.

The election campaign in the spring of 1898 was over-shadowed in the pages of the local press by the events of the Spanish American War. The race for mayor was a typically complicated affair. The Mitchell-Carey Republicans and "the Pennoyer outfit" were backing former Police Chief John Minto, a thoroughgoing machine politician of the old school. The Simon Republicans and sound money Democrats were supporting former Mayor William S. Mason who was currently the president of the Chamber of Commerce. Bourne was back in town and was up to some of his old habits. In a letter to Bourne from co-worker Amedee M. Smith early in May, reference was made to the availability of $2700 which Smith had raised in Astoria. "The money will be used in hiring workers and on election day in securing the floating vote."[67] Two weeks later, Smith advised Bourne to channel the money through Wells Fargo, where it was "least liable to incite suspicion."[68]

Mason was running as a reform candidate. Described by his supporters as "a progressive businessman of positive and well founded convictions," Mason sold out his interests in the Mason-Ehrman Grocery Company, although still maintaining his presidency of the Portland National Bank, and prepared for the fight against Minto, Pennoyer, District Attorney Hume and the North End saloon crowd. The *Oregonian* provided strong support, as Simon had hoped it would. "There is no better, more worthy, more honorable" man.[69] The paper lambasted Hume for criticising Mason whose opponents were depicted as "the pirates of local politics." They were a "gang" devoid of principles.[70]

In an effort to encourage the "positive vote" — to provide maximum support for their Chamber of Commerce leader — most of the larger downtown stores and businesses closed for the Monday, June 6th vote. Mason was overwhelmingly elected, the first and only incumbent chamber president to become mayor in Portland's history, and Joseph Simon regained some of his former authority — not all of it by any means because Mason was strongly independent. He was to be nobody's "man."

Within 11 days after he had re-assumed office in July 1898 Mason replaced the entire police department. The chief, 61 patrolmen, all the detectives, captains, jailers, patrol wagon drivers and special officers were "removed from the force for the betterment of the service. . . . City Hall was humming like a beehive yesterday morning," reported the *Oregonian* on July 2nd. "Many heads were cut off. . . . The ax struck well."[71] Mason told the city council on July 6th: "We have a police commission, and chief of the Department* composed of some of our best citizens, whose aim it will be to carry out your ordinances, to enforce your edicts and to preserve order and give reputation to our city. . . . Some of our current ordinances are practically a dead letter, so far as their enforcement is concerned."[72]

Mason instructed the Board of Police Commissioners to put regular patrolmen back on the beat in the North End. For some years it had been the practice to use the special officers who were working for their employers, not for the public. An espionage system had been created which effectively thwarted vice arrests by the regular patrolmen dispatched on raids from headquarters.**

Mason also told Chief McLaughlan to clean up the brothels and close the gambling establishments, including the Chinese games and lotteries. Board president Hunt ordered police officers to "refrain from collecting any fees from houses of prostitution, gambling houses, or any objectionable class of people." On the same day that these orders were printed, self-proclaimed reformer Thomas N. Strong publicly accused Joe Simon of purchasing a lot at N.W. Davis, between Third and Fourth Avenues, for the purpose of constructing the largest combined gambling house, brothel and saloon in the city.*** Was this to be a "noon rest" or a "refugee home," inquired Strong.[73]

---

*Named as Chief, was D.M. McLaughlan, former mayor of Albina, and a police commissioner for one year under Mayor Frank. Named as the three new commissioners were: James E. Hunt, a hardware merchant; D. Solis Cohen, lawyer and former commissioner under Mason; and George W. Bates. All were Simon men.

**The author was recently informed that some telephone wires have been found, running underground from "The Bishop's House," a Chinese tong in 1898, to the Police Department building, the site of the old smaller headquarters in 1898.

***The accuracy of Strong's charge might well be questioned. He was not known for his analytical talents.

A humorous consequence of Mason's purge was reported in the same issue of the *Oregonian* on July 9th. Many of the dismissed special police and ex-patrolmen were hounding Napoleon Davis, president of the Columbia Telephone Co. and former president of the Board of Police Commissioners, threatening "to beat his head off." Davis was accused of having forced the officers to ante up $25 a month for a special election fund to defeat Mason. The officers gave their combined $2500 contribution to ex-Chief Clohessy who in turn passed it on to Davis who apparently decided to keep the money for his own personal use, "to buy big fat cigars." Little did the public know that Davis had a history of fraudulent behavior which was to be revealed by prosecutor Francis Heney seven years later. He had served under Governor Pennoyer as state land clerk, and it was Mayor Pennoyer who had appointed him to the police board.*

During the following months, Mason's efforts to provide Portland with more effective police protection produced limited results. Community resistance was ingrained and too many profitable commercial enterprises were involved. Furthermore, in the six year period up to 1899, Multnomah County tax assessments had been reduced by almost 50 percent out of fear that the county was being required to pay too high a share of state taxes.[74] The police budget had to be curtailed, at the very time that the city's population was surging ahead by 30 percent. To make matters worse, Mayor Mason died in office on March 29, 1899.

6.

The death of Mayor William S. Mason during the last year of the 19th century symbolized the ending of an era in Portland's business and political development. Leadership was passing to new and younger hands, with only two exceptions: George H. Williams who would be elected mayor in 1902 at the ripe age of 79, and Joseph Simon who would be elected mayor in 1909 at the age of 58. During the previous decade, Aaron Meier, William S. Ladd, Joseph N. Dolph, Frank Dekum, John C. Ainsworth, Simeon G. Reed, Louis Fleischner, Cicero H. Lewis, Donald MacLeay, and Henry Failing had all passed from the scene. Henry Corbett would remain active until his death in 1903.

---

*As someone was to comment on Pennoyer in later years: "He was a prey to evil men."

Although Jonathan Bourne and Joseph Simon still had many active years ahead of them, they were to play a decreasingly significant role in organized politics because the nature of organized politics itself was to undergo a radical change. The enactment of the "Oregon System" in 1902, 1904 and 1908, was to bring about a gradual deterioration of traditional party authority that had operated for years largely through closed and tightly controlled party conventions. Obviously, Simon could not help but be a force in local politics for as long as he was around. But when he went off to Washington in October 1898, to take the seat that was refused Henry Corbett, he left a power vacuum only partially filled by Bourne. The Mitchell forces under the direction of Carey and Matthews wrested control from Bourne and the absent Simon. Their suzerainty would be brief, however, ending suddenly with Mitchell's demise in 1905. Bourne was thus forced to play a more independent role. He would be elected U.S. Senator in 1906, but largely as a result of his personal popularity, not his Republican party credentials. He never returned to live in Portland. After his failure to achieve renomination in 1912, he chose to live out the remaining 28 years of his life in Washington D.C.

In the spring of 1899, the city council took almost two months to select Mason's successor. In 6 of the 13 formal votes, George W. Bates led, but never by as much as the required majority. Finally, Council President William A. Storey was chosen to fill out the remaining 13 months of Mason's term. A woodmill worker by trade, Storey's undistinguished leadership qualities were only exceeded by those of his fellow councilmen. Storey's election initiated a period of weak, ineffective government that was to last at least 6 years. And during this period explosive economic and demographic forces would almost overwhelm the city and the surrounding metropolitan areas.

The Alaska Gold Rush, beginning in the late spring of 1897, together with an increased world wide demand for wheat, ignited an economic boom locally. From 1896 to 1898, over 300 new businesses were incorporated in Oregon, of which 136 were in mining or mining related enterprises. The big investors included some familiar family names: Ladd, Watson, Flanders, Bourne, McCracken, Ainsworth, Rowe, Livingstone, Beebe, Mason, Simon, Knapp and Goode. One fortunate investor whose name was not too familiar to old Portlanders in 1898 was German born Henry Wemme* who had recently brought the first automobile to Portland, a Stanley Steamer. "My automobile was not

---

*(Ca. 1850-1914.)

E. Henry Wemme (right) in 1899 was the proud owner of the state's first auto, emblazoned with the name of his firm. Dan Rosenfeld is his companion.

popular either with horses or their owners," Wemme recalled some years later. "There were more runaways the first year I had it than had occurred in Portland for the twenty preceding years."[75] Wemme was later to bring the first plane to Portland. He was one of the earliest advocates of the renowned Columbia River Highway. Foreseeing the scenic possibilities of Mt. Hood he bought the old Barlow Toll Road for $6000, spent $25,000 of his own money on it, and then gave it to the people of Oregon as a free highway.[76]

Recounting the boom years of 1897-1898, Wemme wrote:

"When the rush to the Alaska gold mines was on, I did an immense business in selling tents. I spent all the money I had and all I could borrow in buying canvas and bolts of cotton. I had more tent material than all the rest of the dealers on the coast put together. Suddenly travel to

216

Alaska quit. I was stuck. I had a big stock of goods on hand, no market and payments for material coming due. I couldn't borrow any more money and I was headed for the rocks. Just at the particular moment the *Maine* was sunk. War was declared. I landed an order for 16,000 shelter tents. I put a big force at work. The Government gave me an additional order for 16,000 more tents and they gave me an open order for hospital tents, telling me to make all I could. Fleischner & Mayer turned their factory over to me. I had 400 people at work turning out tents. When the Government told me to stop making tents for them, I had used up all my material and instead of going broke I had made a clean-up."[77]

When Henry Wemme died in 1914, he left half of his fortune to found and maintain a large home for wayward girls, known today as The White Shield Home in Northwest Portland. Would that other of Wemme's more successful fellow citizens had made similar contributions to the public welfare.

Unfortunately for Portland, the rapid expansion of the private economic sector resulting from the gold rush did not produce comparable benefits to the public sector. Municipal fiscal resources would not expand for at least several years. Portland was saddled with more than $1 million in bonded indebtedness, and the city was operating with a deficit. The public thoroughfares were in miserable condition and the street railways were singled out by the *Oregonian*[78] for "not doing their share." It was common to find the city owed over $100,000 in unpaid taxes. Although the big railroad corporations did pay their taxes, their Oregon properties were way underassessed in comparison with the other states of the Pacific Coast. In 1900, the average value per mile of railroad property, including a fixed proportion of rolling stock, was $3285 for Oregon, $7427 for Washington, and $9719 for California.[79] The ambitious and relentless Harriman railroad empire had become the dominant corporate force in Oregon. It left little to chance. The appointed Multnomah County Court Clerk — the key position for computing tax assessments — was one Frank S. Fields, a Mitchell Republican and the brother of L.R. Fields, general superintendent of the Southern Pacific Lines in Oregon.

The problems that were to face Portland in the early years of the 20th century were clearly evident in 1899, but few people were willing to face them squarely. The private cash registers were too busy.

217

Chapter IX

A Wide Open Town — With Respectability, 1900-1903

1.

During the first decade of the 20th century, Portland was visited by three of the most influential journalists* in the United States. As might be expected, each looked at the city from a different point of view — one that largely reflected the writer's particular interests. The first of the three to arrive in Portland was Ray Stannard Baker who recorded his visual impressions. Upon completing a lengthy trip through the Northwest in January 1903, Baker wrote that what the Easterner really sees "is a fine old city, a bit, as it might be, of central New York — a square with the postoffice in the center, tree shaded streets, comfortable homes, and plenty of churches and clubs, the signs of conservatism and solid respectability. And yet no decay."

"Few cities of the size of Portland can exhibit finer store and office buildings, a better street-car service, or more comfortable residences. Unlike almost any other Western town, save San Francisco perhaps, it has got

---

*Ray Stannard Baker was a regular staff member of *McClure's Magazine* during the time that *McClure's* led the "Muckraking" movement in America. He later became the authorized biographer of Woodrow Wilson. He would occasionally write for other journals as he did about Portland for *Century Magazine.* Burton Hendrick, also a *McClure's* staffer, became better known as an historian and biographer and was to win three Pulitzer prizes. Lincoln Steffens was introduced in chapter 8 and reappears in chapter 10.

beyond its first generation; it has acquired the momentum of stored riches and passed the stage of pioneer crudities. The sons of the pioneers are now coming into power. They have been educated in the East, have traveled in Europe, and they have come back to make homes in their beautiful city. Wealth and education have blossomed, as always, in conservatism and comfort and a greater attention to society, art, music. Portland is noted for the solidity of its financial institutions, its fine clubs and hotels, its good schools and libraries. It is beginning to take a solicitous interest in its history, a true sign of the self-consciousness which comes of assured success."[1]

Baker was impressed by the lively character of the city — its "brisk energy." He also noted that both Seattle and Portland (which had 10,000 more people than Seattle in 1900) gave one the feeling "of being much larger, more important, more metropolitan" than cities of similar size back east. "A Western town of twenty thousand makes more noise than an Eastern city of several times the size. . . . Every citizen possesses an extraordinary knowledge of his city; in five minutes he will give you fifty reasons why it is to be, shortly, the very greatest in the world."[2]

Along with Baker, most of the observers of the Portland scene in the early 1900's mentioned noise and excited street activity as characteristic of city life. Oregon writer Laurence Pratt remembered the traffic as being "congested and noisy":

> "Iron-shod horses clattered along at a good speed with light wagons and buggies. Trucks for heavy transportation hugged the pavement like modern automobiles. Two, four, or six Percheron horses, big as elephants, clanged eight to twenty-four ringing shoes on the cobblestones, aided and abetted by the clash of iron or steel-rimmed wheels.
>
> Today's silent city knows nothing of the decibels emanating from the old street cars. Along Third and Fifth Avenues, up Washington and Morrison Streets almost bumper to bumper the cars ran with the grind and roar of wheels and the constant clang, clang of warning gongs pounded by the motorman's foot as he approached each cross street. And in Portland the cross streets are only two hundred feet apart. Earlier, there had been horse-

S. W. Morrison - Looking East from Third

drawn trams, but I can't remember to have seen any. All were trolley cars. Often the trolley wheel would jump the wire. A common sight was that of the conductor getting off, going back of the car, and by means of a rope attached to the trolley pole, maneuvering the trolley wheel back onto the overhead electric wire."[3]

Another account by engineer Ray L. Stout, recalls the time that he first arrived in Portland in 1900 as a youngster in company with his uncle:

"It was all noise and confusion at Union Station.* As we came out of the building and on to the street many cab drivers were soliciting customers for the various hotels. The horse-drawn cabs, with entrances at the rear, were backed up to the curb as close as they could stand for a full block and the drivers were crowded on the sidewalk shout-

---

*The Union Station had opened, finally, in 1896. The original scheme, promoted by Villard, was the work of McKim, Mead and White, but "the executed building was designed by Van Brunt and Howe of Kansas City, Missouri."[4] The Richardsonian influence was obvious.

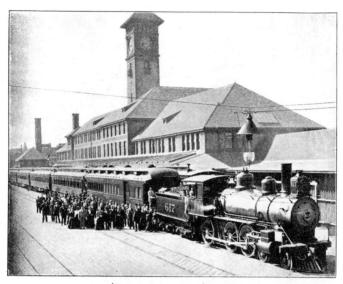
Union depot, Portland.

ing the names of their respective hotels and otherwise trying to induce the people to enter their cab by grabbing
their handbags. I followed my uncle as he pushed through
the crowd, ignoring all of them. He suggested that we
walk uptown, which was satisfactory to me. The seemingly endless rows of buildings on either side of the street
and the noise and confusion from the horse-drawn vehicles and streetcars was bewildering.

During our short stay in Portland, while my uncle was
attending to other matters, I walked around the big city
to see some of the sights. The Portland Hotel, with its
park-like entrance, the Oregonian building with its tall
clock tower and the First Presbyterian Church seemed to
me the outstanding buildings in the city."[5]

Most visitors were singularly impressed by the activity associated
with the river port. Portland was a unique combination of the inland
town and the seaport. As Baker described the setting: "The Willamette River . . . is a majestic stream, so deep that great ocean vessels
come from all the world to load at its docks."[6] In 1901, Portland was
the fifth city in the United States as a wheat exporter, the total ship-
ment being over 13 million bushels — nearly equal to that of San

A rainy day at S. W. 5th & Morrison. Site of Meier and Frank Co. on right; Pioneer Post Office on left; Portland Hotel in background.

Francisco, and largely exceeding those of Seattle and Tacoma put together. The average price of wheat in the United States had risen from 49¢ a bushel in 1894 to 81¢ a bushel in 1897. Portland grain merchants were rapidly becoming wealthy and not far behind them were the owners of the numerous lumber, fruit growing and fish canning enterprises.

The year 1901 was cited "as the greatest year for business in the history of Portland."[7] During the 10 year period ending in 1900, Portland was the third fastest growing of the major cities in the United States. Furthermore, the population would jump by 80 percent in the four year period, 1903 to 1907. The Title Guarantee Trust Co. reported in late 1902: "Never in the history of Portland has the real estate market been in a more healthy . . . and prosperous condition than it is today."[8] Portland was the Pacific Coast's largest city in area size.[9] In the three and a half-year period beginning in 1900, over 25,000 new residents would settle in Portland and over 10,000 in the

225

Portland Statistics

I[10]

Size: 40 sq. miles; 25,600 acres.
Real Estate Value: $90,000,000
Population: 90,426
Street Railways: 105 miles
Sewers: 112 miles
Water mains: 186 miles
Number of street lights: 1320
Public Schools: 32
Private schools: 17
Number of teachers: 340
Number of pupils: 12,000
Library volumes: 30,000
Churches: 126
Number of passenger trains arriving and departing
    at Union Depot daily: 22

II[11]

Occupations in 1900	Male	Female
Agricultural pursuits	1,536	21
Professional	2,313	881
Domestic	12,307	3,068
Trade & Transportation	13,056	1,583
Manufacturing & Mechanical	11,177	1,633
Totals	40,389	7,186

For the period ending in 1899, 61.8% of the county population had been gainfully employed for ten years. In 1900, approximately 4% of the county work force was perpetually unemployed. During the winter season, the unemployment rate rose to nearly 12%.[12]

View of S.W. Portland, from the top of Piggot's Castle. Park Blocks to the left.

adjacent metropolitan areas. Over 5000 new buildings would be constructed, representing an investment of $9 million. Street and sewer improvements would total over $600,000. Manufacturing would more than double and bank deposits would increase one and a half times. The minimum annual return to the average Portland real estate investor would be 18 percent.

Burton Hendrick did not arrive in Portland until eight years after Baker's visit. He was to spend several weeks and write three lengthy articles for *McClure's* about the reforms of the Oregon System. In contrast to his colleague Baker, whom he was heard to characterize as naive, Hendrick looked beneath the surface of visual impressions. He examined the traditional business-political infrastructure and was critical of what he discovered. Although he had the advantage of hind-sight, the basic data was just as available to the reporter in 1903 as it was eight years later. An excerpt from the last of his articles is worth noting:

> "In 1902 [when the Initiative and Referendum were adopted] the Republican machine absolutely controlled the State. In 1901 it sent John H. Mitchell to the United

States Senate for the fourth time, and in 1903 it elected as Mitchell's colleague Charles W. Fulton, a man distinguished for nothing except expert political manipulation. It controlled the governorship, with all its attendant power, and the mayoralty of Portland. On every hand, indeed, the Republican organization held Oregon in its grasp. The real capital of the State was the city of Portland; here were located the public-utility and franchise corporations, the transcontinental railroads, the 'first families,' which for years had usurped the functions of the legislature. The kind of government with which the Republican machine was identified was concretely illustrated in the municipal administration of Portland. Even on the Pacific Coast, Portland enjoyed a peculiar fame as a wide-open town. The machine, by a regular system of monthly fines, had practically licensed gambling and prostitution, and under this system of official encouragement the city had become a popular headquarters for all the vicious characters in the Pacific Northwest."[13]

In the spring of 1902, a week or so before the municipal elections, only a handful of Portland leaders challenged the conditions that were later to be defined and described so accurately by Hendrick. One was Circuit Judge Alfred F. Sears Jr., a prominent attorney whose father, General A.F. Sears, had first proposed the creation of a Port of Portland Commission back in 1883. Judge Sears knew from first hand experience what was ailing Portland civic life. For 10 years* he had been the law partner of Henry McGinn and Nate Simon, Joe Simon's brother. His firm had represented many of the street railway interests, including those of the Markle organization.

Speaking bluntly and to the point, Sears feared "the despotism of the dollar." What we need today, said Sears, "is more of utopia and less of utility . . . more of Plato, less of Edison." Where was all the building construction and real estate development leading Portland? asked the Judge. In what direction was the city heading? Sears concluded his remarks with a stern warning: "The aggregation of property interests . . . confronts us as a menace."[14]

---

*From 1890 to 1900. Sears had also been a member of the city council (1883-1886), assistant district attorney (1886-1890), and an officer of the Portland Railway Co. (1896-1904). Sears served on the bench from 1896 until his death in 1907.

Sears obviously saw what few were willing to admit even if they recognized the problem, that government in the early 1900's was dominated by the very business interests that were booming and simultaneously squeezing maximum profits out of the system. These enterprises contributed practically nothing to the public treasury which was starved for funds. Property values had been increasing while assessments were declining. Little wonder it was that the average real estate investor could enjoy an 18 percent return. In Multnomah County, public pressure in 1901 forced the reassessment of real estate at 50 percent of value, up from 33 percent in 1900.

In 1907, the young *Oregon Journal* was to publish a charge of tax fraud, committed in 1900, involving a practice that apparently had been widespread for many years. According to the *Journal,* the Philip Marquam properties in downtown Portland should have paid a tax of $42,814 (at the 33 percent assessment rate) but instead only paid $15,774. The county had "compromised" at the lower figure. But then it turned out that the county did not receive even the full amount of the lower figure. For some reason, the attorney who represented Marquam received a cash fee of $3,000 which was charged off against the tax. According to the *Journal,* half of the fee was then paid to the county clerk.[15] The lawyer in question was J. Thorburn Ross, state representative and ally of Joe Simon, William M. Ladd, George Bates and Mayor H.S. Rowe. Before the decade was out, Ross would be indicted for numerous fraudulent activities but his first-family associates would escape untouched.

The *Biennial Report* of Secretary of State Frank I. Dunbar,* dated December 1, 1902, contained a number of comments pertinent to Oregon's tax and assessment practices. Republican Dunbar asked his friends in the legislature for a reasonable corporation tax and for a corporate filing fee larger than the then current $5. Oregon counted over 3000 active corporations in 1902, 866** of which had been incorporated since January 1901. According to Dunbar, over half of the states had license taxes. Oregon needed a graduated incorporation fee and a franchise tax. "The assessment and valuation of the property of express, telephone, telegraph, sleeping or Pullman car,

---

*Dunbar himself got into trouble in 1908 when he was convicted of embezzling $100,000 from the state. He was later acquitted by the Oregon Supreme Court.

**Included in the total of 866 new incorporations were:[16]

    308 devoted to mining, oil, coal; capitalized at $220 million.

    77 involved in land and investment; $15.1 million.

    31 railroad enterprises; $23.3 million.

and transportation car companies should receive . . . careful investigation . . . " Such companies, declared Dunbar, "do not contribute to the revenues of the state in proportion to the market value of their property."[17] Oregon, said Dunbar, should assess intangible corporate property, require a license and a tax upon the gross earnings, especially those of the utility companies.[18] The transportation companies should pay for licenses. Finally, Dunbar asserted, Oregon needed an inheritance tax; 27 states already had one in force.[19]

In November 1901, banker Abbot L. Mills must have been aware of the conditions that would be cited by Secretary of State Dunbar in his 1902 report. But in a public speech he revealed a limited understanding of their significance and their relationship to Portland's needs. As a cautious banker who was, himself, deeply involved in the business-political establishment, Mills preferred to tinker with the machinery by advocating some technical refinements. He had no inclination to challenge the basic ingredients of the system itself.

Comparing Portland to other cities of his acquaintance, Mills made the following points. Portland, he said:

(1) Covered too great a geographic area, a condition that was costly.

(2) Was well-lighted (an appropriate comment by an owner of the gas company).

(3) Was ill-protected by a police force that was totally inadequate.

(4) Was well-served by a water system that was one of the healthiest and purest in the nation.

(5) Had been derelict in guarding its rights and franchises in the past (an interesting comment by the chief custodian of private franchise interests).

(6) Was lagging way behind in public kindergartens and municipal libraries.

(7) Was suffering from a tax assessment percentage that was too low.

(8) Needed much greater revenue for municipal services.

Mills concluded his speech with a good banker's warning: "One cannot travel first class on a steerage ticket."[20]

The thought may never have penetrated Mills' consciousness that Portland's elite had for years been travelling first class on a steerage ticket. The leading families wanted the best for their fair city — the "best" as applied to their private, personal lives — but they were unwilling to pay for the trip by providing proportionate compensation to the public treasury. Quality of life was judged in terms of private experiences, and by appearances, politeness, and the kind of surface decoration that came with tidy neighborhoods, well-manicured lawns and rose gardens; by formal parties, and the close fellowship of intimate club life. If the members of urban Portland's upper middle class were thriving and happy, the benefits of their good life would undoubtedly seep down to the working classes whose lives would be enriched accordingly.

Indeed, Portland's upper class society was thriving and happy. As the *Oregonian's* society editor commented some years later: "The period between 1900 and 1914 found Portland gayer than ever before or since in its history."[21] It was not uncommon to plan a four hour luncheon for 30 guests with a program of orchestra music and entertainment scheduled for the later hours of the afternoon. Whereas the young grand dames of New York society would wear skirts and hats for luncheons, not so in Portland where the young ladies were expected to appear in long dresses. One large reception given by Mrs. Henry W. Corbett in 1901 was described as follows: "An orchestra played during the entire afternoon, while women, handsomely dressed in the costume of the time, veiled, gloved and with wasp-waisted skirts sweeping the heavily carpeted floors with their swishing taffeta dust ruffles, called and sipped tea."[22] Card events were quite the vogue and chafingdish parties were particularly popular for winter informal social gatherings.

Waverly Golf Club.

The *Financial Redbook of America,* published in 1903,[23] listed 74 Portlanders with personal assets of over $300,000* — equal to at least $3 million in 1976 buying power. The names are not surprising,** but they do reveal the unusually rapid growth of Portland wealth in only a 50 year period since the city's incorporation. The largest fortunes were directly related to the extent of private property holdings — real estate was still the way to go.

For the men on the select list, golf and shooting became favorite recreational pastimes. In 1899 the Waverly Golf Club leased additional acreage from the Lambert family, and then proceeded to raise $15,000 to purchase the land. The Club's executive committee represented the dominant elite of Portland society: Roderick MacLeay, John C. Ainsworth, Thomas Kerr, Abbot Mills, and William M. Whidden.[24] Small, intimate shooting groups were available to those who felt the need to escape from city and family burdens to wilderness-type enclaves where men could be men. The Morgan's Shooting Club roster included: Mills, Roderick MacLeay, C.F. Adams and Dr. Kenneth A.J. MacKenzie,[25] Portland's most eminent surgeon.

RODERICK L. MACLEAY
President Macleay Estate

---

*Denver listed 46 and Seattle 38.
**See Appendix F.

Exposition Building.

At the other end of the social scale, favorite recreational pastimes included sitting across the street from the Portland Hotel on warm summer afternoons and listening to band music wafting from the parkway area between the wings of the hotel, or taking a leisurely stroll through the Exposition Building which was usually humming with a variety of activities. Sunday afternoon band concerts would draw throngs to City Park. The Park Zoo was equally popular although the conditions under which the animals were kept and displayed were abominable.[26]

Bicycle riding became a craze in 1898 and the United Wheelman's Association promoted the construction of a riding path all the way to the Columbia River across from Vancouver. Dealer Fred T. Merrill sold 8850 bicycles in 1898 alone, making him the largest operator west of the Mississippi. Merrill handled the famous "Pacemaker" which accommodated five riders on its 12 foot, 130 pound frame. According to Merrill, bicycle use began to wane around 1903 when "the favouring women from the North End took to the wheel."[27] They wore bright cycling clothes and "scandalous split skirts," and rode around town ringing their bells. The society girls would have none of this and their loss of patronage hurt the business.

Fred Merrill epitomized a type of businessman-politician who played a crucial role in American city life around the turn of the century. Urban centers like Portland were experiencing traumatic changes that threatened to upset traditional social patterns and personal relationships. Industrialization, technological innovation, business and financial consolidation, immigration, all of these forces and more tended to create separate, specialized units and to fragment society along ethnic and class lines. Street railway expansion redounded in a shattering of older urban boundaries at the same time that power and authority in business and government were becoming more centralized and bureaucratized.

Fred T. Merrill Cycle Co. — Portland's largest cycle house, 1899.

Fred T. Merrill Cycle Co. — South half of mammoth salesroom, 100 x 200 feet in size, the largest bicycle salesroom in the United States.

Conditions of this sort created a sympathetic environment for the urban boss whose machine could meet the changing desires and needs of his constituents. The fact that Portland had proportionately fewer immigrants than eastern cities of the same size made the city less receptive to the classic machine function. And yet a need still existed, of the type often met by the machine, for a personal relationship between the elected official and the voter. Fred Merrill was not a boss by any means, but as a city councilman for six years, 1899-1905, he tried to fulfill a boss-like role for his constituents. He was responsive to their problems and provided services for them. In contrast to many of his fellow councilmen, he was honest. In his opposition to reform, he was pragmatic rather than reactionary. He simply did not believe in trying to change what he considered natural human inclinations. Such efforts, in his mind, were misguided and often doomed to failure. For these reasons, Fred T. Merrill believed in an open town.

In an interview that he granted toward the end of his life, Merrill said that he wanted to be "considered as one of the men who built Portland, made $1.5 million and spent it here." "I have always be-

235

lieved in a lively town," he continued. "In my fifty-four years in Portland I have done my best to keep the place lively."[28] Merrill promoted boxing and wrestling matches, sponsored parades and ballooning events, and built and operated "Twelve Mile House" out on East Division Street, adjacent to which he constructed his own horse racing track. Enjoying a somewhat "questionable reputation," the "House" was a restuarant and hotel that served the growing automobile trade. Merrill had become a Ford dealer following his success with bicycles and he developed a prosperous business.

Merrill believed that the saloon and sporting elements should not be outlawed but rather should pay their fair share through licenses and taxes. Gambling and prostitution would always exist, he felt, but they should be segregated and licensed, be kept open and honest. "There has never been a time during my fifty-four years in Portland when a total stranger couldn't find a gambling game or a sporting house." In 1903, Merrill ran and won on a "Keep Portland wide-open ticket." He considered his initial council race in 1899 "a lark." He never expected to win. All he wanted to do was to promote his bicycles.

He enjoyed his six years representing the Third Ward, from S.W. Washington to N.W. Glisan Streets. "I never took a cent of money from anyone," he recalled. "I became a sort of fixer for people in trouble." He remembered the time that he retrieved "a wild young daughter of a prominent Portland family out of a house of ill-fame."[29] In his council duties he voted against many of the franchise awards which he felt were phony, involving companies that were created for the sole purpose of securing a franchise only to be sold to an out of state investor. He prevented the Standard Oil Co. from establishing an oil storage district on the East side of the river, and he blocked the attempt of Jonathan Bourne's North End crony, Larry Sullivan, to acquire a 50 year garbage collecting franchise.

In most respects, Merrill well represented his lower middle and working class constituents. He was an urban Populist. Open and aboveboard in all of his dealings, he affected no pretentious airs. He was not a part of Portland's plutocracy that enjoyed the financial rewards of vice operations but would not openly admit to it.

Judge Henry McGinn*, on the other hand, was a member of the establishment. In his early life, he not only gave public support to vice and gambling operations, but he actively participated in the

---

*(1859-1933.)

HENRY E. McGINN
Judge, Department No. 3, Circuit Court

"lower pleasures." McGinn won his spurs as a political lieutenant of Senator Corbett and Joseph Simon. One account called him "the most picturesque figure in all Oregon."[30] For years he had been a consort of the notorious Madame P. Shong. He loved booze and women and was not afraid to admit it. Paradoxically, his voice carried authority in a community that ostensibly disdained such activities.

Seven months after Mayor Mason's death, during Mayor Storey's brief tenure, McGinn blithely appeared before the Board of Police Commissioners with a petition from a large number of citizens, merchants, and property owners, requesting the board "to take into consideration all the various interests involved in determining upon a policy as to control and regulation of saloons and gambling within the city." The board's policy should not be too restrictive so as "to become a detriment and injury to the business community."[31] Needless to say, his appeal was effective. Not only was McGinn Nate Simon's partner but the president of the board was Joe Simon's close friend, D. Solis Cohen. C.N. Rankin worked for the *Oregonian* and Harvey Scott was an intimate associate of McGinn's. The third board member was George W. Bates who derived a healthy income from the second floor of his property on Fourth St., over Barnes Market, which he rented out to gamblers. These gentlemen were not about to rock the boat.

By the time of his second election to the circuit court in 1911, McGinn was to have become a thoroughgoing reformer, following a metamorphic path similar to Jonathan Bourne's earlier experience. McGinn publicly confessed his past sins. He admitted that he had been a poor district attorney from 1886-1890. He described the rough politics of those days when "voters were bought openly, . . . [when] the railroads furnished the money for much of the bribery and corruption."[32] Speaking out in the senate one day, McGinn declared:

> "Don't tell me that conditions were better in the past than they are now. I sat next to the right hand of the dealer in the old days of political control in Portland by the bosses. I have sat at the pay window in this place. I watched the voter take the ballot from the judges of election, who deposited it in the ballot box and then the voter appeared at my window and I handed him the five dollar gold piece that he had earned. We have made a start at the cleaning out the Augean stables, but have much yet to do."[33]

Twenty-two years later, having continued to live a life of robust activity, the witty, outspoken Portland born Irishman, the friend of the common people, would die in his favorite brothel and be mourned by Portland's elite. As Walter Pierce* wrote: "He was one of the most striking characters I have ever known."[34]

2.

The administration of Republican Mayor Henry S. Rowe (1900-1902) was a dull, safe businessman's government. Rowe came right out of the traditional mould. Until he was involved in the Albina development he had been a steamship agent and railroad superintendent for the OR&N Company. He continued to maintain strong railroad connections and private real estate interests throughout his term of office, climaxing his career as general agent for the Chicago, Milwaukee and St. Paul Railroad. Throughout his varied and active life in business and government, Rowe maintained a close relationship with Joseph Simon and George W. Bates.

---

*Pierce was Governor, 1923-27; Congressman, 1933-43.

The 11 member city council was entirely new. In socio-economic terms, it was decidedly upper middle class with four lawyers, two of whom were in real estate development, two realtors, four merchants and one accountant. Three councilmen, in addition to Mayor Rowe, were Arlington Club members. The council president was a proper young lawyer named Rodney L. Glisan, grandson of Capt. Couch, nephew of Cicero H. Lewis, and son of Portland's most prominent family doctor during the last quarter of the past century. No innovations or reforms could be expected from this group, whose motto was "business as usual." As Councilman W.T. Branch, an accountant and former city auditor, was quoted as having said: "A city officer . . . [is in a] delicate position, faced with forcing compliance to ordinances . . . [which] makes him many enemies."[35] Councilman E.C. Bronaugh, a leading attorney, phrased similar sentiments when he remarked that there was "too much opposition to the observance of ordinances," especially those relating to sidewalk and street improvement. Bronaugh called for public "cooperation in enforcing city ordinances."[36]

General offices and waiting room — Portland Railway Co., First and Washington Streets.

As with the previous administrations, the city was strapped for funds. The police department ran out of operating revenue two months before the end of the 1900 fiscal year and had to borrow to keep going. Some of the major downtown thoroughfares were in frightful condition, particularly First Avenue, between Burnside and Madison Streets, which was cluttered with railway tracks. But probably the most perplexing headache that the council had to endure was the matter of the city garbage dump and crematorium. Garbage disposal had been a major municipal problem ever since the city was incorporated.* A few years earlier, the *Oregonian* had commented: "The old, old question of 'What shall we do with our garbage?' which, like Banquo's ghost, or the smell of a garbage dump, 'will not down', nor be downed, is . . . coming to the surface again."[37]

In 1900, the "offensive" dump was next to the furnace plant, just north of the depot yards in Northwest Portland. The plant was outmoded and was costing the city $375 a month to operate. Anyone, .including the private haulers, could dump whatever they wanted, whenever they wanted with no charge. Much of the garbage brought in was "thoroughly saturated with water,"[38] a condition that retarded the burning and left several inches of water perpetually in the pans at the bottom of the furnace. The operation was undermanned, with two operators by day and one by night. The foreman quit in September when he was refused a pay increase from $75 to $90 per month. To make matters worse, there were no lights around the dump or within the plant, so that "the employees were compelled to carry lanterns to perform their duties." Refuse dumped at night was apt to end up almost anywhere on the premises.** The plant was moved in 1903 to N.W. 25th, near Guild's Lake, but, as in the past, it would soon prove inadequate for the load, and the operation costs would continue to rise.

One of the most controversial issues to face city government in the winter of 1901-1902 was the purchase by the water committee

---

*It continues to be in 1976. The Portland St. Johns landfill is approaching its limit in 1976. Plans are still unformulated as to future solid waste disposal.

**The Crematory inventory for November 1900 revealed the following:
1480 cubic yards of garbage consumed
15 horses
3 cows
35 dogs

75 loads of sawdust and 16 cords of wood burned; 417 hours of consumption time. In the subsequent months, incinerated animals would include 2 camels, a cougar and a hog.

of the Albina Water Co. property. No clearer example could be offered of the fraudulent nature of the county's tax assessment practices.
It also provided the public with a solid case of conflict of interest.
George W. Bates had been the majority stockholder since the company's founding as the Albina Light & Water Co. in 1889.* Lee
Hoffman, Charles F. Swigert, D.M. McLaughlan and H.S. Rowe
had all been involved with the company one way or another in the
13 year interval. Rowe was now mayor, McLaughlan was chief of
police and an *ex-officio* member of the police board, Bates was a
member of both the police board and the water committee, and Swigert and Hoffman were busy with their various construction projects.

In December 1901, the water company offered to sell out to the Portland Water Committee for $250,000 cash. The engineer's report stated
that the existing system could be duplicated for $172,000; but if the
Albina area were to be served adequately, as opposed to the service
then provided, the cost would total $251,750.[39] The company's assess-
ment record presented a marked contrast to these figures. In 1899, it
was assessed at $11,000; in 1900 at $17,000 and in 1901 at $25,000,[40]
the year in which the rate was supposedly increased to 50 percent of
value. It was obvious to anyone who took the trouble to investigate
the matter, that the Albina Water Co. had been stealing the county
blind for over a decade, because the property was worth at least three
times its listed value. In addition, the company had never paid a
license tax for its operation. Had the company's taxable property
been worth only $50,000, with $20,000 a year net earnings, the company would have been receiving an unheard of return on its investment — at least for a utility.

At the December 24, 1901 meeting, Commissioner L.A. Lewis'
motion for a $157,000 purchase price was defeated 8-3. Commissioner
Joseph Teal's motion for a price of $175,000 was defeated 5-5 with
Chairman Henry W. Corbett voting no. The final vote of 7-3 approved
an offering price of $200,000.[41] George Bates did not attend the Dec-
ember meetings but his interests were well represented. Bates had
enjoyed an intimate association with the water committee as far
back as 1893 when he and Hoffman were chosen to build the $350,000
Bull Run conduit line to Portland. Future mayor George Frank, a
close ally of Bates, happened at the time to be chairman of the construction sub-committee of the water committee and was instrumental in awarding the contract to his friends who already had establish-

---

*See Albina control chart, chapter VI.

ed the competing Albina company. It would be naive to assume that Bates and Hoffman did not plan to sell their Albina property to the city at some future date, when the time was appropriate and the leverage sufficient. Throughout all of the discussion in 1901, the question of competition kept creeping into the arguments. And the more that future competition was viewed as a threatening reality, the more the higher price seemed justified.

In typical fashion, the *Oregonian* praised the deal as a "bargain" for the city.[42] Harvey Scott was on the water committee. But the *Journal* was to attack it in subsequent years as "a sell-out." In the June 1902 election Bates was accused of fraud by his opponents and he lost his bid for the legislature.

3.

A new city charter, approved by the special session of the legislature in October 1898, authorized the establishment of a board of public works, to be appointed by the mayor. This maneuver was a Joe Simon device, designed as an indirect by-pass of the city council which Simon feared might fall under the control of the Mitchell Republicans, particularly during the next five years when he expected to be in Washington as Oregon's junior senator. The board was required to review all city purchases, bids and contracts, as well as all franchise applications, before they were transmitted to the council for final approval. In most cases, the council acted *pro forma* in accordance with the board's recommendations, but it was not obliged to.

The first board of public works appointed by Mayor Mason, included a socially exclusive blue ribbon group of business leaders headed by Chairman Abbot L. Mills. It was heavily weighted toward real estate interests, with Arlington Club members Walter F. Burrell, Otto Breyman and William MacMaster. In theory, the new system was supposed to operate more efficiently and honestly, but in practice it did not. Economy was practically disregarded in purchases because most items were bought on the open market, on orders for less than the limit beyond which a formal bid was required.* Yet, the total purchases from particular companies were enormous; they were simply spread out over the calendar months. Orders were also

---

*Ranged from $100 in 1891 to $250 in 1913.

242

distributed to different dealers with no saving in costs. Collusion was a normal practice when bids were required. Everyone got part of the gravy, a condition that was largely dictated by political influence. Each department did its own purchasing, with board of public works approval. Centralized purchasing, especially for the police and fire departments, would have saved the city thousands of dollars a year. When the proposals reached the council for final approval, they were usually rushed through often at the same meeting at which they were introduced. Because there was no advance printing of the council proceedings to alert the public, the opportunity for corrupt practices was unlimited. Mills remained as chairman through the Rowe and early part of the Williams administrations until the board's functions were replaced by a new agency in January 1903.[43]

Hay, hardware, sawdust and lumber were the major items purchased by the city. The man most often cited in the local press, not the *Oregonian,* as the largest beneficiary of city business was Donald MacKay, president of the North Pacific Lumber Co., chairman of the Republican City and County Central Committees off and on for 10 years and long time member of the state senate. A close political associate of Simon and Corbett, Arlington Club member MacKay was accused publicly of being the major organizer of City Hall graft. "Not a single item enters into the consumption of the two governments [city and county] that has not paid its portion in tribute."[44] MacKay was not only accused of extorting kickbacks, but of furnishing lumber to the two governments at his own price. This latter charge is not verified by the record, although it would appear that there was collusion in bidding for the larger orders.

Furnishing insurance coverage for city properties produced a lucrative income for many of the city's insurance agents. No particular pattern of favoritism was revealed by the list of contracts in force in 1901 although two of the agents were prominent Republicans with close ties to the Simon faction. Street paving contracts, on the other hand, were clearly enmeshed in politics and influence peddling. As was cited earlier, the Ladd & Tilton controlled Trinidad Asphalt Paving Co. secured a number of extremely profitable jobs free of competitive bids. The charter required that the award go to the "lowest *responsible* bidder," with responsibility defined in terms of bonding capacity. The contract to repave S.W. Washington Street for $34,000, awarded in October 1902, was the largest single street paving contract in the city's history to that date.[45]

During 1901, the board of public works increasingly devoted more of its time to franchise applications. The business community was divided on this issue. The council as well as the board had for some time received numerous communications urging that no more franchises be granted to railways and railroads unless the city received reasonable and proper compensation.

On September 4, 1901, prominent attorney Ellis Hughes* sent a remonstrance to the council in which he argued against the awarding of a railroad track franchise to George Weidler along North Front Street. In a most extraordinary document, Hughes declared: "Weidler has no interest in railroads." All he "wants is a valuable franchise to sell." Asked Hughes, "what public interest is there to be served by this franchise?" According to Hughes, if the land was privately owned and used for a similar franchised activity it would be worth $100,000. "I am not seeking to cause any reflections on Mr. Weidler or his associates [one of whom was Judge C.H. Carey**]. No one can blame them for desiring to secure a valuable franchise, or for endeavoring to add such value to their property as will enable them to sell it. I would not be adverse to having a few hundreds of thousands of dollars worth of these franchises myself. . . . There is a wide difference between what Mr. Weidler and his associates may desire and what the public interests require, which public interest is the only ground on which the City should grant this franchise."[46]

Hughes claimed that the franchise was being sought for the Northern Pacific Railroad which wanted to buy Weidler's Mill property and that Weidler already had a contract for sale with representatives of the railroad. "If the Northern Pacific wants this franchise, why does not that company ask for it in its own name?" inquired Hughes. "It is a notorious fact that the Northern Pacific Railroad, ever since the completion of its road to Puget Sound, has been the persistent enemy of this city, seizing every opportunity to injure it, by diverting its trade to its own so-called terminal at Tacoma, or of late to Seattle." Hughes concluded with the declaration that "Portland owes the Northern Pacific no favor."[47]

Through a series of ordinances that were passed, repealed, redrafted and repassed, the franchise was finally approved by the council on December 3, 1901. The board of public works had previously approved the award although chairman Mills had opposed the ac-

---

*A charter member of the Arlington Club, Hughes drafted the legislation that established the Port of Portland Commission in 1891. Hughes was a large property owner in the Irvington District.
**Carey was president of the Weidler Lumber operation while he was also legal counsel to the Northern Pacific Railroad.

tion. In following this course, Mills was true to his own advice that he had given publicly the previous month. But he was also acting against the interests of two close Harvard alumni friends, Northern Pacific diretor William Endicott Jr. of Boston and the railroad's president, Howard Elliott. In later years, when the First National Bank's interests became directly involved in financial dealings with the Northern Pacific, Mr. Mills would support the railroad, but no such conditions prevailed in 1901.

4.

The dirty in-party fighting that characterized the last years of the 1890's continued to afflict the Republicans up through the 1903 legislative session. The Simon candidates for the state senate were badly trounced in the June 1902 election.* Abbot Mills was beaten in his first attempt to seek a House seat. Bourne and Simon decided to rely on Judge Henry McGinn, who retained his unexpired senate seat, to prevent Mitchell from gaining his much desired re-nomination that had been denied him in 1897. Henry W. Corbett was still very much in the fray; at the age of 74, he was prepared to give the U.S. Senate one more try. True to past form, Jonathan Bourne had 32 signed Corbett pledges in his pocket as the legislature opened its doors on January 20, 1901.

In the initial balloting, Corbett held a slight edge over incumbent Senator George McBride who was an ally of Mitchell's. One month later, the issue was still not resolved as George H. Williams had replaced McBride as Corbett's chief contender. On the last regular day of the session, Senator George Brownell, reputedly representing the Southern Pacific, placed John H. Mitchell's name in nomination. After 25 ballots, lasting well into the night, Mitchell was elected,[48] with the aid of 11 Democrats who were rumored to have struck a deal with the Mitchell high command. Democrats were supposedly promised positions on the Portland police and fire boards and some county offices if they would support Mitchell. In 1901, Matthews and Carey had the resources to deliver the votes. As one observer noted, the "S.P. money beat the Corbett money."[49] Ten years later, Brownell publicly referred to the episode and to Corbett whose agents and friends, he said, "bought men and paid them in money and

---

*Donald MacKay, Thorburn Ross, Sylvester Farrell, George Bates.

whiskey and other things for their votes." One House member, a parishioner of a leading church in Portland, was given $100 every time he voted for Corbett plus a slug of whiskey in the cloakroom.[50]

Bourne blamed "four traitors" for breaking their pledges.[51] Representative Matoon, in a state of inebriation, supposedly received $4000 for his switch. Representative A.S. Dresser of Clackamas openly admitted that he broke with Corbett over his campaign methods: "I will never vote for a man who uses the methods Mr. Corbett has used," i.e., threats and bribes.[52] Corbett blamed his loss on the Mitchell machine for having sold the Republican party to the Democrats of Portland for a few offices. As Bourne* said: "They sold out the city government to their political enemies."[53]

The 16 months following the end of the legislative session produced the most remarkable, complicated and paradoxical period in Oregon's tortuous political history. The machinery was already in motion to draft a new charter for Portland. The charter commission, headed by Abbot Mills, included 22 of Portland's most eminent citizens of every stripe and affiliation. For over a year they argued and battled through each provision in an attempt to streamline the governmental process and to grant the mayor more authority for which he could be held accountable. The fire and police boards were to be abolished, a civil service board to be established and the water committee to be limited to 4 members. The board of public works was to be replaced by an executive board of 10 whose members could not hold any other public office. Franchises were to be non-exclusive and limited to 25 years and were to be published before final action was taken by the council.** The city would be authorized to acquire existing utility plants by vote of the people and to issue utility bonds if two-thirds of the voters approved. Total bonded indebtedness could never exceed 7 percent of the assessed value of all real and personal property in the city. The city would also be authorized by popular vote to provide for its own light plant, with a maximum expenditure of $300,000.[54]

While these deliberations were being conducted, William S. U'Ren organized a state non-partisan direct legislation league, with the

---

*On May 15, 1901, Bourne wrote Corbett offering to destroy the "32 pledges."

**A petition signed by 15% of the voters of the last preceding city election could force a public vote on a franchise award. A 15 day grace period was to be allowed after publication for the petition to be received.

help of Bourne and many others,* for the purpose of securing popular approval of an initiative and referendum amendment to the state constitution at the June 1902 election. Support was generated from as diverse a group of individuals as one could imagine:[55] Harvey W. Scott, C.E. Ladd, Abbot L. Mills, Ben Selling, Joe Simon, John H. Mitchell, George H. Williams and all of the liberals and remaining Populists. The Mitchell-Carey group supported it because they knew that Mitchell was the most popular political figure in Oregon and they hoped that the change would end Simon's control once and for all. Most of the other conservative support, including that of Simon, was for a variety of personal reasons — each expected to gain something. Jonathan Bourne was fed up with the old system. He also had senatorial ambitions and was really working for a direct primary system that he knew could only be achieved through the initiative, and not through legislative action. The voters of Oregon gave overwhelming approval to the amendment, 62,024 to 4,668. The "Oregon System" had been launched. Little did the conservatives realize the nature of the popular revolution that they had unleashed.**

In contrast to the spirit of unanimity generated by the initiative and referendum issue, the local city election in June 1902 was more divisive than ever. As the printed election handouts revealed, the Mitchell forces, led by Jack Matthews and Charles H. Carey, were out to get Simon personally. The *Oregonian* had switched its allegiance to Mitchell, an action that would cause Harvey Scott to squirm three years later. There were two reasons for Scott's change of loyalty. First, and most important, he wanted to be elected U.S. Senator to succeed Simon who was not going to seek re-election. Mitchell's support was crucial if his hopes were to be realized. Second, Simon was in the process of creating a fusion ticket of Democrats and anti-Mitchell Republicans, an action that was tantamount to heresy and treason in Scott's book. In April 1902, Scott called the Simon group "a beaten faction . . . desperately trying to hold on to the shreds, rags and remnants of the political power still in their hands."[56]

The Mitchell machine, with Scott's support, was running George H. Williams for mayor. Simon was backing Democrat Robert Inman, one of Oregon's leading lumbermen. Simon's strategy was to create the impression that his ticket was independent of machine control,

---

*Numerous farm and labor groups had been pushing direct legislation as early as 1886.

**See Appendices G and H.

What the Simon Machine Costs the Taxpayers.

SIMON'S MACHINE has been in existence nearly twenty years and has been maintained in power by the criminal use of public funds.

With the exception of the County Judge, everyone of the present City and County officials is indebted to **Simon** for his place, and all of them desire to remain in office. **These are the people** who are clamoring for the election of the "regular," or Simon, delegates in the coming primaries. **These are the men** who are daily and nightly engaged in registering gamblers and thieves, hobos and tramps, loafers, fakirs and men of shady character for the purpose of maintaining the **Simon machine.** Strikers, ward heelers and relatives of officeholders are placed on the payrolls of the City and County and detailed to assist in this work.

Policemen and **firemen** in civilian clothes, aided by their chiefs, may be seen at any hour of the day or night at the North End, where they are rounding up votes of this class. Men who ought to be watched continually by the police are told they can buy immunity by casting their votes as the police direct. The search for votes of this description is incessant and shameless. How long are the people of Portland going to endure a repetition of this unspeakable outrage?

Thousands of dollars are paid out of the public funds to men who never performed an hour's work for the City or County. Contracts are awarded to favorites at exorbitant prices.

Ward workers and strikers are given places in the police, fire and street cleaning departments, and the facts kept from the public. Salaries are increased and the public not informed. Gangs of men who are expected to vote the machine ticket are employed in the various road districts throughout the County. Large sums of money are paid these men and no service rendered.

Whose machine is it and who are working for it? Let us see: W. M. Davis, Deputy City Attorney; Thos. McNamee, Constable; Louis Wagner and Thomas McDevitt, Jr., Deputies; Dr. Harry Mackay, County Physician; S. C. Beach, County Recorder; Lot Q. Swetland, County Clerk; J. P. Kennedy, Circuit Court Clerk; Chas. E. McDonnell, County Assessor; J. G. Mack and Wm. Showers, County Commissioners; D. Solis Cohen, C. N. Rankin and George W. Bates, Police Commissioners; Wm. Fliedner, Richard Everding and T. A. Davey, Fire Commissioners—are the men who are working for it, and all are office holders at the present time, and also lieutenants of Simon in his efforts to maintain the machine and return himself to the U. S. Senate.

These men for the past three weeks have neglected their official duties and have searched in every nook and corner of the City and County for votes, favorable to the machine. Some of them have been in office for years; others are working for the same end. **Taxes** have been largely increased through the extravagant and shameful waste of public funds under their control. Supplies for public use are furnished by themselves and they pass judgment on their own bills.

Why should this machine continue in existence? What right has any man to maintain such a machine at public expense?

This is the opportunity to **smash the ring.** The present primary law permits every voter to cast his vote in secret and in peace and free from the jostling and crowding of the disreputable element.

Every citizen opposed to **Simon and his machine** should see to it that his vote is cast against the "regular," or **Simon ticket,** and in favor of the unpledged delegates nominated by electors in each precinct and whose names appear in The Oregonian as **Anti=Simon Delegates.**

Remember—a vote for the "regular" ticket means the continuance of the Simon machine for at least six years, and the sending of Simon to the United States Senate—a man who has no ability or qualification for the place. He has been tried and found wanting.

THE SHAME OF IT.

The disgraceful spectacle of Oregon's Senior Senator frequenting the slums in the North End of the city in search of votes to carry the coming primaries ought to cause every self-respecting citizen to hang his head in shame.

Why does Senator Simon desert his place in the United States Senate at this time? Is he of no consequence there?

What right has he to *disgrace his high position* by managing ward politics in a primary fight?

Truly, this man, by his own acts, has proven himself *unfitted* to represent the State of Oregon in the United States Senate.

The Simon Machine, under the direction of Joseph Simon, is engaged in rounding up and registering the purchasable element, men who have no property in the city and who pay no taxes. With votes of this class he seeks to carry the primaries and maintain the present machine in power for two years longer, and to secure his re-election to the United States Senate.

Why is it that this man ignores the respectable element of the community? *Does he fear* to go before them on his merits? It seems so.

Scores of men are promised the nomination for Sheriff by Mr. Simon for their influence and vote. Other offices are promised on the same terms. Let him but know what a man wants and he will promise it to him; but Simon sees to it that he gets *his* goods first. The other fe llow—well, *that is the same old story.*

Bribes, threats, promises,—all are being worked by the machine to get votes. If you want this to stop, vote against the "regular," or Simon, delegates and in favor of the independent delegates, as published in the daily papers.

in keeping with the new spirit of popular government sweeping across the state, whereas the Mitchell ticket was depicted as the old type of boss system that was antagonistic to popular government. The *New Age* picked up the theme when it asked: "Does Jack Matthews own the alleged Republican party of Multnomah County?"[57] "Talk about Senator Simon as a boss in years past! Why Simon never attempted or thought of attempting to form so close a political corporation as that now in control of 'Jack' Matthews, nor to be one-tenth as arbitrary in his methods."[58] The Negro paper, of course, was smarting over Matthews' decision to exclude Negroes from the 1902 Republican county convention.

The same election in June 1902 that so heartily approved the initiative and referendum amendment and the new city charter,* barely squeezed the 79 year old political professional George H. Williams into office.** Simon's ticket was decisively beaten and Jack Matthews became the boss of Republican party politics, both locally and statewide. Bourne had purposely remained aloof from the campaign, at least publicly. After the election, he tried to secure Matthews' support for his own senatorial election at the forthcoming 1903 legislative session. When this endeavor failed, he approached Abbot Mills but was turned down.

The story was told that Bourne next sought out Scott through Henry McGinn. He would support Scott in 1903 if Scott would pledge Bourne all the federal patronage and help elect him (Bourne) as Mitchell's successor in 1907. Scott of course later denied that he had ever made any deal with Bourne, and yet Bourne did support Scott during the legislative ballotting after he had dropped his own plans. Scott was finally beaten by Charles W. Fulton from Astoria,*** a long time member of the state senate, Joe Simon's successor as senate president and close political ally of John Mitchell. As in past sessions when senators were to be chosen, much money changed hands. State senator Walter Pierce later commented: "Senator Pierce Mays****
. . . said to me the last night of the session: 'I have $40,000 in the bank.

---

*Approved by Portland voters, 10,810 to 1253, to go into effect upon legislative approval, received on January 23, 1903.
**By 643 votes out of 13,000 cast.
***On the 42nd ballot. Scott entered the running on the 39th ballot. The final vote gave Fulton 46, Scott 21, C.E.S. Wood (Democrat) 17. Wood kept his 17 votes throughout the 42 ballots.
****Mays was the law partner of Judge Charles H. Carey in 1903. The firm represented the N.P.R.R. and the James J. Hill interests. Mays was to be convicted of perjury and fraud in the 1906 timber fraud trials.

I would give all of it to be elected United States Senator, but I do not know how or where to spend it so I shall continue to vote for Charlie Fulton.' "[59] Bourne spent so much money that he overdrew his bank account back in Providence, Rhode Island.

One positive consequence of all this political skirmishing was the founding of the *Oregon Journal.* Established as the *Evening Journal* on March 10, 1902, the paper was bought on July 23, 1902 by Charles S. Jackson, a Virginian by birth who had owned the *East Oregonian* in Pendleton since 1880. He sold the Pendleton paper and moved to Portland and purchased the struggling sheet which he renamed the *Oregon Daily Journal.* The list of his backers included: John C. Ainsworth, William M. Ladd, George W. Bates, Abbot L. Mills and Joseph N. Teal, son-in-law of former mayor David P. Thompson and the paper's attorney. One must assume that most of this group were reacting against Harvey Scott's blatant attack on Joe Simon. In future years, the *Journal* would not always be supportive of the interests of its major backers but at least it would try to be fair and objective. Harvey Scott never really forgave Abbot Mills for his early support of the *Journal.* Four years later he and a reformed Henry McGinn would launch a scathing attack on Mills' Portand Gas Co.

The victorious mayor, George H. Williams,[60] was Oregon's most prominent citizen nationally. Not only had he served one term as U.S. Senator (1865-1871), but he had spent three years in President Grant's cabinet as Attorney General. Born in a log cabin in upper New York State in 1823 and admitted to the bar at 21, Williams practiced law as a Democrat in Iowa in 1845 and was sent to the Oregon Territory in June 1853 as Chief Justice of the Territorial Court that also included Justices Olney and Deady. He entered private practice in Portland in 1859, became a Republican and proclaimed his opposition to the extension of slavery in the territories. As a senator, he played an important role in the passage of the Tenure of Office Act, the Reconstruction Acts and the impeachment proceedings against President Andrew Johnson.

His record as Attorney General was not well regarded by the Bar Associations. He was accused of dereliction of duty in his handling of the scandal investigations. And when he was nominated as Chief Justice, strong opposition developed throughout the east. Henry Corbett and Matthew Deady had long been aware of Williams' personal weaknesses that were only beginning to surface publicly in 1873. Three years earlier, Corbett had written Deady: "I believe him [Williams] wholly insincere, except in one thing, that is his own advancement at all hazard."[61] Corbett felt Williams to be totally self-

251

seeking. "He would sell the state and send it to perdition if in doing so, he could advance himself." A week later, Corbett accused Williams of selling himself out to Ben Holladay over the railroad legislation then under consideration in Congress.[62] Corbett was fighting for Portland as a port of entry for a transcontinental rail line and Williams was blocking his efforts.

Williams' nomination was in trouble from the start. There was natural eastern opposition to a westerner; his wife Kate was considered brash, extravagant and a social climber by Washington society; and the Gibbs affair backfired, referring to his removal of the U.S. Attorney in Portland for prosecuting Mitchell's alleged vote frauds in defiance of his instructions. All of these factors, together with solid Bar opposition, forced Grant to withdraw the nomination by pressuring Williams to take the initiative.

George H. Williams

Williams returned to Portland in 1881, formed a partnership with George H. Durham, William Lair Hill and F. Pierce Mays, and later built himself a lavish home on N.W. 18th and Couch. A new firm was subsequently organized with C.E.S. Wood and S.B. Linthicum. Unfortunately for him, Williams joined the boards of directors of the three major banks which failed in 1893: Dekum's Commercial National, and Markle's Oregon National and Northwest Loan and Trust Co. Williams became the favored speaker at major ceremonies and at 75 joined a confirmation class at Trinity Episcopal Church. He maintained a close tie to the Republican party and gradually gave his support to the Mitchell-Carey faction. When Matthews was searching for a winner in 1902, who better could be chosen to unite the anti-Simon forces. Matthews knew that Williams at 79 would be compliant to his leadership and at the same time would present to the public a steadfast, kindly, fatherly image that would be respected and trusted.

When Mayor Williams delivered his opening remarks to the new council on July 2, 1902, he commented that the existing charter authorized the council "to prevent and suppress bawdy houses." This was an "unpleasant subject" to George Williams who told the council that it might not be able to suppress "this evil." But, he said, "it is in our power and duty to protect public decency. . . . The cribs on streets between the railroad depot and the hotels and elsewhere on our main streets should be suppressed and their inmates compelled to quit their business or to move into more secluded quarters. . . . If these people would [only] occupy houses that have an air of respectability. . . ."[63]

As to gambling, the mayor had no "utopian schemes contemplated." But he felt that the existing ordinances should be enforced for the "more obviously public games such as faro and roulette." He was instructing his police chief to check "rumors" of police pay-offs.[64] The next week when he spoke to the board of police commissioners, he repeated many of the same words. He wanted "the removal of the vicious class from the prominent streets of the city."[65] George W. Bates was still president but William M. Ladd who had inherited his father's mantle now joined the board in place of Simon's protege, D. Solis Cohen.

These words of direction and advice set the tone of the Williams administration. Respectable behavior, decency and tidy appearance in the "prominent" areas of the city were to be given top priority. If gambling and prostitution could not be banished, they could at least be controlled and be subject to a system of "periodic fines." The city treasury would gain some sorely needed compensation that it would not otherwise receive. Councilman Fred T. Merrill staunchly supported the mayor's policy although he preferred more open regulation and less obvious hypocrisy.

Mayor Williams' council counted nine new faces out of eleven. It was decidedly upper middle class in orientation but not prominent socially in terms of elite club membership or place of residence. Included were a banker, tobacconist, cycle shop owner, building materials executive, manufacturer, meat packer, plumbing contractor, insurance agent, lawyer, and two realtors. The board of public works, presided over by Abbot Mills, was still the most prestigious governmental agency within City Hall. And beginning in November 1902, the board was faced with several franchise decisions that put chairman Mills squarely on the hot seat.

From an examination of the available evidence, one is led to conclude that Abbot Mills, representing the First National Bank — and the Corbett, Failing and Lewis interests — and John C. Ainsworth, representing the United States National Bank — and the Crocker and D.O. Mills* interests of San Francisco for which the bank was agent — agreed between them that immediate action had to be taken to protect their street railway investors. The new city charter which was expected to take effect upon legislative approval in January 1903 contained some provisions that might damage future efforts to sell the companies to eastern investors — an action that Mills had been contemplating for some time. Mills and Ainsworth were the closest of friends,** despite their separate institutional loyalties. The fact that Mills had been chairman of the new city charter commission, which had drafted the revised regulations that were meant to provide greater protection to the public interest, did not seem to deter him from what he felt was his primary obligation: to serve the private interests that he represented. What follows was a classic case of conflict of interest.

In November and December 1902, two of the three major street railways that would be combined into the giant Portland Railway Light & Power Co. in 1906 received new franchises from the city council after approval by the board of public works. The much larger of the two, the Portland Railway Co., was the survivor of the old Markle and Dekum properties. Although it had never been a money maker, under John C. Ainsworth's direction it was beginning to show progress. It was granted a 30 year exclusive franchise with a schedule of compensation payments to the city that began at $1500 a year, moving by steps to $5000 a year after 20 years, and in one jump to $12,000 a year after 25 years.[66]*** The Oregon Water Power & Railway Co., the survivor of the Steel Brothers' East Side properties and in 1902 under the control of the Portland General Electric Co., was

---

*No relation to Abbot Mills.
**Some 20 years later, Abbot L. Mills Jr. would marry Katherine Ainsworth.
***Passed by council on November 24, signed by mayor and given final approval by board of public works on November 25. 1902.

granted a 25 year exclusive franchise, requiring car license fees rather than annual fixed payments.[67]*

On January 9, 1903, the city council approved a new 30 year exclusive franchise for Swigert and Corbett's** City & Suburban Railway Co. with a schedule of payments that ran in steps from $3000 to $9000 a year over a 25 year period, moving to $12,000 a year for the last five years. Mills had voted his preliminary approval along with the other board members*** before the franchise was transmitted to the council.[68] The City & Suburban had been doing reasonably well in recent years. In 1901, the 63 mile system had net earnings of $126,692 on gross earnings of $356,000. It had $2.3 million of indebtedness, with $1.5 million out in stock and $860,000 in bonds. It paid $49,000 to the stockholders and $45,000 to the bondholders.[69]

The very day, January 14th, on which the board of public works received the franchise from the mayor for its own final approval, the legislature was in the process of giving final passage to the new city charter which would take effect immediately upon the governor's approval. Working faster than Mills had anticipated, the senate completed action on House Bill 21 on the morning of the 14th,[70] and then a strange thing occurred. For some reason, mysterious at the time, the measure was never transmitted to the governor's office for his signature. Nothing happened for five days. As it was later revealed, the franchise was not valid until it had received both final board of public works approval and acceptance by the company. It was feared that the governor might sign the new charter legislation before company acceptance of the franchise had been received. Had this mishap occurred, the new charter would have taken precedence over the franchise and the City & Suburban Railway, the largest unit of the future monopoly, would have lost its exclusive 30 year franchise. The telephone lines to Salem must have been busy on January 14th. Boss Jack Matthews may have pulled some legislative strings to ensure that someone did not foul-up the deal. In any case, five days later the House passed a new charter measure, House Bill 101.[71] Two days later, a motion was passed unanimously by the House to

---

*Two franchises were granted: on November 10, 1902 and December 18, 1902.

**Corbett had taken over the First National Bank's interest upon Failing's death in 1898.

***Passed by the council on January 9, 1903, approved by the mayor on January 13; given final approval by the board of public works on January 14, carrying Mills' signature, and accepted by the company on the same day.

withhold H.B. 21 from enrollment for reason of a "defective title."[72] The mystery was now cleared up. On the morning of the 23rd the senate unanimously approved H.B. 101 and it was·rushed to Governor Chamberlain for his signature.[73] Portland now had its new charter and the City & Suburban its new franchise.

Over the next few years, the events of January 1903 would be harshly criticized in the local press, especially in the *Oregon Journal.* City Auditor Thomas Devlin on the other hand, a member of the board of public works, staunchly justified the franchise awards, particularly that made to the Portland Railway Co.[79] The new franchises were necessary, Devlin said, because the old ones were a patch quilt of overlapping ordinances awarded at various times under widely differing conditions. Had the rush to secure their passage not been so frantic, Devlin's case might better have withstood historical scrutiny. At least the street railways henceforth were going to have to pay a reasonable compensation to the city for the use of its streets.

There would continue to be dispute over bridge use fees that on the record seem to have been generously low to the transportation companies. The large number of private wholesale, manufacturing and railroad companies that were awarded spur and sidetrack franchises, continued to receive their privileges without any payment or compensation to the city. John Ainsworth's Pacific States Telephone and Telegraph Co.* received two franchises between 1900 and 1902 without paying any compensation other than providing 39 free phones to the city government.** As the decade advanced, the use and misuse of light and phone poles was to pose recurrent problems for City Hall.

In the late afternoon of the date on which the charter legislation was signed by the governor, the newly authorized executive board held its initial session. Charged with approving all city expenditures and franchise applications, the board as appointed by Mayor Williams included 10 prominent citizens who were active in the business and professional life of the city. Four were members of

---

*Incorporated for business in Oregon, May 11, 1900, with Ainsworth as vice president and treasurer, PST&T was a California based company that had absorbed Ainsworth's Oregon Telephone and Telegraph Co. in 1899. The PST&T's listed capitalization was $15 million. It later became part of the Bell (AT&T) System.

**By 1905, the PST&T was paying $1000 a year for its franchise.

John C. Ainsworth

the Arlington Club: Chairman Whitney L. Boise Jr., lawyer and realtor; William MacMaster, realtor; Charles F. Beebe, merchant; and Abbot L. Mills. The new police commission was a sub-committee of the board and it included Beebe, tobacconist Sig Sichel and Mayor Williams.

Police and general budgetary problems were of immediate concern to the Williams administration. The new charter authorized the city to levy a property tax of 11 mills that would raise $417,000, but it would be awhile before these funds would be available. Meanwhile the police department was operating on a $75,000 budget that was $23,000 less than what had been available in 1893 when the city's population was one-half that of 1903. The 50 patrolmen were being paid less than they had received in 1889. Chief C.H. Hunt, who had been out of office for eight years, was a brave man to assume what must have seemed an overwhelming task. Not only was the force way undermanned, but the jail and station house were in deplorable condition. The new civil service code was expected to improve officer quality, but with a base pay scale of only $1020 a year, first rate candidates were hard to recruit.

The police continued to bear the brunt of much of the public criticism of open town activities. This was not a new condition for Chief Hunt to face. The chief was also attacked by the *New Age* for discriminating against Negroes, especially in vice arrests. In his appointment of Hunt, said the paper, the mayor had made "a big mistake . . . with the best of intentions, of course."[75] Williams was chided by the Portland

257

Municipal Association for running a wide-open town. His friend Dr. Thomas Lamb Eliot wrote him, protesting the mayor's tolerance of corruption.[76]

The Portland Municipal Association, organized in July 1903, was to publish a series of reports over the next four years. In its first broadside, it charged that public gambling was "controlled by a trust in league with city government." Brothels and beer halls were flourishing. All this activity was designed "to loosen out the boys when they came to town."[77] The city was deriving over $7,000 monthly from fines, or as the Association called them, "pay-offs." The Portland Club, on S.W. Fifth and Alder, was reported to have grossed $20,000 in December 1903, "with marked cards."[78]

In his *I Remember Portland,* Laurence Pratt recalled:

> "When I first walked north on Fourth Avenue I was startled to find it bordered with one-and-two-story frame buildings like little shops, each with a window against the sidewalk and a woman seated inside. Over each door was a girl's name — Jennie, Lulu, May, Yvonne, The Favorite, or another. I quickly turned around and walked back to Oak Street. Later, when I had a bicycle, I rode down the street, not so close to those windows, and found the rows stretched for blocks on both sides of the street. At that time women and even young girls wore long skirts, sweeping the sidewalk, or at least below their shoetops. It was a jolt when a girl with a skirt above her knees would venture out of her crib and wave at me as I passed on my bicycle.
>
> The Red Light District spread onto other avenues besides Fourth as one came to Davis and Everett Streets. And though these cribs were all in this part of the city, I saw women stand at the side doors of saloons as far south as Salmon street, accost men as they passed, and lead them in and up stairways. The mayor of Portland at that time was the honorable George H. Williams, former U.S. Senator from Oregon. He had inherited the office from Henry S. Rowe. The open operation of vice must have been supported by influential business interests."[79]

The remaining two years of Williams' term were to prove stormy. The city would make great material strides with office building, street and sewer construction, but scandals would accompany such

258

developments. Mayor George Williams was simply not up to the task; he was a weak political leader. He stood his ground and defended his administration with eloquent speeches, but he never faced the issues directly. He disliked contention and preferred to yield to pressure rather than engage in hostilities.

The business establishment generally supported Williams, but it did so by denying that any serious problems existed as long as respectable, parochial, upper class society could function to its own satisfaction. The energies and monies that might have gone into meeting many of Portland's growing urban needs were instead diverted and invested in the planning and building of the prestigious 1905 Lewis and Clark Exposition. Portland's leaders became prisoners of their own booster propaganda as they prepared to put the city on the world map.

Chapter X

Buccaneers
and Boosters,
1903-1905

1.

Much has been written over the years in praise of the renowned
Lewis and Clark Centennial Exposition which opened its gates to the
public on June 1, 1905.[1] Not only did it "place Portland on the map"
so to speak, but it achieved the greatest financial success of anything
of the sort ever held in Oregon up to that date. Over 2,500,000 visitors
passed through the portals, including 135,000 from east of the Mississippi River.

Guild's Lake, site of the Lewis and Clark Centennial Exposition.

Among landscape architects, art historians and urban planners, the exposition has generally been viewed as a natural outgrowth of the reform oriented "City Beautiful" movement that supposedly received its American launching with the Chicago World Columbian Exposition of 1893.* The slow growing all-encompassing reform impulse in American municipal government at the turn of the century was to give birth to a new professional discipline: the art and science of city planning. The initial emphasis was on aesthetics — visual clean-up and civic design — rather than on humanitarian or social planning. With the Chicago Exposition, however, chief architect Daniel Burnham believed that his proposed lakefront development would add a new and beneficial social dimension to the life of the average Chicagoan by permanently restoring the shoreline to the people. Such was not to be the end result of Portland's shoreline development which was ephemeral. After four and one-half months of providing intense enjoyment and gaiety, most of the buildings were to be dismantled, with the hungry land speculators rushing in, transforming the "beautiful Guild's Lake section" of Northwest Portland into a massive rail yard and industrial park. Unlike Paris which still enjoys its Eiffel Tower on the Champ de Mars, Portland's lone surviving monument, the Forestry Building, once the world's largest log cabin, burned to the ground in 1964, depositing its ashes amid a commercial wasteland.

From an examination of the historical records, one must conclude that the dominant motive behind the 1905 exposition was profit — the money that would be generated in the local economy by the attraction of new residents to Portland. As Lewis Mumford has accurately observed:

> "An expanding economy demanded an expanding population; and an expanding population demanded an expanding city. The sky and the horizon were the only limits. On purely commercial terms numerical growth was synonymous with improvement. The census of population was sufficient to establish a city's cultural rank... "[2]

---

*The Paris Exposition of 1889 had a similar effect on the European continent.

Forestry Building

Seattle's population was fast approaching that of Portland's in 1900, a condition that incited panic and horror in the minds of Portland's business leadership.

The first proposal for a Lewis and Clark Exposition was apparently made as early as November 1895 when Portland citizen Daniel McAllen went to see *Oregonian* publisher Henry L. Pittock who heartily endorsed the idea. There were many like McAllen and Pittock who shared George H. Williams' lofty feelings toward his city. Speaking at the corner-stone laying ceremony for the Chamber of Commerce Building in 1892, Williams had waxed eloquent:

> "When I survey from Portland Heights our newly-formed city and its additions, I am reminded of what I have read about Rome upon her seven hills, with the Tiber rolling between; and it has occurred to me that possibly the high lands on the east side of the Willamette, and the hills behind us on the west side, may become as famous in song and story as the Palatine, Quirinal and Capitoline hills of the 'Imperial City.' Ours are the triumphs of peace, and, irrespective of war, Rome had no advantages over us in country, climate or the sources of wealth and power."[3]

263

With words of advice that few people took literally, Williams proclaimed: "Let it be remembered that material prosperity is not all
that makes a city. The intelligence and morality of the people are
the true and enduring elements of greatness."[4] Had Mayor Williams
and his friends adhered to such precepts 10 years later the exposition
would have assumed a different form.

Not much further happened until Col. Henry E. Dosch gave a
lengthy interview to the *Evening Telegram,* on April 22, 1899. German born, ex-Union Army officer Dosch was well regarded in Portland. Having retired in 1889 from a successful shoe wholesale business he was completing a 10 year term of service as the most prominent member of the Oregon Horticultural Commission. Dosch had
also acted as Oregon's official ambassador to national expositions
held at Omaha, Buffalo, Charleston and New Orleans.

> "In the first place," said Dosch, "it means money — lots
> of money. It must be on a grand scale. In fact, the success
> of the whole thing will depend upon its broadness, and
> unless the people of Portland are prepared to go into it in
> a whole-hearted manner and pull together as they have
> never pulled before, further discussion is useless.
>
> I know that such expositions pay — pay immensely.
> I base my opinion upon my experience and observation
> at Chicago and Omaha, particularly the latter place.
> A real estate man from Silverton the other day said to me,
> 'Colonel, they're coming.' 'Who are coming?' I said, 'Why,
> settlers, to be sure,' he answered. 'A number of families
> have lately settled in our section, and every one of them
> had your cards.'
>
> There is the whole thing in a nutsell. Those people were
> among the thousands who visited the Omaha Exposition
> in 1898, and viewed Oregon's exhibits — and got the
> cards.
>
> The trend of immigration is westward. We are taking a
> new start. In conversation with people who make it their
> business to study the immigration of people, I learn that
> the eyes of the eastern states are turned toward the Pac-
> ific northwest. Prof. Wilson of Boston, who devotes his
> life to studying the causes for the shifting about of
> people and is a noted authority on the subject, predicts
> that in fifteen years the population of the Pacific coast
> states will be doubled. He says, further, that in a hundred

years there will be more people living west of the Rocky mountains than on the Atlantic seaboard.

Now is the time for us to strike. The iron is hot. The organization of our new possessions in the Orient will mark an era in the commercial advancement of the Pacific coast. We have the natural resources, climate and everything else needed but people."[5]

In December 1900 the exposition proposal was enthusiastically endorsed by the young Oregon Historical Society whose director, George Himes, became one of the prime movers of the event. The Oregon legislature followed suit in February 1901 a month after Henry W. Corbett had been elected president of the Exposition Association. At the time that Corbett held the first organizational dinner in May, 3035 investors had already subscribed to stock worth over $417,000. Corbett himself bought the largest block, $30,000 worth. Additional funding of $450,000 was to come from the legislature, and $1,775,000 from the U.S. Congress under Senator Mitchell's prodding.

Among the board of directors were some of Portland's most eminent business and professional leaders: Abbot Mills, as second vice-president and treasurer, Henry E. Reed, as secretary and director of promotion, George W. Bates, Charles E. Ladd, John C. Ainsworth Paul Wessinger, William Fenton, P.L. Willis and Harvey W. Scott who would succeed to the presidency upon Corbett's death in late March 1903.

On the recommendation of Col. Dosch, the Guild's Lake site was chosen in July 1902 amid charges of conflict of interest. Forty-six parcels of swamp land were involved, covering 406 acres, of which 220 were in water. All the parcels were leased except for one which was bought for $6000. Major landholders,[6] who received property tax exemption during the period of their lease, included the Stephen Mead Estate (administered by the Ladd family), Amanda Reed, Simeon's widow who owned the neck of land that jutted out into the lake, the T.J. Cottle Estate, and P.L. Willis, friend of Swigert and Bates and also a member of the board. Standing to gain immensely from the site's development was Robert Livingstone's Scottish American Investment Trust Co. of Edinburgh which owned over 7 blocks of prime residential property on lower Willamette Heights, adjacent to the grounds. Livingstone and Mills were of course close friends and golfing companions. Also pushing strongly for the site were the Portland and City & Suburban Railway companies which had major lines already running to within a block of where the main gate would be located. Indeed, it would be hard to believe that Messrs. Mills, Corbett, Bates, Willis, Ladd and Ainsworth were all totally disinterested parties to the site decision.

Most everyone in the upper echelon of Portland society became increasingly enthusiastic over the prospects that lay ahead. As railroad lawyer and historian Joseph Gaston was to comment from first hand experience: "The very decision to hold the exposition, strengthened every man that put down a dollar for it; and from that very day Portland business, Portland real estate, and Portland's great future commenced to move up."[7]

The plan was apparently patterned after the Columbian Exposition but on a smaller and less pretentious scale. The nationally famed Olmsted Brothers of Brookline, Massachusetts and sons of Frederick Law, provided the general landscape design. In John Olmsted's thinking, and in the minds of some of the city park commission members like Dr. Thomas Lamb Eliot and banker L. Leander Hawkins, the exposition should embody a noble planning ideal that might serve as a model for the city of the future. In fact, Olmsted was hope-

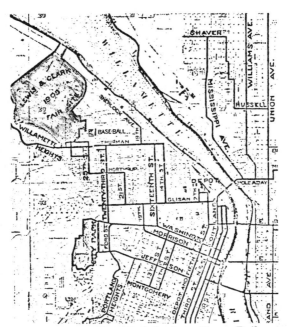

Map showing City & Suburban Street Railway
tracks and Willamette Heights.

267

ful, initially, that the site could be converted to permanent park use after the show was over. But in the minds of Portland's business leadership — including the association's board of directors — such notions were never given serious attention. In his final report to the park board in 1904, Olmsted implied that he already knew what the final decision would be when he wrote: "It is a fair question whether this area may not eventually be dyked and drained and filled and used for manufacturing and other commercial purposes.[8]

Mel Scott, in his thorough study of *American City Planning Since 1890,* has accurately described the feelings held by many Americans, including Portlanders, toward municipal expositions of the early 1900's:

> "If the initial drive was for a city outwardly more pleasing, perhaps it was because Americans needed something more soul-satisfying than trunk sewers, . . . railways, and metropolitan water supply systems to stimulate their local pride and induce them to continue the work of providing the utilitarian essentials of urban growth. . . . They also needed, for their spirits, more parks and playgrounds, and if they could afford them, handsome boulevards, civic centers, and decorative monuments."[9]

Dr. Eliot and his associates had been plugging for more parks and playgrounds for many years. It was fortunate for Portland that he was appointed to the first board of park commissioners, authorized by the legislature and organized by Mayor Rowe in October 1900. Like many American cities, Portland had long been dominated by men of rural background and orientation who could not perceive that as the city grew, nature's presence would be pushed ever further from the urban core. In 1900 unspoiled natural scenery could still be found close at hand. The idea of spending money for parks seemed to many to be impractical and unnecessary. And even as the city population exploded during the early years of the century, the more affluent could always seek natural haven in their exclusive country retreats. In 1902, Portland owned only 136 acres of park land in 10 locations. Compared with Hartford, Connecticut which had 15 percent of its city area dedicated to public parks, Portland had only 1-1/2 percent.

Ironically, it was Dr. Eliot who was responsible for John Olmsted's coming to Portland in the first place, to make a survey of Portland's park potential and to formulate some general plans for future park development. Because of the $10,000 fee involved, Eliot had to devise a joint arrangement to split the costs with the exposition association. Much to the disappointment of the park commissioners, the Guild's Lake site had already been chosen by the time of Olmsted's arrival in May 1903.

> "The Commission put forth a special effort to induce the promoters of the Exposition to adopt one of the parks as a site, or, failing in this, to further some plan by which a new park might be obtained for the city, as part of the outcome of the location and expenditures of the Exposition. It seemed to the Commission that of the many advantages to arise from this celebration, there should be obtained a site which, after use as an Exposition, might with the improvements remain in whole or in large part as a Lewis and Clark Memorial Park, thus insuring a valuable permanent result to the citizens of Portland and the public. Although the site finally adopted is from many points of view an admirable one, it is to be regretted that the ground is almost entirely leased territory, and that most of the improvements will either disappear or revert to private use."[10]

This was a statement of accurate prophecy in 1904. Although the design of the exposition would succeed in stimulating some subsequent interest in city planning among Portland's citizenry, no lasting model would survive in the tradition of Paris, London or Chicago. And even if some of the buildings and landscaping had been preserved, it is doubtful that the combination of Spanish Renaissance and Neo-Classical architecture could have related in any meaningful way to the urban realities and needs of a future American city. As Mumford declared many times, the city of 1905 demanded planning that would at least try to tackle such questions as, how to order business and industry as integral parts of the larger urban scene, or how to structure neighborhoods and family housing within a growing metropolis.

Although the exposition was a lively and luxurious show that was thoroughly enjoyed by all who attended, in terms of furnishing some significant vehicle for meeting basic urban needs it proved useless. It was escapist and cosmetic in character. In keeping with its initial purpose, it did make money; it generated expansive physical growth and it returned a handsome profit to many of the private investors. But it did not produce any lasting investment in the public domain.

In the light of history, it appears that the Lewis and Clark Exposition was a colossal missed chance. It was as important in 1905, as it is in 1976, for a city to own a facility near the urban core to provide a center of varied human activity for all levels of society. The impending development of Portland's downtown waterfront park will hopefully serve such a purpose. By 1907, the only outdoor park which included amusement facilities and that was in easy railway commute to the center of downtown was the privately owned Oaks Park, on the east side of the river adjacent to Sellwood. A similar type of private development was to be constructed atop Portland Heights, at Council Crest. The city was to acquire the 38 acre site 30 years later, clean it up and convert it into one of the most charming small city parks in the Northwest.

Council Crest amusement park, circa 1910.

The Olmsted brothers' final report to the park board received wide publicity in the *Oregonian* in June 1904. As the map reveals, the recommendations were extensive, even radical by 1904 standards. In brief, the report suggested:

> "West of the Willamette River and south of Riverview Cemetery, a large forest reservation, from which an informal picturesque parkway would pass east of Riverview Cemetery, leaving the west bank of the river at Fulton, continue on the hillsides to City Park; thence to MacLeay

MR. OLMSTED'S PLAN FOR PORTLAND'S
PARKS, PARKWAYS AND BOULEVARDS

KEY—
PARKS
AT PRESENT
PROPOSED
PARKS
PROPOSED
PARK WAYS AND
BOULEVARDS

FOREST
RESERVATION

MACLEAY PARK

CITY PARK

Portland
Heights

GOVERNOR
PENOYER
PARK

TERWILLIGER
PARK

FULTON
HEIGHTS

Swan Island

Guild's
Lake

WILLAMETTE
HEIGHTS

Station
Square

Park Square

Reservoir Park

Irvington

Square

Hollada
Park

Hawthorne
Park

Sellwood's Addition

Ross Island

Willamette

University
Bluffs

Columbia Boulevard

Slough

Park; thence along the hillsides to another large forest reservation on the hills northwest of Mountain View Park Addition.

East of the river, a river-bluff parkway from Sellwood, connected by a bridge with the parkway west of the river at Fulton.

Another river-bluff parkway east of the river from a point north of the Oregon Railway & Navigation Company's machine shops to a bluff park west of Columbia University.

A great meadow reservation among the Columbia Sloughs east of the electric railway to Vancouver.

Mount Tabor Park to preserve hill scenery east of the river.

Boulevard from the center of Ladd's Addition to Mount Tabor Park.

Another river-bluff parkway connecting Mt. Tabor Park with Columbia Slough Park.

Ross Island Park would preserve a liberal amount of river scenery.

Swan Island would be a desirable additional reservation of river scenery."[11]

Recognizing that the Guild's Lake area would most likely be developed, the report suggested a plan that would combine a park area on the west with a commercial, dock, railroad area on the east, near the river. But, as with the other proposals, nothing materially was to result from these efforts of Dr. Eliot and John Olmsted. The land in question was too valuable as private investment property to be sacrificed to public use. Would that more of Portland's leaders had shared Dr. Eliot's "vision of the Portland of future generations." He saw the "wisdom and necessity of making liberal provision for a great park system while provision was still possible."[12] Prominent banker L. Leander Hawkins held a similar vision that called for a skyline trail and a scenic driveway through the West Hills that could have been constructed at small expense in 1905.[13] But death was to remove his influential voice within two years after his proposal was published.*

---

*Hawkins (1848-1906) had been president of the Hydraulic Elevator Co., U.S. Electric Lighting & Power Co., Ainsworth National Bank. He was a long-time associate of the Ainsworth family.

Looking east from lower Willamette Heights, to the exposition site and the river beyond.

2.

In rejecting the sound land use proposals of "visionaries" like Olmsted, Eliot and Hawkins, Portland's business-political leadership was pursuing a course of action that was considered normal in most of America's developing urban centers during the early years of the 20th century. In the words of Lewis Mumford:

> "The extension of the speculative gridiron and the public transportation system were the two main activities that gave dominance to capitalist forms in the growing cities. . . . The city . . . was treated not as a public institution, but a private commercial venture to be carved up in any fashion that might increase the turnover and further the rise in . . . values."[14]

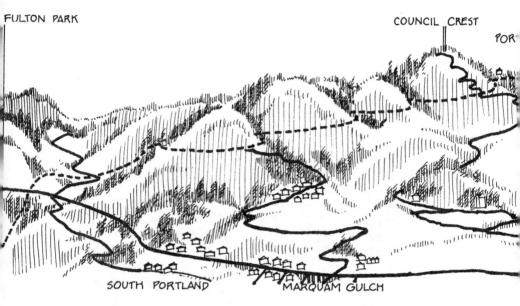

FULTON PARK   COUNCIL CREST
                                                            POR

SOUTH PORTLAND   MARQUAM GULCH

L. Leander Hawkins' plan for a driveway and skyline trail for the Portland
hills. (Reconstruction sketch by Elizabeth Rocchia.)

Mumford's point is clearly illustrated by the events that followed
the awarding of new franchises to the Portland Railway and City &
Suburban Railway companies as described earlier. Banker Abbot
Mills continued to play the leading role. For two years he spent a
major portion of his time putting together the legal and financial
package that was to result in the organization of the giant Portland Consolidated Railway Co. in October 1904. Although the earnings of both railways had been reasonably healthy,* Mills realized
that the companies needed to strengthen their financial position
before a successful merger could be consummated. The City & Suburban stock dividend rate of two percent was too low to make the
securities attractive for sale. Because 1903 was not a good year to
sell railroad bonds in New York, Mills felt he had no alternative but
to plan to issue as much as $2 million in additional City & Suburban
stock and to use the proceeds for purchasing new equipment and

*Net Earnings:	C&S	Pt. Rlwy. [15]
1901	$126,692	$104,336
1902	223,223	119,694

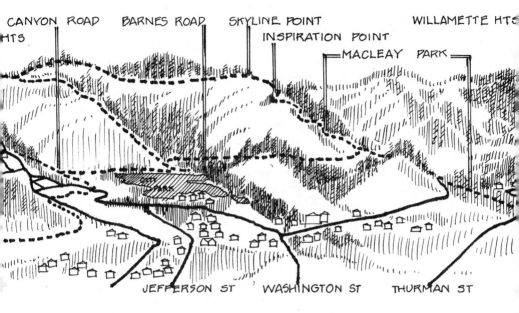

CANYON ROAD   BARNES ROAD   SKYLINE POINT   WILLAMETTE HTS
HTS   INSPIRATION POINT
                                      MACLEAY PARK

JEFFERSON ST   WASHINGTON ST   THURMAN ST

possibly for constructing a new electric generating plant.[16] The major problem facing Abbot Mills, however, was to figure out a scheme "to bail out" the Portland Railway Co. mortgage bondholders, William H. Crocker and Darius Ogden Mills* of San Francisco.

The negotiations were ticklish. Abbot Mills was in almost daily correspondence with his cousin, New York investment counselor and banker, Augustus White. Mills discovered that the Portland Railway Co. was actually a more profitable operation than the statements of earnings indicated. For several years the company had been deducting as operating expenses charges usually listed as fixed by normal accounting procedures. By reducing its listed earnings in this fashion, the company attempted to justify a minimum franchise charge of only $150 a month for use of the Burnside Bridge. When revised operating income figures were published in 1904, the rate was increased to $1000 a month, the same rate that the City & Suburban would be forced to pay for use of the new Morrison Bridge. After nearly 20 years, the public treasury was to receive a reasonable income from its bridge franchises.

---

*D.O. Mills was not related to the Portland banker. The Portland Railway bonded debt was $812,000.

Mills wanted to keep all of the negotiations secret until the final arrangements were settled. He specifically did not want the firm of Moffat and White in New York to issue any circulars showing the current balance sheet and earnings. He was able to convince White that he had the City & Suburban side of the deal well under control, including C.F. Swigert* who was all in favor of issuing more stock, while the nominal president, Tyler Woodward, was opposed. The tentative merger arrangement in March 1904 called for the City & Suburban to acquire the Portland Railway Co. through an exchange of one-third of the existing C & S stock shares for the outstanding Portland Railway mortgage bonds held by W.H. Crocker and D.O. Mills. The newly incorporated Portland Consolidated Railway Co. would then acquire all of the C & S stock through exchange or purchase if necessary. Also in March, plans were being drafted to build a dam, reservoir and generator on the Little White Salmon River, 55 miles away in Washington. Any surplus power generated could always be sold to the Portland General Electric Co. whose expanding needs were rapidly exceeding its generating capacity in 1904. To complete such a project, Mills was aware that the Oregon legislature would have to enact a law to permit power line transmission from Washington to Oregon. Mills was prepared to attend the 1905 session for that purpose.

As final negotiations for the merger began to take shape, Augustus White wrote to his cousin Abbot Mills: "Business is wonderfully facilitated when people have confidence in each other."[18] But Mills' confidence in the Portland Railway outfit was shaken when the California investors revealed that they wanted more than one-third of the total outstanding City & Suburban stock, including any new issue. Mills was prepared to offer no more than 40 percent; if they did not accept, it would be too bad for them as the City & Suburban could survive and operate its own power system as well. Mills was discouraged. He was tired and unhappy with both boards of directors "and their carping criticisms, as if I had been proposing some criminal act."[19] Swigert's uncle Charles Gorrill** of San Francisco, Pacific Construction Co. owner and large stockholder in the City & Suburban, even suggested selling as much as $6 million worth of stock if it would make Crocker and D.O. Mills happier to own considerably

---

*In June 1904, Mills was to write White: "I have every confidence in Mr. Swigert and feel that he will be true to us and our interests."[17]
**Gorrill was described by White as "a well-to-do, elderly Californian."

more shares. This idea was "repugnant" to Abbot Mills; it would result in too small a dividend per share.

To facilitate the merger and at the same time to make it easier for the new company to be sold to eastern investors at some future date, White and his associates began buying up from the minority stockholders some of the existing City & Suburban stock at $80 per share. The majority stockholders were the Failing Estate, the First National Bank of which Mills was now president, the Corbett Estate, Mrs. C.H. Lewis, Henry L. Corbett, Swigert and Gorrill. It was agreed that the Portland Railway bonds would be exchanged for 40 percent of the existing City & Suburban stock plus 40 percent of a new $600,000 offering to be issued at $80 per share. Also contemplated was the sale of an undetermined amount of additional bonds. When Augustus White, who would handle all of the transactions, wrote Mills inquiring about the prospects for selling bonds in Portland, Mills replied that although Portland had a reputation for wealth, to his knowledge "the wealthiest families have little or no ready money at any time, employing every dollar they possess actively."[20]

The Portland Consolidated Railway Co. was incorporated on October 18, 1904 with $5 million of authorized capital stock. Mills was named president, John C. Ainsworth treasurer, and C.A. Dolph and C.F. Swigert vice presidents. Named as general counsel was O.F. Paxton, prominent attorney, former partner of Judge McGinn, original receiver of the former Markle properties, and successor to Ainsworth as president of the Portland Railway Co. In recognition of the vested interest of Portland's two largest banks, the company was to split its banking business between the First National and the U.S. National. One month later, the company was awarded its 30 year exclusive franchise by the city council.* No further consideration was apparently given to the construction of the White Salmon River electric plant as the Portland Railway Co. already held a contract with Portland General Electric that promised to supply adequate power to the Consolidated system for at least two years. By that date, of course, PGE would be merged with the street railway properties to form the Portland Railway Light and Power monopoly.

Abbot Mills had one important task to perform before he could take the next step toward completing the long and arduous assignment that he had undertaken two years previously — to liquidate at max-

---

*As guaranteed by the "events" of mid-January 1903, as described in chapter IX.

imum profit the street railway investments of the First National and U.S. National Banks, and those of the Corbett, Failing, and Lewis families. The previous June he had won election to the state House of Representatives, with the strong support of bosses Jack Matthews and Charles H. Carey. That a man as busy as Mr. Mills would willingly choose to donate one month of his limited time* to serve his state for reasons of civic duty, is indeed a fanciful notion. Mills went to Salem for one reason only and that was to ensure the passage of a law that would benefit the Portland Consolidated Railway Co. Not only that, he went to Salem with the understanding that he would be selected Speaker of the House, an honor that would duly recognize his position as the state's leading banker. He was not to be disappointed.

The laws of Oregon stated that a franchise could not be transferred from one company to another without the consent of the legislature or of the governmental body that had granted the franchise. Mills realized that the existence of such a legal restriction could severely jeopardize the eventual sale of the Portland Consolidated Railway Co. to eastern investors. The properties would not be worth much without a guaranteed 30 year exclusive franchise. Who could predict what a future city council or legislature, or even a mayor or a governor might do?

Senate Bill # 255 was introduced into the February 1905 session by Senator Herbert Holman, a fellow member with Mills of the Waverly Country Club Executive Board. A brief bill, it was passed within three days by the Senate, 19-7, and six days later by the House, 50-10, under the floor leadership of Mills' fellow Arlington Club member, lawyer William T. Muir. Speaker Mills affixed his signature, appropriately, on February 17th, and Governor Chamberlain approved it on February 21st. In essence, the bill stipulated that a franchise of an Oregon corporation may be transferred to another corporation with the consent of the stockholders holding two-thirds of the issued capital stock of the franchised corporation, at a regular or special meeting of said corporation.[21]

The path was now cleared for Augustus White in New York to find a suitable purchaser for the assets of the Portland Consolidated Railway Co. The importance to the company of the Lewis and Clark Exposition's location soon became apparent. In the period from November 1904 to July 1905, the monthly passenger revenues increased 120 percent, from $99,200 to $217,000.[22] The railway properties were

*Especially with his Lewis and Clark Exposition responsibilities.

278

looking more attractive every day. To the utility financier, the real profit was to be made in the manipulation of security prices. The amount of passenger revenue generated obviously had a direct bearing on the utility stock value. It is uncertain whether Augustus White explained to his prospective clients that the huge increase in passenger revenues during the spring and summer of 1905 was due primarily to the influx of visitors to the exposition and not to a normal increase in trade. In any case, White found an interested New York underwriter by the name of Seligman and Co. which in turn found an interested majority stock purchaser by the name of Percy Clark of Philadelphia.

Against the wishes of the Swigert and Gorrill interests who opposed the sale to eastern investors, a new Portland Railway Co. was incorporated under the laws of Oregon on October 13, 1905. The next day the Portland Railway Co. purchased all of the assets of the Portland Consolidated Railway for $6 million.* With 20,000 shares of stock outstanding, and with about $2.5 million in bonded debt,** each share must have realized a sale value of about $160, twice what it had been worth 12 months previously. Some handsome profits resulted*** and the exposition had to share much of the credit. Shortly after its incorporation, Portland Railway issued $3 million in preferred and $4 million in common stock. The whole process was to be repeated, leading to the final merger negotiations that would be inaugurated in 1906 and completed in 1907, resulting in the formation of the $15 million Portland Railway Light and Power Co. Abbot Mills would not be directly involved in this venture. His major task was completed in October 1905. He had fulfilled his private fiduciary responsibilities with extraordinary skill.**** The First National Bank annual dividend rate of more than 30 percent provided adequate testament to his success.[23]

---

*For tax purposes, the Portland Consolidated was only assessed at $850,000.

**Bonded debt included:

Willamette Bridge Railway Co.	$ 100,000
City & Suburban	˙87,000
City & Suburban	1,288,000
Multnomah Street Rlway.	148,000
Portland & Vancouver	100,000
Portland Railway (old co.)	812,000
	$2,535,000

***If Oregon had had a franchise tax like New York, the company would have been taxed on the difference between the total market value of its stocks and bonds and its assessed valuation.

****See Appendix I.

Looking north to Mt. St. Helens. Madison Street Bridge in the foreground.

3.

The election of June 1904 that sent Abbot Mills to the Oregon House of Representatives was as bitter as any that had been held in the previous decade. The Simon regular Republicans and the Mitchell independent Republicans were engaged "in a knockdown, dragout fight," with each faction accusing the other of supporting vice and corruption.[24] Five months earlier, Oregon Water Power & Railway executive, William P. Keady had written Jonathan Bourne Jr: "Matthews is in full swing here, and you know what that means."[25] "Carey and Matthews are to run the machine. . . . You cannot expect good faith in anything controlled by Matthews."[26] According to Keady, Judge Carey was "firmly in Mitchell's camp." Carey would "present his smiling front to the public" while Matthews did the dirty work.[27] In March, the *Oregon Journal* reported that County Clerk Frank S. Fields and Matthews had set an early date for the primary election in an attempt "to harm the Simon faction."[28] According to the *Journal,* the prisoners in the county jail were being registered to vote, using as their residence address the block on which the jail rested.[29]

All of the Matthews-Carey candidates won with a notable exception: honest Tom Word defeated incumbent Sheriff William A. Storey.

Together with District Attorney John Manning, who had been appointed by Governor Chamberlain in 1903, Word would create increasing difficulty for the Matthews-Carey machine, and even for Mayor Williams' administration which would be charged by the grand jury later in the year with malfeasance in office. Unfortunately for the forces of good government, the county judges and attorneys were part of the machine.

The most positive outcome of the election, statewide, was the overwhelming approval of the direct primary amendment to the state constitution, by a vote of 56,285 to 16,354. Because the U.S. Constitution still prevented the direct election of U.S. Senators, the primary amendment had no legal validity *per se*. Senators would still be elected by the legislature. A scheme was devised to make every candidate for the legislature, at the primaries, declare himself on this particular point — to say whether, as a member of the legislature, he would accept as his own, the popular choice for U.S. Senator. The new primary law, therefore, provided that every candidate, in advance of the primary election, should have the privilege of subscribing to one of two pledges: "Statement No. 1," that he would support the popular choice, or "Statement No. 2," that he would consider the popular choice "nothing more than a recommendation." The candidate could, of course, remain silent and refuse to sign either pledge. Public pressure was obviously going to force the great majority of legislative candidates to sign "Statement No. 1" without regard to individual preference.[30]

Jonathan Bourne Jr. worked hard for this change that would help secure his election to the U.S. Senate in 1906. Some years later, Judge Henry McGinn declared: ". . . the Direct Primary law came to us as the result of the most corrupt politics any state has ever known."[31] Prior to that time, said McGinn, anyone could buy a vote for as little as $2.50. The direct primary encouraged the people to speak out against the excesses of corruption that had plagued Oregon political life for over 40 years. Men like Governor George E. Chamberlain and his young state land agent, future governor Oswald West, hoped that the "Oregon System" would stimulate the voters to maintain an enduring interest in public affairs. For too many years, the government had fallen into the hands of politicians like Joe Simon and John Mitchell, or their henchmen, who made it their business to take care of everyone else's business. And "their business" always carried a price tag.

The central problem that the people of Oregon still had to face was the relation of corporate wealth to government. Where profits were

State Land Agent Oswald West.

to be made, the private interest was considered superior to the public interest, especially in Portland during the last two years of Mayor George H. Williams' administration.

Charges of fraud and scandal became increasingly common. The bottom had been left out of the huge Tanner creek sewer. The *Oregon Journal* charged that:

> "Throughout the Tanner creek sewer investigation Mayor Williams uniformly took the side of the contractors against the taxpayers. 'Kickers, knockers, faultfinders' was his designation of the property owners who had the audacity to protest against the acceptance of the sewer. Every possible obstacle was interposed by him to prevent examination of the job, and it was with the utmost reluctance that he finally consented to the removal of Elliott from the office of city engineer. Finally, when the reports of two investigating committees and admissions of Elliott himself no longer left any room to dispute that glaring defects existed in the work, Mayor Williams attempted to have the cost of the repairs advanced by the city, rather than compel the contractor's bondsmen to pay for them.

The cost of these repairs was estimated at nearly $5,000, though it has far exceeded that sum, and Mayor Williams caused an ordinance to be introduced in the council appropriating the amount from the general fund. Only the opposition of a majority of the councilmen prevented this crowning iniquity to the Tanner creek scandal."[32]

Other charges were levelled by the Portland Municipal Association:[33] $52,000 of extra costs had been approved for the new Morrison Bridge without bids; the Front Street fill job had been awarded to the next lowest bidder after the lowest bidder had been supposedly bribed to withdraw; and municipal supply contracts were let to a small clique of political insiders. It was difficult to distinguish "The Beast" from "The Jungle," to use Denver Judge Ben Lindsey's phrase. The resulting public indignation did not seem to bother the principal actors who remained hidden while the audience saw only the shifting of dummies.

The Pacific Bridge Co. was to bear the brunt of many of the accusations directed at the city's public improvement program. It was by far the largest contractor for bridge, landfill and sewer projects, although the Tanner creek fiasco was not its responsibility. Historical investigation has not disclosed any instances of fraud *per se* in the performance of the Pacific Bridge contracts. What has been discovered are cases of interest conflict and slipshod city administration. The company was seldom held to its contract requirements. Bid limits were often exceeded due to specification changes and official completion dates were extended without penalty. Whether such practices constituted a scandal is debatable — they had been permitted for years as normal procedure. The people became aroused when for the first time in the city's history the workings of the system were exposed to public view, particularly in the *Oregon Journal.* Collusion was obviously suspected because the owners of Pacific Bridge were closely tied to the major banking and street railway interests which in turn were well represented on the executive board that had to approve all contracts, revisions and extensions.

The Pacific Bridge Co. was originally a San Francisco based firm, owned by C.F. Swigert's uncle, Charles Gorrill. At some point in the mid-1890's its main office was apparently moved to Portland — the company's books and city directories are unclear in this regard. Apart from building bridges, the company contracted with the city to execute an enormous landfill that stretched from Sullivan's Gulch in the north to the Hawthorne Bridge in the south, and from the river

283

to east Ninth Avenue. Over a period of two years four million cubic yards of sand and gravel were dredged from the river and spread over portions of 27 streets. Much of the area had been a frog pond and swamp over which bridges had been built to carry the through traffic. In some sections, the fill depth was 29 feet.*

During the depression that followed the panic of 1893, the company had to seek business in other regions of the Northwest, mostly in the state of Washington. Two projects in the Puget Sound area resulted in near bankruptcy. The company was forced to reorganize in September 1901 and it borrowed heavily from the First National Bank, George W. Bates and Lee Hoffman. It also borrowed extensively from a new company established by Charles Gorrill in San Francisco, the Pacific Construction Co. As collateral for the initial bank notes, Swigert put up $45,000 in City & Suburban Railway stock.

From 1895 to 1905 the financial affairs of Pacific Bridge and City & Suburban were so completely intermingled that it is almost impossible for an historical researcher to sort them out. Funds were continually shifted from one bank account to another. But one fact is undisputed: Swigert enjoyed a full line of credit with the First National Bank, a major stockholder in the City & Suburban and the chief source of loans for Pacific Bridge. To make matters more confusing, all of the 20 large projects (excluding the East side land fill) undertaken by Swigert from 1901 to 1906 totalling over $350,000, were bid by Pacific Construction of San Francisco.** Pacific Bridge ended up performing the work and sending half of the profits to Pacific Construction. Needless to say the local press had a difficult time reporting accurately on who got what from whom and where when Pacific Bridge was involved.

Pacific Bridge benefited from the city performance bond requirements. For larger projects over $10,000, the bond amount was $5000 plus 25 percent of the improvement cost. Small contractors were automatically excluded. Furthermore, Pacific Bridge always bid for more projects than it could handle, thus it was never able to complete a job by the date stipulated in the contract. This procedure allowed the company to use its large backlog of signed city contracts as collateral for its bank loans. All of the expenses for a given project were covered by a loan, to be repaid upon completion of the job. It was a beautiful

---

*The total amount of fill would have equalled 1/35th of all the material excavated from the Panama Canal. The cost of the project was in excess of $1.3 million.

**The largest contract was for the Irvington Sewer, $152,500 (1905).

East side fill area.

East side frog pond and swamp, looking past the O&CRR to the docks and beyond to Portland Heights.

system. The company could undertake an unlimited number of projects with minimal capital reserves. The City & Suburban tracks were used to transport equipment and supplies to the various construction sites at no additional cost to the traction company and at great saving to the construction company. No competitor could bid successfully against a set-up like this. And of course Abbot Mills' First National Bank was pleased. Each transaction was a source of additional profits. Considering the political clout that Swigert and Mills possessed, the chances of either the city council or the executive board ever upsetting the arrangement were slight indeed.* The job would eventually be completed, usually in a thorough manner, and everyone would get paid.

The case of the new Morrison Bridge contract is perplexing. The Portland voters approved the sale of $400,000 of bridge bonds in June 1903. The 15 submitted bids ranged from $277,000 to $410,000. Pacific Construction's plan # 1 was chosen, for $331,343.[35] The executive board felt this to be the best plan for the type of construction desired by the city engineer. On January 8, 1904, one month after the contract was signed, the company was authorized to substitute steel stringers for wooden stringers, at an additional cost of $37,170. On executive board member Rodney Glisan's motion, the plan was approved without mention of any bid.[36] In November 1904, waiting rooms were added, for $7985, again without bid. In January 1905, the council hired W.C. Elliott as the Morrison Bridge inspector, for $150 a month. Elliott had just been fired as city engineer for incompetence and suspected fraud in the Tanner creek sewer scandal episode. In February 1905, Pacific Construction submitted a claim to the executive board for $66,626, to cover the design changes and additional construction. The board agreed to pay $58,000 and to keep the remainder in reserve until the bridge was completed.[37]

An examination of the record raises some interesting questions about the whole bidding procedure. Did Pacific Construction anticipate the design changes before submitting the original bid? If the

---

*In May 1909 Mayor Harry Lane was to veto council approval to pay Pacific Construction $3640 as its final payment for a job that was completed 18 months beyond the contract limit. Lane said: "We fine the small man and forgive the big one." Pacific Construction, or Bridge, Co. was accused of receiving $250,000 worth of contracts they knew they could not fulfill on time. The council was to override Lane 10-3 after councilman George Baker praised the company as "a public benefactor" entitled "to a little consideration."[34]

company knew that it could secure subsequent approval for the steel stringers, it could well afford to run the risk of submitting a low bid. When a council member requested an opinion from City Attorney L.A. McNary as to the legality of the whole procedure, the council was informed that the legislative act authorizing the executive board to build the bridge, with subsequent voter approval, granted the board very broad powers, independent of ordinary charter provisions. There was no need, said McNary, for the executive board to solicit bids for amounts over $250.[38]

Cases of apparent interest conflict, like this one, did not seem to bother the city fathers. No specific laws were actually being broken as long as the ordinances were not applied literally. Politics, after all, provided the machinery for promoting private economic interests and using political influence was part of the game. As Harvey Scott editorialized in September 1904, "the city of Portland has managed to get on all these years in a steady, plodding sort of way, facing problems with soberness, resolution and sacrifice as they arrive."[39] In truth, the only real sacrifice that was obvious was that of the public interest. The railroads were never refused requests for street easements in order to construct side tracks although the city continually petitioned them to repair the streets on which their existing tracks were built. Mayor Williams recognized no conflict in the city awarding an insurance contract to a company in which he was financially interested. As a matter of fact, councilman John P. Sharkey, one of Portland's largest realtors residing on the East side, approved the award of the city hall's fire insurance coverage to the Orient Insurance Co. of which he was the resident agent.[40]

Portland, as was noted earlier, was the only large city in the country with no meat inspection code. A month before Mayor Williams left office, he vetoed an ordinance regulating the slaughtering of animals by providing for an official meat inspector. The ordinance was "complicated," declared Williams. It was "unnecessarily burdensome and expensive to those engaged in furnishing meat to the people of this city." Of course he failed to note that the company that would have been most adversely affected was the Union Meat Co., owned by council president and long time Williams crony, Louis Zimmerman. Williams continued: "There are too many unnecessary regulations upon meat dealers. . . . I do not believe that as a general rule the meat dealers of Portland are inclined to sell diseased or unwholesome meats to the people. . . . Self-interest . . . would induce them not to engage in that kind of business."[41] Although Upton Sinclair had yet to publish *The Jungle* which made even President Theodore Roosevelt sick to his stomach, the mayor was out of touch with reality and the council knew it. With Zimmerman abstaining, the council voted 8-0 to override the veto. Some limited progress had been achieved.

4.

The greed for private profit at public expense that had characterized so much of Portland's early history was dramatically illustrated by the disclosures of the timber fraud trials which began on November 21, 1904. Although the fraudulent practices themselves had no direct bearing on the physical shaping of the city, the fact that the trials took place in Portland and involved a large number of prominent Oregon leaders, makes the narration of the story essential to an understanding of the code of ethics that dominated much of Portland's business and political life in the early 1900's.

Before special U.S. prosecutor Francis Heney was through, he was to secure 33 convictions out of 34 indictments. Included in the long list would be Senator John H. Mitchell, Congressman John N. Williamson from eastern Oregon, U.S. Attorney John Hall, former U.S. attorney and state senator Franklin Pierce Mays, state Senator Robert A. Booth of the Booth-Kelly Lumber Co., former U.S. deputy surveyor, Henry Meldrum and Stephen A.D. Puter, "The King of the Oregon Land Fraud Ring."[42] Congressman Binger Hermann from southern Oregon was indicted but escaped conviction on a technicality. Thomas B. Walker and Charles A. Smith,* wealthy Minnesota lumbermen and the earliest and biggest crooks of them all, were not indictable due to the expiration of the statute of limitations. Numerous others won their freedom in exchange for turning state's evidence. And literally hundreds more from all over the state should have been indicted had the government provided the time and resources to prosecute the cases effectively.

Writing in the March 1905 *Bulletin* of the Portland Chamber of Commerce, president William D. Wheelwright declared sadly: "We

---

*Walker founded the famed Walker Gallery of Art in Minneapolis. Smith founded the C.A. Smith Lumber & Manufacturing Co. which became the Coos Bay Lumber Co. now owned by the Georgia Pacific Co.

are . . . witness [to] a spectacle of public and private rottenness that is almost without precedent in the annals of the country."[43] Wheelwright believed that the disclosures constituted "a moral indictment" of Oregon's voters. And then he went on to state that "one of the remarkable features of the present situation is the absence of a general sense of humiliation. . . . We go about our business, we talk of the increasing prosperity of our state and city" as if nothing at all had happened. (The time was three months before the Lewis and Clark Exposition.) "How has this come about?" Wheelwright asked. "The answer to the question," he concluded, "is that this state of affairs is the result of carelessness and indifference on the part of the businessmen of this community."[44] Oregon needed the public service of trustworthy businessmen who cared, and the chamber membership should provide them.

The answer to the question was obviously much more complex. Mr. Wheelwright* was an honorable businessman who was sincerely interested in the forces of good government. But like many of his ilk, he tended to blame the bribe receiver and the voters who elected him, rather than the bribe giver and the system that created him. Lincoln Steffens saw the dimensions of the problem far more realistically when he blamed the railroads. "They . . . got lands from the government to help them finance their schemes for the development of the state. They also turned grafters. And this, the inevitable result of grants and grafts, was a pity, for it turned good, great enterprising men into grafters. . . . To get their grafts, and keep them and get more, the grafters have to go into politics and corrupt the government. . . . Oregon . . . was only one state . . . in the development of the System: a system of corruption, by vice and railroads . . ."[45] Steffens concluded the first of his series of articles with the arresting statement: "Bad politicians are mere agents of good businessmen."[46]**

According to Stephen Puter who was personally acquainted with most of the fraudulent transactions that had been conducted since 1890:

---

*Wheelwright was president of the Pacific Export Lumber Co. According to one who remembers him, "he was a great big man in a white suit."

**Corporate officials who have recently been charged with company payoffs to foreign governments would say: "corporate bribes are mere practices of good businessmen." The former Chairman of the Lockheed Corp. recently said: "I didn't do anything wrong. . . . We did it playing the rules of the game as they were then." Daniel J. Haughton blamed the system and not himself. "I went out and increased profits."[47]

"Thousands upon thousands of acres, which included the
very cream of timber claims in Oregon and Washington,
were secured by Eastern lumbermen and capitalists, the
majority of whom came from Wisconsin, Michigan and
Minnesota, and nearly all of these claims, to my certain
knowledge, were fraudulently obtained."[48]

If bribery was necessary to secure a city franchise, then land fraud
was justified to acquire large timber holdings. The Timber and Stone
Act (1878) was designed to save the public lands, not for the large operators, but for small people who wanted small holdings. Shortly after
his arrival in Oregon late in 1903, Francis Heney had the system explained to him by Portland railroad attorney William D. Fenton

at a small dinner party. "So you see, Mr. Heney, it is bad laws* that make men — hum, well, let us say, that make such irregularities necessary." According to Heney, Charles H. Carey nodded his approval. Heney exploded: "You men corrupt all you touch."[49]

Here were two of Portland's leading attorneys and future presidents of the Oregon Historical Society, condoning breakage of the law and debasing themselves in the process. Of course Carey had had long experience with this kind of activity. He was also chief Portland counsel for the Northern Pacific Railroad which received over 57 million acres of land from the public domain. Carey's law partner was F. Pierce Mays who was to be convicted of fraud and perjury. It would be naive to assume that Carey knew nothing of his colleague's shady dealings. William D. Fenton was the chief Portland counsel of the Southern Pacific Railroad, probably the biggest briber in Western American history. The S.P. was reputed to own over 70 billion feet of standing timber in Oregon, most of it legally acquired, but not to be used for the purposes for which it was granted. Carey and Fenton were to be two of the leading defense lawyers during the course of the trials.

Puter related one amusing confrontation that was to occur in 1906 during Mays' trial:

> "At one stage of his impassioned address to the jury, Mr. Heney was interrupted by Judge Fenton, and the Government prosecutor retorted rather belatedly:
>
>> 'It doesn't make any difference, Mr. Fenton, before I get through I will skin you from the top of your head to the soles of your feet.'
>>
>> 'If you do,' responded Fenton with equal warmth, 'I am willing to leave my hide in the jury box where I have six personal friends.' "[50]

According to Puter, Fenton immediately realized the unfortunate nature of his response. The jurors, whose integrity had just been questioned, sat in the box and scowled. As it turned out, Heney did

---

*Fenton, along with most of Portland's successful corporate lawyers like C.H. Carey, believed the Timber Stone Act to be a bad law because, if honestly applied, it would prevent the amassing of large timber tracts by the big operators.

skin Fenton and Mays was convicted following the longest of all the timber fraud trials.

The Northern Pacific Railroad which had come under the control of the James J. Hill interests of St. Paul, Minnesota in 1894, set the pattern of speculative greed that was to be copied by the lesser folk. Along with the other western railroads, the Northern Pacific had benefited from a federal subsidy that granted 20 square miles of public land for each mile of track laid down. The public domain received by the Northern Pacific amounted to a strip up to 40 miles wide, running all the way from the Missouri River to the Pacific Coast, including sections of untimbered mountain peaks. In June 1897, Congress passed the Forest Reserve Lieu Act which permitted the exchange of lands situated in a forest reserve for unsurveyed government lands elsewhere. When Congress later passed the Rainier Mountain Forest Reserve Act, under pressure from the Hill interests, it turned out that the Northern Pacific owned nearly a million acres within the preserve. The Northern Pacific was thereby authorized to select a million acres of choice government timber lands in Washington and Oregon, giving in exchange thousands of worthless timber and barren mountain acreage that was in the Rainier Reserve.

The railroad kept about 500,000 acres for itself, sold 200,000 to speculators for $8 an acre and transferred 260,000 acres to the Weyerhaeuser Syndicate for $6 an acre. By 1908, the Northern Pacific lands in Oregon, received through the exchange, were to be worth over $100 an acre, or $32 million.[51]* The Weyerhaeuser Syndicate proceeded to purchase over half a million more acres from Northern Pacific Grant lands outside of the reserve and over a million and a half acres from James J. Hill's other railroad, The Great Northern. By the time that Frederick Weyerhaeuser died in 1914, Hill's close of timber and be worth a personal fortune of around $300 million.[52]**

The federal government was not quite as generous to the individual settler as it was to the railroad corporation. To encourage settlement in the West, the Homestead Act of 1862 had granted free to each

---

*In his published account of the frauds, Puter actually recorded the location of the 200,000 acres of surveyed lands picked up by the N.P. in the Roseburg and Oregon City Land Districts.

**Today, the largest private landowner in Washington is the Weyerhaeuser Co. with 1.7 million acres. The second is the survivor of Hill's empire, the Burlington Northern Railroad.

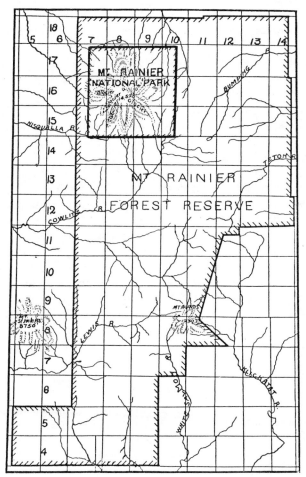

Map of the Mt. Rainier Forest Reserve, showing the position of the Mt. Rainier National Park,
which was created for the special benefit of the Northern Pacific Railroad Company,
that the Hill corporation might be enabled to exchange its worthless holdings for the cream of creation.

settler a one-quarter section of 160 acres with the understanding that the grantee would live on the land for five years. After 14 months, however, the settler could purchase the land for $1.25 an acre. The Timber and Stone Act of 1878 raised the price to $2.50 and modified the residence requirements.

Against a tradition of massive land speculation long established in American history, it did not take much imagination for aspiring lumber barons to sense the profit that could be realized by securing as many as possible of these individual claims and combining them into large contiguous tracts. If one had to resort to fraud and bribery, well, those were "the rules of the game." From Portland and Albina carloads of "settlers" were transported to the various land offices where the dummy applications were filed for sections that had been carefully chosen by Puter and his friends with the connivance of the federal and state surveyors. The land fraud ring did not confine its activities to the federal domain. Oregon's school reserve lands were also plundered, that is until Governor George Chamberlain and Oswald West arrived on the scene. Once the bogus applications were approved, each settler could expect a $200-$300 pay-off in return for the settler's copy of deed. Agents like Puter and Pierce Mays then sold the fraudulent claims to the timber companies and took their commission. The federal and state land office officials were bribed to process the dummy applications quickly, before they handled the bona fide ones. While Binger Hermann was commissioner of the U.S. Land Office in Washington from 1897-1903, he was reputed to have approved thousands of these bogus claims for a price. Mitchell was to be convicted of accepting $2,000 from Puter to grease the bureaucratic machinery in Washington.

It was a sad commentary on the American political and legal system that such thoroughly corrupt characters as Mitchell and Hermann could get away with as much as they did for so long. As early as 1877, San Francisco lawyer Hall McAllister had written Judge Deady that Hermann was a crook. "I told Hermann to leave California because I saw that the Penitentiary was his sure destination — and I preferred, on his family and his account, that he should go to the Pen — of some state other than California."[53] By sneaking into a Portland press photograph alongside President Roosevelt in 1903, Hermann got himself re-elected to Congress. He never did make it to the penitentiary.*

As early as 1903, Secretary of the Interior Ethan Allen Hitchcock had begun to receive tips from Oregon: from the governor's office and from disgruntled bribers who had not been dealt a fair hand. He ordered a quiet investigation and borrowed the famous Secret Service agent William J. Burns from the Treasury Depart-

---

*Born in Maryland in 1843, Hermann came to Oregon in 1859; elected to the state legislature in 1866, state Senate 1868-71; deputy collector of internal revenue for southern Oregon, 1868-71; U.S. Land Office in Roseburg, 1871-3; member of Congress 1885-97, 1903-7; U.S. Land Commissioner 1897-1903. Died in 1926.

Francis J. Heney.

ment. It was not long before Burns had enough evidence to move the Roosevelt administration to take action. The man chosen to direct the probe was Francis J. Heney, a fighting Irishman who had already earned a celebrated reputation as a crime busting special prosecutor in the Arizona Territory. From the very moment that Heney's appointment was announced Oregon's leading politicians and lawyers put every possible obstacle in his path. Senators Charles Fulton and John Mitchell made speeches of protest on the U.S. Senate floor, but to no avail. President Roosevelt announced that he strongly supported the appointment.

Heney and Burns both arrived in Portland together; Heney to work the upper and Burns the nether regions of the business-political world. It took almost a year of relentless investigation before the first indictments were brought, but once the show started on November 21, 1904 the machinery of justice moved swiftly and devastatingly. As William P. Keady wrote to Jonathan Bourne Jr. on January 3, 1905: "The two grand juries in operation are shaking up the political bed rockers and the local machine is gone — with a big 'G'."[54]

Senator Mitchell was summoned from Washington to testify before the grand jury. On his return to the Senate on January 6th, his colleague Senator Fulton, one of the most skillful influence peddlers in Oregon's history, called upon him to convey the confidence and sympathy of his fellow senators. "Mitchell is being outrageously persecuted," declared Fulton vehemently.[55] A few days later, Keady again wrote Bourne: "The machine is done."[56] Mitchell made the mistake of

The late United States Senator John H. Mitchell, of Oregon. Sketched from life during the famous trial by Harry Murphy, the gifted Oregonian cartoonist

attacking Puter openly, whereupon Puter, who had already been convicted but not sentenced, went straight to Heney with the damaging evidence. On February 1st Senator John H. Mitchell was indicted for bribery and perjury. Naturally, Bourne, Keady and Simon were gleeful. Keady wanted Bourne to return from Massachusetts "to help push the downfall of the Matthews machine." According to Keady, Abbot Mills was being mentioned by the "Matthews people . . . who claim that Mills will run as their candidate."[57]

Unbeknown to Keady, Matthews was about to get the official ax. It did not take Heney too long to realize that if he was going to obtain convictions, he would have to give the federal court house a thorough cleansing. He had forced the removal of U.S. Attorney John Hall a few months after his arrival. Heney himself was appointed Acting U.S. Attorney in addition to his special prosecutor's role. Hall was indicted four days after Mitchell. The next major obstacle was U.S. Marshall W.F. "Jack" Matthews, the Republican boss of Oregon. In order to be assured of honest, "unfixed" juries, Matthews would have to be dismissed because impanelling juries and serving subpoenas were his major responsibilities. Heney was forced to carry his fight to a meeting of lawyers in Roosevelt's cabinet and right on up to the President himself. Fulton had been engaged in a full

C.J. Reed, Oregon's new United States Marshal.

scale intrigue in Washington to undermine Heney in support of Matthews. After this victory, Heney had to exert similar pressure within the Roosevelt administration to force the transfer of the recently appointed Oregon Federal Judge, W.W. Cotton. An able lawyer, Cotton had been the chief Portland counsel for the Union Pacific Railroad and Heney did not trust his impartiality.

In seeking a replacement for Matthews, Heney gave serious consideration to a man whom he had met previously through his membership in the Bohemian Club of San Francisco, one Charles Jerome Reed, or C.J. as he was known to his friends. Heney's wife and Mrs. Reed had already formed a close friendship. Reed had good credentials. An insurance agent by trade, he was the son-in-law of the late Henry Green, the founder of the Portland Gas Co., and owner of the luxurious Cedar Hill estate. He had never been involved in partisan politics although he had always been a dissident member of the establishment. Known as a great wit with a sarcastic tongue, Reed nevertheless was accepted in Portland society and had maintained a long time membership in the Arlington Club. When Reed accepted Heney's offer in May 1905, he was denounced as a traitor to his class and ostracized socially and financially. He did not set foot in the club again for several years, or until the day that he took Lincoln Steffens on a personally guided tour and showed him "the crowd that got the timber" sitting around the dining room table.

There was no question that Reed took a real beating from the Portland establishment.[58] His courage in the face of such obstacles made an indelible mark on his young son John who was to become one of the first American journalists to support the Russian Revolution, and the only American to be buried within the Kremlin walls. In the two year period following his removal from office by the Taft Administration, C.J. Reed's financial and physical health deteriorated rapidly. And son John was making a reputation for himself as a nonconformist, the antithesis of the worthy Portlander.[59] When John, called Jack by his family and friends, wrote Roderick MacLeay to thank him for paying his father's delinquent Arlington Club bill, MacLeay noted on the letter that Jack was "a radical of the worst sort."[60]* The Portland establishment had pronounced final judgment. When C.J. died in 1912, Jack blamed the people of Portland for killing his father. He made "a silent vow to justify his death."[61]

5.

In the spring of 1905, Portland was caught in the swirl of two conflicting currents. One, embodying energy, confidence and hope, was generated by the city's boosters in preparation for the June 1st opening of the exposition. The other, combining elements of fear, anger and despair, was a direct consequence of the timber fraud trials. Facing an uncertain future, the timber buccaneers were predicting the end of the free, careless era when forests were cheap and the fast growing West was crying for more and more lumber; when lumbermen had only to set up their mills, slash down their forests, and bank all the proceeds. To make matters worse, the Republican party machinery, which the timber industry had helped to operate for many years, had broken down and was stuck in a state of limbo.

The survivors of the Mitchell, Carey, Matthews forces were searching desperately for viable candidates. At the municipal level, 82 year old Mayor George H. Williams was persuaded to run again, in Keady's words, "as a candidate of what is left of the machine."[62] Referring to federal and state offices, Andrew C. Smith** reported: "Carey, Matthews and the machine crowd join the multitude in roll-

---

*MacLeay would be Arlington Club President in 1913.
**Smith was a wealthy physician, active in Republican politics, a mining partner of Bourne's and president of the Hibernia Trust Co.

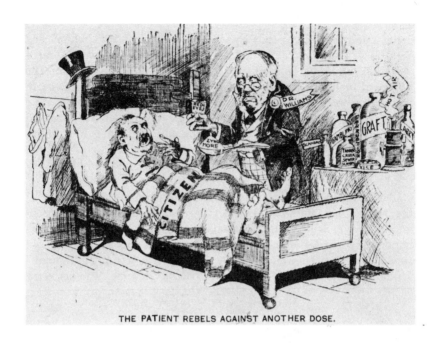

THE PATIENT REBELS AGAINST ANOTHER DOSE.

ing up their eyes in surprise and horror at the developments in regard to Mitchell, and at the same time to be veneering themselves with such thin films of decency as Mills, Linthicum, Ayer (hot air at that) and at the same time holding out bouquets to Wilcox, Fenton and Scott."[63]

The Democrats, with the support of a splinter group of Republicans, nominated Dr. Harry Lane for mayor. Lane was a prominent local physician, grandson of famed Oregon pioneer General Joseph Lane, and a strong environmentalist who had not participated actively in partisan politics. He officially opened his campaign on May 24th with a pledge of "integrity in office." Delivering the keynote speech to 600 eager listeners, 400 of whom were Republicans, Lawyer John Gearin* foreswore any words of personal abuse that might be directed against Williams. "George Williams is an old friend of mine of 30 years standing," declared Gearin, "a man of winning personality, guileless as a child, but he's a foxy old grandpa just the same. . . . He has not been a bad mayor, he's not been a mayor at all."

---

*Gearin was a prominent Democrat, partner in the Dolph, Mallory, Simon firm, and was to be appointed to the U.S. Senate to succeed Mitchell, 1905-1907.

Referring to charges that the Williams administration had used $80,000 in gambling and vice fines "to beautify the city," Gearin asserted: "Hear it! This $80,000, stolen by the gamblers from the homes of foolish men in Portland, or perhaps wrung from the earnings of the poor unfortunate girls who were compelled to pay to their masters the price of their shame — this money Mayor Williams and his executive board took to beautify the city . . . Didn't they realize that every one of those $80,000 was moist with the tears of some mother weeping because the husband and father had gambled away the family's food and clothing money."[64]

George Williams opened his campaign with a stirring defense of his record. He blamed his executive board for the licensing of gambling which he called "a temporary expedient." Asserted Williams: "The board had a secret meeting without my knowledge and consent in which they decided to try this system of fining gamblers." Williams declared that he was tired of being "hounded and persecuted."[65]

"That's the Stuff."

THE GREAT DEMOCRATIC QUARTET GETS READY TO TAKE EVERYTHING IN SIGHT

The newspapers took predictable positions. In supporting Lane, the *Journal* saw the major issue of the campaign as one of good government versus indifferent government, of the rule of right and decency versus that of special privileges.[66] Two days before the election, the *Oregonian* castigated the *Journal* as "the organ of plutocracy.... The plutocratic magnates, ... professed Republicans ... placed their paper in the hands of a couple of Bryan Democrats." Harvey Scott singled out for scorn, "the group of Republican bankers, politicians and monopolists who are running a Democratic newspaper."[67] Scott could never bring himself to accept Republicans who supported Democrats. "The Democrats are a minority party here and can't elect a Mayor except on false pretenses. . . . The most important political office in the state is the office of Mayor of Portland. . . . The allegations against the administration of Mayor Williams are mostly of a trifling nature. Such as are serious, alleged by the grand jury in its published report, in no way or degree affect him. . . . Williams has had to carry the odium of the Matthews machine."[68]

From reading these opinions by the *Oregonian* editor, it is hard to believe that he could have been in full possession of his wits. For a man, long honored in the community and president of the Lewis and Clark Exposition whose doors had just opened, to print such balderdash that totally defied the truth and historical record,* must have left a lot of Portlanders speechless. It proved of little help to Williams. In a predominantly Republican city, Democrat Harry Lane won election on June 5, 1905 by 1217 votes. Scott was to admit some time later that Lane's victory was due to the desire of many Republicans to "get rid of Matthews."[69] The combination of the Williams administration and the timber fraud trials proved to be Portland's "Watergate." Despite the excitement of the exposition, the voters had had enough. They now had an honest mayor and an honest governor, and in John Gearin they would acquire at least one honest U.S. Senator.

Shortly before assuming office, Mayor-elect Lane received a thoughtful letter from prominent real estate investor, Edgar Quackenbush:

> "Never in the history of our city have these things [referring to vice and corruption] been as open, flagrant, shameless, and even virulent as for the past three years or so. Their roots seem to have struck deeper and reached out further into the social life of the community than ever before."[70]

The establishment's final judgment was rendered by General Charles F. Beebe, for three years a leading member of the executive board and a commissioner of police. At the last executive board session of Williams' term, Beebe spoke from his heart:

> "The hour has arrived . . . [The experience has been for each of us] . . . his highest privilege to serve in this intim-

---

*Particularly considering his past relationship with people like Matthews.

ate and confidential capacity the Mayor whose name
more than that of any other occupant of the city's executive chair, has shed lustre on the city's name and cloth-
ed its traditions with honor and renown. . . . It is with pro-
found regret that this close association is about to be
dissolved."

Brigadier General Charles F. Beebe.
(Organized Oregon Brigade.)

Beebe went on to restate the "close" and "intimate relations" that
had existed between "the chief and the cabinet." Beebe had obviously
chosen to overlook Williams' attempt the previous month to blame
the executive board for the decision to exact fines from the vice and
gambling interests. Possibly in that one instance, relations had not
been so intimate. Beebe spoke of the "trying service" of the board
members, involving "unremunerative self-sacrifice and unappreciat-
ed effort." It had been, assured Beebe, "a labor of love." Beebe concluded his eulogy with an expression of great appreciation "to our
venerated and distinguished and beloved chief. . . . His ripe old age
is crowned with honor."[71] As a final gesture, the executive board
presented "The Grand Old Man" with a library chair.

General Beebe's tuneless "requiem" was probably fitting, albeit somewhat pathetic. The old days had come to an end — the period in Portland's history when business and politics were close, intimate activities connected by long established family and social ties. Harry Lane was the first East side resident to be elected mayor. The city would never be quite the same again. Popular government, whatever its pitfalls and weaknesses, was here to stay. The power center was shifting. There would be new buccaneers and boosters but from a different social class.

Chapter XI

The People, Nature and Dr. Lane, 1905-1907

1.

At the time of the First World War, knowledgeable Portlanders would often look back over the previous two decades and date events in terms of those occurring "before Doc Lane was Mayor" or "after Doc Lane was Mayor."[1] Regardless of how one appraised Doc Lane's administration, few could disagree that the period was one of turbulence and excitement, marked by conflicting social forces and philosophies of government. It was also the period of Portland's most explosive population growth: over 80 percent in four years.* As the Chamber of Commerce reported in March 1906, "Portland is at present the Mecca for tourists and large investors."[2]

The city was receiving a plethora of national publicity apart from the political writings of Steffens, Hendrick and Baker. In the *Overland Monthly,* Frederick A. Marriott described "Portland, the Pearl of the Pacific" as a "thoroughly metropolitan city in appearance and in conveniences. . . . Portland has attracted to it men of great wealth, wide business experience and of enterprise. This is seen in the rapid growth in the numerical strength and in the self-evident fact that scarcely anywhere will so much individual wealth be found in a community of the same population."[3] Of particular interest to potential investors was Portland's reputation as a city of substance, "both as to structures and commercial credit."[4] As Marriott stated the case,

*From 110,839 to 207,214. The city boundaries increased by 30 percent.

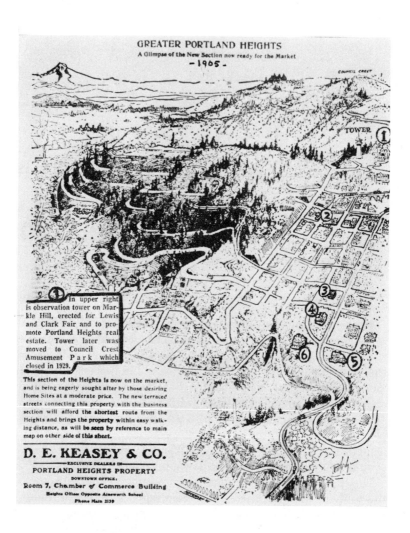

GREATER PORTLAND HEIGHTS
A Glimpse of the New Section now ready for the Market
-1905-

In upper right
is observation tower on Markle Hill, erected for Lewis
and Clark Fair and to promote Portland Heights real
estate. Tower later was
moved to Council Crest
Amusement Park which
closed in 1929.

This section of the Heights is now on the market,
and is being eagerly sought after by those desiring
Home Sites at a moderate price. The new terraced
streets connecting this property with the business
section will afford the shortest route from the
Heights and brings the property within easy walking distance, as will be seen by reference to main
map on other side of this sheet.

D. E. KEASEY & CO.
EXCLUSIVE DEALERS IN
PORTLAND HEIGHTS PROPERTY
DOWNTOWN OFFICE:
Room 7, Chamber of Commerce Building
Heights Office: Opposite Ainsworth School
Phone Main 2159

"Portland's commercial supremacy in the Northwest
rests upon a firm basis, and the basis is the erection of
business houses and public buildings in advance of pressing demands; added conveniences for trade and traffic;
artificial advantages for expediting the accumulation and
distribution of merchandise and factory products, and
ample capital to further all the ways of metropolitan
energy, business capacity, and far-reaching common
sense, and above all, the people are of one accord in their
admiration for their town."[5]

308

Another writer declared "the business men of Portland the fairest on earth."

> "This deserved reputation is now being echoed through-
> out the East and the eyes of investors are turned toward
> Oregon as a state in which they are not likely to be in-
> duced to invest in wild-cat propositions. The conservative-
> ness of Portland is sure to be the conservor of her future
> fortunes.
>
> During the Lewis and Clark Exposition Easterners were
> heard in the electric cars, and on the streets, to comment
> audibly on the politeness and good breeding of the people
> of Portland. The 'Rose City' certainly deserves its reputa-
> tion as being the most polite of American cities."[6]

In *Sunset* magazine, writer Donald Macdonald depicted a "vision of a greater Portland, a city of towering business blocks, of miles of wharves and adjoining industries, of homes filling the Willamette-Columbia peninsula and covering Council Crest and all the lower ridges."[7] According to Macdonald, "the revolution in the lumber trade" was the chief factor in Portland's "marvelous prosperity." Portland was the number one lumber manufacturing city in the United States, reported the *Oregonian* on June 4, 1905. For the year 1905, the city's sawmills cut 541,320,000 board feet, an average of 30 percent over 1904. For 1906, sawmill income was projected to produce revenues in excess of $9 million.*

Next in importance for Portland's burgeoning commercial growth, reported Macdonald, was "the awakening of the value to the farmer of Oregon's cheap and fertile lands."[8] Fifty thousand square miles of the heart of the Oregon territory were being opened up by the extended lines of the Harriman system. The supply and equipment purchases of the Harriman empire, America's longest rail line network, exceeded $100,000 a month just in Portland. From July 1, 1905 until May 1, 1906, almost ten million bushels of wheat and over one million barrels of flour were exported from Portland, much of it brought to the city via the Harriman system. Oregon was the leading state in hop production and its fruit industry was "making amazing

---

*There was a general tapering off of the lumber market beginning in 1907. The major lumber manufacturers were: Inman-Poulson Co, Portland Lumber Co., Portland Manufacturing Co., and North Pacific Lumber Co.

strides." Macdonald noted that "Oregon apples command the highest prices in New York; last season they sold f.o.b. shipping point at $2.50 per box of fifty pounds. The car of pears bringing the highest price on record in the New York Market came last fall from Southern Oregon."[9]

The gold at the end of the agricultural rainbow did not escape the notice of eastern investors. Augustus White in New York, working through his cousin Abbot Mills, handled the financing for the Willamette Valley Traction and Oregon Electric Railroad Companies that were organized in 1906. Willamette Valley Traction was constructing 50 miles of electric lines between Portland and Salem. Somewhat belatedly the Hill interests were beginning to pay more attention to Portland. In 1902, the Northern Pacific R.R. had announced plans to bridge the Columbia and to dig a tunnel under North Portland's Peninsula district, at a total cost of over $3 million.* By 1910, Hill would acquire the properties of the United Railways Co. that was organized by Los Angeles investors to secure valuable city street franchises for a rail line that would connect downtown Portland with 50 miles of electric lines under construction to Forest Grove and Salem. In March, 1906, United Railways purchased 250 acres in the Guild's Lake Exposition site for over $250,000, and was expected to spend upwards of $1 million for additional terminal and industrial real estate in the Guild's Lake area.

All of this economic growth and commercial activity generated jobs, many of which were filled by recent immigrants to Portland. In 1905, the city had over 2,500 manufacturing plants, with $40 million of invested capital, employing 26,000 wage earners.[10] The Harriman lines alone had a monthly payroll in Portland of over $150,000. Newly arrived workers were finding Portland a pleasant city in which to live. The summer climate was "unequalled" and many trades could work outside all the year round.[11] Furthermore, the city advertised its water supply as the best in the United States. And according to the *Journal,* in the two year period from 1907-1909, Portland had the lowest death rate ever recorded in the city to that date.[12]

Several new real estate developments were packaged in 1907, including the Rose City Park section of East Portland, stretching

---

*By 1907, Hill had changed his mind about a tunnel. The Spokane, Portland and Seattle Railroad (SP&S), formed in 1906 by the Northern Pacific and Great Northern Companies, gained approval to cut an open gap through the peninsula. The Harriman controlled Union Pacific R.R. did complete a tunnel on January 14, 1911.

East Irvington district, near N.E. 27th Avenue. The houses were slightly larger than those in Rose City Park to the East but they were sited in a similar fashion. Little imagination or variation was shown. The developers reaped maximum profits from enterprises of this sort.

out N.E. Sandy Boulevard from 45th to 62nd Avenues.[13] Promoted by Theodore B. Wilcox,* Walter F. Burrell, E.L. Thompson and J.L. Hartman,* all prominent downtown businessmen and bankers, the Rose City Park Association planned a strictly residential community of homes that was well within the means of the average skilled craftsman. No house could cost less than $1500 or be closer than 15 feet from the street. Saloons were excluded as was all commercial activity. The Hawthorne Park development on East Hawthorne and Belmont, out to S.E. 20th and beyond, was selling "new and modern homes" for as little as $1500. The Chamber of Commerce even ran ads in the Negro newspaper, the *New Age,*[14] seeking new owners from Portland's slowly expanding Negro population which numbered about 1300 in 1905. The Southeast Hawthorne region was to become the locus of a thriving Italian colony by the time of the First World War.

It was entirely possible for skilled workers to afford such homes. The Oregon Labor Commission issued a report in 1906 entitled: "What It Costs One Family to Live."[15] Citing the experience of an average "first-class Portland carpenter" with a wife and two child-

---

*Wilcox was W.S. Ladd's protege and Hartman was a former Markle associate.

ren, the annual expense was $713.70.* With $15 a month allocated to mortgage payments, the carpenter could purchase a $1500 home, with a 15 year, 7 percent mortgage and minimal cash downpayment. Less skilled members of the working class along with recent immigrants from southeastern Europe occupied lower-grade neighborhoods near the industrial areas. Greek railroad workers found lodging in special low cost housing overlooking Harriman's Union Pacific rail yards, along what is now North Interstate Avenue.

According to the Chamber of Commerce in June 1906, plenty of real estate was available for both residential and commercial uses at reasonable prices. "When we come to consider the availability of land in Portland it is an ideal town for business."[16] In comparing 1906 sale prices of real estate west of 3rd street in downtown Portland with 1898 prices, the increases seemed meteoric. And yet, according to the Chamber, the 1906 prices were not too high; the 1898 prices "were too low." Following the depression of 1893, prices remained depressed until almost 1900. Few sales were made west of Third, "as the best property was held by people** who did not require to sacrifice."[17] By 1905, the center of the retail trade had moved west to Sixth, between Washington and Morrison Streets. The quarter block, on the Southeast corner of Broadway and Stark,*** that had sold for $14,000 in 1898 was bought by Portland lumberman John Yeon for $125,000 in 1906.[18]

Many people thought Yeon was crazy but Yeon knew his history and was thoroughly versed in current population trends. Portland real estate values would continue to advance slowly but surely as long as the city and state continued to grow. And Yeon rightly bet on future growth. In one year, he had purchased a total of three parcels of downtown property for slightly over $400,000.**** Within 20 years they would be worth over $1.5 million.[19] The Sherlock property, a

---

*House pmts. ...	$15.00 per mo.	Insurance	.20 per mo.
Food	19.80 per mo.	Lodge Dues	2.80 per mo.
Water	1.50 per mo.	Hospital and	
Phone	1.25 per mo.	Doctor	16.90 per yr.
Wood	22.30 per yr.	Medicine	18.25 per yr.
Carfare	4.95 per yr.	RR & Steamboat	
Tobacco	4.80 per yr.	fare	2.10 per yr.
Confectionery ..	5.55 per yr.	Services hired:	
Amusement	9.15 per yr.	(washing)	15.20 per yr.
Literature	7.95 per yr.	(shaving)	24.80 per yr.

In addition, the carpenter spent $20.25 annually on tools. Outlay for pots, pans, furniture and a bicycle was $74.90.

**As represented by the Corbett, Failing, Ladd and Lewis Estates.
***Site of the Imperial Hotel.
****Including the sites of the Yeon Building and the Benson Hotel.

Looking north, intersection of 6th & Morrison Streets. Oregonian building in the center. Corner on the right is the current site of Meier & Frank Co.

quarter block at Fourth and Oak, that was bought for $350 in 1858 was sold in 1908 for $140,000. The Corbett and Failing Estates were to realize similar increases in the value of their downtown real property much of which was acquired in the 1850's.

From 1900 to 1910, Multnomah County's property assessments increased by over 500 percent and Portland's total real estate transfers went from $3.5 million a year to $28.5 million.[20] Steel framed, fireproof Class A buildings were authorized to extend 201 feet in height. Consumption of light and power doubled in the three years following 1907. Future First National Bank Chairman E.B. MacNaughton cited the "fever of speculation" in 1907, two years after his arrival as a poor young architect. "It was a riot." He borrowed $5000 on his honest looks, made a downpayment on a $20,000 lot which he sold after two weeks for $25,000. He repeated the same performance one month later.[21]

Despite all of this growth and face lifting the city was presented with numerous housekeeping problems. Blight was beginning to show up in the older buildings along the river adjacent to Front Street. The Chamber of Commerce *Bulletin* ran several articles commenting adversely on the city's broken sidewalks, muddy streets in the winter and dusty unswept roadways in the summer. The eyes of Portland's business community were too easily diverted from the spectacle of poorly maintained streets and older buildings to the overwhelming magnificence of the nearby mountains, rivers and forests.* In an article entitled "Selling Civic Beauty," the *Bulletin* commented:

> "We mercenary sons of Portland have a beautiful city — a city naturally the most beautiful on the Coast, but 'tis like a beautiful woman with a dirty face and a bedraggled skirt — it needs a bath and a new dress. Let us then set the landscape gardener at work making for our Lady Portland a hat, of flower-trimmed street borders and shapely shade trees. Let us put scavengers at work and give her a bath. Let us trim her skirts with parks and driveways and make her in all things a fitting bride for the wealth that comes to woo. Having done this — having robed her natural beauty in fitting garments, then, will outside wealth bejewel her with diamonds and hang upon her ornaments of gold, and we of Portland will sell the diamonds and take toll of the gold.
> Truly, we sons of Portland are mercenary, for we would sell the beauty of our city at a profit. But we can sell it and keep it, too, and that is good business!"[23]

Mayor Harry Lane was to expend much effort during his four years in office attempting to achieve a similar though less pretentious goal. More than just a physically beautiful city, Lane desired a liveable city for all of the people, not simply the affluent; a city that would maintain the human scale in all of its varied activities, and a city that would not sacrifice the natural environment to excessive physical growth by allowing private interests to invade the public

---

*Prominent real estate investor C.K. Henry, in comparing Denver with Portland, liked Denver's enamelled brick buildings that were "easier to keep clean." He also preferred Denver's street paving and street car service. Henry found business location values to be lower in Portland than in Denver and other cities of the same standing.[22]

domain. Lane was to find himself embroiled in many battles. Although the people heartily supported him, especially his fellow Eastsiders, the special interests detested him.* The battleground was the city council chamber.

Fourteen of the fifteen city councilmen were new. They represented the emerging class of business and professional men who were involved directly with Portland's economic growth.** Of the four lawyers, one represented the Harriman interests professionally, one was a Mitchell-Williams crony and one was deeply involved in real estate speculation. The largest realtor was East side resident J.P. Sharkey who was also closely identified with the Southern Pacific-Harriman interests. Businessmen included a druggist, undertaker, farm implement executive, transfer company owner, jeweler, grocer, plumbing contractor and brick manufacturer. The most influential councilman and Mayor Lane's chief antagonist was council president (1905-6) John Annand, the Portland manager of the Postal Telegraph Co. and a close friend and ally of the railroads. During the 1880's Annand had worked variously for the Northern Pacific, Southern Pacific and Oregon Railway and Navigation Companies. The Postal Telegraph Co. had received its initial franchise in 1887 with no compensatory payment to the city. In 1912, the company was to be accused publicly of laying illegal conduits for its message wire service.

In theory, the council system in 1905 appeared democratic, with one representative from each of 10 wards and with five elected at large. In practice, the small constituencies of each ward representative made it relatively easy for the railroads and the liquor interests to secure the election of a council majority, or at least enough votes to override the mayor's veto. During Lane's first year in office, 21 of his 32 vetoes were overridden by a two-thirds vote of the council. During the span of four years, about half of Lane's record 169 vetoes were overridden. Those that were sustained were apt to involve minor procedural or housekeeping matters. The ordinances supporting major private interests were almost always passed. The executive board, composed of 10 Democrats and three Republicans appointed by Mayor Lane, enjoyed only recommendatory powers. The council's decisions were final.

---

*One disgruntled businessman wrote him in October 1905: "I have no more respect for you than I have for a yellow dog.'[24]

**For the first time in over 20 years, not one councilman belonged to the Arlington Club.

2.

Harry Lane was born in Marysville (Corvallis) in 1855, the grandson of General Joseph Lane, Oregon's First Territorial Governor and United States Senator. He received his undergraduate and medical degrees from Willamette University in Salem and took post-graduate work at the College of Physicians and Surgeons in New York City. After practicing briefly in San Francisco, he returned to practice medicine in his home state and became superintendent of the Oregon State Asylum from 1887-91. After a year of further post-graduate study in Europe, Lane settled in Portland where he became attached to the locally prominent Coffey Sanitarium, housed in the old Levi White Mansion on Northwest 20th.

His close friend, lawyer Richard W. Montague said of him:

"No one can forget HARRY LANE who ever came close to that unique and vivid personality. A mind leaping, swift, intuitive, sudden and unpredictable in its way of attack on the commonest questions, a pungent wit, abundant zest of life, genial readiness in intercourse with all sorts and conditions of men, all these were apparent at once, but these were not all, nor was all comprised in these as modified by the human defects, of which he had full share.

His physical appearance contributed no little to the sum of the impression he made. Plain yet very striking features, a prominent, almost aquiline nose, firm, straight, thin-lipped mouth, and keen steel-blue eyes gave rather a grim expression to his face when not lit up by the habitual look of animation that gave it a characteristic charm. His face was finely set off by abundant wavy hair and a peculiar elate carriage of the head that drew the eye at once. Of only middle size, he possessed remarkable muscular strength and activity, and his bearing had an alert readiness that reminded one irresistibly of a swordsman of Dumas and left an impression of perfect physical competence.

I remember that once when a man named Lane was hurt in a street accident the rumor ran that it was Dr. Lane. A shrewd friend of his remarked to me, 'They told me Harry was run over by a street car,' but I said, 'No, not that fellow. Some other Lane, maybe, but no street car will ever run over Harry.'

He was an ardent lover of nature, and was never so happy as when pursuing some inquiry into her secrets. One year he began hunting mushrooms, and before his curiosity was satisfied had made himself a real expert and learned mycologist in the local field, finding and describing many new species, and all in the midst of the day's work which left no leisure to less ardent spirits.

Once, a few hours after the close of a hard political campaign in which he had been defeated, I found him studying a strange bird through his field glasses. 'You see, I have returned to my proper interests in life,' he said, with the look of grave sweetness that unlocked all hearts to him. That look was reserved for his rare moment of sheer friendliness; for the most part he had a cheerful smile which exasperated his enemies, to whom he wore it most gaily, almost beyond endurance. Indeed, he was never in higher spirits than when he went into a fight, and if a forlorn hope so much the better cheer. . . .

Men such as Judge Bellinger and Asahel Bush, at opposite poles of opinion and character, save that both have distinguished intellect and trenchant wit, counted him quite their nearest friend. Children loved him, and I have seen a little boy looking up at him during a cruelly painful minor operation without a wriggle or a murmur while the tears streamed down his little face like rain. . . .

The most notable characteristic of his mind was its unshakable grasp of a few elementary principles of justice and humanity and the sudden and surprising aptness with which he applied them to the case in hand; if to the breaking down of ancient conventions or the shattering of ancient idols, so much the better. From this power of holding fast to the essence amid all the tangle and welter of accident came his flashes of insight as an administrator, when he denied his advisers and defied his enemies — and proved in the end, 'in the teeth of all the schools,' that he was right. A fighting man with an ingrained love of humanity and of basic, uncomplicated justice is pretty sure to be a success in politics, and he was a fighting man in every fiber.

These simple and obvious qualities were the sole source of his political success. Of the arts of the politician he had none, nor any love of wealth or power. For intrigue and combination he had absolutely no aptitude, and for the complicated team play and strategy necessary to carry through large political programs little enough. But the plain people could not be deceived as to the perfect absence in him of acquisitiveness or any disloyalty to them, the depth and utter sincerity of his feeling for common humanity, and his detestation of privilege and power based on privilege; and for these things they gladly ignored any deficiencies in sustained reasonings or far-reaching programs and elevated him again and again to high place in the face of over-whelming majorities."[25]

This was the man who would preside over city hall during four of the most tumultuous years in Portland's history. For the first few weeks of his administration, the council meetings were fairly subdued. The mayor drafted a new committee structure, creating 13 in place of the previous 10. For the first time in 36 years, the First National Bank was not a depository for city funds.* The U.S. Nation-

---

*By August 1906, the First National would again become the fourth depository. The U.S. National Bank had the lion's share of deposits.

al, Merchants National and the Bank of California were the favored institutions. The Ladd & Tilton and the Portland Trust Banks held the city's interest bearing certificates of deposit.

On August 16, 1905 Mayor Lane submitted his second veto of the session, relative to an ordinance amendment allowing saloons and restaurants to operate closed rooms or "boxes" as they were called. Such an amendment, said Lane, would permit combination houses... productive of evil, . . . dives and hiding places for criminals." Portlanders did not want this condition to exist, Lane declared. Turning a deaf ear to such notions, the council overrode his veto 12-3.[26] This was the first of many losing battles that Lane would suffer at the hands of the saloon and liquor interests. The awarding of lucrative liquor licenses* and the regulation of saloons produced the major split in the council for four years. Hours of official time were consumed in heated debate.

The second most divisive issue that kept cropping up at almost every meeting related to requests for granting street vacations, variances and easements for special construction not in compliance with existing ordinances. Lane vetoed practically every one and he was usually overridden 13-2. He was particularly outspoken 18 months later when he denounced the council "for the wholesale giving away of streets" and property that represented "lots of public money if the land were to be bought on the open market." In this particular instance, Lane was referring to an ordinance that granted the vacation of a portion of tiny N.W. Hull Street to the Willamette Iron Works. Majority control of the company had recently been acquired by C.F. Swigert. Lane charged that the city did not even own enough dock space for its new fireboat and yet it was giving away public streets to a private company free of charge.[27]

Neither the council nor the county commission paid much heed to the executive board which was considered to be the "mouthpiece" of Mayor Lane. On October 20, 1905, the board filed a formal protest with the county over the commissioners granting the right to use the draw nests of the bridges on the east side of the river for commercial advertising purposes, i.e., the painting and erection of large signs. The board reminded the county that the city had paid for the bridges even though the county was charged with operating and maintaining them. "The use of any part thereof for commercial advertising purposes is offensive to good taste, civic pride and public decency."[28]

---

*By December 26th, 453 liquor licenses had already been issued since July.

The county refused to order the signs removed, the council took no action,* and after 70 years the issue is still being debated although some progress has recently been achieved toward the gradual removal of bridge ramp advertising obstructions.**

December 1905 was an important month in the life of the mayor and his city council protagonists. On December 6th Lane challenged the head command of the business establishment by vetoing an ordinance that authorized and consented to the franchise transfer of the Portland Consolidated Railway properties to the recently incorporated Portland Railway Co. In his message to the Council, Lane said:

1. If the claim is correct that the company already has the authority to make this transfer independent of this ordinance, then this ordinance is not necessary.

2. If on the other hand, this ordinance does confer rights which the company does not now possess, "it is certainly our duty to exact a corresponding return . . . for the benefit of the City and its inhabitants."

> "It is evident to all that the favors and privileges that have been bestowed in the past as franchises to the several street railways named in this ordinance now have a market value of millions of dollars, all granted without adequate benefit to the City, and it would seem that this excessive generosity with the property of the public should not be continued."[29]

After long debate, the veto was overridden 13-1.

This was the first time that any mayor of Portland had ever expressed such contrary opinions, at least publicly. Abbot Mills and his friends were dismayed but probably not too surprised. They knew that Mayor Lane and the executive board had been studying franchise compensation and comparing Portland's rates with those of other cities. Portland exacted the least compensation of any of the major West Coast cities. In January, the executive board would recommend futilely to the council that the city charge a minimum compensation payment at the rate of 2 percent of gross earnings. San

---

*In October 1907 the council did vote to place some height limits on billboards, against the strong opposition of the Foster-Kleiser Co.

**In April 1976 the city's Sign Review Committee recommended to the council that all billboards be banned in downtown Portland.

Francisco already had a 3 percent rate in effect. Had the Portland Consolidated Railway been charged at a rate of 2 percent of gross earnings in 1905, it would have paid to the public treasury $30,000 instead of a paltry $4500 exclusive of bridge charges which only amounted to $10,000. Mayor Lane had good reason to feel that the city was being, as it had long been, swindled by the street railway companies. But there was nothing he could do about it, as no laws had been broken. In 1906 the Portland Railway Co. would pay a total compensation of $20,000 to the city, equal to about a 1 percent gross revenue charge.

There is nothing in Abbot Mills' correspondence to indicate that he held any doubts as to the correctness of his past actions. Securing the maximum return for his stockholders had always been his primary goal. But had it not been for the extra revenue generated by the exposition, and for the corporate savings resulting from low compensation payments to the city, the per share value of Consolidated Railway stock would have been worth considerably less than the sale price of $160.

As a consequence of such practices, when the council was approached on December 26th and asked to commit the city to the purchase of certain federal government buildings located at the recently closed exposition site, the council did not have the funds to give the matter more than casual consideration. Had the city been able to execute a deal with the federal government and in addition purchase some of the property below Willamette Heights for a park, as recommended by John Olmsted, Portland today might well possess a lasting commemorative monument to Lewis and Clark, instead of a seedy industrial wasteland. In April 1906, the city did manage to scrape together enough money to purchase the Forestry Building and two acres of land. But since the giant log cabin burned in 1964, the site has remained desolately bare, covered with trash and weeds.

When all of the bills were paid, the exposition had netted the Lewis and Clark Centennial Exposition Association $111,456. The city made no formal request for any of the profits, but the state did secure the return of $50,000 of its total $500,000 appropriation as only $450,000 had been spent. Had the association been willing to match the state's $50,000 with its own funds, the state would have released the money, and a permanent memorial building could have been constructed for $100,000. The Oregon Historical Society requested a portion of the profits to build a new headquarters but the bid was rejected. In fact, the association refused to distribute any of the profits for public or community purposes. Placing the interests of the private stockholders above Portland's future welfare,[30] the association's leadership, including Harvey Scott and Abbot Mills, decided to distribute a 21-1/2 percent dividend on an original stock investment that had held no promise of future redemption at any percentage. In truth, Henry W. Corbett's $30,000 "patriotic" contribution was returned to his estate many times over through the vastly improved fortunes of the First National Bank and through the windfall profits derived from the Consolidated Railway Co. sale. The exposition stock dividend was merely the frosting on the cake. Portland's establishment still wanted to travel first class on a steerage ticket.

3.

Three days before Christmas, Mayor Lane and the executive board returned boxes of cigars to August Erickson, the proprietor of the world's longest bar. Thanking him profusely, Lane wrote that he and his administration were obliged to decline the acceptance of any presents or favors as long as they held public office. In another break with tradition, the mayor returned all free railway passes and he instructed the members of his administration to do likewise.[31] The independent council refused to do so.

One more event occurring early in December should be mentioned before passing on to the new year. On December 8, Senator John H. Mitchell died of a diabetic coma following dental surgery. Half-way into his 71st year, Mitchell was facing a six months sentence in the county jail. Many eulogies were offered, including that of lawyer William D. Fenton who denounced the "habit of some classes of people to heap unjustified criticism upon public men."[32] As usual, Fenton missed the ethical point. At least Joseph Gaston tried to find in Mitchell's life "a great lesson." Wrote Gaston: "justice to all and the safety of society requires that those who supported and contributed to the corrupt system, or tamely surrendered to the vicious public opinion that made Mitchell's career possible, should be shown the evil of their own guilty part. . . . Mitchell's political ethics justified any means that would win the battle."[33]

As Mayor Lane prepared his annual address to the council in early January 1906, he was well aware of the financial stringency facing Portland with a projected budget imbalance of $64,000. The city agencies would function but at barely adequate levels. This condition was responsible for his strong feeling that the expanding private industrial and utility sector of the economy should pay a larger share of the growing cost of government. The 53 percent increase in the fire department budget directly reflected the boom in commercial and residential construction. Existing or contemplated revenues could not be expected to cover spiralling public costs that resulted from private development. Furthermore, the city legislators refused to establish a sinking fund for capital improvements or for amortizing past bonded indebtedness.

Speaking to the council on January 17, 1906, Mayor Lane addressed the issues and problems that would concern him during his entire tenure of office. The speech set the tone and direction of his administration. Most of the specific recommendations related to improving the quality of city services and to the equal execution of the laws. Starting with a subject close to his own profession, he recommended the reorganization of the health department. Portland had the second lowest death rate of any major city in the country. There was no reason why it could not achieve the number one rating as America's healthiest city.[34] With this goal in mind Lane decided that the health officer should be a physician, to be assisted by the medical profession. He subsequently appointed Dr. Esther Pohl Lovejoy, the first woman health officer in Portland's history and one of the first such appointments in the United States.

A related issue of concern was the same old garbage problem, referred to previously. The garbagemen were private operators and their wagons were not watertight; spillage was a serious consequence. According to the mayor, the existing system of garbage collection and disposal provided "great inducement to dump at some more convenient place than the city crematorium. . . . I advise that the city take charge of handling the garbage, procure properly built garbage wagons, horses and equipment" and give better service to the public and hopefully profits to the city. The existing crematorium was "inefficient and expensive. . . . The furnaces were too small," always requiring costly repairs.[35]

The board of health was to report later in the year that the city buried 1000 tons of cremated garbage in August 1906 at a cost of $1.50 per ton.* A new plant costing $10,000, incorporating recent technical innovations could, according to the board, handle 35 tons a day at 30¢ per ton. The location of a new plant presented some problems. The Northwest residents wanted the site removed from their

---

*The city dump at St. Johns handles 1000 tons daily in 1976.

neighborhood at the foot of N.W. 25th and Guild's Lake. A special committee of the council was to recommend a downtown site for a more central location. Block 74 on S.W. Front Street* was considered ideal but it cost too much. During his second term, Mayor Lane was to suggest an island in the river but no one took him seriously. Because the existing plant could handle only about half of the garbage collected, much of it was being "dumped alongside roadways, behind hedges and in convenient gulches and ravines." One study that Lane commissioned determined that for the first year it would cost the city $102,000 to run a municipal garbage service but anticipated revenues would total less than $50,000. Needless to say, no official action was forthcoming.

A subject of long standing interest to Harry Lane was that of city planning. Great benefit would accrue to Portland, advised the mayor, "if a plan were devised to terrace the hills, by employing a system of contour approaches . . . in place of the frightfully ugly and costly method now pursued of cutting them up into square blocks and deep cuts, called streets, which are not only expensive but leave the land in many instances almost unapproachable."[36] For the flatter residential districts on the East side that were platted on a grid of 200 foot square blocks Lane was to propose that the city vacate every other street. Except for a 10 foot paved strip in the center, the streets would become park areas with "shade trees and rose vines."** Only light delivery vehicles would be allowed on the strips. Such a plan, declared the mayor, "would make Portland the most beautiful city in the world."[37]

Turning to the riverfront, Lane strongly recommended the replacement of the "unsightly and straggly row of wooden docks." The decaying timbers and open sewers presented a health hazard. The docks should be built of stone and concrete. The following year Lane would comment: "The whole riverfront should be reorganized along lines looking to the betterment of conditions for this city. . . . If necessary, the city should take over the possession of the waterfront to itself by condemnation proceedings."[38]

Moving on to a discussion of the municipal water system, Mayor Lane raised several important issues. Portland's daily per capita consumption was 30 percent higher than 104 other large U.S. cities.***

---

*Site of the new Portland General Electric Co. headquarters building.
**Lane is considered the father of the Rose Festival, a proposal that he made during a speech at the opening of the exposition in 1905.
***During the summer months of 1905, the city used 29 million gallons daily, or 193 gallons daily per person. During the other months, daily city consumption was 26 million gallons; per capita 173 gallons.

The flat fee of $1.50 per month, with reductions to large commercial consumers, encouraged a wastage of water resources and discriminated against the small households and the poorer families. He recommended the installation of a meter system combined with a decrease in the minimum use fee. He also wanted the heavy commercial and industrial users to pay their fair share. More revenue needed to be generated, on a more equitable basis, to pay off the staggering $3.1 million bonded indebtedness which was costing the system $160,000 a year in interest payments.[39]

The mayor reserved his strongest and most pointed comments to the end. The city government must execute the laws equally, to rich and poor alike, "without fear or favor." Too many times he had heard people say, "Oh, what's the use. We go down to city hall and are treated like drunks or tramps." Many people in government were "playing politics or taking graft."[40] The public welfare and the public interest at all times had to be considered "of greater importance than the gain of the private individual." Public franchises or public streets should never be parted with, "without full and proper compensation to the public." Referring to the long standing rather loose practice of allowing time extensions for the completion of city improvement projects, Lane declared that the government must demand "the exact enforcement of all contracts with the city."[41]

4.

The year 1906 was to find Mayor Harry Lane embroiled in simultaneous battle against a number of special interest groups: the vice crowd, the "blanket" franchise beneficiaries, and the Hill and Harriman empires. As Senator Chamberlain was to comment some years later, Mayor Lane "was quick to sense the harmonious relation between powerful figures and the vice ring. With equal celerity he comprehended the inside hold that big institutions maintained in the city and out of which they profited at the expense of the public and the masses."[42] Harry Lane was not opposed to free enterprise or economic growth *per se;* he *was* opposed to illegitimate activities and to business practices that solely benefited the private interests involved. "Grafters were his sport" as someone once commented. The witty pipe smoking doctor, with his "gray eyes, Gladstonian nose and gladiatorial chin" was fearless in combat. He hunted grafters "as other men hunt leopards and bobcats."[43]

Ineffective vice raids had been conducted spasmodically for over a decade. Lane recommended that the council cancel the licenses of the places where such illegal·activities were discovered, as most of them were housed in combined saloon or restaurant facilities. The trial of Thomas Richards brought the issue to a head in January 1906. "Richards Place," a restaurant at the corner of S.W. Park and Alder, was charged with being a front for a bawdy house. When a police investigator called to inquire about arrangements for female company, Richards was quoted as replying: "No problem. Bring your own lady or I can furnish the goods."

According to the *Journal*,[44] the trial was a farce. Both the Municipal Judge George J. Cameron and the Court Clerk Frank Hennessy were openly in sympathy with the liquor interests. Subpoenas were stolen and false ones issued in order to embarrass the prosecutor. No Municipal Association members were permitted to serve on the jury. The defendent's lawyer was allowed by the judge to employ questionable obstructionist tactics. Needless to say, Richards was acquitted. The *Journal* charged that the case was "jobbed." During the course of the trial, the paper had revealed that the building was owned by Lauritz W. Therkelson, President of the North Pacific Lumber Co., one of the city's most prominent business leaders and a 17 year veteran of the Water Committee. Mayor Lane was furious. But when he recommended that the council remove Richards' license, he was rebuffed 8-6.

Over the next year Police Chief Carl Gritzmacher tightened the lid by increasing the number of raids. But in September, 1906, Lane was so incensed by the lack of arrests that he ordered the chief to replace the entire detective force. Success crowned their efforts early in 1907 when the Paris House was closed for good. Opened in late 1904 to entertain visitors to the exposition, Portland's largest bordello occupied the second and third floors of a rambling building on N.W. Davis between Third and Fourth. Each of the more than 100 girls rented her own crib and kept her own earnings and liquor receipts.[45]

Lane's efforts were criticized by former councilman Fred Merrill and future Mayor George Baker.* The mayor was "misguided," said Merrill. The city "could not put down prostitution and gambling;"

*Baker served on the council, 1898-1900, 1906-1913; city commissioner, 1915-1917; mayor 1917-1933.

the sporting element would end up all over town. Regulation by licensing was the only answer.[46] On numerous occasions Lane received petitions from North End and downtown businessmen to remove the red light activities to another district. "Get them away from the business center." Lane would reply that the same policy should be applied unilaterally throughout the city. "Whether we like it or not, the law forbids bawdy houses. . . . I will close up every house in town quite regardless of the consequences."[47] But Merrill's prediction turned out to be accurate. The crusade did little more than scatter the girls throughout the Irvington and exclusive Portland Heights neighborhoods. During Mayor Simon's administration, the girls would float back to the North End as well as to downtown. It was not to be until 1912 that Portland would experience an effective vice crackdown, and then only after Governor Oswald West had replaced the district attorney, empanelled a special grand jury, and brought in a visiting judge on temporary assignment.

Throughout the winter and spring of 1906 Mayor Lane fought one losing battle after another with the railroads and electric railway companies. Existing evidence would seem to indicate that the Hill interests, through their New York bankers including Moffat and White, were behind much of the new interurban electric railway development. Not until 1910, however, after Hill had lost his fight with Harriman over the construction of a rail line from the Columbia River up the Deschutes River to Bend* would the extent of Hill's financial control be revealed.

Moffat and White in New York, along with Abbot Mills and young Henry L. Corbett of the First National Bank, were responsible for the organization of the Oregon Electric and Willamette Valley Traction Companies in March of 1906. Three months later, the Oregon Electric bought out the Willamette Valley Traction and in 1907 began limited operations west of Portland. In 1908, when the Portland to Salem line was completed, Charles F. Swigert was acting President and Guy Talbot the Vice-President and General Manager. Through the efforts of White and Mills, Talbot had come to Oregon Electric from Sidney Z. Mitchell's Electric Bond and Share utility network and would remain in Portland throughout his business career as one of the Northwest's leading utility executives. In 1910, when the Oregon Electric was acquired by Hill's United Railways Co., Talbot

---

*Harriman's Deschutes line won out over Hill's Oregon Trunkline.

moved over to run the Portland Gas Co. which Mills had just sold to Mitchell's American Power & Light Co.*

The story is a complicated one but it needs to be told in order to show the intricate relationship that existed between Portland's business development and the eastern money markets. Abbot Mills of course played a crucial role in many of these negotiations that drew him closer to the Hill interests. Howard Elliott, president of the Northern Pacific, was a former Harvard classmate and close friend of Mills and would be instrumental in securing Mills' election to the Harvard Board of Overseers. In the late 1890's Mills had fought Harriman while he was serving on the board of the OR&N Co. Thus it should not have come as any great surprise to Mills to learn by telegram in November 1908 that Harriman was withdrawing his local business from the First National and would henceforth bank with the U.S. National.[48] Harriman could brook no opposition whatsoever. He looked upon Oregon as his private preserve. To strengthen his local position, Harriman secured election to the Arlington Club in 1907 but it is doubtful that he ever made much use of the facility.

The United Railways Co., which Hill would acquire in 1910 and which would play a crucial role in his attempt to outflank Harriman, created a number of problems for Harry Lane's administration. During the first five months of 1906, the United Railways franchise application consumed much council time before it was finally approved on May 23rd. For several years, Harriman's Southern Pacific had been trying to secure a franchise to run a line down Front Street to the Northern Pacific Terminal Depot. The award of the franchise to United Railways represented a clear defeat for the Harriman interests. Lane's opposition was confined to three provisions: the franchise payment of $1000 a year was much too low; the 25 year term was too long a commitment; and the city's right to future acquisition was not clearly established.[49] At least Lane did succeed in getting the council to write in the provision that the city could purchase any portion of the line, rather than the entire system, if future needs should dictate such a decision.

In August 1908, Lane would recommend to the council that the city initiate suit against United Railways for failure to fulfill the terms of the franchise. Lane felt that the company should forfeit its $100,000 performance bond. The council took no action until April 1909 when it defied the mayor and passed an ordinance allowing Un-

*See chapter VII. Talbot also became president of the Pacific Power & Light Co. (est. 1910) and vice president of the parent American Power & Light Co.

ited Railways to alter the terms of its original franchise; henceforth it would be permitted to operate cars within Portland prior to completing its line to Hillsboro and Mt. Calvary Cemetery by way of N.W. Barnes Road.

The major economic force behind much of this railway expansion within greater Portland was the effort to create a unified belt line system of freight movement, not passenger traffic. As early as January 1906, the *Journal* had noted that the Northern Pacific was buying large tracts of land along the Columbia Slough for future freight yards. Property was selling for $1,000 an acre, ten times its 1905 value. According to the *Journal*,[50] Hill was trying to bottle up Harriman and he had the support of the Weyerhaeusers and some Portland investors including the First National Bank. The N.P. also received several franchise awards for laying side and switching tracks on public streets north of the depot-terminal area. Lane vetoed each of these ordinances because there was no provision for splitting the switching fees with the city, nor any compensation for the use of public property.

In September and early October 1906, Mayor Lane took on both the Hill and Harriman interests. He lost two battles but won the third by sheer ingenuity. For years the city had tried at various times to persuade the Southern Pacific to remove its tracks from S.W. Fourth Street. The legislature had granted this franchise to the Oregon Central Railroad in 1868. Originally designed for passenger traffic, the track was being used entirely for freight and the noise and pollution were extremely irritating to the residents in South Portland. When an ordinance was introduced to repeal the franchise, lawyer William D. Fenton appealed to the council in person. He cited the track's economic benefits to the city's commercial life, that the railroad had no other provision for moving freight through the city on the West side, and that cancelling a legally ordained perpetual franchise and forcing the company to abandon its investment would be tantamount to expropriation of private property without due process of law. With typical arrogance Fenton reminded the councilmen that most of them enjoyed free S.P. rail passes.

As might be expected, on September 19, the council unashamedly failed to support the ordinance by a vote of 10-4. A week later, Mayor Lane transmitted a strong letter to the city legislators to the effect that the old franchise was unconstitutional, that it was in conflict with the current city charter, and that the S.P. had not been the original grantee. Furthermore, the S.P. had a history of not maintaining the streets on which their tracks were laid. This fact alone provided ample legal grounds for cancellation of the franchise, Lane declared.[51] Seven months later, the council adopted a resolution, 6-5, stipulating that the Southern Pacific terminate the use of freight cars and steam locomotives on Fourth St. within 18 months.* The railroad had finally decided to build a bridge at Oswego, to connect the west side traffic with its main line on the east side. Increasing public pressure had forced its hand.

On September 22, 1906, Mayor Lane discovered that the Northern Pacific Terminal Co., owned largely by Harriman and Hill interests, was occupying portions of N.W. Irving and Kearny Streets without a franchise. For years the city had been negotiating with the NPT in an attempt to find a suitable location for a new fire station near the terminal. The previous February, the company had indicated a willingness to lease space but it would not deed ownership to the city. The offer was declined. Now, with this bit of startling information on his desk, Lane called the manager of the Terminal Co. and informed him that all of the tracks running from the depot to the Steel Bridge passed illegally over two city streets. He reported that he had 20 patrolmen with proper tools prepared to dig up the tracks if a deed to the firehouse site was not granted "post haste." No train could enter or leave the terminal grounds if the mayor were to carry out his threat. On September 26, the mayor informed the council that he had his deed for the station, properly executed by the NPT Co. He had personally selected the location at N.W. Third and Glisan Streets. He suggested to the council that in exchange for the building site, a "properly guarded franchise" be enacted to legalize the Terminal Co.'s use of the streets.[53] This was to be Mayor Lane's only substantial victory over the entrenched railroad interests in his two terms of office.

Five days later, Lane vetoed an ordinance granting permission to the Spokane, Portland and Seattle Railroad (SP&S), a joint Northern Pacific-Great Northern enterprise, to excavate a deep cut across North Portland's Peninsula district. Hill had secretly organized the SP&S in 1905 to construct a rail line from Spokane to Portland along the north bank of the Columbia River. The SP&S would also assume

---

*When the deadline arrived, the S.P. refused to discontinue use of Fourth St. for steam locomotives. The city brought suit in U.S. District Court and won. In November 1912, the U.S. Supreme Court upheld the city's inherent police powers. When a franchise renewal application came before the council in December 1912, Judge Charles H. Carey pleaded in behalf of the S.P. The council gave in to pressure and granted the renewal for $500 a year compensation. The Portland *Daily News* said it was worth at least $1000 a month.[52]

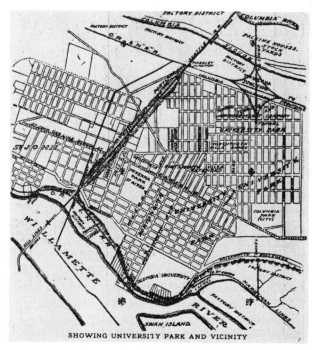

SHOWING UNIVERSITY PARK AND VICINITY

Map showing the SP&S RR cut through North Portland. The
U.P. RR tunnel can be seen to the right.

control of all freight and passenger operations between Seattle and
Portland, using new bridges under construction across both the Columbia and Willamette Rivers. Hill wanted more direct access to the
Northern Pacific Terminal grounds and refused even to consider a
common user arrangement with the Union Pacific that was planning
to build a tunnel under the peninsula, for which it was to receive a
franchise in July 1907.

Lane's veto cited the following objections to the ordinance: (1) no
time limit was included; (2) there was no recall provision; (3) the city's
charter's common user requirement was being violated; (4) the railroad would pay nothing beyond the cost of its own land investment
and that of four steel traffic bridges to be constructed across the cut.
Fourteen existing streets would be closed by the excavation. Although the company promised to replace any of the four bridges
that wore out, Mayor Lane called the whole deal an out and out
"give-away." The cut, said Lane, would be both a "defacement of

332

property and a visual blight." It would also destroy the unity of the district neighborhood.* But Portland business interests were so excited by the prospect of the north bank line and by the realization that for the first time James J. Hill was recognizing Portland as a major terminus, any request by Mr. Hill should be favored. The council overrode Lane's veto 11-1.[54] The previous week, Lane had suffered a similar defeat over a franchise ordinance granted to the SP&S, authorizing the company to lay tracks on several major cross streets in N.W. Portland for freight terminal development with no compensation to the city.

In July 1907, Mayor Lane vetoed the Union Pacific's request** to build its tunnel under the Peninsula district. Citing some of the same reasons he gave in the SP&S case, Lane said, that although the franchise contained a common user clause, there was no right-of-way provision for another user to get into or out of the tunnel, and the franchise was perpetual. Lane deplored the lack of an overall plan for

Southern Pacific tracks — S.E. Salmon Street.

*The SP&S (Burlington-Northern) cut involved a set of conditions and circumstances similar to those of the controversial Mt. Hood freeway project in S.E. Portland, 1974-76. North Portland's experience should offer conclusive proof as to the undesirable consequences that can result from such a barrier. Local residents strongly opposed the decision in 1906 but citizen action groups were non-existent in those days. Environmental impact statements had never been dreamed of.

**Made in the name of the Oregon, Washington Railway Navigation Co.

the area. "The interests of the people are greater than those of any corporation." The council overrode the veto 10-4.[55]

Mayor Harry Lane did not view himself as an enemy of the railroads. He simply wanted an orderly system that would serve both the best interests of the public and the just economic requirements of the companies. On several occasions, he charged that the "railway franchise business represented havoc." With no overall plan, the companies merely placed their tracks in "helter-skelter" fashion wherever they wanted them. City property was chopped up and excessive waste resulted from the failure to enforce the common user requirement of the city charter. Each company jealously and selfishly went its own way with no regard to future consequences. Immediate costs and expected profits provided the only guidelines for decisions that would affect the city for many generations to come. Lane was particularly critical of extended time limits granted by the franchises. In later years the railroads would ignore even these limitations and invest their track franchises with the sacred rights of private property. Whenever Portland was forced to condemn trackage for reasons of bridge ramps or highway construction, the costs to the city were to be astronomical.

Beginning in late June 1906, Harry Lane must have been surprised when he read the *Oregonian's** attack on the street railway and gas company franchises; Abbot Mills most certainly was. Mills had served on the charter commission with Scott. Although Mills might be accused of betraying his public trust, he had at least voted in favor of the new franchise provisions, whereas Harvey Scott had voted against them. Indeed, many people were perplexed — even astounded — by Scott's charge on June 20th that the paper had been duped in 1902-3 when it supported the awarding of the new franchises to the City and Suburban and the old Portland Railway Companies. The event that ostensibly produced this new outburst was the announcement of the incorporation of the Portland Railway Light & Power Co.** The *Oregonian* charged that the sale to eastern financiers was "political jobbery, costing the city millions of dollars."[56] Citing figures to show that the company expected to earn over $200,000 in 1906 and that the city would only receive $13,380 in compensation,

---

*The *Oregonian's* first critical editorial had appeared on May 26, 1905.
**On June 29, 1906. The company did not begin full operation until December 31, 1907. See chapter XII.

THE METROPOLITAN ASSOCIATION, Inc.

PORTLAND, OREGON

520 AMERICAN BANK BLDG.
BEACON 5226

August 21, 1940.

Mr. Marshall N. Dana,
Editor, Oregon Journal,
Portland, Oregon.

Dear Mr. Dana:

       Reference is made to your recent editorial in which you deplore the delay in getting started on the Waterfront Improvement, funds for which were authorized by the voters on May 18th last.

       As you probably know the delay is largely if not wholly due to the obstructionist tactics of the United Railways (S.P.& S.), which is endeavoring to put selfish interests ahead of the public welfare. For a great number of years they have occupied Front Avenue with their tracks, purely on sufferance. Now they are endeavoring to make such use, by sufferance, a vested right. Furthermore, they are doing so by inciting a few shippers to act as "front" for them, on the grounds that, if tracks are removed, those industries affected will be ruined.

       As a matter of fact, most of the industries involved can be as well served by the S.P.Ry., by way of the Oswego bridge. The only exceptions are those shippers whose shipments move only to the north docks and these are for the most part the shippers of scrap iron upon which an virtual embargo has been placed by the Federal government. Of course, if the United Railways and the S.P.Ry. do not see fit to enter into a common user agreement, that is their business, but they have no right to retard or impair an improvement which the electorate has declared to be an improvement for the general good of the entire city. Furthermore, according to figures compiled by one of the shippers and quoted in the Council chamber, the total number of carloads shipped from or consigned to the industries involved is only two thousand cars per year and the switching charges on the majority of this business is now being absorbed by the railroads.

       It would seem that, in view of the favors and concessions which the railroads have received and are receiving from the city, they should be willing, in the public interest, to work out a perfectly simple solution of this problem. If not willing, they should be made to do so.

Very truly yours,

U. L. Upson

ULU-R.   Executive Secretary.

"An example of what Mayor Lane warned would happen. Thirty three years later, the city had to deal with the problem."

the paper charged "fraud." Said Scott: "The tricks of the franchise gang of Portland are coming to light."[57]

The *Oregon Journal* accused the *Oregonian* of hypocrisy.[58] The *Journal* had printed all of the facts in November 1902. It had advised the council to wait until the new charter had taken effect when higher compensation rates and the 25 year limit would be in effect. The *Journal* charged the *Oregonian* with "newspaper treachery. . . . The *Oregonian* has sold itself habitually to the highest bidder for many years." The *Journal* also reported[59] that the Corbett estate still held the balance of power in the *Oregonian** and the 1902-3 franchises were expected to prove profitable to both the Corbetts and the First National Bank. The *Journal* charged further that the *Oregonian* had basely betrayed the people of Portland," because Scott had made a deal with Matthews to make him Senator. "Scott and Matthews were hand in glove" in 1902-1903. Matthews was working with Mills and wanted the *Oregonian* to vigorously support the franchise awards.

Also in late June, the *Oregonian* began a series of attacks on the Portland Gas Co. The first critical piece had actually been printed on January 1, 1906. Then on February 22nd the paper had accused the company of paying taxes on less than half of the value of its property. Dodging $20,000 in taxes was "one of the thrifty methods of the Portland Gas Co." Little more was said until Judge Henry McGinn launched his broadside on June 19th.[60]** Four months later, the *Oregonian* published a further attack under the headline: "Big Grab Plan on River Front."[61] The Gas Co. was accused of making a deal with the Port of Portland to receive dredgings at minimal cost, thereby extending its land into the river and changing the harbor line and narrowing the river in the process. The OR&N and Allen & Lewis Co. were also in on the deal. Gasco President, C.F. Adams, was treasurer of the port, and the port president was Capt. A.L. Pease who was employed by the OR&N. The *Oregonian* charged that this "maneuver" had added over $500,000 in value to the Gas Co.'s property.***

Early in February 1907, a report was issued by a special committee of the city council that had been appointed by Mayor Lane to investigate the *Oregonian's* charges. The three major conclusions were: (1) the gas was of poor quality; (2) the public was being grossly overcharged; and (3) the company's dealings with the public were unsatisfactory. The committee recommended that the council draft and submit a bill to the legislature to revoke the company's franchise. The report was adopted 8-6 and placed on file.[62] No further action was taken but the threat was ever present in Mills' mind and it bothered him constantly. Almost immediately, Mills and Adams started the machinery in motion that would eventually lead to the sale of the company. Augustus White wrote his cousin in March:

---

*There is no evidence in the Corbett papers to support this statement as fact. The Pittock papers, when made available, may shed some light on the question.

**See chapter VII.

***Some 25 years later, Adams' son would marry *Oregonian* owner Henry Pittock's granddaughter.

"I understand perfectly how disagreeable the present slanders of the *Oregonian* must be and do not wish you to stay in the Gas Co. any longer than is necessary to effect a reasonably satisfactory sale of the Co."[63]

Two weeks later, White again wrote Mills: "We do not want to have you tied up in the Gas Co. a day longer than you wish."[64] Mills encouraged White to push ahead with negotiations. But he advised his cousin to work through a third party. The purchaser had to be "considered an entirely independent concern" due to the unpopular-

338

ity in Portland of any "consolidation of interests."[65] The White cousins and other Mills relatives were owners of substantial blocks of Gas Co. securities and Mills did not want this fact to become publicized in the course of the negotiations. The Brooklyn and Franklin Trust Companies, in which the Mills relatives had interests, had just purchased $100,000 in Gas Co. notes at 6-1/2 percent. Despite the charges of the *Oregonian,* the company's 1906 common stock dividend rate of 6 percent was not out of line. Furthermore, the price of the gas per 1000 cubic feet had been reduced from $2.50 in 1892 to 95¢ in 1906. This was a fair rate.

5.

The Street Railway and Gas Company cases raised an obvious question in the minds of many people: was the city, in fact, receiving just treatment from the private companies that were under franchise or contract to provide public services? Of particular concern to Mayor Lane was the bidding procedure for city contracts. He sus-

339

pected collusion. "Bids have been submitted in the name of persons of whose existence no evidence can be obtained." The signatures on the documents were "of varying character."[66] Lane singled out the paving contractors whose work he had personally investigated.

One episode that Lane himself later recounted involved an inspection that he made of some recently paved streets in the Irvington district. In the course of his walk he would stop and bang the curb with a rock. Some neighborhood boys asked him what he was up to. Lane informed them that he was the mayor and would like them to help him with a project. He gave them some chalk and asked them to proceed up and down the street and hammer the curbs with rocks. Whenever they heard a hollow sound they were to mark the spot with a big "x". Lane then went over to his vehicle and took out a pick and a sledghammer. He proceeded to hammer the curb spots himself, leaving the pieces in the gutter. The next morning the contractor stormed into city hall and demanded to know what the mayor was doing, destroying his recently installed concrete curbing. Lane informed him that if he did not immediately rebuild all of the curbs within a specific time period he would have the man thrown in jail and the contract cancelled without any payment for the work completed. A subsequent investigation brought full restitution to the city.[67]

On another occasion, Lane went to inspect the water mains and meters at West Park and Glisan. When he began digging, a man came by and asked him what he was doing. " 'We have to look at this meter,' Lane explained. So the man inquired if he worked for the city. Lane replied in the affirmative. 'I used to do that kind of work,' the man volunteered, 'but I got a better job, and it's a good thing too, what with the mayor's program to make city employees work harder. If he'd quit sitting in his office and come down here and try it himself, he'd see that this is hard work.' "[68]

For over two years Mayor Lane beseeched the council to repeal existing city ordinances requiring hard surfaced streets. He wanted to break up the "concrete pool." He suggested that the city resort to tarred Macadam surfaces, encouraging new companies to bid for the work. The city, said Lane, "is subjected to the shame of being made a shuttlecock by such unclean players" as the concrete contractors.[69]

In March of 1907, Harry Lane embarked on another personal crusade against a fraudulent contractor named Lafe Pence. In the waning months of the Williams administration, Pence had sought permission from the city to construct water conduits across portions of MacLeay Park. With the support of the Board of Trade, Pence planned to sluice dirt off the hills behind Willamette Heights and transport it through wooden flumes to the Guild's Lake area as fill for a projected industrial site. Pence was only one of many hungry land developers who could not wait to get their hands on the soon to be vacated exposition grounds. Within two years, Pence had constructed over 14 miles of sluices, some going way back into the hills of Washington County. Much of the land from which he was dredging dirt was within the incorporated limits of Linnton, an area that would be annexed to the city in 1915 and that someday would be included in the Forest Park preserve. By use of "hydraulic giants", Pence was sluicing as much as 2000 yards a day and he was ruining the approaches to MacLeay Park. During the winter months he used rainfall runoff for most of his water needs, but during the summer he tapped the creeks so that the Balch Creek channel was

practically dry at the foot of Willamette Heights. Pence had great plans to build an electric rail loop through the hills to Linnton and back to Portland on the west side of the exposition grounds. He also planned to terrace the hills adjacent to the rail loop and prepare sites for residential development.

When Mayor Lane discovered that Pence had never received official permission to run flumes over city property, he ordered the operation terminated. After a period of non-compliance, the mayor, in company with a couple of policemen, hiked up to the scene with pick and shovel and personally destroyed the largest of the flumes. But the mayor could not prevent Pence from continuing his rape of the landscape outside of the city limits. And the private landowners who were receiving the dirt welcomed the development that promised to increase their property values.[70]

A week later, the *Oregonian* carried a major front page story on the call for a graft investigation by a coalition of reformers, progressive Republicans and others under the leadership of John B. Coffey.* The group was reported to be raising a fund of $50,000 and negotiating for the return of prosecutor Francis Heney to direct the

---

*Coffey, a prominent tailor by trade, was later to become Registrar of Elections for Multnomah County. He served in the 1907 Assembly.

investigation. "We believe," said the announcement, "that there has been as much graft in Portland as in San Francisco. . . . Corporations and trusts must be dealt a blow for their practice of illegally influencing legislation."[71]

Mayor Lane responded that he doubted the existence of extensive graft in Portland. "It is more a case of careless business records and lack of intelligence" on behalf of past city administrations. Said Lane, "franchises have been blundered away, not grafted away." Lane cited the undue influence and pressure of certain private interests "at the public expense."[72] An example of what Lane was referring to was the report by the *Journal* six weeks later that Councilman H.A. Belding had purchased 12 large parcels of land adjacent to the United Railways right-of-way three months before the council approved its franchise application on May 26, 1906, but during the time, nevertheless, that the matter was under official deliberation. Of course jeweler Belding denied any conflict of interest; it was merely a good investment that came to his attention.[73]

One of the most flagrant examples of shabby contract performance came to light just a few months before Lane left office. In February 1909, the new N.E. 28th Ave. bridge over Sullivan's Gulch was found to be "seriously" defective by the executive board which had to examine it before the city could accept it and pay the contractor his final installment. It was the first reinforced concrete bridge to be constructed in Portland. The inspection found that the bridge was sagging badly, expansion joints had been left out and the concrete was of poor quality. Upon further examination the board discovered that not only had the bridge not been built in accordance with the plans and specifications but that the plans themselves were faulty.[74]

The contractor was Joseph R. Bowles who owned the Northwest Bridge Works, a subsidiary of his Northwest Construction Co.* Bowles agreed to repair the bridge in accordance with revised specifications but the matter was not to be completely resolved for several years and even then the bridge had to be rebuilt after World War I. Bowles' future career was not damaged by this temporary setback. His Northwest Steel Co., organized in 1914, was to become one of the country's largest and most productive First World War shipyards. But in 1920 he was to be accused of bribing a government hull inspector and was to be convicted of contempt of court for refus-

---

*As announced in the Chamber *Bulletin* in August 1906, Northwest Construction erected the most completely equipped steel fabricating plant west of Chicago at the foot of N.W. 15th on the river.

ing to turn over his records to the Justice Department.[75] The story is told on good authority that Bowles would go swimming late at night in the river and remove expensive fittings from the hulls of his ships and then charge the government for replacements. Through such practices, he became a wealthy man and built one of Portland Heights' largest and showiest homes.

6.

Early in April 1907 Harry Lane disclosed that he expected to run for re-election that June. Although he would secure the Democratic nomination the party leadership was not happy with him. He announced that he wanted the freedom — "unfettered hands" — to find and install in city management the best people "regardless of party." Declared Lane: "The rights of the whole people come first."[76] Lane's opponent was to be city auditor, Republican Thomas C. Devlin who was to build his campaign on the theme that "the reformer ultimately fails." He favored applying the soundest business principles to city affairs. Efficiency would breed honesty and such a government would improve morality.

In two years, Harry Lane had antagonized most of the traditional business and political party leadership. Although he looked upon his years in office as "joyful times," he felt frustrated by the weak mayor-council form of government. The main ill of American cities, he said on many occasions, "is decentralized power and authority." Why? Because "nobody is to blame. . . . The public can't put its finger on the guilty man." Everyone sidesteps and "the culprit remains unseen and therefore unwhipped." Lane believed in a strong mayor who could be held accountable. "The eye of the people would be on a single spot. . . . Nobody can watch a dozen ratholes simultaneously."[77]

In spirit, Harry Lane was a Jeffersonian Democrat who had deep faith in the common people whom he found to be "better informed than the businessmen and the University Club members." He realized, however, that a viable democracy depended upon an educated electorate that was concerned with the basic issues. In technique, Lane was a Hamiltonian Federalist. He believed in a strong executive who could act decisively in the people's interest. In temperament, he was emotional and headstrong like a Roosevelt. He knew what was good for the people, and it was not difficult for him to play God, even though he was usually right. At times he could exhibit a degree

344

of audacity — some called it arrogance — that led to strong disagree-ment with his closest friends.

As the election date approached, the press reported that the liquor interests were backing Devlin and the re-election of city Judge George J. Cameron. They had also formed a new political society to repeal the initiative and referendum called "The Patriotic Brother-hood of Liberty Defenders." In no previous municipal campaign of memory had the liquor question created such spirited acrimony. Responding to all the hoopla, the *Journal* declared that "decency and morality" are the only real issues. "There is a solid phalanx of vice, fronting the social order. . . . Is Portland to surrender once more to the audacity of the north end cohorts."[78] The morning of the elec-tion, the *Oregonian* confessed to its readers that "in the present municipal contest" it had "not participated with its customary energy." It was discouraged by the attitude of many regular Repub-licans who had publicly broken ranks in support of a Democrat. "They have failed to cooperate." The paper was also critical of "the Republican management" that was "in league with the interests . . . the franchise operators."[79]

On June 3, 1907, Harry Lane won re-election by 1500 votes. He lost in all of the six wards on the West side. The Downtown, North End and Portland Heights residents gave Devlin a surplus of 1000 votes. Interestingly enough, it turned out that in Ward 2, over 150 voters were prevented from voting — actually turned away at the polls — because they had forgotten to re-register after they had been forced to move by the SP&S freight terminal construction that destroyed 18 blocks of residences, shops, hotels and lodging houses in North-west Portland. Lane might actually have taken the ward that he lost by 200 votes had these unhappy citizens been able to record their displeasure with the railroad. Lane picked up his surplus on the East side, winning handily in all four wards, especially his own Ward 7 in the Southeast. As could be expected, the only council support Lane ever enjoyed came from the East side of the river.[80]

The voters approved a record 11 of 16 amendments to the city charter that had either been proposed by the council or initiated by the voters. The victorious measures included authorization for bond sales as follows: $3 million for a new Bull Run pipe line, $1 million for parks, $500,000 for municipal dock land purchase, $450,000 for a new Madison Street Bridge, and $275,000 for a new fireboat, fire hydrants and water mains. The voters approved the establishment of a free public employment bureau, an increase in the liquor store license fee to $800 a year, further regulations on

WARD MAP OF PORTLAND

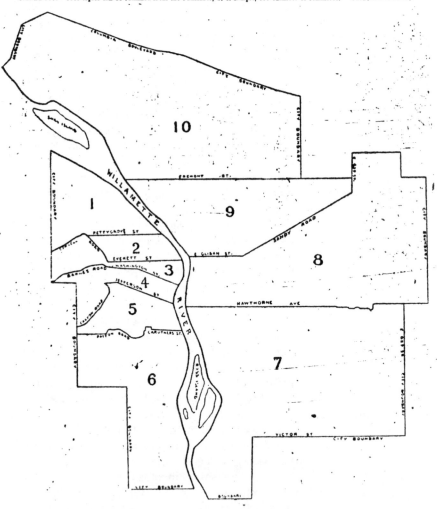

the hours for saloon operations, a 25 year franchise for the Gas Co. and a franchise renewal for the Portland Railway Light & Power Co. that increased the annual compensation to $15,000.[81] The only defeated amendment that Lane had strongly supported provided for salary increases to all of the major city departments.

Reflecting the general tone of discouragement shared by most of Portland's West side establishment, financier Augustus White, who followed Portland events closely, wrote his cousin Abbot Mills on June 4th: "I see by the evening papers that Lane has been re-elected by 1500 — I am sorry."[82]

Not daunted by his failure to attract the support of Portland's business leadership, Harry Lane called for general public interest in the work and decisions of the city council. At the opening of the new council session, Lane declared:

> "The day in which the servants of the people can play 'ducks and drakes' with the people's interests or pay off personal or political debts or other obligations at the expense of the people has gone by, let us hope never to return. . . . The people are now awake . . . [They] . . . expect and demand of their agents . . . true and just service."

Citing instances of gratuities to public officials and the "giving away" of public property by the city fathers, Lane concluded:

> "I have no enemies to punish or friends to reward in the administration of the City's affairs. . . . [My only] desire is to accomplish as much good for the benefit of the people as is possible."[83]

Chapter XII

Some Power Jobbers Among the Natives, 1907-1909

1.

In 1907 Portland had its share of power jobbers, the most skillful of which were the representatives of the major public service corporations — the absentee controlled street railways and railroads. Of the latter group, the Harriman forces led the pack, not only in total track mileage,* but in the unabashed display of arrogance and in the sheer use of force. During a four year period ending in 1909, the Harriman companies invested over $10 million in Oregon according to a self-congratulatory announcement by Harriman's regional manager.** Not detailed was the nature of the local improvements: the building of a tunnel under public land, the laying of side tracks on public streets and the extension of freight services to private companies — all accomplished without payment of compensation.

By 1913, when the federal courts decreed the divorce of the Union Pacific from the Southern Pacific, the Harriman Lines held a total of 56 franchises within the incorporated limits of Portland. With the SP&S, they also shared 34 franchises that had been awarded to the Northern Pacific Terminal Co.[1]***

---

*When Harriman died in 1909, the track mileage was 666.

**The general manager for a number of years was J.P. O'Brien. Villard's early companion and protege, Richard Koehler, played an important role as second vice-president of the Oregon & California division, general purchasing agent for the S.P. and later president of the Oregon, Washington Railway Navigation division. Koehler's signature appeared on all of the franchise applications until 1913.

***The Portland City Charter of 1913 required an annual corporate report of all current franchises.

349

Edward H. Harriman, "the wizard
of Wall Street", (1848-1909)

In 1906, only eight years after Harriman acquired the Southern
Pacific with Rockefeller's help and merged all of his properties, the
Harriman-Rockefeller syndicate noted a 1400 percent increase in the
value of its total holdings. And for the two years of 1906 and 1907,
the railroads reported a combined net profit of $22.2 million.[2] With
economic resources of this magnitude, the major railroad owners like
Harriman and Hill exercised virtually unlimited political power
that they did not hesitate to use for their own benefit. The record of
awarded franchise applications free of public compensation is sufficient proof of their success.

The explosive growth of railroad power, employing vast amounts
of eastern bank and life insurance capital, generated justifiable concern in the minds of many political leaders, including President
Theodore Roosevelt and governors like Charles Evans Hughes of
New York. Beginning with the Elkins Act, passed by Congress in
1903, the next five years were to see a multitude of regulatory laws
enacted, mostly at the state level. The larger railroad conglomerates
actually fostered some of the legislation like the Elkins Act, in an
attempt to preserve their competitive positions by preventing loss
of revenue from rate cutting and rebate practices. Although the
Elkins Act was designed to supplement the authority of the Interstate Commerce Commission by stabilizing rates, it actually permitted the larger railroads to reinforce their existing power. The Hepburn Act of 1906 .went beyond the Elkins Act in an attempt to

350

strengthen the authority of the ICC itself. The ICC could now determine and prescribe just and reasonable maximum rates as well as enforce a uniform system of accounts. The Hepburn Act also restricted the issuance of free passes, a practice that had long been successfully employed in Oregon as a means of assuring sympathetic treatment from state and local governments.

If nothing else, the railroad laws opened the company books to public scrutiny — the exhorbitant profits and some questionable practices became public knowledge. Governor Hughes' investigations of the life insurance and public utility companies in New York had revealed the extent to which many large corporations had employed secret bank accounts for political purposes. Harriman himself had borrowed heavily from the Equitable Life Insurance Co. for political funds; his being a director of Equitable merely made the practice more heinous to Governor Hughes.

The Oregon legislature meeting in February 1907 was not immune to a growing demand by the public and Governor Chamberlain that some formal regulatory agency be created to "guide" the growth of railroad activity. If the legislature did not take action, the public by initiative might produce an instrument that was excessively restrictive. Furthermore, a study that was made of the 1907 House membership revealed an inordinate imbalance in the distribution of state representatives. The existing "election plan [was] way outdated." The electoral districts had been "gerrymandered." According to *Arena* Magazine,[3] the legislature of 59 Republicans and one Democrat, if proportionately elected, would result in a lineup of 33 Republicans, 20 Democrats, four Socialists and three Prohibitionists. The legislature was not about to redraw the electoral district lines, but at the same time its leaders were acutely aware that as the public became more fully informed as to the inequity of the system an initiative reform measure could well result. For these and other reasons, the legislature appeared amenable to Governor Chamberlain's legislative recommendations.

By an act of February 18, 1907, the Railroad Commission of Oregon was re-established* consisting of three members to be appointed by the governor, secretary of state and state treasurer. Representing different regions, the commissioners were to be elected upon expiration of their initial terms. The commission was given power to revise intra-state rates but not to formulate complete rate schedules. In 1911

---

*The 1898 session of the legislature had abolished the original Board of Railroad Commissioners (established in 1887).

James Steel.

its powers were to be enlarged to include the supervision and regulation of all public utilities. Its most effective role, however, was as a collector and publisher of inside corporate information that had never before been a matter of public record.

The second major regulatory agency to be established by the legislature in February 1907 was the State Board of Banking Commissioners, consisting of the governor, secretary of state and the state treasurer. Until the passage of this law that went into effect on May 25th, Oregon had absolutely no state banking regulations; neither a license nor a permission to operate was required. Henceforth, new state banks had to incorporate but existing state banks would be exempted from incorporation until 1925. The law also provided for a state bank examiner, stricter loan regulations and prohibitions against conversion of funds to private use by banks or bank officers.[4]

The man chosen to be Oregon's first bank examiner was none other than the well known Portland banker and former railway executive James Steel, brother-in-law of the late William S. Ladd. Steel's past business attachments also included enterprises related to coal, timber, sewer pipes, ore reduction, woolen manufacturing and real estate. There were few Oregonians alive in 1907 who had been involved in a more varied spread of business careers than the 72 year

George A. Steel.

old native of Ohio. No record exists as to how James Steel secured his appointment; it can only be assumed that Governor Chamberlain would have opposed it.* Obviously the other two state officers chose him; the state treasurer was his younger brother George.

George A. Steel, 12 years junior to James, was the epitome of the eager, second level businessman-politician. Never quite gaining acceptance to the highest social or business stations, George spent his life as an agent of the establishment, always at the service of those who needed his help — for a price. George Steel was a power jobber.

Starting out as an accountant for William S. Ladd, George Steel soon became involved in politics as a member of the Republican State Central Committee. From 1876 forward he was to be one of Joseph Simon's chief lieutenants.** He served in the state senate for two terms and was for eight years the Portland Postmaster, one of the choicest of patronage appointments. He became intimately involved in all of his brother's railway and real estate enterprises, usually as a working treasurer or secretary of the corporation. He was an early junior associate of Jonathan Bourne's in a number of mining ventures. And from 1896 to 1904 he was a Republican nation-

*Steel admitted in 1907 that his old Metropolitan R.R. Co. had kept three sets of books!!!

**In June 1886, Steel had been accused by the *Oregonian* of aiding Simon in a vote fraud scheme that convicted Ralph Dement (*Oregonian,* June 8, 1886).

al committeeman from Oregon. When he ran for election as state treasurer in 1906, he listed himself as a "farmer."

2.

Three weeks after the new banking law went into effect, Abbot Mills addressed the Oregon State Bankers Association on the topic "Doubtful Banking." The major cause of bank failure, said Mills, was "the improper use of funds of a bank in the pet enterprises of its officers and stockholders." Cautioning bank officers and stockholders against being first borrowers Mills also advised against putting "too many eggs in one basket."[5] In no case, warned Mills, should a bank grant excess credits to one borrower.

Mills' speech was highly prophetic. The stock market on Wall Street had been dropping since March. By June it was in sharper decline. Considering the nature of the boom that had swept through the country during the previous three years and the fact that much of it was built upon optimism and extended credit, Mills, the ever cautious banker, could well be alarmed. The "Panic of 1907" hit Portland earlier than it did New York City. On August 21st,the Oregon Trust & Savings Bank closed its doors and went into receivership. A product of the recent bank boom,* Oregon Trust & Savings had been organized by Lonner O. Ralston in 1904. By 1907, the president was W.H Moore and the cashier was W.C. Morris, two gentlemen who did not thoroughly understand the techniques of sound banking. More than most other banks in Portland, it carried many small savings accounts that it had actively solicited from working class women and widows. Needless to say, hundreds of these unfortunate depositors were wiped out.

As the story unfolded, it was discovered that a large portion of the bank's assets, $320,000 worth, was in bonds of newly organized independent telephone systems in Omaha and Tacoma that had not yet even begun to operate. District Attorney Manning further discovered that the bank's officers had shared in the profits of the bond sales to the bank; they had kept $20,000 in bank commissions for their own personal use. When depositors sought to withdraw their

---

*One of the trends in banking in 1906-07 was the founding of ethnic banks. The two leading Portland institutions were the German American and the Scandinavian American Banks. Also founded were Italian American, Japan American and Swiss American Banks.

funds, the bank had insufficient liquidity to meet the demand. Both officers were indicted, convicted and ultimately sent to jail.[6]

By the time that Oregon Trust & Savings collapsed, Bank Examiner James Steel had not had a chance to make any of the annual examinations that were required by the new law. Not until the following May would the machinery be in full operation. But there was no need to worry said the leaders of Portland's banking community. "The banks in Portland have never been in better condition than today,"[7] declared J. Thorburn Ross, president of the Title Guarantee & Trust Co. Generally speaking, Ross was correct. Business was good in Portland. What Ross did not reveal was that a couple of the savings and trust banks in Portland "had been skyrocketing with other people's money in telephone bonds, irrigation bonds and timber land speculations."[8] And Ross' bank was one of them.

During the following fall, six Manhattan and Brooklyn, New York banks went into receivership, including the Brooklyn Trust Co. of which Abbot Mills' father had been an officer. The most spectacular New York failure was that of the old line Knickerbocker Trust Co. on October 22, 1907. The scare was of short duration as the U.S. Treasury Department and J.P. Morgan & Co. each loaned $25 million to the New York Bank Clearing House Association to support any banks in temporary distress. By December, stability had been restored.

In Portland, however, there was more to come. On November 6th Thorburn Ross' Title Guarantee & Trust Co. collapsed with a thud. Writing from New York to Abbot Mills three days later, Augustus White commented: "This looks like the gradual weeding out of the weak points in your local situation. . . . Most of our banks here would envy your having such a large amount of gold in your vaults."[9] By November 10th, the *Journal* was to report that Title Guarantee & Trust's total liabilities amounted to $2.6 million,[10] making it the largest bank failure in Portland's history. Over $600,000 was owed to the Ladd & Tilton Bank and over $400,000 to the State of Oregon, funds that had been deposited by treasurer George Steel. Ross was charged with looting the bank and Steel with incompetence. The state treasurer had put public funds in the one bank that was the poorest risk in the state. As subsequent investigation discovered, Title Guarantee had never been solvent.

Title Guarantee's* failure posed many complications for Portland's

---

*Much of Title Guarantee & Trust's business was in real estate mortgages. Beginning in the late 1890's the firm's name began showing up on titles of property for which loans or mortgages had been issued way earlier by

J. Thorburn Ross.

business community as well as severe consequences for the Ladd family. Until July, 1906 the bank's president had been William M. Ladd, eldest son of the late William S. and the designated successor to his father in the management of the major Ladd family interests. Title Guarantee was an outgrowth of the Real Estate Title & Trust Co. that had been established in 1888 to fulfull a role for the Ladd & Tilton Bank similar to that later played by the Security Savings & Trust Co. for the First National Bank. Ross had been involved for several years as secretary and manager. An examination of Ross'

---

old W.S. Ladd himself. Before Ross' regime, the company had a reputation for ruthless adherence to payment schedules, looking for any excuse to take control of property in cases where payments were in default. One illustrious case involved prominent Portlander, Judge Philip A. Marquam who lost his building, that was to collapse in 1912 while undergoing renovation, and 80 acres of farmland on Sandy Blvd. to Title Guarantee in July 1906 following a State Supreme Court ruling. Under Ross, Title Guarantee went in for more speculative ventures. In the Marquam case, Ross was accused of unethical conduct. The bank was both trustee for the family and creditor of Marquam. The bank got the building for one-third its value and the Oregon Supreme Court upheld the bank.

One young man who lost all of his $1000 savings was E.B. MacNaughton, a recently arrived practicing architect in 1907. Years later he would become chairman of the board of Mills' First National Bank. In exchange for his lost savings, the bank gave MacNaughton five lots from Marquam's former Sandy Blvd. acreage. He developed them and more than got his money back.

career leaves one to wonder about the judgment of William M. Ladd and others who placed a man like Ross in such a position of trust.

J. Thorburn Ross was a minor power jobber, but of an extreme sort. There was little in his past record to commend him for a position of responsibility. From the mid-1890's he had been a political crony of Joe Simon's and former Mayor H.S. Rowe. He had run on several legislative tickets with George W. Bates and Donald MacKay and had served in the 1898 and 1899 sessions of the House. Simon viewed him as an eager and loyal worker who was valuable to his cause. For a number of years he was known to be close to the liquor interests who were fighting Harry Lane in 1907. As an agent of William M. Ladd, he had become involved with insurance as well as mortgage banking, but until mid-1906 he had never exercised top administrative responsibility.

One respected old time banker recalls that Ross was "stupid."[11] A contemporary of Ross' called him "incompetent and extravagant."[12] He was also dishonest. Within two years he would be indicted and convicted for misuse of public funds and for land fraud that did not have anything directly to do with Title Guarantee. After serving a short jail sentence he lapsed into much deserved obscurity for the remainder of his life.

Ross' incompetence was more than matched by that of State Treasurer George Steel. As the *Journal* was to report, "Steel's relations with the Title Guarantee Boys were very close and they were grabbing everything in sight."[13] Steel of course was the brother of William M. Ladd's uncle James and had worked closely with old William S. The relationship was indeed a cozy one, so cozy that George never bothered to find out in what accounts the state funds were placed, nor did he bother with basic essentials such as security that was required by statute. He further violated the law by putting the entire state school fund in one bank. Upon investigation it was found that certain of the state funds were placed in the bank's active account, thus qualifying them as available for loan purposes. According to the *Journal*, there were "many indications that on some of the bank's loans . . . heavy rakeoffs were received by individuals connected with the bank."[14]

To make matters worse, when the state's bonding company, American Surety, paid over the sum of $34,009 to reimburse the state for losses incurred in the Oregon Trust and Savings failure, George Steel "promptly plunked the money into the coffers of the Title Guarantee."[15] Poor American Surety was forced to pay double. With revelations of this sort, Governor George Chamberlain called for

Steel's resignation.[16]*

On December 31st, William M. Ladd publicly offered to assume all credit obligations of the Title Guarantee & Trust Co. As owner of 30 percent of the bank's stock, he had announced initially that he would guarantee payment to cover savings accounts up to a total of $400,000 and that Ladd & Tilton would relinquish the security that it held for a claim of $607,000. But when it was charged in the press that Ladd must have had knowledge of some of Ross' fraudulent transactions and that Ladd & Tilton must have profited from them, Ladd offered to cover everything. This decision was to cost him over $2.5 million. It also was to cost him control of the Ladd & Tilton Bank.

3.

William Mead Ladd's life deserves a close look. In 1907, he was the ranking leader of Portland's native aristocracy. Although not a power jobber by inclination, he had close ties to the power jobber element that operated within the Portland business-political establishment. After his graduation from Amherst College, in Massachusetts, he had returned to Portland to assist his father in the management of the family's extensive business enterprises. His first independent venture was as an investor along with his brother Charles Elliot Ladd in several of Jonathan Bourne's mining operations. When W.S. organized the Real Estate Title & Trust Co. in 1888, William M. was installed as president. Fulfilling a duty that was incumbent upon a Ladd son, William M. won a seat in the Oregon House in 1889. He had officially launched his career in state Republican politics.

Father Ladd must have had some doubts, and rightly so, as to the abilities of this three sons.** The old man was a dominant — almost dictatorial — individual, a shrewd businessman not blinded by family loyalty. He realized that the future health of his holdings

---

*Steel had invested public funds as follows:

$ 35,432 in the Oregon Trust & Savings Bank
  12,478 in the Merchants National Bank
107,483 in the Title Guarantee & Trust Co.
288,426 in the Title Guarantee & Trust Co. (Education Fund)

**C.E. Ladd had some business talent but he much preferred to fish and hunt. He was on the Port of Portland Commission for many years. Youngest son, John Wesley Ladd, was a bit of a scatterbrain who spent a good portion of his time chasing women and enlivening social gatherings.

William M. Ladd
(1856-1931)

would depend upon the quality of their management. W.S.'s close friend, Asahel Bush, the Salem banker, may have had his partner's future needs in mind when he visited his home town of Westfield, Massachusetts in 1877. He spotted a bright young man working in the local bank and made his acquaintance. Shortly thereafter Bush offered Theodore Burney Wilcox* a job as a teller with Ladd & Tilton and Wilcox promptly accepted the offer. Over the next decade, Wilcox more than proved his value to W.S. who had made him his administrative assistant in the early 1880's. When Ladd established the original Albina Flour Mills he installed Wilcox as general manager. The firm ultimately became the extremely profitable Portland Flouring Mills.

When William S. died in the winter of 1893, son William M. became president of Ladd & Tilton, the second largest bank in Portland and still privately controlled by the Ladd family. W.M. was also to become president of the family owned Oregon Iron & Steel Co. According to Martin Winch, Wilcox was cut off from everything but Portland Flouring of which he was president at the time. Apparently Mrs. Ladd and her three sons were jealous of Wilcox who was a hard driving and very able administrator. He was resented by the family who considered him an outsider and a threat to their control. But at the same time, his counsel was required so that he remained a

*Wilcox was born in 1856, in Agawam, Massachusetts, near Springfield.

director of the bank. As Winch wrote to Simeon Reed in June 1893, William M. Ladd "is not very bright but he needs to rely on Wilcox for advice."[17]

In subsequent years, William M. dedicated himself to the worthy causes of Portland life: president of the YMCA, 1895-1922; president of the Art Museum, 1903-1926; treasurer of the Free Bridge Committee, 1891; member of the City Hall Commisison, 1896; treasurer of Riverview Cemetery; president of the Board of Portland Academy; and trustee of Reed College, 1910-1931. Also in the ensuing years, Ladd was to serve briefly on the Board of Police Commissioners* by appointment of Mayor Williams and as a member of the Water Committee from 1897 until he resigned hastily in October 1905. The period from 1905 to 1907 was to produce a series of painful experiences for the seemingly well intentioned but naive leader of Portland's establishment.

On August 30, 1905, William Ladd was accused in court of mishandling the estate of A.H. Johnson, the late owner of the Union Meat Co. At the time of death in 1894, Johnson's estate was valued at $792,000. But he had accumulated debts of $266,000, of which $189,000 was owed to the Ladd & Tilton Bank. Some time before he died, Mr. Johnson had executed a trust deed, turning over to Ladd his property, which, at the time of death, was worth $440,000. Ladd was instructed to sell whatever property was necessary to pay off any existing debts and then to reconvey the remaining property to Johnson's estate for distribution to Johnson's widow and heirs. As it turned out, Johnson's wife pre-deceased him so that the heirs became the sole beneficiaries. All of them were distant relatives, quite poor and widely scattered throughout the country; none resided in or near Portland. To shorten a long and complicated story, Ladd had done absolutely nothing in 11 years to liquidate Johnson's debts. The interest payments to Ladd & Tilton together with Ladd's executor and trustee fees had devoured most of the estate. The court ruled that Ladd had "violated the conditions of trust deed." He had allowed his trustee responsibilities to conflict with his personal interest in the business of the bank. A settlement was arranged out of court and the charges were dropped.[18]

By the fall of 1905, William M. Ladd had become a favorite target of the *Oregonian* in the same way that Mills, Adams and the Gas Company would be singled out in June of 1906. Ladd was a member of the "plutocracy" according to Harvey Scott's unique definition of

---

*From July 1902 until January 1903 when the new charter took effect.

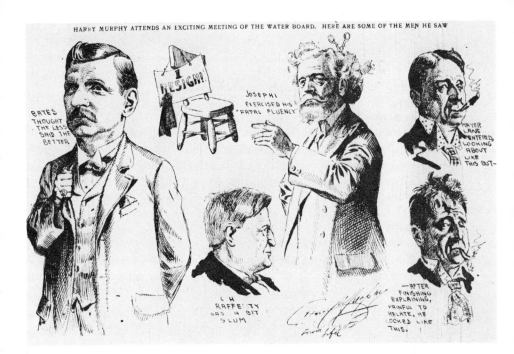

the word. The "plutocrats" were wealthy Republicans who had provided support for the founding of the *Oregon Journal* in 1902, who had assisted in the sale of the street railways to eastern bankers and who dared to vote for a Democrat for public office. Rumor had it that Ladd had endorsed Lane for his first term as mayor.

With glee, the *Oregonian* charged on October 18, 1905, that the Water Committee had accepted an illegal bid of $152,888 from the Oregon Iron and Steel Co. because Ladd was both the president of the company and a member of that esteemed public agency. All of a sudden, Scott was playing the role of a converted Puritan. Oregon Iron and Steel had received over half a million dollars in business from the Water Committee ever since 1894 but no one had bothered to mention it. The company manufactured the only reliable cast iron pipe in the Northwest. It was more costly than steel pipe but according to the engineers it had "better durability." Naturally the losing bidders were furious when the *Oregonian* printed its charges. As one agent remarked: "You might as well look for a snowball in hell as for a square deal here." The next day, Ladd resigned from the Water Board and three days later the Board cancelled all previously submitted bids and ordered a readvertising for new bids. The *Oregonian* was jubilant, especially in noting that Mayor Lane, with whom it differed "in almost everything else," gave the paper credit for exposing the conflict of interest.[19]

361

Once the spigot was turned on it was hard to turn it off. In future months, Ladd was to be charged with a number of cases of conflict of interest. In November, councilman A.G. Rushlight, who would succeed Simon as mayor in 1911, accused Ladd of having used his influence with the Water Committee to provide service for Ladd real estate tracts to the exclusion of others on the East side that were more deserving in terms of resident need. Rushlight represented Harry Lane's Ward 7 which included the eastern part of Portland South of Hawthorne Boulevard. He was also a plumbing contractor so he knew the requirements of the trade. He singled out Ladd's Addition that had practically no homes built on it and which had been provided with full water main service before it was platted for sale.* He also cited Holladay's Addition that was being developed by Title Guarantee & Trust. "Hundreds of requests for service have been denied but not these," said Rushlight.[20]

In September 1906, the *Oregonian,* branching out from its attacks on the Gas Co., blazed forth with a headline on page one that read: "Ladds are smoked out by exposure." The article related to tax assessment practices. Back in January 1905, the paper had charged that the Ladd family had been receiving favored treatment for years. It had also cited a special assessment district that had been established in Southeast Portland for properties held by both the Ladd Estate and the Southern Pacific Railroad. Then, lo and behold, when the new 1906 assessments were published they revealed an increase of more than 220 percent in the total worth of the family's real estate holdings, to over $1.7 million. Portland Flouring likewise went up from $150,000 to $1 million, and Security Savings & Trust from $375,150 to $702,000.[21] The application of public pressure had obviously been effective and the *Oregonian* deserved credit for raising the issue initially even if it did so for personal rather than public reasons. If nothing else, the episode revealed what a newspaper could do, if it tried, to expose such inequities and in the process to help bring about positive changes that would benefit the public as a whole.

William M. Ladd was a prototype of the well educated man of inherited wealth who enjoyed his station in life, who fulfilled community responsibilities thrust upon him by virtue of his position in

---

*The main Bull Run water conduit ran adjacent to Ladd's Addition, under Division Street.

society and who was expected to function successfully in the world
of competitive business that required talents which he did not possess. In contrast to T.B. Wilcox, he was not a power jobber. He rarely
exercised directly the power resources at his command. He has been
described as "a thoughtful, kindly and generous* man" who nevertheless "had a weakness for his own judgment." In this latter regard
he was not unlike his father. Others have called him "stuffy,"[22] a
characteristic that was not applicable to his father.

He lived in a world remote from most Portlanders of lesser status.
One sister, Helen, had been married to the late Henry J. Corbett,
father of Henry L. Corbett. The other, Caroline, was married to
Frederick B. Pratt of Brooklyn, New York, a classmate from Amherst, whose father, Charles Pratt, had been an early associate of
John D. Rockefeller in the Standard Oil Company and was the
founder of Pratt Institute. Ladd was usually running some organization or serving on some executive committee.** He lived comfortably
and was one of the first to develop property in the exclusive Riviera,***
now Dunthorpe, area south of Portland along the Willamette River.
The region was part of and adjacent to the large tract of wooded land
owned by his family's Oregon Iron and Steel Co., the site of the
present Tryon Creek State Park.

The extent of his influence on important public decisions is hard
to determine. He could not help but be a force of some significance
because the Ladd & Tilton Bank, with assets of $14.7 million, exerted
a major influence on the development of Portland. For years the bank
had been the largest purchaser of municipal improvement bonds. By
January 1910, it was to hold over $300,000 worth of Portland Railway
Light & Power Co. bonds. Ladd & Tilton had a definite interest in the
welfare of PRL&P. For a brief spell, at least, Ladd had been a member of Mayor George H. Williams' team. Then he apparently supported Harry Lane but had broken with the mayor by June of 1906 when
Lane fired both him and Wilcox as members of the local San Francisco Relief Committee. As a man of genuinely good intentions, but
of somewhat limited perceptions, William M. Ladd was a symbol of
Portland's genteel, respectable and cultured establishment. He certainly was not going to lead the troops into unchartered territory.

---

*He gave $100,000 to the building of the YMCA (1909); he also gave ex-
tensively to the Art Museum and Reed College.

**In 1906, for example, he was on the executive committee of the Com-
mercial Club with Wilcox, Mills, Ainsworth, Livingstone, W.F. Burrell and
J.F. Watson.

***Where, according to the *Journal,* "the well-to-do build imposing homes."

More than anything else, he was an agent of enlightened stability. His basic sympathies were liberal. But, as with most of his compatriots, the major problems facing urban Portland in 1910 escaped his comprehension.

4.

For some years, Ladd & Tilton had not played as prominent a public role as either the First National or U.S. National Banks. As a private institution it tended to keep a low profile. Under William S. Ladd's firm hand it fulfilled one major purpose: to invest its bank resources in and gain control of potentially profitable business enterprises. In 50 years its assets had grown 30,000 percent. With the passage of the Oregon Banking Act in 1907, it was forced, as a private bank, to incorporate and to make its books available to public scrutiny.

Beginning with 1908, the corporation records are revealing.[23] Aside from the three Ladd sons and their mother, the major local stockholders were T.B. Wilcox, Henry L. Corbett, his mother Helen Ladd Corbett, and Edward Cookingham, the bank's attorney and vice president. By 1909, the Pratt family of Brooklyn, New York had gained control by virtue of owning 5000 of the 9000 capital stock shares. For bailing out William M. Ladd to cover his Title Guarantee & Trust losses, the Pratts took possession of W.M.'s controlling block of stock. At the behest of the Pratts, Cookingham was installed as the chief administrative officer although his title was only that of vice president.

The bank's largest single investments were in the Portland Flouring Mills ($2 million) and the Dexter Horton National Bank of Seattle ($1 million). In fact the Portland Flouring Mills holding constituted one-half of the bank's total stock investment. In October 1910, Ladd & Tilton reduced its holding of $300,000 in Portland Railway Light & Power bonds to $50,000, and bought $338,000 of Portland city improvement bonds. Ladd & Tilton was indeed a profitable institution. The 1908 statement showed a cash surplus of $250,000 and undivided profits for the year of $285,000. By 1910, the combined total would rise to $670,000.

The Ladds, Wilcox and Cookingham were also instrumental in shaping the growth of the Equitable Savings and Loan Association, which was an outgrowth of the old Oregon Building and Loan Association, established in 1890. Ladd & Tilton owned 100 shares of Equitable stock. Charles E. Ladd was president of Equitable during the first decade of the 1900's but by 1912 Wilcox was to become the president and guiding spirit. The company had in force $2.2 million of real estate loans in 38 cities of the Northwest, and by 1910 it had returned to investors more than $2.2 million.[24]

An examination of Ladd & Tilton's operation through 1914, reveals how easy it was for insiders like T.B. Wilcox to make a bucket of money with practically unlimited credit. For example, in September 1911, Portland Flouring and two other Wilcox milling enterprises borrowed $300,000, a sum that was equal to about 5 percent of the bank's outstanding commercial loans. Wilcox of course was a bank director and a major bank stockholder. And, as was noted above, one-half of the bank's own investments were in Portland Flouring. In November 1914, when wheat prices were escalating world wide, Wilcox borrowed $800,000, or 10 percent of the bank's commercial loans. There was nothing really illegal about these transactions in 1914 although they would be expressly prohibited today. On a much smaller scale, Ladd & Tilton was pursuing investment and banking policies similar to those of the New York private banks like J.P. Morgan & Co.

Thus, while William M. Ladd was suffering declining fortunes,* his father's protegé, using his father's bank and other resources, was enjoying rapidly increasing wealth. In contrast to his friend William M. Ladd, Theodore B. Wilcox was admirably suited to taking maximum advantage of his opportunities. Following the example of his mentor W.S. Ladd, Wilcox invested his profits in a variety of real estate packages including the Rose City Park development.** The quarter block at the S.E. corner of Sixth and Washington on which the Wilcox building was to be constructed in 1911 was bought for $250,000 in 1908; it was to be appraised at $675,000 in 1928. Wilcox also purchased two other downtown parcels in 1908 for $300,000. After his death in the spring of 1918, Wilcox's estate was estimated to be worth in excess of $10 million; not bad for a working life*** of 40 years. He apparently left everything to his family and

---

*Relatively speaking. The Ladd Estate realized $2 million from the sale of the Laurelhurst tract in 1909. The estate's real estate holdings were still worth many millions.

**Wilcox and his partners realized an 800 percent profit in this enterprise.

***At a dinner in 1909, railroad magnate James J. Hill praised T.B. Wilcox as the one who had "done more than any other man in Portland . . . to develop the commerce of the Columbia River and gain recognition for the Northwest throughout the world."[26] At the time, Wilcox was president of the

T. B. WILCOX
President Portland Flouring Mills Co.

nothing to charity,* and the tax bite was $2 million.[25]

5.

The "public-be-damned" attitude of the Harriman empire was more than matched by that of the giant Portland Railway Light & Power Co. which was officially incorporated on June 29, 1906 and capitalized at $15 million. As a holding company, PRL&P took over all of the Portland Railway properties plus those of the Oregon Water

Oregon Development League. Shortly before Wilcox's death in 1918, the Ladd interests in Portland Flouring Mills were sold to the Wilcox family. A few months after his death Wilcox's estate sold all of its milling interests to Max Houser, the largest individual grain exporter in the world at that time. Many millions of dollars were involved. With the proceeds, the Wilcox estate acquired an even larger interest in Ladd & Tilton. The bank in turn was acquired by the U.S. National Bank in 1925.

*In 1921, the Wilcox family gave the money to construct the Wilcox Memorial unit of Good Samaritan Hospital for the care of obstetric and gynecologic patients.

Tracks of the Portland Railway Light & Power Co. (1907)

Power and Railway Co. that had been acquired by Portland Railway in May 1906. The company, endowed with 43 franchises, now controlled 28 separate street railway lines that covered the entire city. By the end of December 1907, when it had completed its merger with Portland General Electric, the monopoly comprised 19 companies in control of 161 miles of railway, 431 passenger cars and 6 power plants. In two years, Abbot Mills' $6 million package had been inflated 250 percent in value. By 1910, the year in which it was cited as a monopoly by the *American Banker,* the company carried 16,712,500 passengers and 5,701,000 ton miles of freight.[27]

In keeping with its eastern ownership, new top management was brought in from Baltimore, Maryland, in the person of Benage Stockwell Josselyn.* "B.S.", as he was called, proved to be an effective president of PRL&P, at least for his bosses. As for the City of Portland, he recognized few public obligations. For the six years that he held sway, he fought the city on every franchise award, bridge construction project, and street repair claim. His sole concern as head of a giant public service corporation was the generation of maximum profits.

Privately, Josselyn lived in a style that one might expect of the grand nizam of Portland corporate life. For his home, he purchased the Massachusetts State Building from the Lewis & Clark Exposition and had it moved section by section to a large tract adjacent to Mt. Tabor in East Portland. By one account, it was an "imposing" and "pretentious residence," with "porticoes" and formal gardens. "B.S." was also an avid club man, so naturally he joined the Arlington and Waverly Golf clubs. In interest and temperament, two more different people could not be found than B.S. Josselyn and Mayor Harry Lane. For two years Lane was to battle Josselyn and his giant monopoly, but with little success. With Portland banking, business and social leaders like Abbot Mills, Theodore B. Wilcox, Fred V. Holman and Charles F. Swigert, and with a majority of the council, all lined up in support of Portland Railway Light & Power, Mayor Lane and his "public" had no chance.

Within one month of its incorporation, PRL&P showed that it was going to be a tough negotiator. It refused to meet with the Amalgamated Association of Street and Electric Railway Employees. A strike was narrowly averted when the company unilaterally raised wages. The company's arrogance was fully revealed in September 1908 when it refused to renegotiate its 30 year Madison Street (Hawthorne) Bridge lease with the city. In June 1907, the voters had approved the sale of bonds for a new bridge; they had also authorized the city to charge the PRL&P a fee of $15,000 a year for use of the new structure. The company referred to the 1891 bridge franchise that had been granted to the Mt. Tabor Street Railway for a $1200 annual payment. "We insist that our present franchise be not changed," declared Josselyn in a letter to the executive board.[28] Josselyn admitted that the current payment was low and he indicated a willingness to have it increased "to some extent." But the city could not condemn its tracks; that would amount to "confiscation."

---

*Josselyn succeeded H.W. Goode who had previously been president of PGE. Goode died in 1907.

The city had no right, asserted Josselyn, "to sell bonds before the matter was resolved."[29]

All of Mayor Lane's previously expressed reservations about Portland's "give-away" franchises were clearly illustrated by the case of the 1891 award in which banker William M. Ladd had played such a prominent role as treasurer of the Free Bridge Committee. The franchise ordinance had given the city no authority to change the provisions and the 30 year limit was ridiculously excessive in terms of unforeseen future requirements. The current city charter, however, did grant the city the authority to renegotiate franchise awards and to take legal action if necessary. The executive board ruled that the 1907 charter superseded all previous charter provisions. But the council, under intense pressure from Portland's financial leaders, refused to file suit.[30] For obvious reasons, a majority of councilmen preferred out of court arbitration as a last resort to the uncertainty of trial by a jury of average citizens who could be expected to support the interests of the general public. The council finally voted to resubmit the issue to the electorate in June of 1909 and to proceed to the consideration of a new general franchise excluding bridge use.

The electric light servce of PRL&P now came in for special scrutiny. Back in the fall of 1906, Mayor Lane had vetoed two franchise awards to Portland General Electric that he felt were excessively generous. He was particularly vexed over the provision that the city had no right to regulate or modify the terms for 25 years. The maximum rate, a 2 percent gross revenue tax, was fixed in the franchise. Declared Lane: "Irreparable loss has already been suffered by the city for want of such precautions in granting valuable rights to holders of franchises in past times. . . . The public is . . . groaning under the burdens of excessive charges and inadequate service."[31]

In January 1909, the mayor again cited the excessive charges for municipal lighting services. "The city is paying more than the service is worth." Lane refused to pay some of the bills. He had futilely requested more information from PRL&P.* "The company is difficult to deal with. . . . [It is] an arrogant . . . monopoly."** Furthermore, the company was demanding higher rates for underground wires, a requirement that the council had voted the previous year.

---

*The company published no annual statement.
**A report by Arthur D. Little & Co. filed with the Oregon PUC in April 1976 criticized PGE for its poor public relations and arrogance. Like father, like son, the company's attitude toward the public has changed little in 70 years.[33]

REGULAR ORDER OF BUSINESS IN THE CITY COUNCIL

When They Get Through Wrangling Maybe Something Will Be Done for the Taxpayers

One of the rare occasions when Mayor Lane's veto was sustained.

Lane repeated his earlier caution against long term new contracts. He suggested that Portland consider a municipal plant to provide for the city's own public lighting needs. Although he would prefer to buy power from a competitive private source, none existed in Portland.[32]

The matter of Portland Railway Light & Power Co.'s new franchise came to a final vote in April 1909. A number of legal issues had been raised but the council refused to wait for the city attorney's formal opinion. One question related to the use of PRL&P tracks by C.F. Swigert's Pacific Bridge Co. "By what authority," asked councilman Rushlight, "can Portland Railway Light & Power Co. transport freight over the street railways of the city? . . . By what authority has the Pacific Bridge Co. received exclusive privileges to use the street railways of the city in the performance of public contracts?"[34] No one bothered to answer him.

The council also refused to require a common user clause as stipulated in the charter. Furthermore, it approved an unbelievably low rate of compensation payments, beginning with $500 a year. Excluding bridge charges all the city could expect to receive from a $15 million company over the next 25 years was a total of $20,000.

On April 28th, Harry Lane exploded the heaviest barrage of his four years in office. Likening the ordinance to the 1902 "blanket franchise" that Abbot Mills had wangled, Lane declared: "I do not remember ever before having heard of a case where an incorporated municipality so far lost its self-respect as to voluntarily consent to being assessed and taxed by a private corporation which was its own creature." Apart from the provisions already mentioned, Lane took issue with the company's "guaranteed right to abandon any one of or all 40 streets" anytime it wished, "to maroon any line . . . regardless of the effect of its action on the dependent public." The city had given up any authority to prevent such an eventuality. Furthermore, the city was to be required to keep in repair and good condition all switches for PRL&P use and all elevated roadways and bridges and to pay 75 percent of the cost. A city that acts in this fashion, declared Lane, that "surrenders its sovereign rights . . . is unfit to exist."[35] The council overrode the veto 13-2.

6.

The most prominent member of the Portland establishment who would have applauded Mayor Lane's outburst had he been present in the council chamber was Col. Charles Erskine Scott Wood. "C.E.S." as he was called, was certainly Portland's most colorful figure in terms of his varied interests, talents and wit. His distinguished career was one of marked contrasts: soldier, lawyer, painter and poet.* An unrivaled individualist, he was both a social anarchist and an attorney for the richest and most powerful of clients. Although a lifelong Democrat, he was not a party man except when party represented principle. As a brilliant lawyer, his services were deemed indispensable to those who could not stomach either his politics or his nonconformist causes. As a member of the Arlington Club, he was certainly unique. He could just as happily join anarchist Emma Goldman on the speaking platform as go fishing with banker Charles E. Ladd, one of his closest friends. His law partners were two of the most conservative Republicans in the state: former

---

*(1852-1944.) Born in Erie, Pennsyvania, Wood graduated from West Point in 1874, took a Ph.D. and law degree from Columbia University (1883) while serving in the army in the N.Y. area and was admitted to the Oregon Bar in 1884. He was a former Democratic candidate for district attorney and U.S. Senator.

C.E.S. Wood.

Mayor George H. Williams and S.B. Linthicum. What distinguished him from Harry Lane was his intellectual acuity, sense of humor and skepticism. Regardless of what people thought about his personal habits or social attitudes, he was highly respected and in great demand as a speaker.

Early in February 1909, Col. Wood was asked to say a few words to the monthly meeting of the Portland Chamber of Commerce:

> "Gentlemen of the Chamber of Commerce: The first thing that occurs to me to say is that you wanted Republican weather and you have got it. We have the ice and the cold and the snow and the Legislature all at once."

Proceeding to his main topic, Wood said, "I will talk about the Legislature."

> "Now I want to tell you about these gentlemen, who have gone up into the wilderness to be tempted of the devil for forty days and forty nights. I live near an educational institution, which in a sense, is under the wing of Bishop Scadding, and as no one can live near a sanctuary without receiving some of its droppings, I feel that my great wisdom is furnished by that institution, and just to show you how out of the mouths of babes and sucklings truth

372

is ordained, one of the younger scholars of St. Helens Hall on being asked, 'What are the two houses of Legislature of this state?' answered with an inner wisdom almost terrifying, 'The court house and the jail.' So much for our lawmakers."

Shifting to a second theme, Wood referred to Francis Heney who had visited Oregon the previous spring to campaign against the re-election of Senator Fulton.

"Mr. Heney said that business men were not to be trusted. Now he mustn't mind a little thing like that. I will tell you that there are lawyers not to be trusted by business men. Alas, but I'll not mention names, there are lawyers I wouldn't trust. You don't find lawyers trying to form a law trust. No, gentlemen, there is no monopoly in law.

But this thing of the business men going into politics is something that I want to endorse. I am one of those poor scapegoats and black sheep of a black past who has been trying to get the business men into politics and the professional machine men out of politics for a good many years. . . . The time will come when the business men of this state and this Chamber will accept the inevitable with a good grace and get down to business, adopt the present primary law in substance and see that we get good, respectable senators, good respectable officials of all kinds."

Col. Wood ended his extended remarks with a plea to Portland's business leaders to take more of an active interest in eastern Oregon's agricultural possibilities — the future wealth of the state. Referring to Episcopal Bishop Scadding who preceded him to the podium, Wood said:

"I was going to suggest that Bishop Scadding take his lantern slide and map of Oregon and go East and give a lecture to Mr. Harriman, using the map of Oregon as a basis for his talk."[36]

C.E.S. Wood was the antithesis of the power jobber. Portland was indeed fortunate to have a leader of such perception and humanity, with a mind that could put public affairs in balanced perspective, and with a fearlessly free spirit that was not afraid to burst the bubble of business or professional pretentiousness.

7.

Col. Wood's comments were appropriate to the 1909 political season that was already upon the Oregon voters. The legislature was faced with selecting a new U.S. Senator to replace the repudiated Charles W. Fulton. Popular Democratic Governor George E. Chamberlain was opposing Republican candidate Harold M. Cake, prominent Portland attorney who was also identified with the Equitable Savings & Loan Association. Fulton, the epitome of the power jobber lawyer, had proven himself blind to the machinations of the timber barons and railroad magnates. Francis Heney had made three speeches attacking Fulton as an agent of those who "had squandered the nation's heritage of natural resources."[37]* Cake's campaign suffered from both a split party and the stigma of the timber fraud trials although Cake himself was not in any way identified with the lumber interests. Following the requirements of "Proposition #1", the heavily Republican legislature swallowed hard and elected Chamberlain by a solid majority.**

In April of 1909, the voters of Portland were confronted with an approaching mayoralty election. Harry Lane had already indicated that he was tired and did not feel up to the physical requirements of running again. The Democratic leadership had definitely decided not to support him even were he to change his mind — which he did at the last moment, running as an Independent Democrat.

Portland's business leadership*** wanted a sure bet, someone who could be trusted and who was an integral part of the major corporate complex. Who better than the experienced veteran of many political battles, Joseph Simon? Since retiring from the U.S. Senate in 1903, Simon had kept a low political profile while concentrating on his law practice and his downtown investments. As the *Oregon Journal* reported on May 4th, "every public service corporation president, dir-

---

*Heney called Fulton "unfit for office," and Fulton called Heney a "liar and a viper."

**When Chamberlain resigned to go to Washington D.C. on March 1, 1909, Secretary of State Frank W. Benson succeeded to the governorship.

***With at least two notable exceptions: W.M. Ladd and lumberman W.B. Ayer who supported Rushlight along with the *Journal.*

ector, officer and agent is for Simon." Portland, said the *Journal* editorially, "will be scuttled if Simon is elected Mayor."[38]

The *Oregonian* supported Simon in his primary campaign against councilman Rushlight who was running as an Independent Republican. Simon was picked by the regular Republicans in a party convention that, according to the *Journal*, "was appointed by a handful of manipulators. The rank and file of Republican voters did not have opportunity to name a single delegate out of the whole number chosen."[39] During the succeeding week, the *Journal* pulled out all of the stops; it printed old editorials and articles from the June 1886 issues of the *Oregonian* that had attacked Simon with a degree of savagery seldom encountered in the history of American journalism. Finally, the *Journal* headlined its May 7th edition: "Boss Rule or Rule by the People — Which?" Two days later Simon defeated Rushlight in a light primary vote that saw an overwhelming turnout from the West Side and the North End. Judge M.G. Munly secured the Democratic nomination.

Banker Abbot Mills was a strong supporter of Joe Simon. The Dolph, Simon firm was handling the legal affairs of the Gas Company, particularly those that related to the forthcoming sale of the company to eastern investors. In fact, the election entered into some of the pre-conditions of sale. All during the spring, Augustus White kept writing Mills that the company's current earnings were not attractive for the price being asked. "New York can't understand why, with the growth of the gas system, the company does not show better earnings."[40] Mills replied to White that no price change could be contemplated before the election. "We hope that Simon will be elected.... We can't afford to embarrass Simon."

Mills had little to fear. Joe Simon won his return to political office with ease. In a light turn-out, the Republicans swept to victory on June 7, 1909, carrying all of the municipal offices. Over 20,000 voters had chosen not to go to the polls. The power jobbers were now back in command after a four year exile. As the conservative *Spectator* gleefully commented: "the city's affairs [would now be] conducted in a businesslike way," meaning of course the way business wants to conduct them. The paper viewed the election result as a "protest against the skyrocketing, fussy-wussy administration that Portland has had for a few years."[41]

The election ballot contained 32 measures for voter consideration, including 19 charter revisions. The most far reaching of the amendments, one that would have provided for a commission form of government based on the Galveston plan, was defeated 2-1. Not only had the *Oregonian* opposed the commission plan, but the influential Taxpay-

THE GLASGOW VOTER
(Scotland)

My city is governed by the Council and my ballot contains just the single office Councilor from my ward. I have one man to choose and it's so easy for me to know what I'm voting for that I never get buncoed. That's why Glasgow is the best governed city in the world.

THE DES MOINES (IOWA)
VOTER

My city is governed by a commission of Five, and my ballot contains just those five offices. I have just five men to choose and you can't fool me into voting for a man I don't really want. No long ready-made tickets for me—I'm boss myself with this Short Ballot, and the politicians in this town are out of jobs.

THE PORTLAND, OREGON VOTER, WITH A BALLOT THREE FEET LONG

My city, county and state are governed by hundreds of elective officers and my ballot is so long with seventy-five candidates and thirty-two initiative laws, that no one but a professional politician can vote it intelligently. I'm voting half the time for men I wouldn't vote for if I could find out about them. My ballot is designed to favor the expert politicians and befudge the plain voter, and it succeeds. That's why I have government by politicians instead of government by the people.

ers League threw its weight against the proposed changes that it considered "too radical" for the time.

A number of significant measures were approved, however. The construction of the new Broadway Bridge was authorized; a 7 percent limitation was placed on bonded indebtedness and a 6 percent limit on taxes; authority was granted to levy a 1 percent tax for a special bridge fund and a one-half percent tax for a much needed sinking fund; bonds were authorized for parks and boulevards ($1 million), docks ($500,000) and the Broadway Bridge ($450,000). Several major franchise provisions were approved that tightened up the old procedures. New franchises to public utilities were to be subject to popular vote; no territorial or side track franchises could be issued to a railroad with a time limit that extended beyond the term of the company's original franchise; the articles of every public utility franchise application would have to be specifically set forth and would have to include a 25 year maximum term and fair compensation to the city; quarterly reports would have to be submitted to the auditor with a $500 fine for failure to comply; and franchised property was to be subject to county property taxes.[42] Harry Lane could well take credit for many of the above proposals that he had been advocating vainly for four years. They were all placed on the ballot by initiative.

As Lane's term drew to a close, Simon publicized his appointments to the executive and water boards. U.S. Bank president John C. Ainsworth and Theodore B. Wilcox were named to the water board with Wilcox as chairman, and Henry L. (Harry) Corbett, the 26 year old manager of the Corbett Estate, was appointed to the executive board which was composed entirely of businessmen. The four newly elected members of the council included a wealthy realtor-contractor, a lawyer, a wealthy grain executive and Thomas C. Devlin the former auditor and mayoralty candidate. The council was an average middle class, merchant oriented political body. Pacific Grain president Gay Lombard was the only councilman to be a member of an exclusive club, in this case Waverly. On the executive board, however, were four Waverly members, two of whom were also members of the Arlington Club. Abbot Mills was offered a position on the executive board but he declined in favor of his young associate, Harry Corbett, who at the time was vice president of the First National Bank among his many and varied responsibilities. The Port of Portland Commission, whose members were appointed by the legislature, was the blue ribbon business panel of 1909. Headed by Charles F. Swigert, with Gasco's C.F. Adams as treasurer, the group included John C. Ainsworth and former Chamber president William D. Wheelwright.

Mayor Joseph Simon's term of office was going to be safe for the Portland business community. West Side, downtown Portland was back in control. In his first major message to the council in October, Simon reassured his supporters when he declared: "The functions of city government relate almost wholly to business and little to politics. Modern business methods should be applied to their execution," and the departments of government "kept within appropriate limits."[43] This was an amazing statement for one whose life had been devoted almost entirely to party politics. Perhaps Simon had mellowed during his years of political retirement. In 1909, he liked to think of himself as a man of moderation and stability. The future would tell. At least the official relationships within city hall and between city hall and the port would be much closer and more cordial than those of the previous administration.

8.

When Harry Lane left office on June 30, 1909, he received predictably contrary evaluations. The *Oregonian* blistered him. The *Journal* praised him for leaving Portland "a clean city." Declared the *Journal*, Lane was a man "of great integrity" who had no political machine ties whatsoever.[44] In the history of the city to 1976, Lane's four years as mayor clearly stand out. "They were not inane administrations," as Senator Chamberlain was later to comment. They were not to be forgotten as most have been that have stood for nothing. The Lane-Simon differences were as pronounced as any that have ever afflicted Portland — two men with totally different backgrounds, professions, temperaments and sets of interests. Lane did not accomplish much in a material sense. He was not a great builder of brick and mortar structures. In many ways he was a failure if one were to use tangible measurements. But he was a positive leader who was not afraid to tell the people the truth as he saw it. He did not flinch from trying to lead the people in directions that he believed were important and necessary for the city's future survival. He was more concerned with human values than material values, with "soft ware" rather than hardware. "He opened the closed eyes of the public to what was going on. . . . Without a Lane, Portland might still be in the mire of those rotten times."

In retrospect Portland has seen some rotten times since George Chamberlain uttered these words in 1917.[45] Harry Lane did not succeed in cleaning up the city once and for all. But at least he tried, and he cared. He valued people as ends in themselves, and not as instruments to be used by others. He was a thoroughly ethical man and therein lies his great distinction.

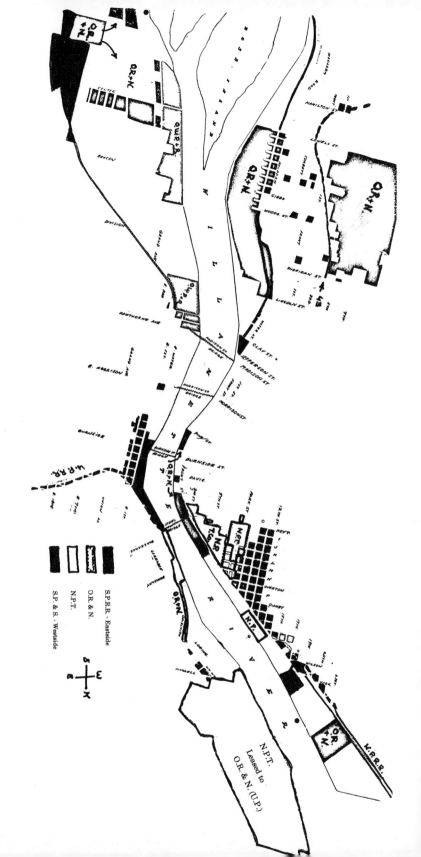

Map of Portland's waterfront, showing the immense amount of river frontage in possession of the railroads.

Chapter XIII.

One Step Backward, Two Steps Forward, 1910-1913

1.

"[A] peculiarity of American conditions is the extraordinary vigor and activity of private enterprise, which has stood ready on all occasions to assume the semi-public functions of the city and exploit them for private gain. American cities have not only unlimited suffrage and heterogeneous population to control, but also the powerful combination of private interests banded together to gain riches from special privileges in the streets and ready if need be to apply an almost resistless power of organized greed to corrupt the sources of the civic polity."[1]

This statement by Delos F. Wilcox* in 1910 could just as easily have been applied to Portland as to the major eastern cities that he was examining. Mayor Simon's administration was a business regime, run by the most experienced political professional in Oregon. Not only was he a master of the art of compromise, but he was thoroughly versed in the techniques of self promotion and public relations. After only six months in office, he received a glowing evaluation by the *Oregonian* and the heartiest of congratulations from Portland's business leadership.

---

*Wilcox (1873-1928) was one of America's leading public utility experts. In 1910, he was Chief of the Bureau of Franchises of the New York Public Service Commisison, New York City District.

A memorandum in Simon's "Papers" lists five accomplishments that he wanted preserved for the historical record: (1) the establishment of a "hard surface" policy relating to street paving — concrete over asphalt; (2) the decision to build a new garbage crematorium* at the old Guild's Lake site; (3) the promotion of underground utility wires; (4) the expansion of the Bull Run pipeline; and (5) the purchase and location of sites for additional children's playgrounds.[2] In later life, Simon was to comment: " . . . the thing I personally took the greatest pride in was the swimming pools and the playgrounds we established."[3] The *Oregonian* added further praise by citing the mayor's efforts to clean up the waterfront by eliminating scows, his initiative in lowering the property tax levy from 6.6 mills to 4.9 mills, his promotion of a city beautiful fund, his sponsorship of a huge new reservoir and park at Mt. Tabor, and his success in abolishing the red light district in North Portland by eliminating restricted sections for such activities.[4] As the *Oregonian* was to comment a few months later: "Vice can never be extirpated, but at Portland it is held now under closest possible restraint."[5]

Except for sponsoring the city beautiful fund and moving to reduce the tax rate — an action that did not really lower the dollar amount paid because of rapidly increasing assessment values — most of Mayor Simon's positive accomplishments were actions that simply carried out programs already approved by the voters. In fact, the park acquisition program had moved slowly. Two hundred acres** in six months seemed like a huge amount by comparison with the city's previous total park acreage, but the voters had authorized a much larger increase to be effected as rapidly as possible before the available sites were gobbled up by speculators. Along with the park board, Simon deserved credit for negotiating donations of park property in Ladd's and Holladay's additions and for acquiring through donation and condemnation enough parcels of land to begin the Hillside Parkway,*** a 200-400 foot strip that would run from Fulton Park on the south to the base of Marquam Hill on the north — part of the current Terwilliger Boulevard. Beginning in January 1911, Simon was authorized by the council to negotiate further with the OR&N Co. for the acquisition of an additional 65 acres that would

---

*Opened in November 1910 at a cost of $100,000.
**Parks acquired: Sellwood (15 acres), Kenilworth (9 acres), Mt. Tabor (125 acres plus 45 acres for the reservoir), Laurelhurst (30 acres), Peninsula (20 acres). Approximate cost $500,000. The voters authorized $1 million. (See map — circled areas).
***As recommended by John Olmsted in 1907.

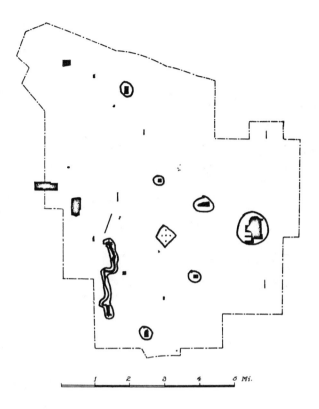

connect South Portland to the Hillside Parkway.* The city offered
to pay one-half the appraised value, or $195,000, plus $65,000 for the
railroad's property under the east ramp of the new Broadway Bridge.
Also figured into the deal was the worth to the city of some vacated
streets granted to the OR&N in May 1910 as part of the company's
Steel Bridge replacement needs — an explosive issue that will be
discussed later in the chapter.

*This parcel of land near Duniway Park, was part of a much larger tract
that Henry Villard had acquired in the early 1880's. In the mid-1920's *Oregon
Journal* owner C.S. Jackson's widow and family would purchase approximately 89 acres of the Villard property on Marquam Hill and donate it to
the State of Oregon. The area is now included in the site of the Sam Jackson
Memorial Park and the University of Oregon Medical School—Veterans Hospital complex.

Mayor Simon's relatively effortless success in forming a city beautiful fund in November 1909 revealed the degree of support given his administration by Portland's old guard establishment. Included among the $500 contributors were: Charles F. Adams, John C. Ainsworth, Jonathan Bourne Jr., Rodney L. Glisan, Mrs. G.F. Lewis, The Portland Lumber Co., The Portland Railway Light & Power Co., Theodore B. Wilcox, and brewer Paul Wessinger who gave $250. Additional support for the cause was provided by the *Oregon Journal* which subscribed for $500.[6] Physical improvement had now become an accepted need that could and should be supported by liberals and conservatives alike. The basic business-economic relationships would not be disrupted — any threat in that direction could easily be diverted. The old docks along the downtown waterfront had already exceeded their useful life; furthermore, current dock activity was moving down river where extra space and rail connections were more readily available.

No less an institution than the *Oregonian* supported the proposition that it might be advisable for the city to hire an "expert consultant" who would examine the city, especially the downtown waterfront. Portland "needs a program of improvement by plan, by anticipating congestion of traffic, the poor housing and too narrow streets. . . . " The city needed guidance as to the costs involved and

Mayor Joseph Simon.

directions in "how to go about it."[7] The city beautiful fund was to be used to hire Edward H. Bennett, a former associate of Daniel Burnham's of Chicago. Bennett would have his final proposal ready for public examination in October 1912.

To Mayor Simon, his supporters and the *Oregonian*, it was one thing to clean out dilapidated private docks at public expense, but it was quite another matter to build public docks, at public expense, that would compete with newer private docks and other profitable operating facilities many of which were controlled by the railroads. On May 25, 1910, Simon vetoed a council ordinance that would have authorized the sale of $500,000 in dock bonds as approved by the voters in June 1909. The council sustained his action. Simon's reasons were a bit specious to say the least: the bond market "was dull"; the project needed more preparation and study; the amount approved was insufficient; and there was already "too much public debt."[8] The real reason for the veto was revealed by the *Oregonian*'s supporting editorial: "Every city should leave to private enterprise the active industries, on which development depends," otherwise "waste, corruption and politics" would result.[9]

A few months later, Mayor Simon openly admitted to the council that he was opposed to municipal ownership, despite the evidence contained in a widely publicized Federal Commissioner of Corporations report that the railroads largely controlled the nation's water terminals to the disadvantage of water traffic generally. Of the 50 foremost ports, there were 21 "in which railroad ownership and occupancy" covered over 50 percent of the active frontage. The only ports where considerable public control existed were New Orleans, San Francisco, Baltimore and New York. The commissioner found Portland to have adequate wharf space in fair condition but no public city dock. Portland's frontage was all privately owned, almost entirely by the railroads.[10] Being a veteran OR&N lawyer, Joe Simon had no intention of threatening the status quo. The OR&N, after all, owned six miles of waterfront, split almost fifty-fifty between the West and East sides of the Willamette.

Mayor Simon's veto of the public dock bond sale provoked an unanticipated reaction with surprising consequences. Both the Chamber of Commerce and the Taxpayers League launched a study of waterfront ownership, and various groups interested in promoting increased water traffic sponsored an initiative charter amendment to be placed on the November 1910 ballot. Not only did the amendment provide for the establishment of the Portland Commission of Public Docks, but it authorized the commission, not the council, to levy taxes and execute the sale of $2.5 million worth of bonds, five times the original authorization that Simon and the council had refused to approve. The funds were to be used for dock construction, a belt line railway, and the purchase back from the owners of as much as possible of the 1850 levee land that had been taken from the public domain by political skulduggery. A month before the election, prominent lawyer Joseph N. Teal, son-in-law of former Mayor David P. Thompson, submitted to the chamber a detailed report with an attached map* that showed all current docks in working order to be owned by the railroads, including the dock space being used by large industry. On the basis of this kind of evidence, with strong *Oregon Journal* support, the public overwhelmingly voted its approval. This case is only one of many in Portland's history that reveals the enormously wasteful consequences of earlier decisions which were made

---

*See page 380.

Construction of the new Steel Bridge; the old bridge in the foreground. The building and dock belong to the OR&N Co.

with total lack of foresight; decisions that placed the sacred rights of private property over those of the public domain.[11]

At the same meeting of the council to which Simon submitted his veto of the dock bond sale, the mayor proudly announced the tentative agreement that he had negotiated with the OR&N and NPT companies relative to the eastern approach ramps for the Broadway and new Steel Bridges. He had engineered a trade whereby the Harriman lines would give up some existing trackage in exchange for 14 street vacancies that the railroad had long wanted. Also as part of the deal, Simon indicated that the OR&N would probably be willing to sell some of its South Portland land to the city for a parkway at one-half the appraised value. The council not only approved these arrangements but seven additional street vacancies for Harriman's Oregon & California line on East First and Second Streets.

Over the next month the public reacted strongly against what the *Oregon Journal* called "this blunder." The *Journal* charged that the railroad was going ahead "with the Steel Bridge ramp foundation on the East side before the completion of a formal agreement and in spite of the protests of thousands for an initiative election."[12] Petitions were already circulating that would ultimately place the issue on the June 1911 ballot but the city attorney refused to issue a formal complaint against the company. Oregon and Adams streets had al-

Railroad tracks along the east bank of the river.

ready been vacated to the railroad by June 14th. Five days later, the *Journal* editorialized: "The city affairs of Portland are becoming badly muddled. The stormiest days of Mayor Lane did not approximate the controversies and disturbances of the government in these days of Mayor Simon."[13]

The *Journal* continued to print repeated charges that Simon's deal would harm the city's public dock potential. "The railroads control North Portland. . . . The Oregon Railway and Navigation Co. gets the best of the deal by far."[14] The city had agreed to vacate the ends of 14 streets to the OR&N for both its new Steel Bridge ramps and some additional freight yard space while the company in turn had only to move a small section of double track to make room for the city's Broadway Bridge ramps. "Condemnation is the preferred route," said the *Journal,* "not exchange." The East side was angry with Simon over his negotiations and compromises which were viewed as devices for exchanging East side rights for benefits to West side residents. The East side riverfront was being traded away for West side park land. The reaction "paid off" in June 1911 when the voters by almost 2-1 approved an initiative charter amendment that prohibited future street vacations within 2000 feet of the water front and 1000 feet of a terminal yard. City approval of any other vacations would require a three-fourths vote of the council and the signature of the mayor. In commenting upon the fact that the city had already given away much of the property named in the amendment, one prominent political scientist labeled the action "belated — locking the door after the cow's left."[15]

Oregon Journal Building—S.W. Broadway
and Yamhill Streets. Currently Jackson
Tower. Corner of the Hotel Portland on left.

2.

"The extraordinary vigor and activity of private enterprise," to
requote Delos Wilcox, was clearly exemplified by Portland's experience during the decade that ended in 1910. In terms of population
growth, which was the usual yardstick for measuring economic
progress, no other city in the country of corresponding size, except
Seattle and Los Angeles,* had done anywhere nearly as well.[16] In
1910, Portland was exceeded in population by only 27 other cities.
This enormous expansion of population and business created a large
amount of new construction. As Herbert Croly reported: "During the
past ten years the aspect of Portland has been almost completely
transformed." In 1910 alone, over $20 million of new construction
was begun. Croly arrived in Portland the year following the publication of his *Promise of American Life* (1909), one of the most important

---

*Ten year percentage growth for cities over 100,000: Seattle 194, Spo-
kane 183, Portland 129, Los Angeles 113.

Hotel Benson on Broadway. Property owned by John Yeon.

and influential books to be published in pre-World War America.*
Croly described what he saw:

> "A very large number of new business buildings have
> been erected, and inasmuch as the interests of the city are
> rather commercial than industrial, these new business

---

*Croly (1869-1930) had been editor of the *Architectural Record* (1900-
1906) and founded the *New Republic* (1914) with Walter Lippmann as one of
his editors; Croly was a leading progressive intellectual.

edifices are not factories or furnaces, but office buildings and warehouses. Portland is extraordinarly well equipped with house room for the transaction of its affairs. Indeed, unless we are very much mistaken, it is better equipped than is any city of corresponding size in the country, which is presumably a result of the comparatively abundant supply of capital, which is controlled by the business men of Portland.

Portland, moreover, unlike any other city on the Pacific Coast, San Francisco excepted, has an architectural history. It has been erecting comparatively large business buildings ever since the essentially modern movement in American architecture began late in the eighties. The different phases of that movement can be studied to better advantage in Portland than in many middle western cities of larger population. Many of its earlier buildings were, indeed, designed by eastern or middle western architects, and at the present time an unusually large proportion of them are still so designed. Some of its earlier buildings are of exceptional interest and merit, and de-

The Hotel Portland, on S.W. Sixth, in its prime. Demolished in the early 1950's. The site is known as the Meier & Frank parking lot. The city plans to develop the block as a park.

serve a place of their own on any complete account of the development of American business architecture."

Croly commented upon the fact that Portland, like other large American cities, had very few public buildings. He singled out for praise the old Pioneer Post Office and the new County Court House. But, he said:

> "Portland is to be congratulated on the fact that its new business structures are as good, if not better, than are the average of those erected in the Middle West or in the East. If the prevailing level of design is maintained or improved during the coming generation, it will become a city which will possess in the mass the dignity and the solidity, which follow inevitably from an architecture based frankly on utilitarian considerations and limitations."

Croly was the first major American writer to emphasize Portland's Middle Western antecedents in contrast to the New England roots and influences so often mentioned.*

> "Oregon is substantially a Middle Western state transplanted to the Pacific Coast. It is homogeneous in population. It is predominantly agricultural in interest. It is Puritan in temper. At the same time its resources are unusually diversified for an agricultural state, and in the course of time its social and business life will be enriched by a larger variety of commercial interests and agricultural pursuits than is that of any of the farming communities west of the Mississippi river."[17]

Writing at about the same time, Henry E. Reed, the county assessor and inveterate compiler of statistical data, carried Croly's prediction one step further when he said: "Portland will . . . become the chief city in the American section of the Pacific Coast. It has the advantages, and its people are improving them to the fullest possible extent."[18] To illustrate "what Portland has accomplished since it struck its gait," Reed listed the following evidence:

---

*The 1910 Census showed the largest states of birth as Iowa, Illinois, Missouri and Ohio. For Oregon, only 1.8 percent had been born in New England. The importance of New England as a formative influence stemmed more from the quality of contribution to Portland development than from the quantity of ex-New Englanders. The common thread — or link to New England — was Portland's "Puritan Temper."

	1905	1910
Population	110,929	207,214
Telephones in use	14,734	46,556
Building permits	$ 4,183,368	$ 19,152,370
Bank clearings	228,402,712	557,933,736
Real estate transfers	15,102,185	25,269,549
Post office receipts	416,052	1,002,610
Manufacturing output	28,651,000	46,861,000

The 1910 U.S. Census,[19] from which Reed took some of his data, revealed further information of interest:

One-sixth of Oregon's population was foreign born: German 22.4%, Canadian 11.2%, English 9.5%.

Ethnic minority totals (less than 3% of the state population)

Negroes	1492 (1264 urban)
Indian	5090
Chinese	7363 (5787 urban)
Japanese	3418

Males outnumbered females 384,265 to 288,500.
45.6% of Oregon's population lived in cities of over 2500 population.
44% of Portland's residents owned their own homes — far above the national average.

Joseph Gaston was an even more voluminous compiler of statistical information. Reporting 1910* figures, he noted:

Portland was the number two city in the United States for wheat exports** after New York: 5,571,000 bushels.
Wool and Salmon were being exported by rail, no longer by ship.
Lumber manufacturing and shipping was the largest local wealth producer. In 1910, over 700 million board feet were cut,*** producing $10 million in revenue. One-third went by ship to foreign markets, one-third by rail to Calif-

*See Appendix J for additional 1910 economic data.
**In 1913, Portland was the fourth ranking U.S. city in total exports.
***Enough lumber to build a plank road from Portland to Chicago 30 feet wide.

ornia and the east, and one-third was used locally. Oregon counted three billion board feet of standing timber.

Portland manufacturing establishments numbered in excess of 2200, with 713 related to wood products. Invested capital amounted to over $32 million. Over 23,000 workers earned $9 million annually, producing manufactured goods of close to $50 million. One third of Portland's work force was unionized.[20]

"Expansion of General Business"

"In one day this month of October, 1910, eight steamships, all bringing cargo for Portland, came into the Columbia river. The fleet included two big freighters from European ports, bringing nearly 5,000 tons of cargo, two passenger liners from San Francisco, a big Standard Oil tanker, and three freighters, which ply regularly between Portland and San Francisco. During the day an American-Hawaiian liner and a lumber carrier crossed out to sea, both loaded to their capacity.

This fleet of ten vessels registered 14,312 tons, and had a carrying capacity of nearly 30,000 tons. All of the craft came along in the regular order of business. While the tonnage was short of record proportions for a day, it

Harbor view, Municipal Terminal No. 1.

afforded a good illustration of the growth of the shipping business of the port.

Seventy steam railroad passenger trains and 164 electric trains, not including local service to Mt. Scott, St. Johns, Troutdale and other nearby points — and not including freight trains — move in and out of Portland every twenty-four hours. This is an average of one steam passenger train arriving or departing every twenty minutes, and one electric train every nine minutes.

October is not regarded as a month in which freight traffic moves in record quantities; but in the first three weeks of this month (1910), the railroads hauled into this city, among other commodities, 1,551 carloads of wheat, barley, flour, oats and hay. They also brought into this city in the first twenty-one days of the month, 8,755 hogs, 8,505 sheep and goats, 4,629 cattle, 1,140 calves and 210 horses; a total of 23,239 animals, or something more than 1,000 head per day. And during the year 1910 the Portland Union depot and North Bank Railroad handled in and out of the city two hundred and twenty thousand freight cars."[21]

3.

In contrast to the vigor and momentum of Oregon economic activity in the early spring of 1910, the old Republican machine, paradoxically, was "virtually shipwrecked." As Burton Hendrick reported, "the whole state was strewn with political cadavers."[22] There were still some smoldering fires of opposition to the Oregon System — those who still believed that the old order could be restored. "Not inappropriately, Harvey W. Scott came forth as the spokesman" of the malcontents. "The Republicans of Oregon," said the *Oregonian*, "intend to repudiate 'Statement No. 1.' " Hendrick reported that Scott's group proposed an even more ambitious long range campaign: to call for a state constitutional convention to abolish the direct primary as well as the initiative and referendum. They kept their plans secret.[23]

According to one report, the Harriman and Hill railroads, the Portland Railway Light & Power Co., and the Gas Co. banded together under the chairmanship of Abbot Mills. Included in the group were former Mayor Rowe, Franklin T. Griffith who would be the next

President of PRL&P and Judge M.C. George, a long time party stalwart and former congressman. Mayor Simon gave tacit support.*

The strategy called for the convening of local assemblies all over the state at which the various legislative candidates could be hand-picked. They would still have to run in the direct primary but they would carry the strong support of the party high command. According to Hendrick, just before the meeting of the Multnomah County Assembly, "one of the public-utility law offices of Portland held a meeting, where the local slate was fixed and 'slipped' to the bosses in control."[24] The State Assembly that followed in Portland was, in Hendrick's words, "a museum of political antiquities. . . . All the old political war-horses whom the voters had repudiated . . . occupied the front benches on the stage. The legislative agents of the corporations had favored positions and regularly led the applause." The enthusiasm reached its highest pitch when the candidate for governor, Jay Bowerman,** was escorted to the platform where he accepted his role to lead Oregon's "return to representative government."[25]

As the assembly disbanded and proceeded out into the street for a parade, one of the most interested spectators was "a tall, boyish figure, leaning in the darkness against a telegraph pole."[26] The curious onlooker was 37 year old Oswald West who was bemused by what he saw. Many of the faces were familiar, from as far back as 1897 when, as a teller in the Ladd & Bush Bank in Salem, he had deposited much of the cash that had changed hands between the bosses, the lobbyists and the legislators. As a respected member of the state railroad commission, West had entertained the notion that someday he might like to follow in the footsteps of his mentor George Chamberlain and run for governor. As West later recounted the episode to Hendrick, "he watched this noisy crowd of old political ringsters marching triumphantly through the streets of Portland."[27] He thought to himself, why not run now? The next morning he filed his intention of becoming a candidate for the Democratic nomination.

The kind of campaign that West ran established the basis for the West legend. Historians have often wondered whether or not West was a phenomenon peculiar to Oregon. There is no question that 66 years later he is still revered as the one governor in Oregon's history who was the true man of the people — especially the little people. He found

---

*Simon was very close to Mills in 1910. He was a director of the Security Savings & Trust Co.

**Bowerman was acting governor for six months following Benson's resignation in June 1910 for reasons of ill-health.

Declaration of Principles

If I am nominated and elected, I will, during my term of office, always keep in mind those principles of the social compact found in our Constitution which declare this to be a government absolutely by the people, and will fight to a finish any attempt of the legislature to repeal or nullify the Initiative and Referendum, Direct Primary Law, Corrupt Practices Act, or the Recall.

The people must rule the corporations or the corporations will rule the State. I believe had God intended that the corporations, and not the people, should rule he would have created the corporations first.

I wish to have printed after my name on the nominating ballot the following words: I favor the Initiative and Referendum, Direct Primary, Corrupt Practices Act, and Recall.

1910   *Oswald West*

Record as State Land Agent:

He broke down the barriers erected around the State Land Office by the old school land ring and made it possible for every citizen of the state to transact business with that office in a legitimate way and receive decent treatment.

He exposed forgeries and other bogus transactions affecting the purchase of hundreds of thousands of acres of state land and brought about the cancellation of scores of certificates and the recovery to the state of thousands of acres of its lands.

He prepared for the office suitable records, and put upon the statute books the best land law to be found in any state in the Union, thereby securing to the school fund intended benefits, and assuring every applicant for state land a square deal.

Record as State Railroad Commissioner:

He has been instrumental in having the railroads of the state improve their roadbeds and furnish better equipment and service, and in bringing about the erection of new depots and the installation of better side-track facilities at many points.

He has made a fight for better train service and facilities for live-stock shippers and better freight rates for the wool men. He has been instrumental in securing reductions of freight, passenger and express rates on many roads, thereby saving hundreds of thousands of dollars annually to the shippers of Oregon.

He has been active in securing the physical valuation of all railroad properties in Oregon, which will be of inestimable value for rate making purposes and in bringing about a more equitable distribution of the burdens of taxation.

himself at 37 without money or influential friends, with no political machine and a Democrat in an overwhelmingly Republican state. He secured the names of 20,000 registered Democrats and sent a personal letter to 15,000 of them. From the responses, he put together groups of enthusiastic workers from all over the state. This was the West "machine."

West had little difficulty obtaining the nomination. For the next four and one-half months he traveled to the far corners of the state, visiting hamlets that had never seen a gubernatorial candidate. He was already fairly well known in many of the rural sections because as a young man he had driven cattle and sheep down the valley and through Eastern Oregon. His four years as state land agent, 1903-07, had further extended his circle of friendships. He concentrated on meeting people and limited himself to few formal speeches. To win, he obviously had to count on the cross-over vote of a number of Republicans. Senator Jonathan Bourne Jr. returned from Washington D.C. to help rally the progressive Republicans to West's support. The old guard leadership never forgave Bourne for this treason and two years later, with help from Bowerman and his old crony Joe Simon, the party regulars defeated his effort to gain renomination.

Early in August, Harvey W. Scott died half way through his 72nd year. This event was in itself an omen of things to come for the Republican cause. In many respects, Scott's death signified the passing of the traditional frontier style of Republican politics. The old machine would be replaced by new machines, with new parts, but the direction of travel would remain the same. At least with Oswald West's overwhelming victory which cost him less than $3,000, the state could be assured an honest and forthright administration for four years. West would make mistakes. He had some of Harry Lane's emotional, headstrong qualities. They would be clearly revealed two years later, on his arrival in Portland to provide personal leadership of the anti-vice, anti-saloon crusade.

4.

When Mayor Simon delivered his annual report to the council in early January 1911 he appeared in good spirits. He was the sole survivor of the old rough-and-ready school of Republican party politics. There is no record of how he reacted to Oswald West's election but one cannot help but surmise that he must have felt some concern about what the future held in store not only for him but for all of the varied enterprises to which he had long been attached. Nearing the age of 60, he was beginning to mellow. He no longer thrived on controversy. Compromise was preferable to litigation. Because he was now the grand old man of the state Republican party,* he assumed a

*The original "Grand Old Man," George H. Williams, had died the previous April, ten days after his 87th birthday.

sort of patriarch's role. It was difficult for him not to be patronizing. He knew how things should be done, in addition to knowing *what* should be done.

Simon presented a glowing report on the state of the city. Portland was experiencing a "period of great prosperity and health." There was, however, "a need to economize in public expenditures," he warned.[28] The city's accumulated bonded indebtedness totalled $8,875,000.* Improvement bonds totalling $5,572,989 were not included as part of the bonded indebtedness. Although he evidenced some concern about the size of the bonded indebtedness,** he had never favored a policy of increasing taxes either to pay the full cost of some of the projects initially or to increase the rate of amortization of the existing debts. To pursue such a course would have been unthinkable in the business minds of men like Simon and Mills. And yet, from the point of what constituted good business sense for the city government, a tax raise to the charter limit of 6 percent would have proven more beneficial over the long haul. Of course, the banks and investment houses made handsome profits off the city's bond issues.

In the early 1940's Mayor Earl Riley was to criticize severely the bond and tax policies that were to leave the city still heavily in debt years later. Commenting upon a 30 year $1 million bond issue voted by the people in 1909, Riley noted that the city had paid $1.225 million in interest. Maintaining the real property tax rate at 6 percent, or amending the charter to a higher limit, would have cost the voters "much less" over the same span of time.[29] But what was considered good for the banks was deemed beneficial for the city. In lieu of raising taxes and floating more bonds to meet increasing public needs produced by an exploding population, the city would simply have to economize on future service. This was, after all, the only sound, businesslike policy to follow.

Evidence was not available in 1910 to show what some recent research has revealed, that expanding the economy of a city does not solve a crisis in urban government finance. On the contrary it makes it worse. If the gross income of a city goes up 100 percent, revenue rises only 90 percent at the most, and expenditures, or the

---

*Water system	$4.2 million	Ferry	$115,000
City Hall	$675,000	E. Port.	$300,000
Bridges	$1.8 million	Albina	$140,000
Parks & Blvds.	$500,000	Crematory	$ 50,000

**Only 3 percent of the assessed value of property in 1910. The Charter limitation was 7%.

need for expenditures, rise 110 percent. "Consequently, when a city's economy grows, the city's budget is in a worse fix than before."[30]

An interesting "businesslike" transaction worked out by Mayor Simon involved the new Hawthorne Bridge. The original bid came in at $459,000. The final cost at the time of its opening in early 1911 was at least $490,000 — some accounts show the total as high as $511,000. According to the Portland Municipal Association[31] most of the increase was due to a delayed decision to widen the bridge to accomodate the newer and larger cars of the Portland Railway Light and Power Co. The original contract with the Mt. Tabor street Railway had required a $100 per month payment for the use of the first bridge. The company had refused to negotiate a new contract despite an initiated ordinance setting the annual fee at $15,000. The unresolved issue was carried over from Lane's to Simon's administration. Having been authorized by the council to "make a deal," Simon allowed the company to continue paying the old rate of $1200 a year. The council ordinance that approved this arrangement provided, however, that the city could, at its own expense, sue the company for the additional $13,800, an action that did not occur for two years.

In at least two other matters, Mayor Simon compromised away the rights of city government for the benefit of private enterprise. One involved a lighting contract that called for certain requirements that had not been met. Mayor Lane had held back $29,000 until the terms were fulfilled. Not long after Simon's arrival in office he instructed the city to pay the utility $20,000 before any of the changes had been made. A second episode related to the ill-fated Brooklyn sewer in Southeast Portland. Lane had refused to accept the job as the stone bottom had been laid in dirt rather than concrete. Simon accepted the project on grounds of public necessity and the companies* were paid. The city was to endure years of costly repairs as the bottom washed away with regularity.

As the June 1911 municipal election loomed on the horizon, Mayor Simon was unsure whether or not to run again. The Municipal Association together with the *Oregon Journal* kept up a steady barrage of criticism. One charge involved Simon's "hard surface" policy. The costs of street paving had soared, all to the benefit of the paving "trust," and then the property owners were stuck with the bills. One

---

*C.F. Swigert's Pacific Bridge Co. was one of the prime contractors.

job in Portland Heights, on upper S.W. Hall St. and Heights Terrace, cost the adjacent property owners $30,000. The city did not pay one penny.[32] Another series of charges related to vice conditions. On April 29th, Chief of Police A.M. Cox had been indicted by the grand jury for malfeasance in office, for permitting certain disorderly houses to operate without molestation. The Municipal Association cited 98 known houses that were doing a booming business. Cox denied any responsibility — the decision was made higher up. He was, he said, "a victim of circumstances."[33] The association blamed Simon for appointing Cox in the first place — a man with a known prior record of blindness to vice conditions.

By the middle of May Simon had decided to seek re-election as an Independent Republican. Veteran Councilman, A.G. Rushlight, the East side plumbing contractor, had already been assured the support of the regular Republicans and he won the primary easily. The remnants of the old Harvey Scott group, West-siders like Mills, Beebe, Rowe and even Henry E. Reed came out for Simon. The *Oregonian* of course strongly endorsed him, citing Rushlight as the "minority candidate without business support."[34] At the June 5th election Simon was retired for good by almost 2-1. The Democratic candidate ran a poor third.

The election of June 1911 was significant on several counts, above and beyond the marking of Joseph Simon's departure from public life after an extraordinary career spanning 34 years. The voters considered a number of measures that had been long debated and that would prove to have a determining influence on the future physical shape of the city. In addition to the charter amendment that prohibited street vacations on the waterfront, other measures receiving voter approval included: the establishment of a municipal garbage collection system ($75,000); the construction of a new city jail downtown at Second and Oak ($200,000); the construction of the city's first public auditorium ($600,000); the regulation of the erection, construction and maintenance of billboards; and the requirement that a three percent tax be applied to the gross receipts from the sale of gas and electricity. The voters rejected the purchase of Council Crest for a city park, a South Portland high bridge, a municipal paving plant and the establishment of a municipal public service commission.[35]

The last 15 member city council that would serve before the creation of the five member commission form of government two years hence varied little in character from those of the previous decade except that realtor representation was doubled to four in number. Nine of the 15 councilmen were new and only one was a member of an elite social organization. It was an average chamber of commerce or commercial club group. The dominant figure was theater owner-manager George L. Baker, a colorful council veteran and council president since 1909. Baker would serve 16 years as mayor beginning in 1917. The appointments to the last executive board were also drawn from a similar group of business and commercial intersts — none from the upper echelon of Portland society. For the first time two representatives of organized labor — the longshoremen and railway workers — were invited to participate in the higher levels of city government. Following a pattern that marked the Lane and Simon periods, the divisive saloon issue would continue to plague city hall. As for executive leadership, Mayor Rushlight was a colorless figure but he was a dedicated public servant. His opening message to the council called for harmony and cooperation. "We must gauge all of our acts by what is best for the city."[36] Unfortunately for the mayor and for the city, his two years in office would prove to be turbulent as a result of conditions and problems that were not really of his making and over which he could exercise little control.

Within a month after Mayor Rushlight had assumed office public pressure for an official vice investigation began to build up a head of steam. Even the *Oregonian* started to take notice of local conditions by complaining: "The trains are loaded with gamblers, macquereaux, touts, pimps,confidence men, common women . . . who have heard that the town is wide open, the pastures are green, and the feeding good."[37] On August 23, 1911, the council passed an ordinance that authorized the mayor to appoint a group of inquiry. Within hours, Rushlight created the 15 member Vice Commission of the City of Portland, headed by the Rev. Henry R. Talbott of St. David's Episcopal Church and including three additional ministers and four doctors.[38] Almost immediately the good citizens, armed with badges of authority, as distinct from earlier privately conducted investigations, proceeded about their work, block by block, building by building, in quest of direct evidence.

Not much was heard about the quiet activities of the Rev. Talbott and his cohorts until they presented the council with their first report the following January. The briefest of the three that they would make over the period of a year, the commission's initial findings related largely to the incidence of venereal disease which was discovered to be 21 percent of the total reported diseases in the city. There were 1360 cases recorded in October alone. The commission believed

Governor West and Mayor Rushlight confer on anti-vice campaign.

the figures to be low as only one-third of the doctors had responded. The commission noted that the city had no public facility to handle the problem.[39] Neither the mayor nor the council felt any need for urgent action so the report was filed away. The following April, however, the council did pass an ordinance, on recommendation of the commission, to prohibit the employment of women in shooting galleries. The commission had noted that 16 year old girls employed in the galleries were particularly vulnerable "marks for prostitution." Also in April, a citizens group launched a recall drive against District Attorney George Cameron, a long time friend of the liquor interests.

Matters came to a low boil on August 20th when Governor Oswald West announced from Salem: "I am going to clean up Portland next."[40] He had just concluded two successful anti-vice campaigns in Redmond and Huntington. Mayor Rushlight responded: "I have no knowledge of any conditions in Portland that require cleaning up by the Governor . . . but I will assist him."[41] Two days later, the vice commission published its second report and the police raided 13 establishments in the downtown and North End. The following day Governor West swept into Portland with a flourish, "to wage relentless war upon vice," to quote from the *Journal's* headline. The Portland *Daily News* gave the action big play: "Maybe you thought this a clean town; say, read this."[42] "Shocking moral status shown by the Vice Commisison," charged the *Journal*. "Fashionable districts" were also included plus the "Tenderloin" area of the North End. "Prominent citizens profit from vice."[43]

On August 24th the tempo increased. Governor West exclaimed: "I will clean the city or quit my job."[44] He appointed young attorney Walter H. Evans as special prosecutor and all candidates for the 1912 sheriff's election as special agents. Declared West: "There is a great deal of property held by people of means that is rented for houses of prostitution. . . . That property is held by corporations organized for the purpose of covering up the real ownership. . . . I am going to take steps to take away the charters and dissolve such corporations at once."[45] The *Journal* editorialized: "The secret and silent gentlemen who buy automobiles and mansions from the tainted profits of the underworld . . . are the ramparts of the system." Indeed, the profits were great as the commission discovered. The owners of vice property could count on an investment return of between 84 and 540 percent. One owner invested $10,000 and made $5400 the first year. A $250 fine was not going to deter him.

Editor Edgar Piper of the *Oregonian* could not get very excited. He counseled his readers to "face the facts — reality: . . . Social vice is a large and powerful business, and that it exists and spreads is because it pays heavy profits." Anti-vice laws prove little, said Piper; all they lead to "is the propagation of more vice by increasing its profits. . . . Bad as we are, we are no worse than our neighbors."[46] The *Oregonian* seemed to take delight in one of the *Report's* observations "that a person might stand on the roof of one of the principal churches of the city and throw a stone into any one of 14 places, 10 of which are wholly immoral."[47] Such comments neither amused nor excited Mayor Rushlight who suggested to a *Daily News* reporter that perhaps the best solution after all might be for the city to establish " a restricted district for prostitution activities."[48] This pronouncement did little to endear the mayor to Governor West.

The vice commission's *Report* covered a thorough nine month examination of all aspects of the problem. The "operatives" visited 547 hotels, apartments, and rooming and lodging houses in downtown and the North End. They discovered 431 of them to be immoral, classifying them as places "wholly given up to immorality," places where "immoral tenants [are] desired or preferred," and places where "immorality [is] countenanced or ignored."[49] The commission drew a map and located each establishment with an appropriate circle or square. The red, purple and black colors indicated their classification. The map did not locate the streets or any other distinguishing physical characteristics — this being an attempt to protect the names and reputations of the property owners. The commission later destroyed its files so that no one would ever know with certainty exactly who owned what. But by careful reconstruction, it has been possible to determine with a high degree of accuracy the names of the owners. The list is interesting, even fascinating, but not totally surprising. Some of the "best people" in Portland were included. One eager observer was pleased to see from his calculations that the Union Station did not appear in color. Another was relieved to know that none of the girls had taken up residence on the river bridges. According to Fred Merrill, the map brought apoplexy to some and a good deal of humor to others.[50]

Partial List of Identified Property Owners
1912 Vice Report

.Banks owning or managing property in their names:
Security Savings & Trust, C.F. Adams, Pres., Mills and Simon, directors.
Hibernia Savings Bank, Dr. A.C. Smith, Lansing Stout, officers.

Estates Managed by Banks:

Failing	)	
Corbett	)	
Reed, S.G.	)	First National Bank
Dolph, J.N.	)	
Thompson, R.R.	)	
Kamm	)	
Thompson, D.P.	)	U.S. National Bank
Weinhard	)	

Small Trust and Investment Companies:
Union Trust Investment Co., MacMaster, Wm.
General Investment
Beaver Investment
Beck Investment Co.
Nichols Investment Co.
J.C. Ainsworth Co.

MAP

SHOWING HOTELS APARTMENTS LODGING & ROOMING HO

WITHIN A GIVEN AREA ON THE WEST SIDE OF THE CITY

PORTLAND INVESTIGATED BY THE VICE COMMISSION

PHYSICAL CLASSIFICATION

	MORAL	DOUBTFUL
HOTELS	■	
APARTMENT HOUSES	●	
LODGING AND ROOMING HOUSES	⊙	

MORAL CLASSIFICATION

GREEN INDICATES MORAL HOUSES
BLUE " MORAL STATUS NOT DETERMINED
BLACK " IMMORALITY COUNTENANCED OR IGNORED
PURPLE " IMMORAL TENANTS DESIRED OR PREFERRED
RED " HOUSES WHOLLY GIVEN UP TO IMMORALITY

Realty Firms:
Fliedner, Morgan & Boyce, 14 properties
Columbia Realty, W.L. Morgan

Prominent Family Names:

Alisky	Cardwell	Woodward, T.
Cardinell	Harrington	Hawkins, W.J.
Durkheimer	Nicolai	Dolph, C.A.
Hirsch, J.	Fried	Blyth
Warren, F.M.	Blumauer	Spencer
Therkelson	Wemme	Wilson, C.C.
Leadbetter	Watson, J.F.	Ainsworth
Cook, J.W.	Bates	Glisan
Holman, J.	Holbrook	Teal
Ralston	Seller	Henry
	Mayer	Sinnott

What all of these names revealed, of course, was that the property owners came from the highest social and business levels in the city. The Waverly, Arlington and Concordia Clubs were well represented. Interestingly enough, Joseph Simon's name did not appear. He had apparently sold his property following the publicity of earlier anti-vice campaigns. An examination of the police records revealed the ineffectiveness of police raids and arrests. The established power was too strong. The business-political leadership had closed its eyes to the problem, collected its profits and prevented any effective reform. As Governor West declared: "The real prostitutes I am after in Portland are the prostitutes in office."[51] And he meant not only political but corporate office. The blame was to be attached to the investors whose sole concern was money. Greed and vice went hand in hand, even for those who attended church regularly on Sunday mornings.

The *Oregon Journal* spoke to the heart of the matter when it declared that the real issue "is the struggle between two systems of government. It is a contest which has been in every city since the beginning. . . . One system holds that the law means what it says and says what it means, the other system holds that the law is only to be enforced sometimes."[52] The same double standard that was applied to matters of private and public interest in business and political affairs was also applied to matters of private and public morality.

To many upper class Portlanders, prostitution was a necessary "evil" — a process by which the young men of the family could achieve initiation into the mysteries of sex before entering upon marriage. The historical record in Portland is replete with stories of fathers introducing their sons to such experiences. After all, nice girls were not meant to be exposed to the joys of premarital sex. Furthermore, for adult males, the "lower pleasures" were considered an acceptable, even a necessary amusement, and for the unhappily married, an indispensable relief. In the minds of some Portlanders, prostitution was a required device to stave off social chaos and prevent harm from befalling the nicer young ladies of the community. It was a social safety valve for the thousands of employed men who came to Portland each winter from the logging camps and lumber mills adjacent to the city. Many would remain until their funds ran out. The saloons were full and the company of available women was eagerly sought. In January 1912, the chief of police had requested and secured permission from the council to add 50 new patrolmen just to maintain basic law and order. Had prostitution facilities not been accessible, the chief would have needed even more officers. The whole process was a vicious circle, and, like a slot machine, too profitable to destroy.

Little thought was ever given to the prostitute, to the conditions that drove women into the profession, or to the disastrous health and psychological consequences. As the *Report* said, "the prostitute . . . is a woman who is being knocked about with the butt of stupid laws." She is in many cases "a nuisance to herself; in all cases a menace to the community, and in no case with any chance for improvement." Low wages and large-scale unemployment in Portland were to blame for forcing over 3000 women into the profession. They had become profitable tools — or slaves — to the system. Commission Chairman Talbott told a large public audience that society needed to pay living wages to young women. Furthermore, the city needed juvenile facilities and programs of recreation and guidance. "Even little children are thrown into the surroundings of vice."[53] For the prostitute the commission recommended a program of detention and social rehabilitation in lieu of fines and short jail sentences.

The vice report linked the "commercial prosperity of the houses" with the "sale of liquor by the inmates." It was common for liquor to be sold on the premises by the proprietors of the houses. Where the entertainment was on the second floor with the saloon underneath liquor was brought to the rooms by the girls and sold to the customers at a tidy profit. Beer was especially popular at $1 a bottle.

A POPULAR BEVERAGE

In this edition is a picture of the City brewery, H. Weinhard, proprietor. This is the largest brewing establishment on the coast, and Weinhard's lager beer is favorably known and extensively used all through this section. It is the choice of the connoisseur, being clear as

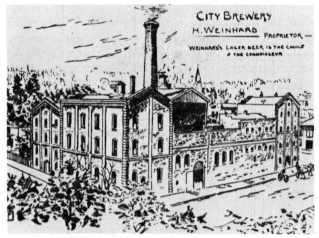

amber, and unequaled for "a nice, exhilarating drink." Orders for any quantity should be directed to H. Weinhard, corner Twelfth and B streets. The telephone number is 72.

(From the Oregonian, *January 1, (1891). The brewery building still stands on West Burnside Street.*

Conditions of this sort led Governor West to level charges against the breweries* as accessories and promoters of vice activities. Before a mass meeting of 3500, held in the evening of September 4th at the Gypsy Smith Tabernacle, the governor blamed Mayor Rushlight, the breweries and the "higher-ups." He accused the breweries of running the city. At least, declared West, "Weinhard's brewery won't rule the state of Oregon . . . There isn't a brick in the brewery down here that doesn't represent a broken heart."[54] West took the onus of blame for any criticism of his current campaign.** Ex-Mayor and Sheriff W.A. Storey had just launched a recall effort against the governor whom he charged with "hurting the economy and business."[55]

---

*The breweries, especially Weinhard's, owned a number of saloons in the "Sin City" area.

**West's aversion to all alcoholic beverages stemmed from his having experienced his father's serious addiction to alcohol while West was growing up.

West continued: "I may be down here a week or ten days, or I may be here for two years, but I'm going to keep hammering away all the time I am here until a lot of this law breaking has been cleaned up. . . . I am not here to get these poor unfortunate women. . . . I'm here after the men crooks." West concluded his remarks by stating that if the papers would not print the names, "I am going to get out on a soapbox in the streets and do a little publishing of my own."[56] Before the campaign had begun, the liquor dealers had turned down West's invitation to meet with him. In so doing, "they lost their chance."

The *Journal* editorialized that "the Governor may not be able to rid Portland of her jungle. But, Oregon will for a time have more officials on the jump than in many a long year."[57] Before West headed back to Salem he publicly charged prominent lawyer Waldemar Seton with conflict of interest. Seton was a member of Rushlight's executive board and one of four police commissioners. West accused Seton of appearing in court as attorney for an indicted saloon keeper. When West discovered that Seton had disciplined two officers who had brought charges against saloon keepers in the past, the governor had the men reassigned to his vice investigation unit. Seton denied any wrong intentions. These people were simply "old clients." And furthermore, he had not sought the executive board position in the first place.[58]

West returned to the Capitol with a pledge to seek a statewide abatement law from the 1913 Legislature. Portland had experienced a busy two weeks but there was more to follow in subsequent months. Three days after West left, Theodore Roosevelt arrived in town to promote his Progressive party candidacy. On hand to greet him was Harry Lane who had been providing West with strong vocal support. Lane, of course, was the Democratic candidate for the U.S. Senate but he was a warm admirer of Roosevelt. The Portland press now had other issues to occupy its attention.

Early in October the council began heated debate on two ordinances that had been strongly recommended by the vice commission. One, which became known as the "Tin Plate Law,"* required the owners of hotel, rooming and lodging houses and saloons to maintain a plate or sign in a conspicuous location, giving the owner's name and address. For non-compliance a fine of up to $100 a day could be assessed. The second ordinance was designed to regulate hotels, rooming and

---

*The first in the United States.

lodging houses, by requiring a business permit and the posting of a $1000 performance bond. Apartment houses were deleted from coverage early in the discussion. Both measures passed on October 23rd with large majorities but Councilman George L. Baker, the future mayor, led the futile opposition. He used the same argument that had been voiced by Fred Merrill a decade earlier, that the low class women would be dispersed either into high class neighborhoods or into the cheapest of accommodations. Baker's argument raised the question that no one could or would try to answer: where should the sporting women go?[59]

During the five week interval before the laws went into effect, some of the owners devised ingenious tactics to protect their reputations. Properties suddenly became owned by groups of mysteriously formed companies. Some plates went up in Arabic, Hebrew and French, although the city ruled subsequently that they had to be in English. By the end of November over 40 indictments had been handed down and the papers reported that most of the property owners were in compliance. Some had even forced the occupants to move and were remodelling their buildings. And the Weinhard Brewery had cancelled contracts with five major saloon outlets. Some slight progress had been achieved.

November 1912 was plagued by one more scandal that was reported only in the *Portland Daily News:* "Sex activities at the YMCA." The headlines ran as follows: "Eleven arrested, one attempted suicide.... Forty men and boys in scandal.... Prominent people involved.... Confessions galore.... Many leave town quickly.... Thirteen out of forty in jail.... Twenty-one indictments...."[60] Most of the cases were settled out of court, a few lesser known characters served short jail sentences, some were shipped out of town and no one of prominence was convicted. Portland had experienced enough vice revelations to satisfly even the most curious. The attention of city government, henceforth, was to be fixed on franchises, docks, city planning and municipal finance.

5.

Much council time was expended on franchise applications during the last year of Rushlight's administration. The same companies and many of the same problems seemed to keep reappearing on the agenda. For the first time in the council's history, however, strong opposition was beginning to develop, in support of the kinds of policy

S. W. Washington Street looking east from 6th Street, Portland
Railway Light & Power streetcar.

concerns advocated by Mayor Harry Lane. The East-siders were
leading the attack, particularly against the Portland Railway Light &
Power Co. whose service in certain areas left much to be desired. The
company was a giant, with over 250 miles of lines (175 miles in Portland proper), 600 cars, 4000 employees (cut back a thousand in the
winter), and an annual payroll of almost $3 million.* Since 1907, the
company stated that it had spent nearly $5 million on updating ser-
vices, financed by stock and bond sales.[61] Considering the fact,
though, that the city boundaries had expanded by almost 40 percent
since the end of the exposition, and that the population had doubled,
$5 million was not a large capital investment. And looking at the

*Wages were: 25¢ per hour for new men; 30¢ with five years experience;
50¢ for experienced linemen who worked an eight hour day with generous
overtime pay.

five year earnings record since the time that Abbot Mills sold out
to the East, the profits had been very substantial. As reported to the
city council:[62]

1906-1911

Gross Earnings	$25,000,000
Net Operating Earnings	12,271,000
Average increase in	
Net Op. Earnings, yrly.	821,990

Operating Statement for 1911

Gross Revenue	$6,267,094
Expenses	3,026,769
Taxes	340,267
Bridge rentals	30,062
Adjustments	27,992
Depreciation	385,981
Net Operating revenue	2,456,000
Bond interest and discount	1,480,000
Net revenue (15% of Gross Revenue)	975,803
Dividends (6% on capital stock worth $16,246,875)	999,777

Several questions were raised in council about these figures. No
income was shown for interest on funded debt owned by the company, estimated at $5 million. The $16.2 million value of capital
stock was probably not worth that much as the company had been
issuing increasing amounts of new stock, thus diluting its value per
share — or "watering it" to quote the critics.

Another interesting item was brought to the council's attention.
An advertisement in the *London Daily Mail* early in 1912, used as an
enticement for the sale of $16 million in bonds, listed 1911 gross
revenue as $69,608 higher than the above statement, and listed net
operating revenue as $810,784 higher.

On February 20, 1913, a formal complaint was filed with the city
council and the Oregon State Public Service Commission against the
Portland Railway Light & Power Co. by some 30 organizations in-

414

cluding the Sunnyside and Laurelhurst Improvement clubs. The document cited the need for four cross town lines, 33 miles in length. "The
trouble with the Railway Co. is that they want it all velvet—all income
and no outlay; they want valuable franchises, without money and
without price; upon the strength of which they can water, and float
their stocks and bonds; with the least possible public accommodation
and service." The complaint was particularly aimed at a recent
franchise grant, covering 22 miles but with no cross town line provided. The document cited the further facts that in the 1902-1913 period,
over 35,000 residences had been built on the East side as opposed to
only 4100 on the West side. The East side population was now 235,000
as opposed to 41,000 on the West side. Also mentioned was the lack of
any service to the new Reed College site in Eastmoreland.[63]

Eliot Hall — Reed College (1913).

The previous month the council had received a petition from the Portsmouth Commercial Club in North Portland about the company's "poor service." Several months earlier councilman Clyde had made a strong speech in chamber in favor of the city taking over the company but he received little support beyond that of councilman Maguire* who felt the service to be "rotten." Even Mayor Rushlight, in his annual message of January 1913, had strongly urged the city to acquire its own lighting plant for purely municipal needs. Portland was paying the company $160,000 a year in street light charges.

Public pressure was building slowly but Portland Railway Light & Power would fight all the way. It was conditions such as were described in the complaint that would force people increasingly to use the automobile. After World War I, as passenger use dropped off, the quality of service also declined. From the vantage point of today, some 60 years later, it should be obvious to the well-informed that a public transportation system, or any public utility system for that matter, cannot survive through private ownership if it is to meet fully the service and environmental needs of an expanding population, keep its rates low in the face of inflated energy costs, and pay a healthy dividend to the stockholders. Except for the early years, most

---

*Councilman Maguire proposed an ordinance to grant half-fare for straphangers. He cited the case of one East-sider who had secured a seat only six times in ten years during rush hours.

private municipal transportation companies never really netted much on passenger revenue if their service was adequate. The largest return to owner-investors came from the manipulation of security prices. The companies always borrowed against anticipated future revenues derived from expansion. The day of reckoning was bound to come.* Portland's experience in 1913 provided a clear indication of the kinds of problems that lay ahead, but few people were able or willing to read the signs. Local business and banking pressures were too great. Municipal ownership, with centralized planning, was socialism — a fate worse than death.

6.

Paradoxically, the very kind of comprehensive planning that was needed for municipal public utility services, and that was rejected outright by the private sector, was generally accepted by the business-political leadership when it came to the management of port and dock services. Where private profits could not be anticipated, public funding and management were apparently justified. The introduction to the Commission of Public Docks' *Second Annual Report* is interesting when one realizes that the five member commission included some of the most conservative — albeit public-spirited — business leaders** in Portland:

> "In presenting an immediate and comprehensive plan for a port development of any harbor, there are certain essential principles that must be recognized and given due consideration. A port should be developed not as an aggregation of individual piers or wharves, indiscriminately constructed to serve various kinds of shipping as the immediate needs demand, but rather a port should be developed as a terminal, each pier or wharf should have some logical relation to those already constructed, to the upland immediately adjacent, and should be but a definite step forward in a well defined plan.
>
> In a port partially developed, especially by private interests, it is exceedingly difficult to follow this principle.

---

*See Appendix K, for street railway passenger and track mileage data (1907-20).

**Chairman was lawyer and Arlington Club resident Fred W. Mulkey. Others included merchant Ben Selling and banker Charles B. Moores. Henry L. Corbett and William MacMaster had served for the first two years.

The expense is often seemingly prohibitive and leads to makeshift policies on the part of public harbor commissions. In the long run, the larger expenditures for these improvements under a logical plan are the more economic, and therefore should be insisted upon, even if it is necessary to undertake the difficult task of educating the public opinion to such an extent that it will demand the larger expenditures. The economic justification of this assertion is shown by a brief consideration of the attitude and accomplishments of the great ports of North Europe and this country."[64]

This was bold thinking! The same argument could just as easily have been applied to city planning and management problems, to prevent what Barbara Ward has called "the inadvertent city."[65] "Lack of Plan on Waterfront" was the headline of a letter submitted to the *Oregon Journal* in September 1912 by citizen-activist J.B. Ziegler, the father of the waterfront anti-street vacation amendment passed in November 1911:

"Following up the story of the plundering of the public properties capable of producing revenue, we will now cross to the east side of the river. As we do, I will ask the citizen with sufficient concern, to stop at the top of the arc of the great new steel bridge* and take a look around. He sees about him the organic heart of Portland. The transportation arteries, land and water, converge beneath his feet. The features he contemplates are not so beautiful as the same landscape presented to the Indian before the advent of the pioneer.

There is no impression of symmetry, of unity, no agreeable hint of the perfection of nature in her patient toil weaving her magic web. There is instead a gratifying sense of utility, but it is marred by the lack of plan and presage of completeness.

Between the old towns of Portland and East Portland, the Willamette is constricted and choked, the impression of adequacy which obtains above and below this point is replaced by the ugly and dirty warehouses with their

---

*The new Steel Bridge, built by the OR&N—UP for $1.7 million was opened in August 1912. It was the largest telescope bridge of its type in the world.

New Steel Bridge, looking south.

backs to the river. They look inconsequential and insufficient as they crowd in upon the noble stream. The sawmills, unused slovenly banks, the scows and docks protruding intrusively here and there, suggest individual sordidness, selfish insistence and public wastefulness, rather than a calm and benign development.

There is no evidence of a harmonizing and unwasteful supervision. A casual observation will detect along the east boundary of Front street the line of the old river banks which made in the old days Front street what it was called, Water street. The old steamship and railroad docks occupy what was once navigable water and public property. Natural and artificial filling among the piling is converting this to private title.

On the east side, just south of the old steel bridge, is the Southern Pacific hop warehouse and dock. This dock projected beyond the harbor line (channel line) established in 1892, and was reported against by Mayor Hanbury as cutting off with the bridge piers adjacent, 12 percent of the cross section area of the river. But it still persists.

The Harriman tracks run up and down the river throughout the extent of East Portland and Albina with-

419

out any attempt to utilize the waterfront except to fence it off as a private exclusive domain."[66]

Carrying out its public mandate, the Commission of Public Docks ran headlong into the stubborn Northern Pacific Terminal Co. The commission wanted to get the track of the NPT on North Front Street either removed or open to common use for the reason that North Front furnished the best access between the heart of the city and Public Dock No. 1 that was shortly to be constructed. The commission was either going to build its own belt freight line or rent the use of the NPT track. The commission contended that the NPT had no franchise for the track and City Attorney Grant supported this position before the council in October 1912. Said Grant: "The Northern Pacific Terminal Co. has played fast and loose with its original franchise" that did not extend beyond the city limits at the time of its approval. The company argued that the later extension of the boundary northward automatically extended the franchise northward. The original franchise, like the ones granted to C.F. Swigert's Willamette Bridge Railway Co. in Albina, was a general ordinance — a blanket grant — containing the words "may be extended to the city limits." To the company this wording implied automatic extension. The matter was resolved through compromise in 1914, when the first dock opened, but it proved again how public rights that had been given away free could only be retrieved at heavy public expense. As a matter of fact, after the dock commission first approached the NPT, the company went ahead and laid a second track on North Front street, thus doubling the commission's problems.[67]

The commission had further difficulties with the property owners occupying the site chosen for Dock No. 1. Suits of condemnation had to be filed after the owners rejected offers of twice the properties' assessed valuation. Even with court adjudication, the Pacific Milling and Elevator Co. received $310,250 and the Star Sand Co. $300,000. Joseph Bowles, the notorious N.W. Steel Co. owner who had defrauded the city when he built the N.E. 28th Avenue viaduct, demanded $77,000 for a tiny strip of land that was part of the site; he was awarded $35,000.[68]

One of the major reasons for the dock commission's establishment was to provide a locally controlled public agency for the fostering of maritime commerce. As Joseph Teal had reported to the chamber, wheat and lumber were not enough to make Portland a great commercial port. With the old private docks fading into disuse and the intercoastal trade dropping off, only foreign cargo would provide the essential basis for a thriving Portland trade. In late 1912, a number of Portland's business leaders expressed concern with the apparent overlap of authority between the dock and port commissions. Which agency was to exercise responsibility for straightening the harbor line? Who would decide ownership of the waterfront tidelands between low and high water? Was this public or private land? Who was going to tackle the railroads which were a continual pain in the neck to any public body they could not control?[69] Friction and jealously, it was feared, were going to develop between the port and the dock commissions. The port had long viewed itself as the major promoter of maritime commerce, but over the years it had been accused of indifference* and with showing too much favoritism to the railroads.[70] In 1912, Portland still had no Oriental steamship line providing service on any regular basis. Pacific Mail, with home port in San Francisco, was owned by railroader E.H. Harriman, and James J. Hill owned the major steamship service out of Seattle and Tacoma.

The port commission had been established by the legislature in 1891 to "promote the maritime shipping and commercial interests" of the city. "To accomplish the results sought it was necessary," in the words of the 1915-16 *Biennial Report:*

"First. To make and maintain in the Willamette and Columbia Rivers between Portland and the sea, a channel that will accommodate the shipping of the Port, and to improve the harbor of Portland.

Second. To construct and operate a large sectional floating dry dock in Portland harbor.

Third. To establish and maintain an efficient towage and pilotage service between Portland and the Pacific Ocean.

Fourth. To sell coal and supplies to ships in the interest of the Port.

For the carrying out of these purposes very broad powers have been conferred, principal among which are:

Full control of the Willamette and Columbia Rivers between Portland and the sea to the extent of the State's control; the right of eminent domain; the power to levy regular and special taxes upon the property within the

*As reported in a speech to the chamber by *Journal* publisher C.S. Jackson who was especially critical of the chamber's indifference.

district and to bond the district to provide funds for carrying on its operations."[71]

From its inception, membership on the Port of Portland Commission was considered a high honor, reserved for representatives of the city's leading families. William S. Ladd, appropriately, was named as the first president. John McCracken followed him for six years. Other familiar names included: Henry Failing, Cicero H. Lewis, James Steel, Ellis Hughes, George B. Markle, J. C. Flanders, T.B. Wilcox, George Weidler, Ben Selling, John C. Ainsworth, Charles E. Ladd, William Wheelwright, C.F. Adams and last but not least by any means, Charles F. Swigert. As a matter of fact, for the decade ending in 1911, Swigert was the dominant spirit on the port commission, serving as vice president in 1901-2, president in 1904, and president again from 1908 to 1911. During much of that time, of course, Swigert was wrapped up in his construction projects, some of which had an indirect relationship to river activity. Initially the 15 member commission had been appointed by the legislature. After consolidation, the group was reduced in size and made self-perpetuating. From 1903 on the seven members were again appointed by the legislature.

The port began its existence with a 25 foot channel dredging project for Portland harbor. It next engaged in constructing dikes and revetments along the Willamette and Columbia rivers and in dredging and permanently maintaining a 25 foot ship channel from Portland to the sea. In 1902-3 it spent $377,342 on the first floating dry dock,* located in the St. Johns district. By 1910, it had spent a total of over $2.5 million on river improvement, dredges, dry dock and administration. From 1892 to 1908 five different bond issues were authorized by special acts of the legislature. These totaled $1.2 million. The rest of the funds were raised by annual tax levies

---

*On November 27, 1902 the port was sued over the dry dock contract that was awarded to the Wakefield Co. of which Swigert was a director. In a closed session, the commisison had changed the specifications after the Wakefield bid had been accepted. The company was accused of receiving preferred treatment, a charge similar to that levied against the Pacific Bridge Co. The suit claimed that the bid was illegal. The matter was settled out of court.

(as shown below).* In contrast to what had been a fairly quiescent existence heretofore, after 1915 the port was to play a far more active role in Portland's political and physical development.[72]

7.

A dream that never came true was the product of C.F. Swigert's imagination and initiative. Before leaving for Europe on an extended family vacation in 1905, Swigert had given some thought to the future use of Guild's Lake that was then the locus of the exposition. Always interested in new ideas and novel ways of doing things, Swigert was opposed to the total abandonment of the area to future industrial development. While in Paris, he contracted with an urban designer who had worked for Baron Haussmann to draw up a plan to make Guild's Lake into a ship harbor with a turn-around. He also had the designer draft a scheme for the construction of a waterfront esplanade to replace the old docks on the West bank of the river south of Guild's Lake. Behind the esplanade would be two wide boulevards leading to two large circular plazas. By the time that Swigert returned to Portland the future of Guild's Lake had already been sealed, but many of the features of his "dream" were to be incorporated in the Greater Portland Plan that was unveiled to the city fathers in October 1912.[73]

No master plan for Portland has drawn more interest over the years than the 1912 Bennett Plan. In May 1928, the city planning staff unearthed some old maps pertaining to the Bennett Plan and shortly thereafter published a memorandum with the following comments:

*Tax Year	$ Amount	Tax Year	$ Amount
1892	82,203	1904	138,968
1893	62,487	1905	148,177
1894	14,938	1906	112,063
1895	31,724	1907	141,106
1896	38,262	1908	272,549
1897	30,210	1909	276,917
1898	42,867	1910	417,747
1899	62,817	1911	470,997
1900	46,287	1912	475,178
1901	47,654	1913	359,958
1902	70,034	1914	616,887
1903	71,163	1915	360,681

"It is interesting to see the proposals that have been made at various past times for a reformation of the street system of Portland. How much effort has been put into devising proposals to give Portland a few wide and imposing streets! How far any actual construction has always fallen short of the projected plans!

There is a fairly large and decidedly influential body of citizens who are prone to criticize all plans of the least vision or imagination on the score that, 'It's better to wait until the city of a million or more is here and let them provide their own wide streets and parks. It will be easier for the people of 1980 to pay the high price of that day than it is for us to pay the present price.'

A few instances of what has happened in other cities where business methods have prevailed over visionary plans, might be illustrative of just how much can be lost by trying to save at the wrong time. In 1875, it was proposed to widen Grand Avenue, St. Louis, at a cost of $5,000. In 1925, a less extensive widening was being done at a cost of 1 ½ millions."[74]

Twenty years later, veteran City Commissioner William A. Bowes was to comment: "The City of Portland has a long, somewhat unbalanced history of planning extending from the year 1903 when the Olmsted Brothers . . . were invited to Portland. . . . "[74] Indeed, Portland did have an erratic record of planning. Prior to 1912, the real estate developers dominated the platting of urban property. Plans and plats were hastily drafted with no check by any planning agency. In the words of architect Ellis Lawrence, "it was chaos." Public Works Commissioner A.L. Barbur noted in 1919 that "Portland's development, economically, has been along the lines of least resistance."[76] The cheapest sites were always sought, and the results were the product of chance and private judgment.

Lawrence, who was one of Oregon's leading architects, noted the lack of city parks, the widely scattered civic buildings, the narrow gridiron street system and the fact that Olmsted's boulevard scheme had never been developed beyond the Hillside Parkway section. He and Barbur agreed that the "real estate developers [had always been] in charge."[77] Two months before the Bennett Plan was published, another report by a well known park consultant, L.H. Weir, declared: "Portland Parks Lacking. . . . Portland far behind Seattle,

City Park (now Washington Park).

Tacoma* or the cities of California." Commenting upon the fact that many of the city's parks were adjacent to public school sites, Weir said: "The schools are bare and unlovely, poorly located and unfamiliarly designed." The other parks "are beautiful but too limited in area."[78] Weir judged Portland's recreational facilities to be "too commercialized." For many lower class Portlanders, recreation was to be found in the city's 252 pool and billiard halls, 75 of which were connected to saloons. Mayor Rushlight had long been advocating the purchase of more public park land. In fact he secured an option to purchase 400 acres of Ross Island for $300,000 but the voters rejected the proposal in November 1912.

The city beautiful fund that Mayor Simon had raised was supplemented by additional contributions in 1911 when Mayor Rushlight formed the Greater Portland Plan Association. The council retained Edward H. Bennett of Chicago, a collaborator with Chicago's Daniel H. Burnham, to develop a scheme for the entire city. As drafted, Bennett's plan bore much similarity to Burnham's plan for Chicago. The time had arrived, said Bennett, "when the cities of the earth are planning for the future."[79]

---

*Park acreage: Portland 653, Tacoma 1700, Seattle 1500.

425

PORTLAND
OREGON
GENERAL PLAN
of
PROPOSED DEVELOPMENT OF STREET AND PARK SYSTEM
ALSO, BUSINESS DISTRICT, PRESENT AND FUTURE.

KEY 1ST PERIOD OF EXECUTION

E. H. BENNETT · ARCHITECT
CHICAGO.

D. H. BURNHAM

PROPOSED PARK DEVELOPMENT
OF THE RIVER
AND ROSS ISLAND

Bennett Plan — 1912 — Proposed intersection of West Burnside Street, North Park Blocks, and extended Park Blocks looking north, to a new station and bridge.

427

The key recommendations, that were amply illustrated, are summarized as follows:

(1) Place the dock and harbor facilities for wholesale and light industry activities north of the central downtown, as far as St. Johns and beyond to the Columbia River — the current rivergate district. Develop a deep water harbor north of St. Johns. Place ship slips into part of Guild's Lake as well as at Swan Island across the river.

(2) Restore public ownership to the downtown waterfront area. Construct continuous parkways near the river banks, conserving views of the river. Where necessary, build elevated boulevards over those warehouses and railroad tracks that must remain and connect them to the bridges by elevated ramps. Plant the banks of the river with trees.

(3) Open up the congested downtown with its narrow streets and commercial-warehouse concentration near the river. Citing the well known fact that the "growth of a city tends more and more to the segregation of its elements," Bennett advocated greater variety of human activity in the downtown area with adequate provision for residential and recreational use. Not only should the Park Blocks be extended, but several wide boulevards should be constructed diagonally as radial traffic arteries with large plazas that could also serve as traffic circles. Provision should be made for a more rapid and efficient transit system.

(4) Begin to plan for suburban highway systems by widening "the great Canyon Road" and by considering the construction of a tunnel through the hills to the Tualatin Valley. Bennett envisioned the growth of suburban towns like Beaverton, Hillsboro, and Milwaukie as "garden cities" that would need efficient connection to downtown Portland. But in no case should new transit ways disturb residential units.[80]

A civic rally was held on October 29th at the Gypsy Smith Tabernacle, a temporary structure erected in the vicinity of Multnomah Field to accommodate a visiting evangelist. Frank Branch Riley,

Portland's nationally famous ambassador of good will, addressed the assembled throng in his usual florid style:

"Did you notice the streets in the plan upon the screen? In the admirable system of street circulation, there is provision for the swift, rapid transit from the extreme ends and corners of the city to its intense business and civic centers, by great direct traffic arteries, broadened to receive the flow from parallel streets.

There are axial arteries, connecting laterals and traffic circuits, into which is diverted the traffic which must cross the city but does not seek the center — admirable schemes of street circulation to relieve the increasing congestion of the main centers. . . . Examine the plan again and see the connected boulevards that stretch along the banks of the Willamette, wind through the wooded canyons, climb to the heights in majestic sweeps, and then follow the crest of the river hills, unfolding panoramas unrivalled in the world.

Most interesting of all, perhaps, are the long diagonal arteries that lead in straight lines from the circumference of the city to the center, and these the architect has wisely made the extensions of the main trunk rural highways — the Powell Valley, the Canyon Road, the Pacific Highway, the Base Line, the Sandy Boulevard. I said 'boulevard,' but I had my fingers crossed. (Laughter) It is knee-deep tonight!

This is the age of the highway, not the railroad; the age of the motor car, not the locomotive. The motor car is both feeding and competing with the railroad. Connecting up the empire that lies at our back door is just as important as developing our commerce upon the ocean that lies at our front door."[81]

Although the voters of Portland approved the concept of the Bennett Plan by the overwhelming margin of 16,202 to 7,996, in November 1912, nothing substantial resulted from all of the energy and funding that had gone into the preparation of the grand scheme. As one writer was to comment in 1945: "Portland ended up with little more than some beautiful illustrations now almost forgotten, and a sense of frustration."[82] A number of Portland critics, including Ellis Lawrence, felt that the plan was out of scale with

PORTLAND ORE.

Park area proposed by Mr. E. H. Bennett in his plans for Greater Portland
(Black indicates parks)

Portland; it was too massive. Bennett's buildings had a "Parisian look," and the waterfront an air of old "Budapest."

Bennett should not have been blamed for planning a downtown of such great density as all of the official predictions had shown that Portland's growth would continue to be explosive. In 1912, the dock commission was reporting: "While a continuation of the present rate of growth would result in a population of 3,000,000 in 1950, it is much more likely that this population will not exceed 1,500,000."[83] As Commissioner Bowes noted in 1945: "The Bennett plan was founded on the usual over-estimate of the potential growth of the city, characteristic of plans and planners, even up to the present time."[84] Bowes, along with the critics of 1912, believed that Bennett's wide boule-

430

vards would have been excessively expensive to construct. The violent, almost chaotic real estate boom* that placed Portland 13th in the country in the amount of new construction,** created forces that "were in direct conflict with the plan . . . since land values had grown very high and staid old Portlanders have always feared bonds and high taxes."[85]

One of the "staid old Portlanders" was banker Abbot Mills who represented an important segment of Portland's established leadership that was evolving second thoughts — even serious doubts — about the desirability of Portland's rapid development pace. One of the ingredients of growth was the attraction of new industry and the consequent increase in the potential job market. In the spring of 1912, the Ford Motor Co. was considering locating a plant in Portland until it ran into what it called Portland's "antiquated business methods." Secretary-treasurer James Couzens wrote Mills in July 1912 that he was appalled at the "ultra-conservatism of the men that ought to be big in Portland."[86] The future mayor of Detroit and U.S. Senator from Michigan was reacting against the first National Bank's refusal to pay interest on business checking account balances, a practice that Mills labeled "pernicious." Couzens told Mills that the Ford Motor Co. received 2-2 ½ percent interest on bank balances maintained in all 35 cities in which they did business, "even in conservative London and Manchester England." He accused Portland's bankers of being in collusion by their joint refusal to adopt currently accepted banking practices. Furthermore, the Ford Motor Co. was not about to open savings accounts and buy certificates of deposit in order to receive interest on balances that might run at any time to $50,000 or more. The company could not be bothered.

Six months later, Couzens apparently changed his mind. The banks had made some kind of accommodation with the Ford Company which was unique in America for its policy of depositing company funds in communities where Ford had assembly plants or important dealerships. Couzens was responsible for Ford's establishing a financial influence in every region of the country. By 1912 the company already had a network of 7000 dealers. On the West Coast it had assembly plants in Seattle, Los Angeles and San Francisco. It was absurd for Portland not to be included. By the time that the

---

*365 real estate brokers received licenses in 1912.
**Portland led the Pacific coast in July 1912.

Steel Bridge, 1914.

Portland assembly plant was opened in February 1914, at Southeast 12th and Division Streets, Couzens had left Ford in a huff.* Portland's large three story plant, one of 17 in the country, represented an investment of over $200,000. Using all local labor, it started production with ten cars a day.

---

*When Couzens sold his company stock to Henry Ford six years later, he received $30 million — not bad for an 18 year business relationship.

Ford Motor Co. assembly plant, S.E. 12th and Division
Street, current site of the Metropolitan Press.

Also in February 1914, the Commission enacted Portland's first
comprehensive code for automobile and pedestrian traffic. Henceforth, pedestrians would be required to use regular crossings. The
age of the motor car had finally arrived.*

Daily Bridge Traffic, November 1914

Bridge	Streetcars	Streetcar Passengers	Auto & Train Vehicles	Bikes & Cycles	Horse Driven Vehicles	Pedestrians
Broadway	1,046	20,947	1,192	291	478	2,379
Steel	1,267	25,336	1,486	166	661	3,162
Burnside	494	9,877	1,389	289	1,365	6,939
Morrison	1,309	25,088	1,671	397	1,572	9,957
Hawthorne	1,818	36,273	1,630	177	1,240	4,486
TOTALS	5,934	117,521	7,368	320	5,316	26,923

(From the Portland Department of Public Works Traffic Survey.)

*See Appendix L.

Lewis Building, right, center. Third and Oak Streets, 1910.

Chapter XIV

The Fruits
of Progressivism,
1913-1915

1.

"In temper, like Philadelphia, Portland is solid, strong, venerable, dignified, and self-sufficient. Freeman Tilden once wrote that in order to know how Portland, Oregon, would react in any given situation, it was only necessary to know how Calvin Coolidge would react."[1]

Written 20 years after the period, this depiction of Portland by Glenn Chesney Quiett accurately portrayed the character of Portland's traditional leadership that was being challenged in the last years of the Progressive Era. These particular qualities of dignity, solidity and strength were given distinctive expression in the architectural styles of over 20 major private and public buildings that were erected in downtown Portland, from 1907 to 1915. No comparable period in Portland's history witnessed so substantial an amount of new construction in terms of quality and investment.*

---

*Downtown buildings included: Wells Fargo (Porter), Failing, Corbett, Stevens, Selling, Wilcox, Spalding, Yeon, Oregon Journal, Meier & Frank, Lipman-Wolfe, Imperial, Multnomah and Benson Hotels, Northwestern National Bank, U. S. Customs House, County Court House, Police Headquarters, Library, Lincoln High School, Couch and Shattuck Elementary Schools, Arlington, University and Multnomah Athletic Clubs, and the Pittock Block, the city's first full block office structure. Elsewhere, Reed College, Westminster Presbyterian Church, Jefferson, Washington and Franklin High Schools. Over $17 million was expended.

The Wells Fargo (Porter) Building, currently the
U.S. National Bank Building, on S.W. 6th and
Oak. The Benson Hotel in the right background.

Public Library — Main Branch.

Lipman, Wolfe Department Store, S.W. 5th between Alder and Washington, built by the Corbett Estate.

Henry L. Pittock bought this block of land in 1856 for $300. It is worth over $1 million today. It contained Pittock's small residence until November 1912 when he leased the site to Herbert Fleishacker of San Francisco for 99 years for a total net ground rent of $8,310,000 — nearly 28,000 times the original cost of the block in 1856. Fleishacker was to construct a building for not less than $650,000 with the ownership reverting to the lessor at the end of the lease. The increasing yearly rent scale was based on Pittock's estimate of the increasing value of the land. As it has turned out, the *Oregonian* publisher was amazingly accurate in his prediction.

Likening the reactions of Portlanders to those of Calvin Coolidge reminds one of the late Samuel Eliot Morrison's characterization of our 30th president as "a man of respectable mediocrity" who "lived parsimoniously but admired men of wealth."[2] In terms of providing municipal services as opposed to the building of concrete monuments, however stylish, Portlanders were niggardly. The city was "operating by the seat of its pants" according to a survey made by the New York Bureau of Municipal Research in 1913. Most public expenditures were kept to as low a level as possible and the caliber of most services was only respectably mediocre. Portlanders still wanted to travel first class on a steerage ticket.

Oregon Journal publisher C.S. Jackson had taken the lead in trying to organize a bureau of municipal research for Portland. He had formed a committee of civic minded citizens that included W.B. Ayer, James B. Kerr, Richard W. Montague and Kingman Brewster. To show their Portland friends the value of such an institution, the committee contracted with the New York bureau for a general survey of the city's governmental organization and business methods. Jackson hoped that the resulting report would generate more enthusiasm for both a new city charter and a new form of city government.

As published in April 1913, the report[3] was a shocker. Better than Jackson had expected, the impact was to be immediate and decisive. The survey's findings clearly revealed that antiquated business methods were not confined to the city's banking institutions. With $3 million in general fund income and $15 million in total receipts, Portland was managing its municipal affairs in much the same manner as they had been handled at the time of consolidation in 1891 when the city's population and municipal fund totals were less than 25 percent as large. A brief summary follows:

> **1. The Police Department:** The survey discovered "practically not one single earmark of proper organization or efficient method." The administrative structure was "very poor." The new police headquarters had been planned without seeking the country's best experience and judgement and without ascertaining the needs of the department. Vice control was found to be "vicious for its irresponsibility." Police records were faulty and information non-existent. The lay board of police commissioners was making too many decisions and the civil service procedures were not functioning well.

2. The Fire Department: Generally good equipment was observed but there was no program for fire prevention other than monthly inspections. The financial accounting procedures were poor. The department needed one fire house replacement.

3. The Department of Buildings: As established by the Lane administration, the department was found to be well organized and efficiently operated. But, its effectiveness was restricted by poor support for its recommendations from both the mayor and city council. The council had issued too many "special permits", with an average of two a year from 1905 through 1910, then eight in 1911 and 24 in 1912. Referring to the department's original responsibility for billboards, the report cited a recent ordinance that split jurisdiction among several departments. The consequent supervision was "lax and the results unsatisfactory."

4. The Health Department: The report cited Portland for nearly one-third more deaths from typhoid fever than New York City, in proportion to population. The department was criticized for its generally poor administration and deficient reporting system, especially with regard to tuberculosis which was Portland's leading cause of death. School inspections were deemed inadequate. In blunt terms, the *Report* called Portland "a sanctuary for rats, flies and mosquitoes." The city was violating "with seeming impunity the laws of cleanliness and health protection." Portland was lucky because its natural "climate was good to the city," allowing the "city to get away with" such unsanitary conditions. Portland only had three inspectors, one before 1913, who were unable to provide adequate supervision. The milk inspection program was all but non-existent. In 1909, when the milk inspection standards were established, one-third of all samples tested were found to be adulterated. A local survey, examined by the New York group, found filth and dirt in food handling areas of restaurants and bakeries. In one slaughterhouse, manure, entrails and mud were piled four feet high. Rats and flies were in evidence and a slimy scum clung to the walls. The slaughterhouse was closed four months later.[4]

439

5. Garbage Collection: In unequivocable terms, the *Report* declared that "private collection of garbage is always a failure." In the long run "the costs are much higher to the city." Because the costs are not shown as official expenditures in the city budget, it is easy to deduce, falsely, that the city is saving money. Portland was encouraged to develop a new city owned dump and build a second incinerator plant, despite the fact that the existing plant was only three years old. The city was producing 250 tons of garbage daily and only incinerating 133 tons on the average. On the positive side, Portland's rate for garbage disposal was less than 34 cents a ton, the lowest rate in the nation.

6. Street Cleaning: Portland's streets were clean. This pleasing condition was mostly the result of relatively little population congestion in comparison with eastern cities, smooth surface streets and an evenly distributed annual rainfall.

7. Department of Engineering (Public Works): This department received the most severe criticism. To begin with, its divisional organization did not conform to the functions performed. There was very little overall planning and progress reporting on street pavement jobs. Singled out for particular censure were the construction methods used in laying railroad tracks through the city streets. The companies, with city approval, had employed the cheapest materials. The rails should have been set in concrete foundations rather than in loose stone blocks. Cost records were non-existent and accounting records neglected. There was no central filing system and no coordination between street and sewer work. As to maintenance, the city was wasting thousands of dollars every year. Economy in purchases was totally disregarded. Because orders were split and kept small, under $250, bids were not used. All suppliers received their share. Sewer repair costs were found to be excessive, using private contractors rather than the city's own labor force. And finally, the city engineer's estimates were found to be seldom accurate.

8. Water Department: The report confirmed that Portland had one of the finest water systems in the country. Meters had recently bee.. installed in approximately 30 percent of the dwellings. Non-metered users were charged flat rates* in accordance with the number of outlets. In the 25 years of its existence, the Water Department had collected over $14.4 million from water sales and bond revenues. In December 1912, the books showed a balance of $6,349. The report found a deficiency of $238,000 that could not be accounted for. Was there a big leak? Were the inspections adequate? Chairman Theodore B. Wilcox commented that the deficiency was "of no matter."

9. Finances: Budgeting procedures were judged to be weak. No publicity was given to the budget hearings or even to the approved budget for that matter. It was published a year after the fact in the mayor's annual report. The charter contained too many specific funds.** Estimated expenditures were unreal and not based on actual need projections. A unit cost system was lacking and the department heads were continually overspending amounts previously appropriated. There was "an utter lack of accounting procedures" in the management of city contracts. The council adopted over 90 percent of the city ordinances involving expenditure of funds at the same meetings in which they were introduced. The whole procedure was too rushed. The council calendar was not published. The opportunity for corrupt practices was unlimited. The city could save over $100,000 a year by centralized purchasing, standardized specifications and large quantity purchasing by competitive bids.

10. Municipal Offices: The one office that was severely criticized was that of the municipal judge. Being a part time position at $1800 a year, the judge only worked when his presence was needed. The bank account system, furthermore, was "too open for misuse by the judge."

The New York survey was injected with full force into a two phased struggle: one that involved consideration of a new charter, in

---

*The average charge per dwelling was $9 per year versus the average of $13.68 for 369 other cities in the United States.
**Even with the new charter, there were still 40 special funds in 1914.

stituting the non-partisan commission form of government known as the Galveston Plan; and one that related to the partisan race for mayor that would proceed along traditional lines even if the new charter were to be adopted. The charter and primary votes were set for May 3rd and the election of city officers for June 2nd. Regardless of the outcome of the charter plebiscite, the month of May was going to be frantic with political activity.

The Galveston Plan called for the replacement of part time councilmen with four full time commissioners, each assigned a major department of city government by the full time mayor who also administered at least one department, usually the police. The commissioners and the mayor held equal votes in legislative matters; the veto was abolished. District or ward representation was also abolished, with each commissioner elected city wide by following a system of preferential voting. City elections were no longer conducted on a partisan basis. The preferential system provided for first, second and third choices. A candidate receiving a majority of first choices would win. If no majority was achieved, the second choice votes would be added and then the third choices if necessary. One of the purposes of this system was to eliminate the need for run-off elections. With the Galveston Plan, the mayor and the commissioners assumed both legislative and administrative responsibilities. All citizen boards were abolished except for the civil service board.

Councilman Gay Lombard, millionaire president of the Pacific Grain Co., was both the chief opponent of the new charter and the leading candidate for the Republican mayoralty nomination. A close ally of Joseph Simon's, Lombard charged that the new charter was "compiled largely by men who have increased taxation, failed to make good in the conduct of the city's business, and who allow departments to purchase goods and supplies at higher rates than private industry pays." He specifically accused seven members of the Rushlight administration with failure to perform their duties.[5]

The existing charter was not to blame for the criticisms contained in the *Research Survey,* declared Lombard. Mayor Rushlight was to blame, as was council president George L. Baker, a leading advocate of the Galveston Plan. The new charter would grant too much power to the mayor, claimed Lombard. It would downplay the party, abolish the direct primary and substitute an experimental preferential voting system that was still not fully tested. The mayor's ability to transfer departments would threaten civil service procedures. The opponents blamed the people's apathy, not the instrument of government. How naive to believe that with the new charter, "lions will lie down with lambs in the streets of Portland," and that "all of a sudden, badly run departments will blossom," and "Nirvana" will be attained.

By late April the political fray became intensely personal. Running against Lombard, Rushlight accused his opponent of favoring the big corporations like the Portland Railway Light & Power Co. George L. Baker supported Rushlight and the new charter which, he said, was "particularly fitted to meet the needs and problems of a city that has outgrown its old charter." The example of the $238,000 water department deficiency was cited as the sort of problem that resulted from insufficient control by elected city officials. T.B. Wilcox was not responsible to the voters. Baker discussed the overlap of authority that was embodied in the present charter. It now "takes 30 men to kill a fly," he said.[6]

The white collar Democrats led by Col. C.E.S. Wood became active proponents while the blue collar Democratic *Labor Press* was not satisfied. "Let's wait and get a better one," declared the *Press* five days before the election.[7] The state's leading women's suffragist, Harvey Scott's sister Abigail Scott Duniway, strongly opposed the measure that had been drafted by an all male charter commission. The more conservative Republican business elements also opposed the charter, whereas liberal Republicans of the stamp of W.B. Ayer, William M. Ladd, Joseph Teal, William L. Brewster and James B. Kerr joined *Journal* publisher C.S. Jackson in providing strong endorsement. The Roosevelt Progressives, the Portland Municipal Association, the Greater Portland Plans Association and the more enlightened members of the educational-religious community led by Dr. Thomas Lamb Eliot provided active assistance. In the midst of the campaign, the Broadway Bridge opened with great fanfare and enthusiasm that did not diminish the political acrimony one bit.[8]

A week prior to the charter vote, the *Oregonian* had as yet taken no position on the measure. The day before the election, editor Edgar Piper admitted that he could not get too excited. There was probably some need for change — the idea of a commission appealed to him — but the issues were "overdrawn. . . The people are [the] most important [element]. . . . Beware," said Piper, "of creating a fetish over governmental forms."[9] The paper was critical of the manner in which the charter was presented to the public. It also questioned the merits of a non-partisan preferential voting system. To the *Oregonian,* especially under the late Harvey Scott, Republican partisanship was as sacred as motherhood.

On May 3, 1913, the new charter providing for a commission form of government passed by only 722 votes out of 33,406 cast.[10] This certainly was no great display of reform enthusiasm.

	Yes	No
West Side	4,832	6,114
East Side	12,232	10,728
	17,064	16,842

Barely 22 percent of the eligible electorate had bothered to vote and barely 12 percent were responsible for the passage of the new charter. As with the previous elections of Harry Lane and Allen Rushlight, the East side vote made the difference. But East side charter sentiment was more a reflection of past dissatisfaction with the old charter — with the degree of unbalanced council representation — than an expression of the reform spirit. After all, the Republicans outnumbered the Democrats by almost three to one on a city wide basis. East side support was also responsible for Rushlight's overwhelming defeat of West-sider Gay Lombard for the Republican mayoralty nomination. In June he would face Democrat H. Russell Albee, a prominent insurance executive who had served on the council during Mayor Williams' term. Albee had endorsed the new charter but not with great enthusiasm.

Immediately after the election, the predicted scramble for new offices created a condition of sheer bedlam. A group of leading businessmen organized the "Committee of 100" for the purpose of securing and endorsing the most qualified candidates, particularly those with business experience and ability. As the group expanded, not only included were such familiar figures as Abbot Mills, Theodore Wilcox, Ben Selling, Rodney Glisan, William Wheelwright, Joseph Teal and W.B. Ayer, but several women, ministers, educators, and the perennial reformers Col. C.E.S. Wood and Thomas N. Strong. All meetings were open to the public and every candidate was invited to submit a statement of intention and qualifications. Before the week was out, 84 candidates had surfaced. Three men were also in the running for city auditor, the only other remaining elective position." In his usual overstatement of the case, Thomas N. Strong told the *Oregonian:* "We have smashed the political bosses."[12] Few took this naive declaration seriously. But still, some limited reform had been achieved. And even Strong won agreement from his peers when he expressed concern lest the city commission end up peopled with "incompetents."

The June 2nd election had to be considered a victory for the forces of "better government" despite the less than 30 percent of the 146,000 eligible voters who went to the polls. Although voter participation did increase by 9000 over the previous month the total level of involvement was low. One reason for this state of apparent apathy may have been the decline in party organization and discipline that had been largely responsible for getting out the vote in previous years. The enormous influx of new residents who were not familiar with the names of candidates outside of their own districts was also a factor.

Mayor H. R. Albee, 1913-1917.

Elected to a four year term as mayor was insurance executive H. Russell Albee. Born in Rockford Illinois in 1867, Albee had come to Portland in 1895 to accept employment with the Northwestern Mutual Life Insurance Co. During the course of the campaign, he had secured the endorsement of many progressive Republicans by advocating the municipal ownership of public utilities. The people of Portland, he said, were paying 25 to 50 percent too much for telephone, electric, gas and street car service. He proposed that the city proceed "rationally and carefully" toward the goal that he had outlined. Albee was joined in this issue by successful commission candidate Will H. Daly, manager of the Portland Monotype Co., former councilman-at-large and a warm friend of organized labor. Daly would, appropriately enough, become commissioner of public utilities.

As the incoming commissioner of public works, 37 year old Robert G. Dieck was highly qualified. A civil engineering graduate of the University of Pennsylvania with special training in hydraulics, Dieck had been a past consultant to the city. He was particularly interested in planning. The new commissioner of finance was to be C.A. Bigelow, a well regarded department store official who had just spent two years on the executive board. The fourth commissioner, William L. Brewster, the one who needed the most encouragement to run, was a highly respected liberal attorney* with excellent professional and social credentials. A graduate of Wesleyan University and Columbia Law School, the 47 year old lawyer had served on the civil service board since 1905. He was involved in library and art museum affairs and was a member of both the Arlington and Waverly Golf Clubs. As commissioner of public affairs, Brewster assumed as his major task responsibility for the city park bureau. Elected as city auditor, A. L. Barbur would subsequently serve 16 years as a commissioner. Former council president George L. Baker, the colorful theater owner and manager, was denied his commission bid in 1913, but two years later he would unseat Brewster and move on to the mayor's office, succeeding Albee in 1917.

2.

The Albee administration endorsed a number of projects that were to have a determining influence on the physical shaping of Portland. In October 1913, the commission of public docks publicized its future comprehensive plan. To quote from the *Annual Report:*

> "This plan provides for a development and installation of piers, slips, quays and warehouses on property known as 'Bridgeport' and 'Mock's Bottom'; also the acquisition of Swan Island and the removal thereof, and the development of the 'Bridgeport' and 'Mock's Bottom' properties. This comprehensive plan it is estimated will require an expenditure of $14,475,000, and these two installations will furnish berthing space at one time for thirty-eight vessels of 500 feet each in length, and would have classification, assembling and storage railroad yards accommodating 780 cars. Industrial sections in the rear of the warehouses would contain about 180 acres for factory development. To acquire these properties at fair

---

*Member of the firm of Cotton, Teal and Minor.

values and construct piers and slips to accommodate twelve vessels has been estimated to cost about $4,500,000. The commission at one time had under consideration the submission of a measure to the people at the December, 1913, city election asking for between three and four million dollars as an initial appropriation for this work, but it was decided that sufficient time did not remain for publicity for such a project, and the Commission contemplates submitting such a measure during the year 1914 if a city election is held during that year.

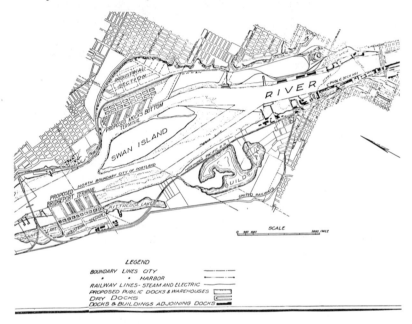

This comprehensive plan made public by the Commission during the year 1913 also included the contemplated development of the waterfront of the Public Levee property at a cost estimated to be $102,000, the plan being to make the installation at the Public Levee property one serving two purposes: first, for river craft; second, as a lumber dock to take care of the Willamette Valley lumber shipments."[13]

In February of 1913, under Governor West's prodding, the legislature had passed a law providing for the old public levee at the foot of S.W. Jefferson Street to revert from the Southern Pacific Railroad

Slip No. 1 at Municipal Terminal No. 1. Pier "A" is at right, Pier "B" at left.

to the State of Oregon which in turn passed title to the City of Portland. The dock commission assumed jurisdiction over the waterfront portion of the property and leased the remainder to the S.P. for 25 years.* A steamboat landing at the foot of S.W. Stark St. was completed in January 1914. On March 28, 1914, the commission opened the first unit, Pier A, of Municipal Dock No. 1, stretching 663 feet along North Front Street. When completed, the dock would be one fifth of a mile in length. A thousand people were on hand for the momentous occasion. They heard attorney Joseph Teal, introduced as the "father of the public dock ideal in Portland," speak to the significance of the event for Portland's economic life. "Upon the water," declared Teal, "rests the foundation of Portland's future."[14] A second public dock was being planned for construction in the St. Johns district in 1915.

The people of Portland did not provide the degree of support for public parks that they did for public docks. In many respects this attitude was understandable, for the docks produced revenue. Bennett's plan for Greater Portland had recommended 7791 acres for the city's park system within an eight mile radius of downtown, in the expectation that the ultimate population would exceed two

---

*See Governor West's statement at the end of chapter IV. This portion of the levee, which for many years lay underneath one of the Hawthorne Bridge ramps, is included in the current waterfront plan as a small boat docking area.

million. Obviously the Portland taxpayers were not going to embark willingly on so ambitious and costly a venture, at least not all at once. Under the direction of Park Superintendent E. T. Mische and Commissioner Brewster, a $2 million bond measure was prepared, similar to one that had failed earlier. With these funds the city could begin to acquire some of Bennett's recommended park land property and it would also attempt to complete the Hillside-Terwilliger Parkway segment of Bennett's proposed belt boulevard scheme. (See Map A.) Portland's boulevard or parkway mileage was small — only three miles — in fact it was the least of any city in its class. For comparison, Seattle had 32 miles. In December 1913, the voters again rejected the issue, thus dooming for over a decade any further efforts that required major public funding.

Mische became discouraged and had a falling out with Brewster over a minor park regulation matter. He resigned from his job and assumed the role of a consultant to the Park Bureau while at the same time establishing his own landscape architecture service. According to one who knew him well, Mische was a most extraordinary

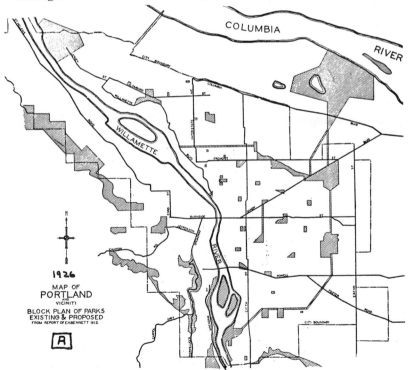

1926
MAP OF
PORTLAND
AND
VICINITY
BLOCK PLAN OF PARKS
EXISTING & PROPOSED
FROM REPORT OF E.H.BENNETT 1912

[A]

THIS MAP SHOWS THE SYSTEM OF PARKS THAT WOULD HAVE BEEN ACQUIRED IN PORTLAND IF THE BENNETT PLAN HAD BEEN ADHERED TO. THE PROPOSED BELT BOULEVARDS AS SHOWN WERE RENDERED SOMEWHAT LESS DESIRABLE BY THE RAPID GROWTH OF THE AUTOMOBILE AND THE PAVED HIGHWAY.

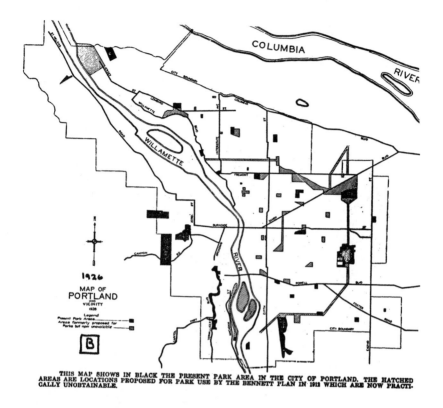

THIS MAP SHOWS IN BLACK THE PRESENT PARK AREA IN THE CITY OF PORTLAND. THE HATCHED AREAS ARE LOCATIONS PROPOSED FOR PARK USE BY THE BENNETT PLAN IN 1912 WHICH ARE NOW PRACTICALLY UNOBTAINABLE.

man. As a product of the Olmsted firm in Brookline, Massachusetts, "his vision, his talent and his enthusiasm in five years . . . made the citizens aware of their God-given opportunity to have one of the finest places in the world to enjoy urban living."[15] Unfortunately for the future of urban Portland, not enough citizens were willing to pay the price.* And Map B documents the consequences. By 1926, when another bond issue went down to defeat, a sizeable number of locations recommended by Bennett in 1912 were already practically unobtainable.

Before leaving office in 1911, Mayor Simon had appointed an auditorium commission to locate a site and choose an architect for the construction of Portland's long awaited public auditorium, a project that the voters had just approved. Almost two years later, the location was still a matter of dispute. As with other issues the East side was

---

*From 1900 to 1915, private investments in saloon properties totalled $1,899,172; public investment in parks totalled $575,640.

VANCOUVER

MAP OF
PORTLAND
SHOWING
PARK PROPERTIES
PARK DEPT. CITY OF PORTLAND
MARCH 1913
SCALE OF MILES

Courtesy of
Rumbers Portner
Map Publishers

Annual Reports of the Park Commission
1908-12 March 1913

fighting the West side. The then current West side public market block was a tempting choice as the city already owned it, but there was a legal question that needed to be resolved. Could the property be used for another purpose? The most desirable West side location was the site of the late Joseph N. Dolph's home,* but the price of $175,000 was considered too high.

In August 1913, the Greater East Side Improvement Club recommended the purchase of a centrally located block near the river that would cost only $55,000.[16] Inasmuch as the intersection of East Burnside and Grand Avenues represented the population center of Portland, the city's needs would best be served by placing the structure in that general area. The club proposed a ten story building, with a 12,000 seat auditorium, and with four stories dedicated to the use of the Oregon Historical Society which badly needed a home as well as adequate storage space for its records. A number of Historical Society members were still smouldering over the exposition board of directors' decision not to turn over some of the profits to help build a society headquarters. West-siders reacted with fury to this wild scheme. The Portland Symphony Orchestra was adamant; it refused to play on the East side.**

In February 1914, the city attorney ruled that the Market Block, between Southwest Second and Third and Clay and Market Streets, could be used for a public auditorium. The commissioners were evenly split: Bigelow and Daly favored the East side and Brewster and Dieck the West side. Mayor Albee had been wavering for some time. He finally voted with the West side for the reason that the property would be free and the resultant savings could be applied to the building. The voters had approved a bond issue of $600,000. Now another delaying complication arose when chairman T.B. Wilcox revealed that the auditorium commission had directed the architects to design a two block structure. The city commissioners were angry. By formal vote, they ordered the architects to redesign the plans or forfeit payment of their $16,000 fee. The two block auditorium was way out of scale and the projected cost was $200,000 over the bond limit.[17] Three years later the civic auditorium was finally opened, with a capacity of 4500. Only 17 percent of the original

*The present site of the Equitable Savings & Loan headquarters.
**Ironically, from 1965-1968, when the auditorium was being rebuilt, the Symphony did perform on the East side, in the old Oriental Theater not far from where the Improvement Club wanted to locate the auditorium in the first place.

452

The old Mechanics Fair Pavilion which was rebuilt and enlarged into the Metropolitan Public Market in 1890. The site was known as the Market Block, the current location of the Portland Civic Auditorium.

structure was salvaged when the facility was rebuilt from 1965-68 at a cost of nearly $4 million.

To accommodate the public markets which had to be moved from the new auditorium block, the city purchased locations on both sides of Southwest Yamhill Street from Fifth to Third, with the large central market covering a quarter block at Yamhill and Fourth. The public markets were an integral part of Portland's thriving street life for many years.

3.

Probably the most troublesome issue to face the new commission was the water meter question. Approximately 30 percent of the city's dwellings, most of them of recent construction, were fitted with meter hook-ups. Mayor Albee's administration was firmly committed to water meter installation throughout the entire city. Commissioners Brewster and Daly actively promoted the program, using the ar-

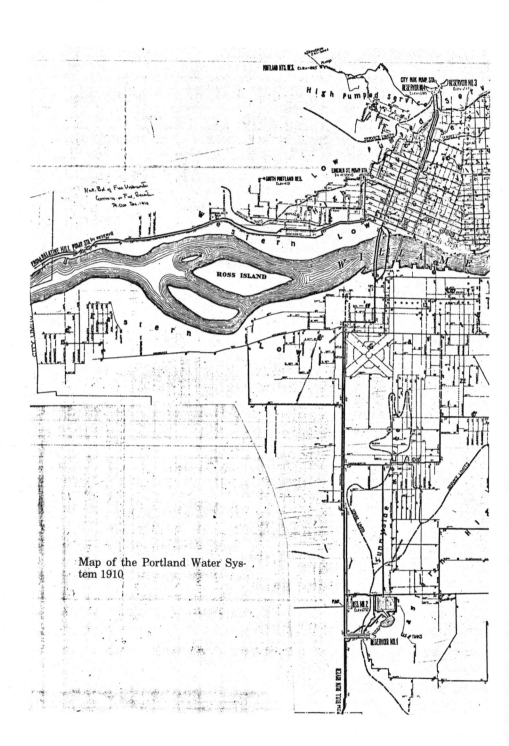

Map of the Portland Water System 1910

gument that with meters the consumers pay for what they use and not for what others waste. The flat rate discriminated against the lower income families and heavily favored the larger commercial users including the owners of apartments and multi-family units. Many of this latter group could be expected to be charged as much as $350 a month by use of a meter system whereas they were only paying $30 by flat rate.[18]

One of the leading opponents of meters was Attorney Whitney L. Boise, the most powerful member of former Mayor Williams' administration.* Boise had been an active and prominent Republican for many years, and under the old city council system he had enjoyed considerable power and influence which he did not hesitate to use for his own benefit. Thirty years earlier he had been the attorney for the Northwestern Mutual Life Insurance Co. for which Mayor Albee was later to become the general agent. Boise was a specialist in realty law and developed a large mortgage loan business on the side. As the son-in-law of J.C. Hawthorne he managed the extensive East side properties of the Hawthorne Estate. Many of these holdings enjoyed flat rate hook-ups. In some cases, the structures were in such bad repair that the ancient plumbing would have had to be replaced before meters could be attached. The costs involved, plus the projected rate increases, threatened to remove a huge slice of income from a thoroughly lucrative investment. The city was expected to pay for the meters and their attachment but not for the repair of outworn plumbing.

The most influential opponent of water meters was the *Oregonian,* the supposed champion of the people back in 1906 when the paper was crusading against the gas company's high rates as discriminatory to low income families. Commissioner Daly thought he knew why the paper had taken an adversary position on this issue. Shortly after he assumed office, Daly found a contract, signed by the city, obligating the municipality to lay a water main from Southwest Monte Vista Terrace to Henry L. Pittock's new mansion that the *Oregonian* publisher was in the process of building high up on a promontory above MacLeay Park.** Checking further, Daly dis-

---

*There were some who thought that Boise controlled Williams. Boise had been president of the executive board.

**Little did Commissioner Daly, or Henry Pittock for that matter, ever dream that almost exactly 50 years later the Pittock estate, a 22 room mansion and 46 acre woodland, would become the property of the city park bureau. About a third of the reduced purchase price of some $250,000 was raised by private contributions.

Henry L. Pittock and his mansion.

covered a letter dated May 12, 1913, written one month before the end of T.B. Wilcox's term as president of the water department board, an agency that was soon to be abolished. Addressed to Wilcox and signed by Pittock and Wilcox's close associate William M. Ladd, the letter requested the installation of the water line at the city's expense. At an estimated cost of $17,000 the project was approved by the board in total disregard of the fact that the mansion lay half a mile outside of the city limits.* The pipe would have extended through a large area of idle land and the city would have found itself as a cooperative partner in a real estate promotion scheme. Daly cancelled the contract. If Mr. Pittock wanted Bull Run water he would have to install his own main and meter, and pay the city for any costs incurred by the special service. From that day forward the *Oregonian* went on the attack.

The *Oregonian* could not be blamed, at least directly, for the mysterious series of events that occurred in late February and early March of 1914. Petitions were circulating for the recall of Mayor

---

*The "minutes" of the Water Board show no record of this transaction.

Albee and commissioners Brewster and Dieck. It was rumored that the water meter controversy was the root cause of the whole effort, although the auditorium decision must have been a factor, as the movement was initiated on the East side. The *Oregon Journal* labeled the endeavor an "ambush" by unknown persons.[19] The mayor was charged with conflict of interest for not having severed his ties with the Northwestern Mutual Life Insurance Co. He was also accused of violating civil service procedures by approving the discharge of a number of city employees for no justifiable or even apparent reason. Brewster and Dieck were charged with being extravagant and lacking in good judgment.

The *Journal* was appalled by the whole procedure. "We cannot conduct government if we get a recall movement every time an official does something which some of us do not approve. Nor can we get anywhere with government if we start a referendum on every city ordinance with which some of us are not suited."[20] The fragility of the "Oregon System" was beginning to show up. If devices that were designed as safeguards for the people, and for use only in the most extreme instances, were to be employed with such reckless abandon the whole system itself might be jeopardized and eventually suffer destruction. By mid-March each of the petitions had secured more than the required number of names to authorize a recall election — over 9,000. But no immediate action was to be forthcoming until candidates could be found who would be willing to contest for the positions of the present incumbents should they be recalled. The challengers were placed in a tough spot. They put the petitions in "cold storage" for seven months, but, as the *Journal* suggested, they should have thrown them in the river.[21]

The rest of the story can best be told by quoting from Percy Maddux' account:

"On Friday, October 2, 1914, recall petitions were filed with the city auditor against Mayor Albee and Commissioners W.L. Brewster and Robert G. Dieck.

At the filing of the petition Mayor Albee stated: 'If it is the will of the people that I should be removed as mayor, I am ready to step down. But I do not believe that is the will of the people. The whole recall movement has come because certain persons and certain interests have not got what they wanted. . . . '

The recall law provided that any official whose recall was sought might resign within five days after the filing of the petition and so avoid an election on the issue. In the event that resignation was not tendered, it was the duty of the city auditor to call a special election within twenty-five days after the filing of the recall petition. Since no resignations were received, City Auditor Barbur fixed October 27 as the day of the election. Mayor Albee said he wanted the recall election held; he would not favor any move to stop it. 'I am not afraid to face voters in a recall,' he said, 'but I do regret that this election will cost the city about $20,000.'

There was great excitement about it during October; there were many surmises as to who would be candidates if recall were successful. Some mentioned the name of ex-Mayor Rushlight, who definitely refused to be a candidate. Eugene E. Smith and B.E. Kennedy filed for mayor, W.E. Leet for commissioner against Brewster, and H.E. Abry and Dr. George Parrish against Dieck. These candidates were asked to speak at a luncheon of the Oregon Civic League at the Multnomah Hotel on October 10 and state their platforms giving reasons for opposing incumbent officers.

Anxiety was experienced as to whether or not Oregon's new recall law was actually in effect. At this time a Columbia County recall election was being challenged in the state supreme court. Preparations for the Portland election were held up as long as possible. On Saturday, October 18, the supreme court ruled that the Oregon recall law was legal. As soon as this news was received, the city hall became a busy place, with the entire force working on recall arrangements. The employees generally worked only half a day on Saturday, but this Saturday they were kept all day. At five o'clock 3,516 letters were sent out to election judges and clerks. Starting Monday, election notices were being posted all over the city.

Little disturbance marked election day. Voting began heavy, dropped off in the afternoon, became heavy again in the evening. The information desk at the city hall was swamped with calls, some from election board members who had not thought to ask in advance about eating arrangements and were now hungry. Could they close the polls during the noon period so they could go out and eat? Commissioner Dieck received a telephone call from a woman who asked him where he stood on the dog muzzling question. He said that he was for muzzles. Whereupon she told him, 'Then I and all my friends will vote against you.'

The results upheld the mayor by a two to one vote (15,455 for recall; 33,687 against). The two commissioners were also sustained by a heavy majority. Nearly fifty-six per cent of the registered voters had turned out."[22]

4.

Many of the problems facing Mayor Albee and the new commission in the 1913-1915 period were, like the water main issue, inherited from previous administrations. City government was never a free agent — able to pick and choose those matters it would take and those it would leave untouched. There were always unresolved questions, unfulfilled earlier programs and new pressures from every corner of the community. City government was seldom master of its own fate. It could and did provide constructive leadership. It could and did develop priorities of need. But it was always constrained by limited financial resources. Instead of being able to plan out rational programs and proceed in some orderly fashion toward implementing them, city government was usually caught in the role of the emergency fireman, rushing around frantically putting out spontaneous or man made conflagrations. It was usually reacting to conditions rather than creating them. To all but the stout hearted city administration could be a most frustrating experience. That of the recall election must have been totally discomforting to the entire commission, let alone to the Mayor. It was distracting to say the least.

One inherited problem related to vice. On Governor West's urging, the 1913 legislature passed what became known as the Abatement Law. Anyone owning a building used for immoral purposes was guilty of maintaining a public nuisance. The offensive practices did not have to be observed. Common fame was sufficient evidence of guilt and there was no need to prove that the owner had any previous knowledge of what was happening on his property. The penalties were severe: the building could be closed for a year, furnishings could be confiscated and the offenders could be fined and jailed. Exceptions could be granted by the courts in those cases where the owners promised to clean up the premises within a stated period of time. On August 12, 1913, District Attorney Walter Evans filed

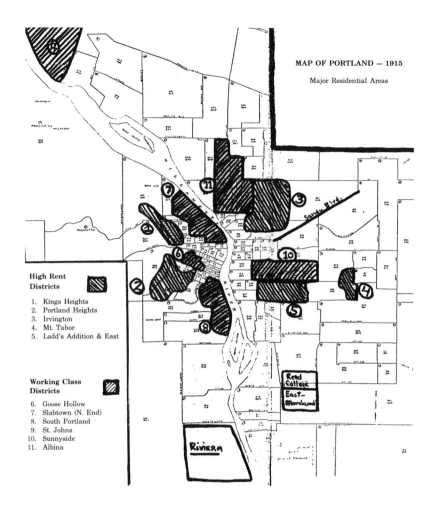

MAP OF PORTLAND — 1915

Major Residential Areas

High Rent Districts

1. Kings Heights
2. Portland Heights
3. Irvington
4. Mt. Tabor
5. Ladd's Addition & East

Working Class Districts

6. Goose Hollow
7. Slabtown (N. End)
8. South Portland
9. St. Johns
10. Sunnyside
11. Albina

the first of many suits under the new law against a variety of guilty parties which included a number of prominent family estates. Within 18 months he would file a total of 68 and none of them would be appealed. According to one account, he was still at it in 1917,[23] when Mayor George L. Baker withdrew the active support of city government. In Baker's mind, the vice crusade had lasted long enough.

Apart from the extra police costs involved, the main problem facing the Albee administration was what to do with the convicted prostitutes. The vice commission had recommended the use of a detention home where physical and emotional rehabilitation would be provided. The council approved a sum of $15,000 which was used for the purchase of property near the county farm and for the design of a proper facility. But, through 1915 at least, additional appropriations were to be deleted from the budget due to financial stringency.* It was the same old story — never enough money to support vital human services. Portland would struggle along somehow and the prostitutes would end up back on the street.

Sunnyside district, S.E. 33rd and Belmont. A working class residential area by 1915.

Portland was afflicted by other kinds of social problems over which it had little control and no available means to help resolve. During the winters of 1913 and 1914 the city attracted increasingly larger numbers of the seasonally unemployed. Emergency benefits were non-existent except to a limited group of trade union members. The city had finally established a free employment service bureau but it could not meet the need.** On several occasions conditions became so desperate, with hundreds literally crying for food, that restaurant raiding, or "rushing," became a necessity.[24] The police would be called out and a few of the more obstreperous would be arrested.

It was during this two year period that Portland for the first time experienced the development of hard core slum conditions, especially

---

*Income from all sources went down $2 million in 1914 and general fund income was reduced from $3.5 million to $3.2 million.

**In 1914, jobs were found for 28,133 men and 2,320 women.

in the Slabtown and North End districts. Albina, South Portland and Slabtown were experiencing the introduction of new industry to their areas. All three districts suffered a drop in population from 1910-1916. For the better off working classes, the major population shift was to North Portland and to the south central East side. For the least fortunate, accommodations could be found in some of the run-down old residences in South Portland, Goosehollow and the near East side that had long since lost their original owners and had been converted into cheap rooming houses.

Large, inexpensively constructed apartment houses were rising adjacent to the industrial areas, especially on the East side of the new Broadway Bridge, near lower Albina. Although less than eight percent of Portland's population would be residing in apartments by 1916, the number was growing rapidly for a city that had possessed practically no apartment dwellers ten years earlier. These were not wooden tenements, but large one hundred room masonry structures with few windows and little ventilation. In some areas, city blocks became overbuilt, yard space restricted and increased congestion became a fact of life.

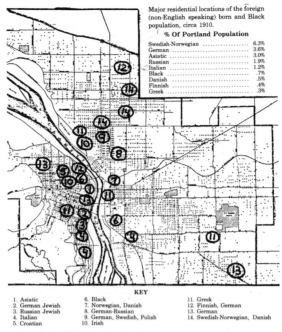

Major residential locations of the foreign (non-English speaking) born and Black population, circa 1910.

% Of Portland Population

Swedish-Norwegian	6.3%
German	3.6%
Asiatic	3.0%
Russian	1.9%
Italian	1.2%
Black	.7%
Danish	.5%
Finnish	.4%
Greek	.3%

KEY

1. Asiatic	6. Black	11. Greek
2. German Jewish	7. Norwegian, Danish	12. Finnish, German
3. Russian Jewish	8. German-Russian	13. German
4. Italian	9. German, Swedish, Polish	14. Swedish-Norwegian, Danish
5. Croatian	10. Irish	

Sources: *Portland Public Schools, Annual Reports.*
Ethnicity in Portland 1850-1970: A Brief Demographic History, to be published in 1976 by the Center for Urban Education.

For Portland's population generally, life was more than bearable. A family of four could live comfortably on $1580 a year which was Portland's average per capita wealth in 1914.* The state legislature had been doing its share to raise wages to a liveable level, especially since the advent of Governor West's administration. By 1914, according to one account, Oregon had "gone further than any other state . . . to regulate hours and conditions of labor for women and girls." Oregon was the first state to designate wages for particular classes of employment.[25]

The ten hour working day had been enacted in 1903 when women were prohbited from employment in mechanical establishments, factories and industrial laundries. Future Justice Louis D. Brandeis had won that decision before the U.S. Supreme Court in 1908.** In 1911, the legislature had enacted a ten hour law for men and women as well as a minimum wage law that prescribed time and a half pay-

---

*In 1917, the average per capita wealth for Oregon was $1257; Washington $920 and California $1730.

**Muller v. Oregon, 208(U.S.) 412, (1908).

ment for overtime. A number of Portland concerns were subsequently fined for violating the ten hour law. The Portland Cordage Co., the largest rope manufacturing outfit on the West Coast, founded by Henry Failing, H.W. Corbett and C.H. Lewis whose estates still controlled it, was convicted in August 1912. In 1913, the legislature established the Industrial Welfare Commission which was authorized to set maximum hours and minimum wages for women and girls. In September 1913, the commission ordered an eight hour maximum working day at a minimum wage of $8.64 per week. The U.S. Supreme Court upheld this ruling in 1917.* Through the appeal process local industry was obviously fighting to the last ditch, but at least some slow progress was being achieved. The workers were not going to become rich on these wages, but they could survive with a minimal level of decency.

In one instance, even the city government became entrapped in the web of the new regulations. Early in 1914, the state labor commissioner ruled that the eight hour regulation applied to all workers, public as well as private.** Albee protested. He refused to include the members of the police and fire departments who, he felt, should be excluded from compliance. The approved city budget was already strained. To abide by the recent order would force the city to hire new employees for which there were no funds. A circuit court judge found the mayor guilty of contempt and sentenced him to jail although he told Mayor Albee that he did not intend to enforce the sentence. The mayor was to be confined in theory only. Several days later, the state labor commissioner reversed his previous ruling and Mayor Albee was released from his theoretical detention.

The high watermark of progressive legislation in Oregon was reached during the 1913 session of the legislature. Although Portland benefited from these enactments, the city government played no direct role in securing their passage. Portland legislators, especially senate president Dan J. Malarkey and Dan Kellaher, provided key leadership as did Governor Oswald West. With the backing of the federal courts, the State of Oregon now had the constitutional authority to prescribe decent conditions for employment. In other matters pertaining to corporate regulation the state legislature had been moving slowly but firmly since 1907, enacting a series of laws designed to force business and industry to accept more open and responsible patterns of behavior and to recognize obligations beyond

---

*Bunting v. Oregon, 243 (U.S.) 426, (1917)
**The 1909 legislature had passed an eight hour law for public employees but it had not been enforced in Portland.

the mere accumulation of maximum profits to private shareholders. In addition to banking, railroad and public service corporation regulation, tax assessment policy became a matter of proper state concern. The first tax commission report in 1911 revealed the new program for assessing the property of public service corporations. They would now be assessed by the state, as units; the old county system which had functioned unevenly and inconsistently was to be abolished.

The establishment in 1913 of the state department of corporations and the office of corporations commissioner proved to be a landmark in Oregon history. Known as the Blue Sky law, the legislation compelled investment companies and corporations to file a full description of their business and prohibited their selling of securities until authorized by the commissioner of corporations. Stock promotion had long been the curse of Oregon from the viewpoint of corporate abuses. The sky had been the only limit to the claims of fraudulent promoters. Misrepresentation had been widely practiced. Companies were deliberately over-capitalized, with often as much as 90 percent of the stock "in water."[26]

During its first year of existence, the department of corporations reduced authorized capitalization of newly formed corporations from $17,555,000 to $12,462,000. It also denied 33 permits to sell securities.[27] As the commissioner reported, "the first year, the . . . Department drove from the markets of the State an aggregate total of $59,564,104 of worthless, doubtful or unproven securities." It also dissolved a number of corporations.[28]

Portland felt the impact of this legislation that was rigorously enforced by Governor West. Changes in corporate leadership were beginning to reveal a more enlightened approach to business responsibility, particularly in the case of the Portland Railway Light & Power Co. On June 1, 1913, Franklin T. Griffith succeeded B.S. Josselyn as president and chief administrative officer of the giant monopoly. In his first official act after assuming office he granted a one percent per hour increase in pay to the entire labor force. Operational efficiency was to be his major long range goal. In many respects, Griffith was ahead of his time. His immediate concern was the company's attitude toward the public. "The public must know all the facts," he declared. "We need an open air policy" and "a new era of understanding between corporations and the public." Then, in a statement that must have shaken a few of the old guard from Portland's business establishment, Griffith exclaimed: "Public service corporations are no longer private enterprises."[29]

465

Harry lane had only been out of office four years and here was the chief administrator of the city's largest corporation expressing thoughts similar to those that had condemned the former mayor in the minds of most Portland business leaders. In 1915, franchise payments to the city were now a matter of course. The rates would be debated, but few would question their justification. For 1915, bridge use fees totalled $123,378 and other franchise payments came to $19,782. Franchise income had risen 900 percent in ten years.

5.

During the first year of the European War, Portland's economy experienced a decline for the first time in nearly a decade, but real estate investment continued to grow. The Kenton district in North Portland, just south of the Columbia Slough, was expanding rapidly as a company "town" serving the executives and employees of the Swift & Co. meat packing plant. The plant itself was located outside of the city limits by city ordinance. Former president B.S. Josselyn of the Portland Railway Light & Power Co. had been an active promoter of the development which was served by one of his street car lines. For several years he had just happened to be president of the Kenton Construction Co.

SWIFT AND COMPANY MEAT PACKING PLANT, COVERING ONE HUNDRED AND FIFTY ACRES

Walnut Park
Only $40
A Front Foot, 1909

Brooklyn
Now Called
Portland's Business
Center,
1909

bove Portrait John Jacob Astor   This Picture Shows Future Portland,---The New York of The Pacific---as depicted by   Above Portrait W. M. Killingsworth
W. M. KILLINGSWORTH
Central Office, Walnut Park.   Suburban Office. 538 Chamber of Commerce.   Phone Main 7974

In August 1913, the president of the National Association of Real Estate Exchanges had declared that "Portland has the greatest future of any city on the Pacific Coast." Portland prices were undervalued; for those with capital Portland offered excellent investment opportunities. A large tract adjacent to Sullivan's Gulch, running from the river east to 18th Street and including Holladay's addition, had just been sold to the out-of-state Pacific Anglo Realty Co. for $2.5 million.[30] The Irvington District continued to expand with the construction of 50 new residences in the spring of 1914, ranging in price from $3500 to $10,000.

Walnut Park near North Rodney Street in the Albina area, was being promoted as a desirable location for middle income families. By the end of 1914, the "phenomenal" Laurelhurst development, located on the former site of William S. Ladd's Hazel Fern Farm, had finished construction of 500 homes in just three and a half years.

Perhaps the most unique land use project involved a double development: the creation of the Westover Terraces in Northwest Portland and the filling of Guild's Lake by dirt and gravel transferred from

467

Northeast quarter of the Laurelhurst
tract. The plat revealed an imaginative
break from the traditional square grid
that characterized much of the East
side development, especially Irvington.
Orientals and blacks were excluded.

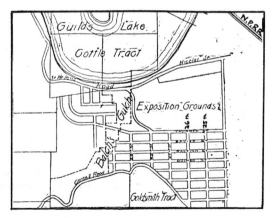

the Terraces to the lake by hydraulic sluices. In September 1909, over 90 acres of the undeveloped and inaccessible Goldsmith Hill Tract had been purchased for $500,000 by a syndicate that included bankers John C. Ainsworth and Henry L. Corbett, *Oregonian* owner Henry L. Pittock, realtor Dorr Keasey and the Lewis & Wiley Hydraulic Co. of Seattle. A portion of the lower Westover area on N.W. Cornell Road had been owned by the Ladd Estate. The water requirements of the sluicing operation were enormous — more than twice the daily consumption of the entire city. The developers built a 12 million gallon pumping station at the lake side. Over the next few years, Lewis & Wiley proceeded to transform the rough and steeply graded hillside into potentially attractive but bare residential sites and at the same time to convey enough fill material over the distance of more than a mile to convert much of Portland's largest lake into 50 acres of dry land. To quote from a 1913 *Oregon Journal* account:

469

"Quietly and without ostentation, . . . Guild's Lake has been transformed from a muddy and unattractive sheet of water into a modern up-to-date industrial center. . . . The result has been that the greater part of Guild's Lake is today a manufacturing district, or an industrial center, as the owners call it, which is rapidly filling up with the manufacturing and industrial plants that have been operating for years in other parts of the city.

Kings Heights and Westover Terraces, Northwest of the Uptown Shopping Center (1915).

Industrial center embraces an area of about 50 acres and contains something like 125 individual sites, each fronting on a broad street and having in the rear a 30 foot alley. Each site contains 10,000 square feet. Up to date 10 well known manufacturing plants located in the down town district have acquired sites in Industrial Center and are hastening preparations to move their enterprises to the new location.

For many years the consensus of Portland opinion has been that some day Guild's lake would be the manufacturing district of Portland. Everybody realized that it would be a huge undertaking to transform this body of water into dry land, but that it would be done some day no one doubted.

That this development means much to Portland, no one who is at all familiar with the difficulty heretofore attending the securing of desirable manufacturing and industrial sites, will deny. The property separates the wholesale district and the industrial section extending down the river from Portland to Linnton. Its exact location is Twenty-ninth and Nicolai streets and it is so near in that it is quickly reached by the west side carlines and is supplied with abundant rail shipping facilities."[31]

A decade earlier few people would have agreed with the *Journal's* description of Guild's Lake as "a muddy and unattractive sheet of water." Since the end of the exposition, the lake had suffered from industrial and other forms of pollution. It had become an unofficial dumping swamp. The roadbeds of both the Northern Pacific on the

927 aerial survey of Guild's Lake district, showing the fill on the upper left. The Northern Pacific R.R. racks bisect the scene. Terminal No. 1 is on the lower right; Swan Island in the upper background.

east and Great Northern's United Railway on the west had added to its unkempt state. By the time that the Lewis & Wiley Company came along, the area was ripe for a good fill job which it duly received and would continue to receive for over 30 years. By the end of 1915, the tract would cover over five hundred acres, filled to a depth of from fifteen to twenty-five feet. Every lot would have railroad trackage. In the 1920's the Port of Portland would contract with the property owners to permit the port to dump dredging material from the new main channel west of Swan Island. In return for the fill, the port would accept a large tract of waterfront to be held for public dock space.[32]

The extension of the industrial center north from Guild's Lake was hastened by the rapid growth of the Linnton district which became heavily industrialized and commercialized in the period following the exposition. Led by such companies as the Portland Gas & Coke and Standard Oil of California, over 15 major industries had settled in Linnton by the end of 1912. Within three years, Linnton would be annexed to Portland, bringing with it much of what 30 years later became the Forest Park Reserve.*

---

*Both Linnton and St. Johns were annexed in 1915, increasing the geographic size of Portland by 25%.

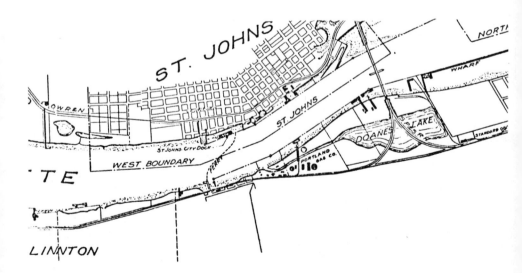

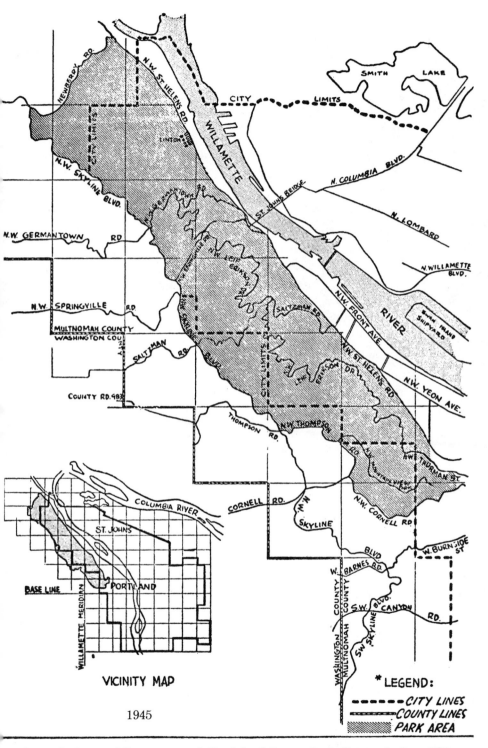

SMITH LAKE

CITY — — LIMITS

WILLAMETTE

NEWBERRY RD.

N.W. ST. HELENS RD.

LINTON #96

N.W. SKYLINE BLVD.

N.W. GERMANTOWN RD.

N.W. GERMANTOWN RD.

N.W. SPRINGVILLE RD.

MULTNOMAH COUNTY
WASHINGTON COU

SALTZMAN RD.

N.W. SALTZMAN BLVD.

COUNTY RD. 989

N. COLUMBIA BLVD.

ST. JOHNS BRIDGE

N. LOMBARD

N. WILLAMETTE BLVD.

SWAN ISLAND SHIPYARD

RIVER

N.W. FRONT AVE.

N.W. ST. HELENS RD.

N.W. YEON AVE.

N.W. ERICKSON DR.

N.W. ECK
N.W. KNOX DR.

CITY LIMITS

THOMPSON RD.

N.W. THOMPSON RD.

N.W. MOUNTAIN VIEW RD.

N.W. THURMAN ST.

CORNELL RD.

N.W. SKYLINE

N.W. CORNELL RD.

W. BURNSIDE ST.

COLUMBIA RIVER

ST. JOHNS

BASE LINE

WILLAMETTE MERIDIAN

PORTLAND

BLVD.

W. BARNES RD.

WASHINGTON COUNTY
MULTNOMAH COUNTY

S.W. SKYLINE BLVD. CANYON

S.W. CANYON RD.

VICINITY MAP

1945

**Area designated for proposed Municipal Forest-Park lies entirely within
Multnomah County while 70% of it is within the City of Portland.**

1915 downtown aerial survey. The County Courthouse is in the bottom center. To the west and north can be seen the Failing and Corbett residential blocks, further to the west and north can be seen the YMCA and the Hotel Portland. Directly to the north of the Hotel Portland is the Northwest National Bank Building that replaced the Marquam Building, currently known as the American Bank Building. The Broadway Bridge can be seen in the upper right corner.

Chapter XV

In Retrospect

The decision to establish an industrial center at Guild's Lake and the process by which the center was put together, symbolized the general pattern of decision making and inadvertent development that shaped much of Portland during the period from 1885 to 1915. Public interest was secondary to private interest. Few questioned the traditional notion that private development was synonymous with progress and the public welfare. Only when community health, fire hazard and similar issues were at stake, or when projects were not considered profitable to the private investor, did Portland's business-political leadership appear willing to accept public planning or public management. Although many decisions reached in the 30 year period proved, in retrospect, to have been wise, few of them were made for legitimate public policy reasons.

The record is fairly clear. Human greed was the dominant motive in determining the physical shape of the average American city, particularly during the 50 years following the Civil War. Decisions involved choices, but in Portland's case the choices were not difficult. The path of least resistance was the chosen route — hasty decisions based on immediate profit expectation or lowest public expenditure. This was the "businesslike" approach that was in the long run to produce excessive waste of human and economic resources. In recent years millions of dollars of public tax funds have been spent to remedy the mistakes made by previous generations. It is doubtful that future generations will be able to afford this luxury.*

---

*Urban renewal programs provide the clearest and most costly examples. Only recently has urban conservation become an acceptable public program. In August 1976, the Portland city council approved the establishment of a fund for this purpose, to help restore designated city landmarks.

When Lewis Mumford addressed the Portland City Club in 1938, he was especially critical of industrial developments like Guild's Lake. He suggested the acquisition of lands not immediately on the river, to be developed as model industrial cities, or towns within cities. Neglect of this type of public planning, Mumford declared, "is nothing short of a public disgrace." Directing his comments to a cross section of Portland's business-political leadership, Mumford stated: "You have an opportunity for setting an example to the rest of the world." Mumford accurately predicted that most American cities "will have to be rebuilt within the century, because they will be obsolete if for no other reason."[1]

The subsequent history of Portland's industrial development, at least until the 1960's, showed that few took Mumford seriously. As the planning commission staff wrote almost 50 years ago:

> "The history of city building is a history of what might have been; and the present seems always to be unwilling to learn from the past and to try to avoid the pitfalls in which the past has perished. The dreamer of yesterday, scoffed at by his own contemporaries, is lauded as a prophet by the people of today, who are just as foolish in their ridicule of the planner of today who will surely be appreciated some day in the future when it's too late to use his wisdom."[2]

The voices of a Bennett, Olmsted or Mumford went unheeded. So did the voice of the *Oregon Journal* when it pleaded for the preservation of the old Chamber of Commerce Building in 1933. "The forward course of progress pays no heed to values of a sentimental nature. The fact that the building is rich in history is of no consequence."[3] The real estate developers and the bankers shared much of the responsibility for local decisions of this sort. As prominent

---

The initial authorization calls for the expenditure of $450,000 from local tax increment and federal Housing and Community Development funds. Additional millions of federal dollars have been and will be spent to restore deteriorated neighborhood districts in St. Johns, Kenton, Linnton and Albina.

Southeast Portland, from Burnside Street to Powell Boulevard, from the river to 12th Avenue is being considered for redevelopment as an inner-city light industrial park. Millions of dollars of public and private money will be involved. Approximately 20 percent of the existing buildings are considered functionally obsolete. This is the area that was literally given away to the railroads 75 years ago. Sadly, the waterfront along the southeast river bank is almost beyond repair. The location of the interstate freeway "resolved" that problem.

realtor Chester A. Moores stated in 1939: "If older buildings that are losing money were torn down and new ground areas made available for parking space, the remaining office buildings would reap still further advantage."[4] Few building owners made any attempt to maintain or upgrade their older properties. A building was valued solely for the income that it would produce; the less spent on it the more income to be realized.

On a broader scale, the absentee owned utilities, railroads and street railways exercised the crucial influence, particularly over the councils of state and city government. Knowing the caliber of many of Portland's councilmen and mayors, one may rightly question whether the city would have done a better job than private enterprise had its leaders elected to pursue a more active municipal role in planning and management. Perhaps not, but at least the consequences could not have been any worse and the public resources might have been better protected. Certainly the private interests would have been forced much earlier to share a larger percentage of the profits with the total community.

The overall quality of Portland's fiscal management and political leadership was poor. The city councilmen, county officers and most of the mayors were limited in vision and primarily committed to the service of particular private interests. In 65 years Portland had only four public spirited mayors who placed the people's welfare foremost: Henry Failing, William S. Mason, Harry Lane and H. Russell Albee. Portland's old council system — as with its present commission form — was susceptible to dispersed accountability. Portland's mayors traditionally functioned with limited power. Whereas public authority was diffused and weak, private authority was more highly structured and better organized, in addition to being more adequately financed. It is little wonder, therefore, that private interests tended to dominate public interests. This condition led to a type of city development that was concerned primarily with physical structure rather than social structure, with building new buildings rather than new people. The profits proved to be greater and the expected results more durable.

Historians who attempt a critical evaluation of the business ethic that so completely dominated cities like Portland in the early 1900's often encounter the response, "So what! That was the system in 1910; it was only human nature. Those businessmen should not be judged by 1976 standards." As someone recently wrote in *Fortune*, critics today seem to be "going through a period of moral seizure."[5] Perhaps we are, but perhaps it is time that we do. Some recent statements in self-defense made by officers of multi-national corporations, by members of Congress, and even by a former Vice President, raise serious questions in the minds of many Americans as to just what are the 1976 standards of ethical conduct. The need to compete for profits and the apparent compulsion to preserve power status and job security seem to justify almost any course of action short of murder.

The notion that acceptable ethical standards in 1910 were different is a specious one. Acceptable to whom? The record of 65 years ago reveals a number of outspoken citizens who were appalled by what they saw: Thomas Lamb Eliot, Stephen Wise, George E. Chamberlain, Oswald West, Harry Lane, Richard Montague, C.E.S. Wood, William D. Wheelwright, and Joseph Gaston just to mention a few of the more prominent local figures. On the national scene, besides Theodore Roosevelt, Francis Heney and Lincoln Steffens, were a number of able and forthright governors: Charles Evans Hughes of New York, Woodrow Wilson of New Jersey, Robert LaFollette of Wisconsin, John F. Shafroth of Colorado and Hiram Johnson of California. These gentlemen could not be accused of being gripped by "moral seizure." They were simply demanding an honest deal for the American public.

It is fitting to conclude this work with some relevant comments that were written in 1910 by Joseph Gaston. Gaston was a remarkable person: early railroad builder; successful farmer, journalist and lawyer; respected friend of many of Portland's leading business and political figures; independent Republican who on occasion expressed Populist sentiments; and eloquent author of an exhaustive multi-volume history of Portland.

Joseph Gaston.

478

"The one chief factor that has changed the standards of character and rectitude in modern times, from the standards of the pioneer days, east and west, is the corrupting influence of corruptly accumulated wealth. The old Jewish prophet was not mistaken when he declared that 'the *love* of money was the root of all evil.' Go back as far as you please, and you will find that the pioneer founders of all the abiding benefits of American civilization, were satisfied with a very modest amount of this world's goods and gear, as compared with their descendants of the third generation.

What do we see now? Greater inequalities of wealth and position in the United States within 134 years after its founding, than in any European nation that is a thousand years old. Direct poverty alongside of single fortunes of two hundred million dollars accumulated in forty years. . . . Combinations of capital to fix prices, and raise or depress wages, increase or decrease the supply of commodities, and drive out competition, with a more effective and autocratic power than was ever exercised by any absolute monarch of any old world dynasty. Unscrupulous adventurers, casting behind them all the restrictions of honor, decency and fair play, with millions accumulated from reckless gambling or downright extortion, buying their way to the highest legislative or executive offices, to disport their vanity and corrupt the public conscience."

"Is this progress? Has all the experience of two thousand years, the statesmanship of Pericles, the wisdom of Cato, the learning of Bacon, the patriotism of Washington and the great heart of Lincoln — all are gone for nothing? Is there no wisdom in counsel; no great heart in combination? Is it now to be a factional scramble for place and power by antagonistic and diverse interests; great capitalists, great corporations, multi-millionaires, deft political schemers, all appealing to the ignorance, prejudices or self-interest of rival and incoherent bodies of unorganized voters?

Civil government is now on trial in Oregon, as never before, and the end is not yet."[7]

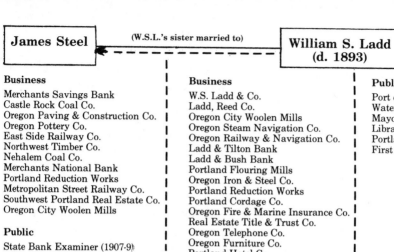

James Steel

(W.S.L.'s sister married to)

Business

Merchants Savings Bank
Castle Rock Coal Co.
Oregon Paving & Construction Co.
Oregon Pottery Co.
East Side Railway Co.
Northwest Timber Co.
Nehalem Coal Co.
Merchants National Bank
Portland Reduction Works
Metropolitan Street Railway Co.
Southwest Portland Real Estate Co.
Oregon City Woolen Mills

Public

State Bank Examiner (1907-9)

William S. Ladd (d. 1893)

Business

W.S. Ladd & Co.
Ladd, Reed Co.
Oregon City Woolen Mills
Oregon Steam Navigation Co.
Oregon Railway & Navigation Co.
Ladd & Tilton Bank
Ladd & Bush Bank
Portland Flouring Mills
Oregon Iron & Steel Co.
Portland Reduction Works
Portland Cordage Co.
Oregon Fire & Marine Insurance Co.
Real Estate Title & Trust Co.
Oregon Telephone Co.
Oregon Furniture Co.
Portland Hotel Co.
Riverview Cemetery Inc.

Real Estate holdings:

Oswego
Palatine Hill
Eastmoreland
Canyon Road Highlands
Burlingame
Laurelhurst
Cornell Road
Ladd's Addition
East Portland lots
Mead Estate

Public & Other

Port of Portland (1891-3)
Water Committee (1885-93)
Mayor (1854-55)
Library Association
Portland School Board
First President, Board of Tr

Brother George A. Steel

Business

Farming
Portland Stock & Mining Exchange
Metropolitan Street Railway Co.
East Side Railway Co.
East Side Electric Co.
J.K. Gill Co.

Public

Oregon State Senate
Portland Postmaster
National Republican Committee
Oregon State Treasurer (1907-11)

Protégé Theodore B. Wilcox

Business

Portland Flouring Mills
Ladd & Tilton Bank
Willamette Valley Milling Co.
Western Warehouse Co.
Equitable Savings & Loan Assoc.
U.S. National Bank
Tepustete Iron Co.
Columbia Life & Trust Co.
Arlington Building Assoc.
Rose City Park Assoc.
Downtown real estate holdings

Public & Other

Water Committee
Oregon Development League
Commercial Club

Sons

William M. Ladd

Business

Ladd & Tilton Bank
Oregon Iron & Steel Co.
Title Guarantee & Trust Co.
Oregon Improvement Co.
Washington Reduction Works
Columbia Life & Trust Co.
Portland General Electric Co.
Portland Railway Light & Power Co.

Public

Oregon House of Representatives
Executive Board
Water Committee
Treasurer, Free Bridge Committee
New City Hall Commission

Community & Other

Portland School Board
Portland Academy
Art Museum
Library Association
YMCA
Reed Institute
Commercial Club
San Francisco Relief Committee

Charles E. Ladd

Business

Adamant Co.
Trinidad Asphalt Paving Co
Numerous Mining Companie
Equitable Savings & Loan A
Willamette Valley Milling Cc

Public

Port of Portland

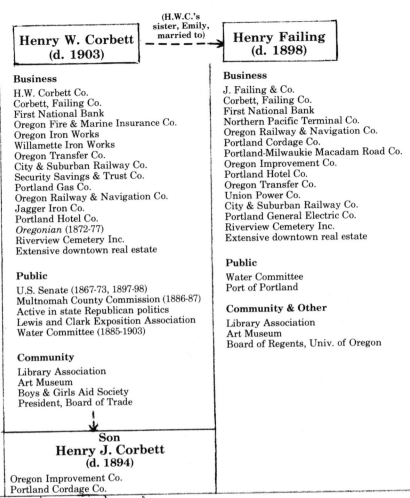

Henry W. Corbett
(d. 1903)

(H.W.C.'s sister, Emily, married to) → **Henry Failing (d. 1898)**

Business

H.W. Corbett Co.
Corbett, Failing Co.
First National Bank
Oregon Fire & Marine Insurance Co.
Oregon Iron Works
Willamette Iron Works
Oregon Transfer Co.
City & Suburban Railway Co.
Security Savings & Trust Co.
Portland Gas Co.
Oregon Railway & Navigation Co.
Jagger Iron Co.
Portland Hotel Co.
Oregonian (1872-77)
Riverview Cemetery Inc.
Extensive downtown real estate

Public

U.S. Senate (1867-73, 1897-98)
Multnomah County Commission (1886-87)
Active in state Republican politics
Lewis and Clark Exposition Association
Water Committee (1885-1903)

Community

Library Association
Art Museum
Boys & Girls Aid Society
President, Board of Trade

Business

J. Failing & Co.
Corbett, Failing Co.
First National Bank
Northern Pacific Terminal Co.
Oregon Railway & Navigation Co.
Portland Cordage Co.
Portland-Milwaukie Macadam Road Co.
Oregon Improvement Co.
Portland Hotel Co.
Oregon Transfer Co.
Union Power Co.
City & Suburban Railway Co.
Portland General Electric Co.
Riverview Cemetery Inc.
Extensive downtown real estate

Public

Water Committee
Port of Portland

Community & Other

Library Association
Art Museum
Board of Regents, Univ. of Oregon

Son
Henry J. Corbett
(d. 1894)

Oregon Improvement Co.
Portland Cordage Co.

Daughter
Helen Ladd

Son
Henry Ladd Corbett

Business

Ladd & Tilton Bank
First National Bank
Home Telephone Co.
U. S. National Bank
Oregon Electric Railroad Co.
Equitable Savings & Loan Assoc.
Commonwealth Inc.
Oregon Mutual Life Insurance Co.
Portland Gas & Coke Co.
Portland Consolidated Railway Co.
Portland Railway Light & Power Co.
Southern Pacific Railroad
Corbett Investment Co.

Public & Other

Portland Dock Commission
Executive Board
Port of Portland
Oregon State Senate
President, Portland Chamber
   of Commerce
Red Cross
War Bond Drive, WWI
Library Association
Art Museum
Portland Symphony Society

APPENDIX A

Corbett, Failing, Ladd & Relatives — Corporate Family Tree

APPENDIX B

List of the Mayors of Portland from 1851 to 1915:

1851	Hugh D. O'Bryant	1876-7	J. A. Chapman
1852	A.C. Bonnell, to November	1877-8	W. S. Newberry
1852	S.B. Marye, elected in Nov.	1878-9	W. S. Newberry
1853	Josiah Failing	1879-80	D. P. Thompson
1854	W.S. Ladd	1880-81	D. P. Thompson
1855	George W. Vaughn	1881-2	D. P. Thompson
1856-7	James O'Neill	1882-3	J. A. Chapman
1858	L. M. Starr	1883-4	J. A. Chapman
1859	S.J. McCormick	1884-5	J. A. Chapman
1860	George C. Robbins	1885-6	John Gates
1861	J. M. Breck	1886-7	John Gates
1862-3	W. H. Farrar	1887-8	John Gates
1863-4	David Logan	1888-9	Van B. DeLashmutt
1864-5	Henry Failing	1889-90	Van B. DeLashmutt
1865-6	Henry Failing	1891	W. S. Mason
1866-7	Thos. J. Holmes	1894	Geo. P. Frank
1867-8	J. A. Chapman	1896	Sylvester Pennoyer
1868-9	Hamilton Boyd	1898	W. S. Mason
1869-70	B. Goldsmith	1899	W. A. Storey
1870-71	B. Goldsmith	1900	H. S. Rowe
1871-2	Phillip Wasserman	1902	George H. Williams
1872-3	Phillip Wasserman	1905	Harry Lane
1873-4	Henry Failing	1907	Harry Lane
1874-5	Henry Failing	1909	Joseph Simon
1875-6	J. A. Chapman	1911	A. G. Rushlight
		1913-17	H. R. Albee

APPENDIX C

List of Governors and U.S. Senators (Oregon)

Governors

1882-87	Zenas F. Moody (Rep.)
1887-95	Sylvester Pennoyer (Dem.)
1895-99	William P. Lord (Rep.)
1899-1903	Theodore T. Geer (Rep.)
1903-09	George E. Chamberlain (Dem.)
1909-10	Frank W. Benson (Rep.)
1910-11	Jay Bowerman (Rep.)
1911-15	Oswald West (Dem.)

U.S. Senators

1865-71	George H. Williams (Rep.)	1867-73	Henry W. Corbett (Rep.)
1871-77	James K. Kelly (Dem.)	1873-79	John H. Mitchell (Rep.)
1877-83	Lafayette Grover (Dem.)	1879-85	James H. Slater (Dem.)
1883-95	Joseph N. Dolph (Rep.)	1885-97	John H. Mitchell (Rep.)
1895-1901	George W. McBride (Rep.)	1897-98	Henry W. Corbett (Rep.)
1901-05	John H. Mitchell (Rep.)	1898-1903	Joseph Simon (Rep.)
1905-07	John M. Gearin (Dem.)	1903-09	Charles W. Fulton (Rep.)
1907-	Fred W. Mulkey (Rep.)	1909-21	George E. Chamberlain
1907-13	Jonathan Bourne, Jr. (Rep.)		(Dem.)
1913-17	Harry Lane (Dem.)		

APPENDIX D

Description of the Fulton Park Real Estate Development in 1888.

[From *The West Shore*, 14 (August, 1888), pp. 442-43]

Upon the gently sloping hills lying between the cemetery and the city the Southern Portland Real Estate Company, composed of some of the most prominent business men of the city, has laid out the town of Fulton Park, whose many advantages as a place of residence can not be overestimated. Along one side of the tract passes the Portland & Willamette Valley road, while the west side line of the Southern Pacific runs directly through it. From the depot of either, any portion of the tract can be reached in a few minutes. Winding through the tract, so as to reach every portion of it, the company is constructing a system of grand boulevards, at an expense of $15,000.00, and the plat is so laid out that a large proportion of the lots face the boulevard, which has a total length of five miles. All the other lots can be reached from the boulevard by cross streets of from one to three blocks in length. The ravines and steep hillsides are not included in the plat, and there is not a lot of the thirteen hundred and ninety-three embraced in the tract which does not afford a fine building site; nor is there one from which cannot be obtained a fine view of the city, the river and the entire country to the north and east, the landscape culminating in the Cascade mountains and the great snow peaks, for which the scenery of Portland is famous. The slope of the hills, while sufficiently gentle to render their ascent by foot or carriage easy or convenient, affords splendid natural drainage, insuring freedom from malaria, while pure air and springs of clear mountain water conduce to health and comfort. The chief difficulty in the way of such suburban tracts is the fact that houses are erected and improvements made so slowly that it takes a number of years to render them the convenient and desirable places of residence that they eventually become. In this case, as has already been stated, the means of frequent cheap and rapid transportation already exist, a convenience for which such tracts are usually compelled to wait several years. Trains on the two roads reach the tract in seven and eight minutes, a shorter time than is required to reach many portions of the city by street cars, and the fare is but five cents, the same as is charged by the latter. To accomplish the other point, that of avoiding the usual delay in building, the company has adopted the plan of erecting one hundred houses at its own expense, which will be given away to purchasers of lots. The company is reimbursed for this outlay by the added value of the tract by reason of the building upon it of one hundred houses, which will be more than the cost of construction. This added value will attach to the lots sold as well as to those still remaining in the company's hands. In order to give these houses to purchasers of lots so as to avoid partiality, it has been determined to distribute them by lot. For this purpose one thousand lots have been set aside for sale at a uniform price of $400.00 each, payable in installments of $50.00 at the time of purchase and $25.00 per month thereafter, beginning with the first of next September. On the fifteenth of November the drawing will be held, and, of course, every tenth lot will include a house, many of which will have been completed by that time. Those who fail to draw a lot with a house upon it, will have the satisfaction of knowing that their land is at least worth the money, and that they have received full value for their investment. Of these houses, ninety-eight will be cottages, of four different styles, costing $1,000.00 each, and two will be elegant $5,000.00 houses, each occupying more than one lot. All the lots are fifty by one hundred feet, or larger, owing to the contour of the tract. The company has reserved three hundred and ninety-two lots, selected indiscriminately throughout the tract, which are for sale on easy terms at prices ranging from $300.00 to $500.00 each, the purchaser, of course, having no interest in the drawing.

Here is, undoubtedly, the best opportunity the man of small or large means will have to secure a good suburban home on the confines of Portland. By building these houses and constructing the boulevards, the company practically annihilates fully five years of time, and gives to the land at once the value it would ordinarily acquire during that period by gradual improvement. Fulton Park will begin its career with one hundred houses, all of which will, in the nature of things, soon be occupied, and splendid transportation facilities, a stage in its growth which no other tract can hope to reach in the period mentioned. Undoubtedly, before a year has passed Fulton Park will be universally admired as the most beautiful and pleasant residence district in the city of Portland.

Henry Pittock, James Steel, and others, incorporated the Metropolitan Railway Company to provide electric street car service from Second St. to Fulton Park. When some citizens complained that Pittock was putting up rails, poles, and wires which would be unsightly, he replied with his usual good humor that they were a lot less unsightly than a tired horse pulling a car up the hill. The day of the horse-drawn street cars in Portland was drawing to a close.

APPENDIX E

Statistical Table of Manufactures

[From *The West Shore*, 14 (August 1888), p. 414]

Industry.	Capital Invested.	Hands Employed.	Annual Wages.	Annual Product.
Bags, Tents, Sails, etc.	$ 130,000	57	$ 36,340	$ 531,000
Beer	700,000	56	54,000	430,000
Billiard Tables	1,000	2	1,800	2,500
Book Binding	14,500	34	20,800	36,000
Boots and Shoes	19,000	105	93,480	189,000
Brick	40,000	150	36,000	120,000
Brooms, Wooden and Willow Ware, and Brushes	39,500	73	23,250	82,000
Car Shops	765,000	183	161,147	300,000
Carpentering	23,000	107	96,000	146,000
Carpets	300	2	700	2,000
Carriage and Wagon Manufacturing and Blacksmithing	88,100	191	164,816	379,000
Cement and Artificial Stone—Building and Paving	125,000	40	29,500	125,000
Cigars	14,300	40	25,580	80,000
Clothing—Gentlemen's	70,700	208	185,390	363,000
Ladies'	54,000	309	86,424	444,000
Coffee and Spices	47,000	19	17,000	108,000
Confectionery	85,000	75	29,130	339,500
Cooperage	36,700	46	27,300	59,000
Cordage	100,000	30	25,000	125,000
Crackers, Bread, etc.	131,000	138	88,970	471,000
Electrical Goods	5,000	7	6,000	8,000
Electrotypes	1,000	2	1,500	2,500
Engraving	300	2	1,800	2,500
Flour	730,000	78	57,720	2,040,000
Foundries and Machine Shops, Boiler Works etc.	468,100	412	276,020	834,000
Fruit and Vegetable Canning and Drying	43,000	253	42,000	115,000
Furniture	391,900	306	182,200	557,500
Furs	45,000	34	11,000	55,000
Gas	1,006,500	26	31,000	400,000
Glass Decorating	500	1	1,000	2,000
Gloves	5,000	5	3,000	10,000
Glue	2,000	6	2,500	6,000
Hair Goods and Feathers	4,500	15	4,750	21,000
Ice (Artificial)	55,000	25	12,500	65,000
Iron	1,500,000	350	250,000	700,000
Jewelry	18,200	27	19,484	79,500
Lime	25,000	11	7,200	55,000
Lumber	960,000	526	356,200	1,705,000
Marble Works	16,000	20	25,700	64,000
Matches	20,000	60	35,000	100,000
Meat Packing	165,000	103	41,000	900,000
Musical Instruments	1,000	3	2,160	3,500
Paints and Oils	155,000	36	34,000	400,000
Paper	200,000	80	36,000	200,000
Paper Boxes	2,500	7	3,000	7,000
Photographs	45,000	37	33,100	79,200
Picture Frames, Mirrors, etc	12,500	14	12,000	50,000
Planing Mills, Sash, Stairs, Boxes, etc.	419,000	269	220,400	932,200
Pottery	75,000	30	8,275	50,000
Printing, Lithographing and Publishing	323,500	306	244,877	863,000
Reduction Works	50,000	25	22,000	500,000
Rubber Stamps, Stencils, Models and Locksmithing	22,000	31	22,450	52,500
Saddlery and Harness	128,600	80	47,820	217,000
Ship Building	96,000	95	79,600	195,000
Show Cases	6,000	8	6,000	24,000
Signs	7,000	18	16,000	40,000
Soap	25,000	11	6,200	52,000
Soda and Mineral Water, Extracts, Cider and Vinegar	32,500	28	20,830	74,500
Solder and Babbitt Metal	10,000	3	2,500	20,000
Stoves	160,000	195	52,000	175,000
Straw Works	300	4	1,800	2,700
Stucco Ornaments	4,000	2	2,100	4,600
Tanning and Wool Pulling	49,500	42	29,800	266,000
Tin, Sheet Iron and Zinc	107,000	125	77,540	287,000
Trunks	14,000	7	6,120	22,000
Wire Works	500	4	1,800	2,700
Woolen Mills	575,000	300	135,000	725,000
Total	10,457,000	4891	2,693,573	17,293,900

APPENDIX F

Names of Portland residents, cited in the *Financial Redbook of America,*
reputed to be worth more than $300,000, taken from the *Oregonian,* October 14, 1903. (See S.B. #259, OHS Library).

Ainsworth, John C,
Ayer, W.B.
Bates, G.W.
Bickel, Fred
Blyth, Percy
Bourne, Jonathan, Jr.
Breyman, O.
Burns, W.J.
Corbett, Helen Ladd
Corbett, H.W., Estate
Cotton, W.W.
Dekum, Frank, Estate
Everding, Henry
Failing, Henry, Estate
  and three daughters
Farrell, Sylvester
Flanders, J.C.
Fleischner, I.N.

Frank, Sigmund
Goode, H.W.
Hirsch, Solomon
Honeyman, T.D.
Kohn, Charles
Ladd, J.W.
Ladd, William M.
Ladd, W.S., Estate
Leonard, H.C.
Lewis, C.H., Estate,
  and five children
Lipman Family
MacLeay Estate
MacLeay, Roderick
MacKay, Donald
Mears, S.
Meier, Mrs. Aaron
Myers, George T.

Mills, A.L.
Morey, P.F.
Mulkey, F.W.
O'Reilly, D.C.
Pittock, Henry L.
Prescott, C.H.
Scott, H.W.
Shelby, Eugene
Simon, Joseph
Smith, W.K.
Therkelson, L.W.
Thompson, D.P., Estate
Warren, F.M.
Watson, J.F.
Weinhard, Henry
Wilcox, T.B.
Wolfe, Adolph

APPENDIX G
Oregonian Editorial, March 10, 1976:

I & R upheld

Joseph Gaston, the Oregon historian, called the Initiative and Referendum, adopted as a constitutional amendment 62,024 to 5,668 in 1902, "the most remarkable application of civil government since the formation of the federal union in 1789."

Efforts have been made down through the years to dilute the legislative powers of the people. The courts have sometimes vacillated, but in the end they usually have upheld the I & R, just as the state Supreme Court did when it reversed a lower court and sustained the vote of the people cast in 1902.

This week the Oregon Court of Appeals held that zoning ordinances and county-wide land use plans are subject to the vote of the people in the entire county, not just in a neighborhood. The case arose from a suit brought by James B. Allison, who has been opposing the state's land use laws and comprehensive county planning. Allison both won and lost his appeal from a lower court. He was told he could sue the county over its comprehensive plan but that if he sought a vote on the issue he could not restrict the voting to a narrow rural section but must let urban area residents vote on the county's plans.

The court overturned also a 1974 Court of Appeals decision in Clackamas County that said additional legislation would be needed before the I & R could be applied. That decision, written by Judge Robert Y. Thornton, sought in a case where voters wanted to establish a wild river, declared that the I & R was not "self-executing" without legislative action.

This week's opinion, coupled with a half-dozen others issued by the Appeals Court in recent months, has set a new direction for land use planning in Oregon, a direction that mostly affirms the concepts behind Senate Bill 100. In traveling over new ground, the courts are trying to cut through legal tangles and decide what is primarily of local concern and what the state has preempted. The Fasano decision established that judicial review, rather than legislative action through the I & R, would apply in zoning cases, and that the comprehensive plan would prevail over local zoning decisions.

Litigation may go on for some years. Undoubtedly the Allison case will be appealed to the state Supreme Court, but the expectation is that the Court of Appeals is now tracking along lines that will be upheld on appeal. That the courts are able to do this, while sustaining the rights of people to vote on issues of either city or county concern, has made a new ball game of land use planning and zoning laws in Oregon.

485

APPENDIX H

Under the Initiative and Referendum amendment to the Oregon Constitution in 1902, laws have been proposed by the people, or adopted or rejected by the people on referendum from the legislature as follows:

	YES	NO
1904.		
Direct primary law with direct selection of United States Senator — a	56,205	16,354
Local-option liquor law — a	43,316	40,198
1906.		
Omnibus appropriation bill, state institution — b	43,918	26,758
Equal suffrage constitutional amendment — a	36,902	47,075
Local-option bill proposed by liquor people — a	35,297	45,144
Bill for purchase by state of Barlow toll road — a	31,525	44,527
Amendment requiring referendum on an act calling constitutional convention — a	47,661	18,751
Amendment giving cities sole power to amend their charters—a ..	52,567	19,852
Legislature authorized to fix pay of state printer — a	63,749	9,571
Initiative and referendum to apply to all local, special, and municipal laws — a	47,678	16,735
Bill prohibiting free passes on railroads —	57,281	16,779
Gross earnings tax on sleeping, refrigerator, and oil car companies — a	69,635	6,441
Gross earnings tax on express, telephone, and telegraph companies — a	70,872	6,360
1908.		
Amendment increasing pay of legislators from $120 to $400 per session — c	19,691	68,892
Amendment permitting location of state institutions at places other than the capital — c	41,971	40,868
Amendment re-organizing system of courts and increasing supreme judges from 3 to 5 — c	30,243	50,591
Amendment changing general election from June to November — c	65,728	18,590
Bill giving sheriffs control of county prisoners — b	60,443	30,033
Railroads required to give public officials free passes — b	28,856	59,406
Bill appropriating $100,000 for armories — b	33,507	54,848
Bill increasing fixed appropriation for State university from $47,500 to $125,000 annually — b	44,115	40,535
Equal suffrage amendment — a	36,858	58,670
Fishery bill proposed by fish wheel operators — a	46,582	40,720
Fishery bill proposed by gill net operators — a	56,130	30,280
Amendment giving cities control of liquor selling, pool rooms, theatres, etc., subject to local-option law — a	39,442	52,346
Modified form of single tax amendment — a	32,066	60,871
Recall power on public officials — a	58,381	31,002
Bill instructing legislators to vote for people's choice for United States senators — a	69,668	21,162
Amendment authorizing proportional-representation law — a ..	48,868	34,128
Corrupt-practices act governing election — a	54,042	31,301
Amendment requiring indictment to be by grand jury — a	52,214	28,487
Bill creating Hood River County — a	43,948	26,778

— Submitted under the initiative.
— Submitted under the referendum upon legislative act.
— Submitted to the people by the legislature.

From Joseph Gaston, *Portland, Its History and Builders,* (Portland, 1911), vol. 1, p. 564.

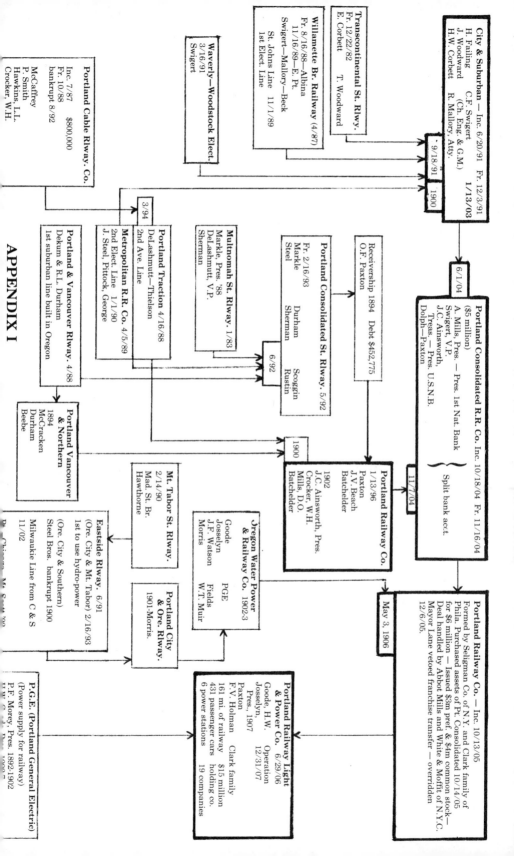

APPENDIX I

City & Suburban — Inc. 6/20/91
H. Failing C.F. Swigert
J. Woodward (Ch. Eng. & G.M.)
H.W. Corbett R. Mallory, Atty.
Fr. 12/3/91 1/13/03

Transcontinental St. Rlwy.
Fr. 12/22/82
E. Corbett T. Woodward

Willamette Br. Railway (4/87)
Fr. 8/16/88—Albina
11/16/89–E. Pt.
Swigert—Mallory—Beck
St. Johns Line 11/1/89
1st Elect. Line

Waverly–Woodstock Elect.
3/16/91
Swigert

Portland Cable Rlwy. Co.
Inc. 7/87 $800,000
Fr. 10/88
bankrupt 8/92
McCaffrey
P. Smith
Hawkins, L.L.
Crocker, W.H.

9/18/91 — 1900

Portland Consolidated R.R. Co. Inc. 10/18/04 Fr. 11/16/04
($5 million)
A. Mills, Pres. — Pres. 1st Nat. Bank
Swigert, V.P.
J.C. Ainsworth,
Treas. — Pres. U.S.N.B.
Dolph–Paxton

6/1/04

11/7/04 — Split bank acct.

Portland Railway Co. — Inc. 10/13/05
Formed by Seligman Co. of N.Y. and Clark family of
Phila. Purchased assets of Pt. Consolidated 10/14/05
for $6 million — Issued $3m pref. & $4m common stock—
Deal handled by Abbot Mills and White & Moffit of N.Y.C.
Mayor Lane vetoed franchise transfer — overridden
12/6/05.

Portland Consolidated St. Rlwy. 5/92
Markle Durham Scoggin
Steel Sherman Rustin

Fr. 2/16/93
Markle
Steel

Receivership 1894 Debt $452,775
O.F. Paxton

Multnomah St. Rlwy. 1/83
Markle, Pres '88
DeLashmutt, V.P.
Sherman

Portland Traction 4/16/88
DeLashmutt–Thielson
2nd Ave. Line

Metropolitan R.R. Co. 4/5/89
2nd Elect. Line 1/1/90
J. Steel, Pittock, George

3/94

6/92

Portland & Vancouver Rlway. 4/88
Dekum & R.L. Durham
1st suburban line built in Oregon

Portland Vancouver & Northern
1894
McCracken
Durham
Beebe

1900

Portland Railway Co.
1/13/96
Paxton
J.V. Beach
Batchelder
1902
Paxton
Crocker, W.H.
Mills, D.O.
Batchelder

Oregon Water Power & Railway Co. 1902-3
Goode PGE
Josselyn Fields
J.F. Watson W.T. Muir
Morris

Mt. Tabor St. Rlwy.
2/14/90
Mad. St. Br.
Hawthorne

Eastside Rlway. 6/91
(Ore. City & Mt. Tabor) 2/16/93
1st to use hydro-power
(Ore. City & Southern)
Steel Bros. bankrupt 1900
Milwaukie Line from C & S
11/02

Portland City & Ore. Rlway.
1901-Morris.

May 3, 1906

Portland Railway Light & Power Co. 6/29/06
Goode, H.W. Operation
Josselyn, 12/31/07
Pres., 1907
F.V. Holman Clark family
Paxton
161 mi. of railway $15 million
431 passenger cars holding co.
6 power stations 19 companies

P.G.E. (Portland General Electric)
(Power supply for railway)
P.F. Morey, Pres. 1892-1902

APPENDIX J

From Gaston, *op. cit.*, Vol. 1, p. 632.

Business — Retail Liquor: 1910	Number of licenses issued.
Breweries	4
Wholesale liquor dealers	20
Wholesale liquor dealers and rectifiers	10
Saloons, dram drinking places	419
Groceries—liquor	10
Restaurants selling liquor	35
Theaters, first-class	8
Nickelodeons	8
Nickelodeons	24

And as showing the size and influence of the liquor traffic in Portland and its close relations with the city government, the following statistics are quoted:

"Liquor licenses last year in Portland made up $360,800 of the general fund of $630,299.47, or $101,300.53 more than all other licenses, fees and moneys which go to make up the city's general fund.

"Liquor licenses have borne about the same ratio to the general fund in previous years as last year and the present year. In 1901, liquor licenses made up $169,730.96 of the $234,422.40 in the general fund; in 1902, $193,084.06 of the $225,655.89 in the general fund; in 1903, $140,683.35 of the $294,280.98 in the general fund; in 1904, $163,799.75 of the $330,957.20; in 1905, $208,891.95 of the $383,464.75 in the general fund; in 1906, $218,166.60 of the $392,114.02 in the general fund; in 1907, $330,241.46 of the $504,065.25 in the general fund; in 1908, $367,425 of the $577,655.82 in the general fund; in 1909, $390,800 of the $630,299.47 in the general fund; in 1910, $364,939.95 of the $672,088 in the general fund."

RAILROAD MILEAGE TRIBUTARY TO PORTLAND, 1910.

Astoria & Columbia River Railroad	122 miles
California Northeastern Railway Company, Klamath Falls to Weed, California	86 miles
Corvallis & Alsea river (Corvallis to Monroe)	21 miles
Corvallis & Eastern (Yaquina Bay to Cascade Mts.)	140 miles
Columbia River & Oregon Central (Arlington to Condon)	45 miles
Columbia Southern Railway (Biggs to Shaniko)	64 miles
Great Southern R. R. Co. (The Dalles to Dufur)	30 miles
Independence & Monmouth, Airlie and Dallas	19 miles
Malheur Valley R. R. Co. (Malheur to Vale)	14 miles
Mt. Hood Railroad (Hood River valley)	16 miles
Northern Pacific to Puget Sound and branches	300 miles
Oregon & California and branches	666 miles
Oregon Railroad & Navigation Co. and branches	1,327 miles
Oregon Short Line and branches	1,508 miles
Oregon & Southeastern (Cottage Grove to Disston)	20 miles
Pacific & Eastern (Medford to Crater Lake)	31 miles
Pacific Railway & Navigation (Hillsboro to Tillamook)	98 miles
Rogue River Valley (Jacksonville to Medford)	66 miles
Salem & Falls City, Black Rock & Dallas	23 miles
Spokane, Portland & Seattle and branches	421 miles
Sumpter Valley Railroad (Baker City to Prairie City)	95 miles
Umatilla (Pilot Rock Junction to Pilot Rock)	14 miles
Oregon Electric (Portland to Salem and Forest Grove)	69 miles
Portland Railway (electric, Portland to Cazadero)	37 miles
United Railways (Portland into Washington county)	37 miles
Columbia river logging roads	60 miles
Total mileage	5,269 miles

To the above should be added the new roads being constructed through the Des Chutes canyon:

The Oregon Trunk Line (Hill road)	150 miles
The Des Chutes Road (Harriman line)	150 miles
Grand total to be in operation by May, 1911	5,569 miles

	1850	1870	1890	1910
Apples, dried, per pound	$ .50	$ .07	$ .06	$ .08
Peaches, dried, per pound	.50	...	.12	.15
Beef, fresh at block, per pound	.18	.12	.12	.20
Pork, fresh at block, per pound	.16	.10	.07	.20
Hams	...	.16	.12	.20
Butter, fresh, per pound	1.00	.30	.25	.36
Cheese, per pound	.50	.20	.14	.18
Flour, per pound	.10	.03	.02	.03
Coffee, green, per pound	.18	.25	.22	.20
Sugar, brown, per pound	.20	.12	.05	.10
Sugar, loaf, white, per pound	.50	.18	.07	.07
Tea, per pound	1.00	1.00	1.00	1.00
Molasses, per gallon	1.50	.75	.75	1.00
Tobacco, per pound	.75	1.00	1.50	2.00
Rice, per pound	.20	.15	.06	.05
Lard, per pound	.40	.18	.10	.20
Salt, per pound	.06	.03	.02	.01
Iron, per pound	.16	.04	.04	.02½
Nails, per pound	.18	.06	.05	.04
Chickens, per dozen	...	4.00	6.00	7.50
Eggs, per dozen	1.00	.35	.15	.35
Wheat, per bushel	3.00	.80	.65	.90
Potatoes, per bushel	6.00	.75	1.50	1.25
Oats, per bushel	1.50	.40	.38	.50
Baled hay, per ton	...	11.00	16.00	20.00
Rough lumber, per thousand	75.00	14.00	10.00	14.00
Cooking stoves	75.00	30.00	25.00	30.00
Hops	...	.20	.10	.15
Whiskey, good, per gallon	1.50	4.00	5.00	6.00

WAGES IN PORTLAND, 1910

Portland, Oregon.	Wages.	Working hours per day.
Barbers, per week	$16.00	10
Bartenders, per week	18.50	10-12
Carpenters, per day	3.50	8
Cigarmakers, per day	3.50	8
Electricians, per day	3.50	8
Longshoremen, per day	4.95	9—10
Painters, per day	3.50	8
Plasterers, per day	5.50	8
Plumbers, per day	5.00	8
Printers, per day	5.00	7—7½—8
Steamfitters, per day	5.00	8
Structural iron workers, per day	4.50	8
Tailors, per day	3.00	8—10
Teamsters, per day	2.75	9—10—11
Tilesetters, per day	5.50	8
Waiters, per week	12.50	10—12
Waitresses, per week	9.00	10

From Gaston, *op. cit.*, Vol. 1, p. 629.

APPENDIX K

Street Car Lines — Portland

Year	Total Passengers Carried	Total Miles Track owned & operated	Car Miles run
1907	60,115,222	159.50	9,026,652
1908	61,896,868	160.14	9,813,035
1909	68,585,762	161.68	9,984,613
1910	78,296,246	167.68	10,696,192
1911	85,996,686	172.13	12,385,612
1912	89,849,096	178.89	13,001,817
1913	89,518,665	195.17	14,273,196
1914	89,597,657	105.04	14,362,682
1915	78,670,631	196.25	14,193,671
1916	74,494,197	196.36	14,911,422
1917	84,478,997	198.19	15,703,426
1918	95,194,639	198.22	15,919,450
1919	100,301,793	197.17	15,668,670
1920	96,852,120	197.65	15,012,542

Length of Main Lines, Business Center, West Side to End of Lines.

	Miles
North and South Portland —	
North Terminal	2.77
South Terminal	2.37
Williams Avenue	3.69
Mississippi Avenue	5.33
Fulton	3.89
Irvington	4.70
Broadway	4.40
Montavilla	6.11
Rose City Park	5.50
Woodstock	6.04
Richmond	3.60
Brooklyn	2.92
Depot-Morrison	3.74
Mt. Tabor	6.20
23rd Street	2.56
16th Street —	
North Terminal	2.06
South Terminal	1.72
Portland Heights	3.50
Alberta	5.07
Woodlawn	5.11
Sellwood	5.29
Mt. Scott	7.84
Hawthorne Avenue	5.38
St. Johns	9.75
Vancouver	8.07
Average length of line	4.70
Average possible length of ride with transfer	9.40
Longest ride for single fare	19.20

City Club Bulletin 42 (July 1, 1921).

APPENDIX L

Relative Usage of Transportation Modes in Portland.*

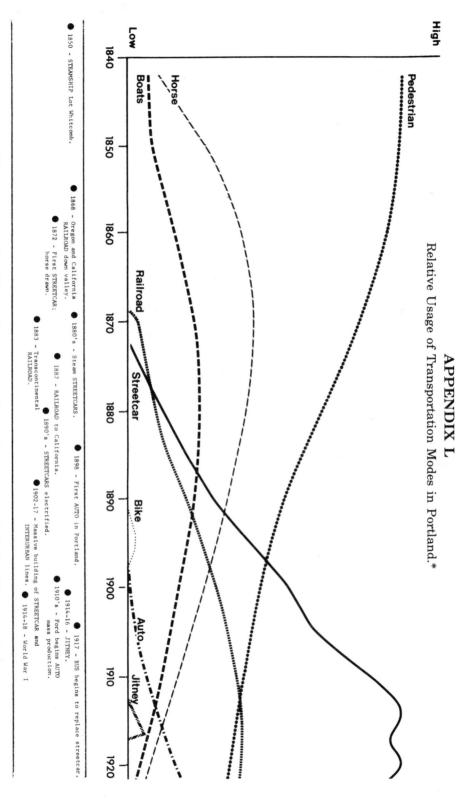

High

Low

1840 1850 1860 1870 1880 1890 1900 1910 1920

Pedestrian

Boats

Horse

Railroad

Streetcar

Bike

Auto..., Jitney

● 1850 - STEAMSHIP Lot Whitcomb.

● 1868 - Oregon and California RAILROAD down valley.

● 1880's - Steam STREETCARS.

● 1898 - First AUTO in Portland.

● 1914-16 - JITNEY.

● 1917 - BUS begins to replace streetcar.

● 1872 - First STREETCAR; horse drawn.

● 1887 - RAILROAD to California.

● 1890's - STREETCARS electrified.

● 1902-17 - Massive building of STREETCAR and INTERURBAN lines.

● 1910's - Ford begins AUTO mass production.

● 1883 - Transcontinental RAILROAD.

● 1914-18 - World War I

*(Figure 4, page 5, *I-80N Draft, Environmental Impact Statement*, by the Federal Highway Administration & Oregon State Highway Department.

APPENDIX M

Table Showing Area, Population and Density of Occupation
at Various Dates of City of Portland.

Date	Area in Square Miles	People per Sq. Mile	People per Acre	Population
1851	2.100	489	.76	1027
1882	6.594	3258	5.1	21500
1885	6.138	5212	8.1	31990
1891	25.977	1946	3.0	50560
1893	38.845	1528	2.4	59370
1898	36.872	2214	3.5	81637
1905	35.900	4156	6.5	149200
1906	40.475	3955	6.2	160100
1907	41.275	4162	6.5	171809
1908	41.525	4420	6.9	183570
1909	47.300	4148	6.5	196224
1911	48.447	4381	6.9	212290
1913	50.067	4444	6.9	222547
1915	66.025	3521	5.5	232500

APPENDIX N

Presidents of the Portland Board of Trade

William S. Ladd
1870

W.H. Corbett
1875-1877

Donald MacLeay
1881-1889

T.F. Osborn
1890

Presidents of the Portland Chamber of Commerce

T.F. Osborn
1891-1892

George B. Markle, Jr.
1893

E.J. DeHart
1893-1894

John McCracken
1894

D.D. Oliphant
1895

Charles F. Beebe
1895, 1897

Charles H. Dodd
1896

Gus Simon
1896

William S. Mason
1897-1898

W.L. Boise
1898

Charles F. Beebe
1899

E.T. Williams
1899

George Taylor
1900

H.M. Cake
1900-1905 Inc.

Henry Hahn
1901

Frank E. Beach
1902-1903

Robert Livingstone
1903

Walter J. Burns
1904

William D. Wheelwright
1905

R.R. Hoge
1906

F.W. Leadbetter
1906

Samuel G. Reed
1907

C.W. Hodson
1907-1908

C.F. Swigert
1908

Dr. J.R. Weatherbee
1909

William MacMaster
1909-1910

H. Beckwith
1910-1911

H.M. Haller
1911

F.C. Knapp
1912

E.B. Piper
1912-1913

A.H. Averill
1913-1914

Horace Ramsdell
1914

C.C. Colt
1915

J.H. Burgard
1915

APPENDIX O
Leading Law Firms

1900	1915
Dolph, Mallory, Simon (J.), & Gearin	Same
Paxton, Beach & Simon (N.)	Beach, Simon & Nelson
Carey & Mays	Carey & Kerr
Williams, Wood & Linthicum	Wood, Montague & Hunt
Cotton, Teal & Minor	Teal, Minor & Winfree
Bronaugh & Bronaugh	Same
Cake & Cake	Same
Mitchell & Tanner	Disbanded
Fenton & Muir	Disbanded
	Malarkey, Seabrook & Dibble

Leading Individual Lawyers (1900-1915)

John Caples	Fred W. Mulkey
J.C. Flanders	Robert L. Sabin
Rodney L. Glisan	Dan J. Malarkey
George H. Durham	Richard Montague
Wallace McCamant	Arthur C. Spencer (OR&N)
Fred V. Holman	Wilson T. Hume
Thomas O'Day	Henry E. McGinn
Ellis Hughes	D. Solis Cohen

APPENDIX P

A selected list of 100 local banks, businesses, associations and partnerships (including officers and chief stockholders), the titles of which, with a few exceptions, are not identified with the founding members. Period, approx. 1885-1915.

Adamant Co.
C.F. Beebe
C.E. Ladd

Ainsworth Bank
J.C. Ainsworth
L.L. Hawkins
W.K. Smith

Albina Light & Water Co.
G.W. Bates
C.F. Swigert
L. Hoffman
D.M. McLaughlan

Albina Real Estate Co.
G.H. Durham
R.L. Durham

Albina Savings Bank
Bates
H.S. Rowe

Baggage & Omnibus Transfer Co.
R.B. Knapp

Bank of Albina
Bates
V.B. DeLashmutt

City & Suburban Railway Co.
T. Woodward
Swigert
H. Failing
H.W. Corbett
H. Campbell

Columbia Fire & Marine Insurance Co.

F. Dekum	W.K. Smith
R.L. Durham	G.H. Williams
G.B. Markle	J.F. Watson
D.P. Thompson	W. Burrell

Columbia Investment Co.
Dekum
M.C. George

Columbia Life & Trust Co.
W.M. Ladd
T.B. Wilcox

Columbia River Paper Co.
F.W. Leadbetter   Pittock

Columbia Street Bridge Co.
DeLashmutt
C.M. Forbes
W.S. Ladd

Commercial National Bank
R.L. Durham
D.P. Thompson
C.A. Dolph
J. McCracken
G.H. Williams

East Side Railway Co.
James Steel
George A. Steel

Eastern & Western Lumber Co.
W.B. Ayer

Electric Land Co.
Swigert
P.L. Willis

Electric Steel Foundry Co.
Swigert

Equitable Savings & Loan Assoc.
Wilcox   H.L. Corbett
H.M. Cake
Edward Cookingham
C.E. Ladd
S.B. Mears
W. MacMaster

First National Bank
Henry Failing   H.L. Corbett
H.W. Corbett
C.H. Lewis
C.A. Dolph
Abbot Mills

Greater Portland Realty Co.
J.V. Beach

Hibernia Trust Co. (also Savings Bank)
Dr. A.C. Smith
W.S. Mason

Home Telephone Co.
Mills
H.L. Corbett

Investment Co., The
E. Quackenbush

Ladd & Tilton Bank
Ladd Family   H.L. Corbett
Cookingham
Wilcox

Lumberman's National Bank
Bates
C.K. Wentworth
Dr. K.A.J. McKenzie

Merchants National Bank
R.L. Durham
J. Lowenberg
J.F. Watson
J. Steel

Merchants Savings & Trust Co.
R.L. Durham
J.F. Watson

Metropolitan Street Railway Co. (Fulton Park Line)
J. Steel
G.A. Steel

Mining Partnerships:
DeLashmutt   R.B. Knapp
Goldsmith   J. Simon
Lowenberg

J. Bourne   S.G. Reed
Lowenberg   R.R. Thompson
Goldsmith

Bourne   Bourne
W.M. Ladd   C.E. Ladd

Nehalem Coal Co.
Steel brothers

North Pacific Lumber Co.
D. MacKay
L. Therkelson
R. Inman

Northwest Cold Storage Co.
C.H. Prescott

Northwest Fidelity Co.
Pittock

Northwest Fire & Marine Insurance Co.
Lowenberg
McCracken
F. Warren

Northern Pacific Terminal Co.
Failing
C.A. Dolph
J. Simon

Northwest Loan & Trust Co.
G.B. Markle   D.F. Sherman
DeLashmutt   Hartman
G.H. Williams
C.F. Beebe
J.T. Ross

Northwest Steel Co.
J.R. Bowles
W.B. Beebe

Northwest Trading Co.
Lowenberg
D.P. Thompson

Northwestern National Bank
Pittock
Leadbetter

Oregon City Woolen Mills
D.P. Thompson
Ladd Family   J. Steel

Oregon Electric Railway Co.
Swigert   G. Talbot
Mills   H.L. Corbett

Oregon Fire & Marine Insurance Co.
H.W. Corbett
W.S. Ladd

Oregon Improvement Co.
H. Villard   C.A. Dolph
S.G. Reed   J. Simon
C.H. Lewis   Failing
C.H. Prescott   J. Bourne

Oregon Iron & Steel Co.
Ladd family
S.G Reed
H. Villard
J.F. Watson

Oregon Land Investment Co.
F. Dekum
R.L. Durham

Oregon Life Insurance Co.
A. Mills
C.F. Adams
L. Samuel

Oregon Lumber Co.
DeLashmutt
R.L. Durham

Oregon Mortgage Co.
Robert Livingstone

Oregon National Bank
Markle
DeLashmutt
D.F. Sherman
G.H. Williams

Oregon Paving & Contracting Co.
J. Steel
Ladd family

Oregon Pottery Co.
J. Steel
Ladd family

Oregon Railway & Navigation Co.
Ainsworth family   Corbett family
Ladd family   H. Failing
Lewis family   Rowe
S.G. Reed   Prescott
J. Kamm   Mills
Dolph brothers   W.B. Ayer
D.P. Thompson

Oregon Real Estate Co.
C.H. Lewis
D.P. Thompson

Oregon Telephone & Telegraph Co.
J.C. Ainsworth
W.S. Ladd
S.G. Reed
McCracken

Oregon Transfer Co.
H.W. Corbett
Failing
G. Weidler
Kiernan

Pacific Bridge Co.
C.F. Swigert
H. Campbell

Pacific Export Lumber Co.
W.D. Wheelwright

Pacific Grain Co.
Gay Lombard

Pioneer Real Estate Co.
C.H. Lewis

Portland Cable Railway Co.
J.C. McCaffrey
P.C. Smith
L.L. Hawkins

Portland Canning Co.
C.H. Prescott

Portland Coast Steamship Co.
D. MacLeay
C.F. Beebe

Portland Consolidated Street Railway Co.
Markle
Dekum
R. Durham
J. Steel
Scroggin

Portland Consolidated Railway Co.
Mills   H.L. Corbett
Ainsworth
Swigert
C.A. Dolph

Portland Cordage Co.
W.B. Ayer
Failing
C.H. Lewis
H.J. Corbett
W.S. Ladd
S.B. Mears
D. MacLeay

Portland Flouring Mills
W.S. Ladd
Wilcox

Portland Gas Co. (Gas & Coke Co.)
J.D. Green   G. Talbot
H. Green   H.L. Corbett
H.C. Leonard
Adams
Mills
C.H. Lewis

Portland General Electric Co.
F.V. Holman   W.M. Ladd
P.F. Morey
Failing
Ainsworth
Goode
W.M. Ladd
T. Woodward
Swigert

Portland Hotel Co.
Failing
H.W. Corbett
Ladd family
C.H. Lewis
C.A. Dolph

Portland Hydraulic Elevator Co.
L.L. Hawkins

Portland Lumber Co.
G.K. Wentworth

Portland Manufacturing Co.
Peter Autzen

Portland National Bank
W.S. Mason
W. Reid

Portland, Nehalem & Tillamook Railroad Co.

McCracken	Rowe
G.T. Myers	J. Fliedner
Reid	
Pittock	

Portland Railway Co.
Ainsworth
Sears
Paxton
J.F. Batchelor

Portland Railway Light & Power Co.

Goode	H.L. Corbett
Holman, F.V.	W.M. Ladd
Paxton	
B. Josselyn	
F. Griffith	

Portland Real Estate Co.
J.C. Moreland

Portland Reduction Works
W.S. Ladd
J. Steel

Portland Savings Bank
Dekum
C.A. Dolph
W.K. Smith
D.P. Thompson

Portland Smelting & Refining Co.
J. McCracken

Portland Stock & Mining Exchange

Ayer	Prescott
DeLashmutt	S.G. Reed
J.C. Flanders	T. Woodward
Goldsmith	Bourne
J.C. Lewis	G.A. Steel

Portland Traction Co.
DeLashmutt
Markle
D.F. Sherman
Thielson

Portland Trust Co.

A. Noyes	J. Steel
B.I. Cohen	A.S. Nichols
F.W. Leadbetter	Ben Selling

Portland, Vancouver & Northern Railway Co.
R.L. Durham
J. McCracken
C.F. Beebe

Rose City Park Assoc.
Wilcox
E. Thompson
Hartman

Security Savings & Trust Co.
Adams
Mills
Corbett family
Failing
Lewis family
J. Simon
C.A. Dolph
J. Teal

Sellwood Real Estate Co.
Pittock

Southeast Portland Realty Co.
Bourne

Southwest Portland Realty Co. (Fulton Park)
Steel brothers
Pittock
J. Simon
C.E. Ladd

Tepustete Iron Co.
Ladd family
Wilcox
J.F. Watson

Title Guarantee & Trust Co.
W.M. Ladd
J.T. Ross

Transcontinental Street Railway Co.
T. Woodward
E. Corbett
L.W. Therkelson

Trinidad Asphalt Paving Co.
C.E. Ladd
Dekum

Union Laundry Co.
Bates

Union Power Co.
Failing
Swigert

U.S. Electric Lighting & Power Co.
Morey
Weidler
F.V. Holman
L.L. Hawkins

U.S. National Bank
D. MacLeay
T. Woodward
R. Mallory
Ainsworth
Kamm
J.E. Haseltine
Wilcox
Ayer

University Park Co.
Swigert

Willamette Falls Electric Co.

Morey	D.P. Thompson
L.L. Hawkins	W.K. Smith
F.V. Holman	J.C. Moreland

Willamette Bridge Railway Co.
Mallory   Swigert
Beck

Willamette Iron Works (& Steel Co.)
Corbett family
J. Lotan
P. Taylor
Swigert

Willamette Valley Lumber Co.
Pittock

Willamette Valley Milling Co.
Wilcox
C.E. Ladd

ACKNOWLEDGEMENTS
I. Published Materials

The author wishes to acknowledge permission to publish materials from the Manuscript Collections of the Oregon Historical Society and Reed College, and from the Special Collections Library of the University of Oregon. He also acknowledges permission to publish excerpts from letters contained in these and other collections as granted by the heirs of the writers. Finally, he acknowledges permission to reprint from the following published works:

American Heritage History of American Business, by Alex Groner, © 1972 by American Heritage Publishing Co.
Arlington Club and the Men Who Built It, 1967.
City on the Willamette, by Percy Maddux, © 1952 by Binford & Mort.
"The Electric Power Industry", by Sheldon Novick, *Environment,* vol. 17, No. 8, p. 37, © 1975 by the Scientists' Institute for Public Information.
The City in History, by Lewis Mumford, © 1961 by Lewis Mumford and Harcourt, Brace & World.
Interpretations and Forecasts, by Lewis Mumford, © 1973 by Lewis Mumford and Harcourt Brace Jovanovich.
They Built the West, by Glenn Chesney Quiett, © 1934 by Appleton, Century, permission to reprint by Hawthorn Books.
Challenging Years, by Stephen S. Wise, © 1949 by G.P. Putnam's Sons.
I Remember Portland, 1899 — 1915, by Laurence Pratt, © 1965 by Laurence Pratt.
The Making of Urban America: A History of City Planning in the United States, by John Reps, © 1965 by Princeton University Press.
Romantic Revolutionary: A Biography of John Reed, by Robert A. Rosenstone, © 1975 by Alfred A. Knopf.
Success Story, The Life and Times of S.S. McClure, by Peter Lyon, © 1963 by Charles Scribner's Sons.
American City Planning Since 1890, by Mel Scott, © 1969 by The Regents of the University of California.
Early Transportation in Oregon, by Henry Villard, ed. by Oswald Garrison Villard, © 1944 by the University of Oregon.
Gold in the Woodpile, by O.K. Burrell, © 1967 by the University of Oregon.
Centers For The Urban Environment, by Victor Gruen, © 1973 by Litton Educational Publishing, Inc., permission to reprint by Van Nostrand Reinhold Co.
Pharisee Among Philistines, The Diary of Judge Matthew P. Deady, 1871-1892, ed. by Malcolm Clark, Jr., © 1975 by Malcolm Clark, Jr., permission to reprint by the Oregon Historical Society and Malcolm Clark, Jr.
"Jefferson Street Public Levee and the Railroads", by Oswald West, *Oregon Historical Quarterly,* vol. 43, June 1962, © 1962 by the Oregon Historical Society.
"Over the Bush and Through the Trees: Surveying, 1900-1909", by Ray L. Stout, *Oregon Historical Quarterly,* vol. 73, December 1972, © 1972 by the Oregon Historical Society.

II. Photographic Reproductions (cited by page number)

OREGON HISTORICAL SOCIETY PHOTOGRAPHIC LIBRARY: Inside front cover, xii, 2, 3, 11, 13, 19, 21, 23, 31, 46, 52, 55, 63, 79 (top), 81, 85, 86 (bottom), 88, 89, 90, 96, 113, 114 (top), 116 (bottom), 121, 122, 124, 132, 146, 165, 166, 170, 171, 172, 176, 178, 183, 190, 193, 196, 198, 211, 218, 219, 223, 225, 231, 233, 257, 261, 265, 267, 270, 272, 280, 282, 284, 311, 313, 325, 333, 340, 352, 353, 356, 359, 372, 384, 385, 387, 388, 389, 390, 391, 397, 403, 413, 415, 416, 419, 425, 426, 427, 432, 433, 436, 437, 445, 453, 461, 462, 469, 471, 474.

AUTHOR'S COLLECTION: 8, 22, 27, 29, 34, 41, 42, 48, 53, 61, 70, 83, 84, 93, 107, 110, 116 (top), 120, 123, 140, 143, 152, 154, 159, 173, 177, 179, 197, 202, 224, 227, 232, 234, 235, 237, 239, 252, 263, 290, 295, 296, 303, 316, 350, 366, 376, 394, 434, 456 (right), 466, 470.

WEST SHORE (Author's Collection): 5, 20, 25, 26, 28, 30, 35, 37, 56, 57, 59, 71, 79 (bottom), 80, 86 (top), 91, 103, 106, 114 (bottom), 115, 119, 125, 134, 135, 144, 148, 150, 177.

ARLINGTON CLUB: 175.

GREEN DOLPHIN BOOKSTORE: 44, 118.

NORTHWEST NATURAL GAS CO.: 169.

OREGON JOURNAL: 299, 300, 305, 370.

OREGONIAN: Cover, 50, 76, 117, 208, 216, 271, 297, 301, 308, 326, 332, 336, 338, 339, 342, 361, 410.

PHOTO ART: Inside back cover, 456 (left).

PORTLAND CITY CLUB BULLETIN: 473.

PORTLAND CITY WATER BUREAU: 66.

PORTLAND COMMISSION OF PUBLIC DOCKS: 447,448.

PORTLAND DEVELOPMENT COMMISISON: 136.

PRESERVATION OPTIONS FOR PORTLAND NEIGHBORHOODS: 467.

UNIVERSITY OF OREGON SPECIAL COLLECTIONS LIBRARY, ABBOT L. MILLS PAPERS: 205,248,249.

NOTES

The Oregon Historical Society Library Materials are cited OHS.

CHAPTER I.

1. Henry Villard, *Early Transportation in Oregon,* ed. by Oswald G. Villard, (Eugene, 1944), pp. 43-44.
2. Quoted in John F. Scheck, "Transporting a Tradition: Thomas Lamb Eliot and the Unitarian Conscience in the Pacific Northwest, 1864-1905", (Eugene, 1969), p. 212. (Unpublished Dissertation, Department of History, University of Oregon).
3. *Pacific Banker and Investor,* 2(September, 1894), p. 42. See also, Edward Roberts, "The Western Portland", *Harper's Weekly Supplement,* 33(April 6, 1889), p. 276.
4. *Oregonian,* June 19, 1889.
5. *West Shore,* combined vols. 16-17, (August, 1890-January, 1891), p. 146.
6. *Oregonian, January 1, 1891.*
7. *West Shore,* 14(May, 1888), p. 263.
8. H.K. Hines, *An Illustrated History of the State of Oregon,* (Chicago, 1893), p. 230.
9. *Oregonian,* March 14, 1888; also *West Shore,* 14(May, 1888), p. 236.
10. Letter from Oswald West to Dorothy Johansen, March 15, 1960. Oswald West Papers, OHS.
11. Stephen Wise, *Challenging Years,* (New York, 1949), pp. 7-8.
12. Quoted by Lincoln Steffens, "The Taming of the West", *American Magazine, 64(September, 1907), p. 590.*
13. Henry E. Reed Papers, Box 3, "Historical Notes", "History of Oregon Railroads", ch. 19, p. 29, OHS.
14. *Ekistics,* 39(March, 1975), p. 134.
15. *Oregonian,* May 18, 1910.
16. Joseph Gaston, *Portland, Its History and Builders,* (Portland, 1911), vol. 2, p. 442.
17. *Oregon Journal,* July 15, 1938.
18. Victor Gruen, *Centers for the Urban Environment,* (New York, 1973), p. 211.
19. See George Cabot Lodge, *The New American Ideology,* (New York, 1975).
20. Gruen, *loc. cit.*
21. *American Banker,* May 28, 1910.
22. See Marshall Dana and Ellis Lawrence, *The Greater Portland Plan,* (Portland, 1912).
23. *Pacific Banker, op. cit.,* p. 42.
24. *Portland Chamber of Commerce Bulletin,* 4(June, 1906), p. 9.
25. Harvey W. Scott, *History of Portland* (Portland, 1890), p. 434.
26. *Oregonian,* September 11, 1898.
27. H. Reed Papers, "Real Estate Folder", *op. cit.*

CHAPTER II.

1. *Oregonian,* November 27, 1910.
2. Benjamin M. Whitesmith, "Henry Villard and the Development of Oregon", unpublished M.A. Thesis, University of Oregon, Eugene, 1931, p. 42.
3. Malcolm Clark, Jr., ed., *Pharisee Among Philistines, The Diary of Judge Matthew P. Deady, 1871-1892,* (Portland, 1975), vol. 1, p. 59.
4. O.K. Burrell, *Gold in the Woodpile — An Informal History of Banking in Oregon,* (Eugene, 1967), p. 61.
5. One of the most thorough and readable accounts of Portland's early investors is still to be found in Glenn Chesney Quiett, *They Built the West, An Epic of Rails and Cities,* (New York, 1934), ch. 13.
6. Earl M. Wilbur, *Thomas Lamb Eliot,* (Portland, 1937), pp. 91-92.
7. Simeon G. Reed Papers, Reed College Library, Misc. file. Cited hereafter as S.G.R.
8. See Marion D. Ross, "Architecture in Oregon," *Oregon Historical Quarterly,* 57(1956), p. 33.
9. See Irvin G. Wyllie, *The Self-Made Man in America,* (New York, 1954).
10. W.S. Ladd Papers, OHS. Cited hereafter as W.S.L.
11. *Ibid.,* "Financial Records."
12. West Papers, *op. cit.* Letter to Dorothy Johansen, March 15, 1960.
13. W.S.L., *op. cit.*

14. Letter to J.W. Ladd, quoted in D. Johansen, and F.B. Gill, "A Chapter in the History of the Oregon Steam Navigation Co.," *Oregon Historical Quarterly*, 38(March, 1937), p. 36.

15. S.G.R., "Letters", vol. 2. Letter dated May 6, 1871.

16. "Abstract of Title", Lots 2 & 3, Block 11, Tilton's Addition, Title Guarantee & Trust Co., Portland, 1926.

17. Matthew P. Deady, "Journal", vol. 1, p. 65, OHS. Entry dated May 10, 1871; *ibid.,* p.21. Cited hereafter as D.J.

18. D.J., *op. cit.,* p. 93; entry dated August 12, 1871.

19. Quoted in Burrell, *op. cit.,* p. 54.

20. Much of the factual information for this sketch came from C.H. Lewis Papers, OHS. See also, article by Louise Aaron, *Oregon Journal,* May 31, 1959. Also, private discussions with his grandchildren.

21. See Scrapbook #122, p. 163-1/2, OHS.

22. Henry E. Reed, *Cavalcade of Front Avenue, 1866-1941,* (Portland, 1941), p. 2.

23. Much of the factual information for this sketch came from an unidentified newspaper account, contained in Scrapbook #38, p. 181, dated December 21, 1889, OHS. See also Henry Failing Papers, OHS. Cited hereafter as H.F.

24. Much of the information for this sketch was found in the H.W. Corbett Papers, OHS. Cited hereafter as H.W.C. Also, The Corbett Investment Co. Papers, OHS. Also, Arthur L. Throckmorton, "The Role of the Merchant on the Oregon Frontier: The Early Business Career of Henry W. Corbett, 1851-1869", *Journal of Economic History,* 16(1956), pp. 539-550. Also conversations with members of the Corbett family, most especially an interview with Mrs. Henry L. Corbett, March 29, 1975.

25. *H.W.C., loc. cit.*

27. Interview with Mrs. Henry L. Corbett, March 29, 1975.

26. Quoted in Quiett, *op. cit.,* pp. 351-52.

28. H. Reed, "Railroads", *op. cit.,* ch. 20, p. 25.

29. See Wyllie, *op. cit.,* p. 123.

30. James H. Polhemus, *Oregon — Its Resources, Its People, and Its Future!,* (New York, 1951), pp. 17-18.

31. Joseph N. Dolph Papers, Scrapbook #5, University of Oregon, Special Collections Library. See also, Frederick W. Roth, "A Biographical Sketch of Joseph North Dolph", University of Oregon Thesis, Series #13, OHS.

32. Matthew P. Deady, Letters, no. 61, dated July 13, 1886, OHS.

CHAPTER III.

1. See Villard, *op. cit.* Also H. Reed Papers, *op. cit.;* Gaston, *op. cit.,* vol. 1, pp. 288-90; Quiett, *op. cit.;* Robert G. Athearn, *Union Pacific Country,* (New York, 1971); James B. Hedges, *Henry Villard and the Railways of the Northwest,* (New Haven, 1930), a thorough account of Villard's dealings with the Northern and Union Pacific Railroads.

2. Villard, *op. cit.,* p. 40.

3. Clark, *Deady, op. cit.,* vol. 1, p. 80.

4. Villard, *op. cit.,* p. 45.

5. Villard, *op. cit.,* p. 40.

6. *H. Reed,* "Railroads", *op. cit.,* ch. 19, p.22.

7. Cited by H. Reed, *ibid.*

8. D.J., *op. cit.,* vol. 1, p. 155.

9. *Ibid.,* vol. 2, pp. 174, 322. See Clark, *Deady, op. cit.,* vol. 1, p. 128.

10. *H. Reed,* "Railroads", *op. cit.,* ch. 19, pp. 32-33.

11. Villard's words, Villard, *op. cit.,* p. 45.

12. Burrell, *op. cit.,* p. 61. See *H. Reed,* "Railroads", *op. cit.,* ch. 20.

13. Villard, *op. cit.,* p. 91.

14. *Ibid.*

15. Hedges, *op. cit.,* p. 81.

16. Villard, *op. cit.,* p. 94.

17. John S. Cochran, "Economic Importance of Early Transcontinental Railroads: Pacific Northwest", *Oregon Historical Quarterly,* 71(March, 1970), p. 73.

18. Clark, *Deady, op. cit.,* vol. 2, p. 413.

19. *Ibid.,* p. 452.

20. *Oregonian,* September 12, 1883.
21. H. Reed, *Cavalcade, op. cit.,* p. 2.
22. Leslie M. Scott, *History of the Oregon Country,* (Cambridge, 1924), vol. 4, p. 169.
23. *H. Reed,* "Railroads", *op. cit.,* ch. 19, p. 27.
24. Sheldon Novick, "The Electric Power Industry", *Environment,* 17(December, 1975), p. 28.
25. John W. Reps, *The Making of Urban America: A History of City Planning in the United States,* (Princeton, 1965), p. 412.

CHAPTER IV.

1. Scrapbook, #257, p. 179, OHS.
2. See 10th & 11th *Annual Reports of the Portland Chamber of Commerce,* (Portland Board of Trade until 1891), Portland Public Library.
3. *Oregonian,* February 28, 1886.
4. *Oregonian,* September 4, 1898. Also, H.W. Scott, *op. cit.,* pp. 612-615. Some of Scott's factual data is incorrect. Additional information on Robert Livingstone and William Reid was provided the author by Robert Livingstone's son, of the same name, at various meetings during 1975 in Portland.
5. Ross, *op. cit.,* p. 54.
6. H.W. Scott, *op. cit.,* p. 431.
7. *Ibid.,* pp. 432-433.
8. Jean Muir, "The Elegant Eighties", *Oregon Journal Sunday Magazine,* April 14, 1940. See also, Robert A. Rosenstone, *Romantic Revolutionary, A Biography of John Reed, (New York, 1975),* ch. 2.
9. Thomas B. Merry, "Portland, the Beautiful Metropolis of the Pacific Northwest", *The Northwest,* 3(November, 1885), p. 29.
10. *West Shore,* 14(September, 1888), pp. 459-60.
11. Joseph Simon Papers, OHS. Cited hereafter as J.S.
12. *Oregon Journal,* May 2, 1909.
13. *Oregonian,* June 8, 1886.
14. *Oregon Journal, loc. cit.*
15. See D.J., *op. cit.,* 1880, p. 954; Clark, *Deady, op. cit.,* vol. 1, p. 327.
16. Clark, *Deady, op. cit.,* vol. 2, p. 324.
17. The material for this sketch was gleaned from the *Minutes of the Board of Police Commissioners,* Portland City Hall Archives, cited hereafter as "Police Board". Jonathan Bourne, Jr. Papers, Special Collections Library, University of Oregon, cited hereafter as J.B. J.S., *loc. cit.*
18. The material for this sketch was taken from the "Minutes of the Proceedings of the City Council", vol. 8, pp. 664-668, meeting of November 18, 1885. Cited hereafter as "Council".
19. *Ibid.*
20. *Ibid.,* vol. 1, p. 328.
21. "City Water Works Scrapbook", OHS, p. 4. Also "Records of the Proceedings of the Water Committee of Portland", vol. 1, p. 55, Portland City Hall Archives. Cited hereafter as "Water Committee".
22. "Waterworks Scrapbook", *op. cit.,* p. 18.
23. *Ibid.*
24. Clark, *Deady, op. cit.,* vol. 2, p. 551. Entry dated February 23, 1889.
25. "Waterworks Scrapbook", *loc. cit.*
26. See: Leslie M. Scott, "History of the Narrow Gauge Railroad in the Willamette Valley, *Oregon Historical Quarterly,* 20(June 1919), 141-158; also, B.B. Branson, *The Dayton & Sheridan Narrow Gauge Railroad, A True History,* Portland, 1884, OHS; also Oswald West, "Jefferson Street Public Levee and the Railroads", *OHQ,* 43(June, 1962), pp. 135-138.
27. See W. Turrentine Jackson, *The Enterprising Scot,* (Edinburgh, 1968), p. 32.
28. West, "Public Levee", *op. cit.,* p. 136.
29. See *Sixth Annual Report of the OR&N Co.,* Boston, 1885.
30. *Fortune,* 16(November, 1937), p. 98.
31. H.W. Scott, *op. cit.,* pp. 135-136.
32. *West Shore,* 14(December, 1888), p. 651.
33. West, "Public Levee", *op. cit.,* pp. 137-138.

CHAPTER V.

1. *Oregonian,* April 21, 1887.
2. See *West Shore,* 14(May, 1888), 236.
3. Published in June, 1888. For an account of the Portland Stock Exchange, see Marian V. Sears, "Jonathan Bourne, Jr., Capital Market and the Portland Stock Exchange . . . 1887", *Oregon Historical Quarterly,* 69(September, 1968), 197.
.4. *West Shore,* 15(March, 1889), 153.
5. *Ibid.,*
6. Background information on Markle and his family was gained through personal communication (letter and phone) between the author and the late Alvan Markle, Jr. of Hazelton and Henry Wilkins Rustin of N.Y.C., nephews of GBM, Jr.
7. For an interesting account of the construction and opening of the hotel, see Carl Gohs, "There Stood the Portland Hotel", *Sunday Oregonian, Northwest Magazine,* May 25, 1975.
8. "As it Looks from Here", *Oregonian Magazine Section,* September 12, 1948, p. 2.
9. For documentation of Markle's private financial affairs relating to real estate and mortgage loans, see: *Abstract of Title, Property of F.F. and B.C. Pittock,* Block 115, Grover's Addition, Multnomah County, 1926, in the possession of the current owner of the former Markle home, Robert Autrey.
10. Ross, *op. cit.,* p. 62.
11. H.W. Scott, *op. cit.,* pp. 434-435.
12. Clark, *Deady, op. cit.,* vol. 2, p. 614.
13. *Oregon Journal,* December 17, 1933.
14. H.W. Scott, *op. cit.,* p. 630.
15. Information on DeLashmutt's life was discovered in a variety of sources: newspapers, *City Directories,* the Simeon G. Reed Papers. See also his obituary, *Oregonian,* October 6, 1921.
16. *Oregonian,* October 6, 1921.
17. Letter of February 1, 1893. "Correspondence to Simeon Reed", vol. 31, S.G.R.
18. See Scrapbook #50, p. 122, OHS; *Oregonian,* February 23, 1914.
19. Documentation for these activities is to be found in "Council", *op. cit.;* also "Council Papers", filed by year, under "Franchises", Portland City Hall Archives.
20. Interview with C.F. Swigert's son Ernest G. Swigert, Nov. 25, 1975.
21. S.G.R., "Correspondence . . . Reed", *op. cit.,* vol. 35, Dec. 15, 1892.
22. *19th Annual Report* of the Portland Chamber of Commerce, 1893, p. 17.
23. *Pacific Banker & Investor,* 1(March 1893), 7.
24. H.W. Rustin to author, Dec. 21, 1975.
25. "Abstract of Title . . . Pittock", *loc. cit.,*
26. S.G.R., "Correspondence . . . Reed", *op. cit.,* vol. 35.
27. *Oregonian,* July 28, 1893.
28. October 12, 1910. See Scrapbook #54, OHS, p. 45.
29. *Oregonian,* January 1, 1895.
30. Clark, *Deady, op. cit.,* vol. 1, p. 17.
31. As told to the author by Max's son, Harold Hirsch. Also, Mrs. H.L. Corbett to author.
32. *Pacific Banker & Investor,* 1(August, 1893), 43.
33. S.G.R., "Correspondence . . . Reed", *op. cit.,* vol. 35.
34. "Abstract of Title . . . Pittock", *loc. cit.,*
35. *Pacific Banker & Investor,* 1(September, 1893), 54.
36. For a thorough survey of the effect of the panic on the banks, see Burrell, *op. cit.,* chapter entitled "Trouble in July", pp. 129-167.
37. Rustin to author, Dec. 21, 1975.
38. *Portland Evening Telegram,* Dec. 9, 1893.
39. Gaston, *op. cit.,* vol. 1, p. 610.
40. *Oregonian,* January 3, 1932, Sect. 1, p. 21.
41. Henry L. Pittock to George T. Myers, Letter of October 17, 1893, OHS.
42. *Oregonian,* December 23, 1893.
43. *Arlington Club and The Men Who Built It,* (Portland, 1967), p. 81.
44. *Pacific Banker & Investor,* 1(November, 1893), 54.
45. *Oregonian,* September 4, 1898.
46. Clark, *Deady, op. cit.,* vol. 2, p. 555.
47. H. Reed, "Railroads", *op. cit.,* ch. 17, p. 2.
48. *Oregonian,* May 15, 1902.

CHAPTER VI.

1. *Daily Journal of Commerce,* November 9, 1926.
2. William J. Hawkins III, "Befriending Your Cast Iron District", *Old Portland Today,* Spring 1975.
3. See Eugene E. Snyder, *Skidmore's Portland: His Fountain and its Sculptor,* (Portland, 1973).
4. *Oregon Business Directory and State Gazetteer, 1873,* copy in the Harry Lane Papers, OHS.
5. *Ibid.*
6. *West Shore,* 14(December, 1888), p. 651.
7. "Eastside History", *Sunday Oregonian,* July 9, 1893.
8. "Real Estate Appraisals, A transcription of Lectures and Discussions Given at the Real Estate Classes of the General Education Division, Oregon State System of Higher Education, in cooperation with the Portland Realty Board", (Portland, 1939), p. 144. From the Chester A. Moores Papers (presently in the possession of Mrs. Wayne Rogers, Portland).
9. "Eastside History", *loc. cit.,*
10. Portland City Hall Archives.
11. "Eastside History", *loc. cit.,*
12. Albina Pioneer Society, Papers, "Minutes of the Annual Meeting", March 16, 1934, OHS.
13. April 2, 1887. For additional background and information, see *Oregonian,* January 9, 1961, sect. 2, p. 6; January 10, p. 7; *Oregon Journal,* February 4, 1939, p. 4.
14. March 6, 1888.
15. *Ibid.*
16. H.W. Scott, *op. cit.,* pp. 428-29.
17. As quoted in the *Oregonian,* January 10, 1961, p. 7.
18. See article by Oz Hopkins, *Oregon Journal,* February 6, 1975.
19. Moores Papers, "Real Estate Appraisals", *op. cit.,* p. 206.
20. *Portland City Club Bulletins,* "The Negro in Portland", vol. 26, no. 12, July 20, 1945; "The Negro in Portland: A Progress Report 1945-1957", vol. 37, no. 36, April 19, 1957; "Problems of Racial Justice in Portland", vol. 49, no. 2, June 14, 1968.
21. *Oregonian,* March 10, 1903.
22. *Laws and Ordinances of the City of Portland (1892),* pp. 851-852.
23. *Ibid.,* pp. 815-854.
24. *Oregonian,* March 28, 1896.
25. Information on Bates was derived from news files, official records, interviews, *The Portrait and Biographical Record, Portland and Vicinity,* (Portland, 1903), pp. 172-73, OHS. The information in these sources is not entirely accurate.
26. Anonymous source #1, to the author, April 3, 1975.
27. *Portrait and Biographical Record, op. cit.,* p. 170.
28. "Council", *op. cit.,* vol. 12, July 23, 1891.
29. Percy Maddux, *City on the Willamette,* (Portland, 1952), p. 132.
30. Julian Hawthorne, *The Story of Oregon,* (New York, 1892), vol. 2, p. 266.
31. See the Earl Riley Papers, OHS, article on the history of city finances, undated.
32. *Ibid.*
33. *Oregonian,* January 1, 1891.
34. See "Police Board", *op. cit.,* pp. 78, 89.
35. *Laws and Ordinances . . . 1892, op. cit.,* pp. 78, 89.
36. *Oregon Journal,* October 11, 1925, p. 4.
37. Marion D. Ross, "Portland's Architectural History", *Old Portland Today,* January 1, 1975.

CHAPTER VII.

1. "Council", *op. cit.,* vol. 12.
2. Henry Reed, "Know Your City and State", from an undated 1927 issue of the *Oregonian* contained in the "Moores Papers", *op. cit.,*
3. Charles E. Sawyer, "Concerning Portland's Bridges", *Portland Chamber of Commerce Bulletin,* (December 12, 1912), p. 306. (No vol. #).
4. Alice Wheeler Grove, "Morrison Tie First to Span Willamette", *Oregonian,* October 27, 1963.
5. Sawyer, *loc. cit.,*

6. H. Reed Papers, "Historical Notes", *op. cit.,*

7. "Insurance Man Celebrates Fortieth Year With Firm", *Oregonian,* October 20, 1929.

8. Sawyer, *loc. cit.,*

9. "Council", vol. 12, November 11, 1891.

10. *Ordinances . . . Portland, 1892, op. cit.,* pp. 541-544.

11. *Oregonian,* April 7, 1926.

12. The Oregon Bank, *It Seems Like Yesterday,* (Portland, 1962), OHS. No page number.

13. For background information on Lotan, see articles also relating to his crony, W.F. (Jack) Matthews: S.B. #53, p. 75; #55, p. 125; #261, pp. 141-142, OHS. Also *Oregon Journal,* May 28, 1909, and various *City Directories.*

14. *Oregonian,* December 3, 1893.

15. *Ibid.,* December 24, 1893.

16. *Oregonian,* March 3, 1896.

17. *Oregon Journal,* May 28, 1909.

18. Pacific Bridge Co. Papers, "Journals", (several volumes in varying condition, not well identified), OHS.

19. "Council", *op. cit.,* vol. 12; see especially ordinances passed 8/6/91; 11/21/91; 9/25/91; also "Ordinances, City of Portland", vol. 10, City Hall Archives.

20. "Council", *op. cit.,* vol. 15, March 1, 1893.

21. See O.B. Coldwell, "Early Days of Electricity in Portland", *Oregon Historical Quarterly,* 42(December, 1941), pp. 279-294; also R.R. Robley, *Portland Electric Power Company with its Predecessor Companies,* 1860-1935, (Portland, 1935), OHS.

22. *Arlington Club, op. cit.,* p. 70.

23. Novick, *op. cit.,* p. 37.

24. H.W.S., *op. cit.,* January 26 1899.

25. *Ibid.,* "Proposal for Installation of a Municipal Lighting Plant", submitted by W. Stuart Smith, February 14, 1899.

26. See *Sunday Oregonian,* January 4, 1959; *Sunday Journal,* January 11, 1959; *Portland Magazine,* (November, 1975), p. 21. Also, *The Blue Flame,* 16(January, 1959), pp. 1-8.

27. "Portland Gas & Coke Co., History", no date of issue; provided the author by the N.W. Natural Gas Co.

28. "Origin, Growth and Development of the Northwest Natural Gas Co.", November 13, 1972; statement issued by the Company.

29. Mimeographed account of Leonard and Green, dated October 3, 1955, provided the author by the company.

30. *Ibid.*

31. Abbot L. Mills Papers, Portland Gas Co., Folder #3, Special Collections Library, University of Oregon.

32. Alex Groner, *American Business & Industry,* (New York, 1972), p. 201.

33. *Ibid.,* p. 180.

34. As told to the author by Charles F. Adams, Jr., January 27, 1976.

35. Mills Papers, *op. cit.* Impression gained from a thorough examination of the whole collection.

36. "Stock Registration for the Security Savings & Trust Co.", in the custody of the First National Bank of Oregon, main branch vault.

37. *Oregonian,* June 19, 20, 1906.

38. *Ibid.,* June 20, 1906.

39. *Ibid.,* June 24, 1906.

40. Letter of William A. White to C.F. Adams, March 13, 1908, Mills Papers, *op. cit.*

41. For accounts of the flood, see, "The Flood of 1894 or Venice of the Northwest", *Old Portland Today,* 3(March 1, 1975); *Oregon Journal,* March 29, 1972, sec. 2, p. 1.

42. "Flood of 1894 . . . ", *op. cit.,* p. 4.

43. Michael P. Jones, "The History of Third and Burnside is the History of the North nd," *Metropolis,* January, 1975, p. 6.

44. *Albina Weekly Courier,* June 9, 1894.

45. "Flood of 1894. . . . ", *loc. cit.,*

46. *Albina Weekly Courier,* June 9, 1891.

47. *Ibid.*

48. *Oregonian,* January 3, 1932, sec. 1, p. 21.

49. *Arlington Club, op. cit.,* p. 80.

50. *Ibid.,* p. 1.

51. *Ibid.,* p. iv.

52. Lewis Mumford, *Interpretations and Forecasts, 1922-1972,* (New York, 1973), p. 83.

53. Portland Blue Book, 1890, (San Francisco, 1890), p. 31.

54. Wilbur, *op. cit.,* p. 85.

55. D.J., *op. cit.,* vol. 1888-1889, p. 131. Also, Clark, *Deady, op. cit.,* vol. 2, p. 531.

56.Taped interview with Mrs. Henry L. Corbett, 1967, on file at the Oregon Historical Society Library.

57. *Ibid.*

58. *Ibid.*

59. Editorial by Harvey W. Scott in the *Oregonian,* January 1, 1891.

CHAPTER VIII.

1. From *The Crusade Against Vice,* (New York, 1902). As quoted in *Bartlett's Familiar Quotations,* (Boston, 1968), p. 891a.

2. *Oregonian,* March 16, 1896.

3. Peter Lyon, *Success Story, The Life and Times of S.S. McClure,* (New York, 1963), p. 215.

4. *Ibid.,* p. 221.

5. Lincoln Steffens, *The Shame of the Cities,* new edition, (New York, 1969), pp. 4-5.

6. *New York Times,* February 17, 1976, pp. 45, 47.

7. *Oregon Journal,* July 15, 1910.

8. *Ibid.,* July 19, 1910, Sect. 5, p. 1.

9. According to Jonathan Bourne, as related to Cornelia Marvin Pierce, recorded in her diary, *Capitol Journal,* September 29, 1955, p. 4. Cited hereafter as C.M.P. Material taken from chapter 3, p. 3., of manuscript in preparation, entitled "The Memoirs of Walter Pierce", OHS.

10. *Ibid.*

11. Oswald West, "Them Were the Days", undated clipping, "Memoirs . . . Pierce", *op. cit.,* p. 3.

12. *Oregon Journal,* June 10, 1910, Sect. 5, p. 1.

13. C.M.P., *op. cit.,* p. 5.

14. Dolph Papers, Scrapbook #5, *op. cit.*

15. *Oregonian,* April 24, 1902.

16. Charles H. Carey, "New Responsibilities of Citizenship", *Proceedings of the Oregon State Bar, 1908-1909, 1909-1910,* (Portland, 1910), pp. 19, 21, 22.

17. *Ibid.,* p. 29.

18. Steffens, *op. cit.,* pp. 8-9.

19. Carey, "Responsibilities . . . ", *op. cit.,* pp. 36-37.

20. S.B. #253, OHS.

21. *Oregon Journal,* June 19, 1910.

22. Author's notes, taken from a conversation with Charles Evans Hughes in July, 1947, covering the period of his life up to 1910.

23. "Council . . . ," *op. cit.,* vol. 12, p. 375.

24. Letter of December 8, 1891, William Lair Hill Papers, OHS.

25. George H. Williams, "Speech in support of Charles F. Beebe for Mayor", Special Collections Library, University of Oregon, Eugene. No exact date. During May, 1896.

26. According to Mrs. Henry L. Corbett, whose husband was persuaded by Matthews to enter politics.

27. See obituary accounts following Matthews' death on July 14, 1915. Scrapbook #53, p. 75; #55, p. 125; #26, p. 141-2, OHS.

28. "Committee Report . . . To The Ministerial Association of Portland", no date, Mss. 1286, OHS Library. No page numbers.

29. *Ibid.*

30. *Ibid.*

31. Terence O'Donnell and Thomas Vaughan, *Portland, a Historical Sketch and Guide,* (Portland, 1976), p. 20.

32. As qutoed in Bartlett's, *op. cit.,* p. 454b.

33. *Oregonian,* January 1, 1891.

34. See series of articles by Stewart Holbrook in *Sunday Oregonian,* "Portland's Greatest Moral Crusade", August 2, 1936—September 9, 1936. Quotation, August 2, 1936.

35. *Oregonian,* August 2, 1936.

36. *Oregonian,* April 10, 1895.
37. As reported later in the *Oregonian,* March 15, 1896.
38. *Ibid.,* March 8, 1896.
39. *Ibid.*
40. *Ibid.,* April 5, 1896.
41. *Ibid.,* March 12, 1896.
42. For a detailed account, see Clark, *Deady, op. cit.,* vol. 1, pp. 151-52.
43. Burton J. Hendrick, "Initiative and Referendum and How Oregon Got Them", *McClure's Magazine,* 37(July, 1911), p. 243.
44. *Ibid.*
45. D.J., vol. 1872, p. 174.
46. For a detailed account, see Clark, *Deady, op. cit.,* vol. 1, pp. 154-155.
47. As contained in Dolph Scrapbook, #5, *op. cit.,*
48. S.G.R., "Letters to . . . ," *op. cit.,* vol. 33.
49. Hendrick, "Initiative . . . ", *op. cit.,* p. 244.
50. Bourne Papers, *op. cit.,*
51. West to Dorothy Johansen, October 30, 1952, West Papers, *op. cit.,*
52. C.M.P., "Memoirs . . . Pierce", *op. cit.,* p. 5.
53. *Oregonian,* November 27, 1896.
54. "Memoirs . . . Pierce", *op. cit.,* p. 6.
55. H. Reed, "Railroads", *op. cit.,* ch. 19, p. 28.
56. *Oregon Journal,* June 19, 1910.
57. Printed in a Portland paper, no masthead or date, S.B. #274, p. 52, OHS.
58. Letter to the Editor of the *Oregonian,* March 20, 1898.
59. See West Papers, *op. cit.,* "History of the Republican Party Split, 1895-97".
60. Letter from Henry Corbett, dated October 6, 1898, found by the author to be filed mistakenly in the H. Reed Papers, OHS.
61. Bourne, *op. cit.,* March 11, 1897.
62. *Ibid.,* August 17, 1897.
63. *Ibid.,* August 30, 1897.
64. *Ibid.,* December 9, 1897.
65. *Ibid.,* October 13, 1897.
66. *Ibid.,* December 23, 1897.
67. *Ibid.,* May 7, 1898.
68. *Ibid.,* May 20, 1898.
69. *Oregonian,* May 15, 1898.
70. *Ibid.*
71. *Oregonian,* July 21, 1898.
72. "Council", *op. cit.,* vol. 18, p. 32.
73. *Oregonian,* July 9, 1898.
74. *Biennial Report of the Secretary of State of the State of Oregon, 1899-1900,* (Salem, 1900), p. 37.
75. As quoted in Fred Lockley, *History of the Columbia River Valley,* (Chicago, 1928), vol. 1, p. 677.
76. Account of Henry Wemme's life in Henry Hanzen Papers, pp. 7-9, OHS.
77. Lockley, *op. cit.,* p. 678.
78. *Oregonian,* August 9, 1886.
79. Secretary of State, *Biennial Report . . . 1899-1900, op. cit.,* p. 40.

CHAPTER IX.

1. R.S. Baker, "The Great Northwest", *Century Magazine,* 65(March, 1903), pp. 658-59.
2. *Ibid.,* p. 659.
3. Laurence Pratt, *I Remember Portland, 1899-1915,* (Portland, 1965), p. 9.
4. Ross, "Architecture in Oregon", *op. cit.,* p. 63.
5. Ray L. Stout, "Over the Bush and Through the Trees: Surveying, 1900-1909", *Oregon Historical Quarterly,* 73(December, 1972), p. 333.
6. Baker, *op. cit.,* p. 659.
7. Newspaper account, January 17, 1902, from S.B. #48, p. 86, OHS.
8. Newspaper account, 1902, S.B. #48, p. 111, OHS.
9. See *Portland Chamber of Commerce Bulletin,* 5(August, 1906), p. 10.
10. City of Portland, *Mayor's Message and Annual Report, 1901.*
11. H. Reed Papers, *op. cit.,* "Statistical Notes".

12. Frank O'Hara, "Unemployment in Oregon", *Report to the Oregon Committee on Seasonal Unemployment*, (Salem, 1914).

13. Burton J. Hendrick, " 'Statement No. 1', How the Oregon Democracy, Working under the Direct Primary, has destroyed the political machine", *McClure's Magazine*, 37(September, 1911), p. 506.

14. Newspaper article, unidentified, May 20, 1902, S.B. #48, p. 5, OHS

15. *Oregon Journal*, December 27, 1907.

16. *Biennial Report of the Secretary of State of the State of Oregon, 1901-1902)*, (Salem, 1903), p. lxxvi.

17. *Ibid.*, p. xxviii.

18. *Ibid.*, p. xliv.

19. *Ibid.*, p. xlv.

20. As reported in the *Oregonian*, November 10, 1901. from the Mills Scrapbooks, Mills Papers, *op. cit.*,

21. Gwladys Bowen, "Socially Speaking," *The Sunday Oregonian*, February 23, 1936, p. 8.

22. *Ibid.*

23. As reported in the *Oregonian*, October 14, 1903, S.B. #259, OHS.

24. Scrapbook of Roderick MacLeay, in the possession of Mrs. Richard Phillippi.

25. *Ibid.*

26. Pratt, *op. cit.*, p. 28.

27. Stewart Holbrook, "The Life of Fred T. Merrill", *Oregonian*, March 22, 1936, Magazine Section, p. 6.

28. *Ibid.*

29. *Ibid.*

30. "S.B." #261, p. 104, OHS.

31. "Police Board", *op. cit.*, vol. 2, pp. 185, 186, October 30, 1899.

32. "S.B." #261, p. 104, OHS.

33. "Memoirs . . . Pierce", *op. cit.*, ch. 4, p. 4.

34. *Ibid.*

35. Unidentified newspaper account, June 16, 1902, from S.B. #48, p. 27, OHS.

36. Unidentified newspaper account, June 12, 1902, from S.B. #48, p. 29, OHS.

37. *Oregonian*, December 12, 1894.

38. Information gathered from "Minutes of the Board of Public Works", vol. 1, pp. 364, 381, 418, City Hall Archives. Cited hereafter as "Public Works".

39. "Water Committee", *op. cit.*, vol. 2, pp. 114-115.

40. *Oregonian*, October 10, 1901.

41. "Water Committee", *op. cit.*, vol. 2, p. 116.

42. Undated article, S.B. #48, p. 24, OHS.

43. See "Public Works", 2 vols., *op. cit.*, .

44. *The Daily Times*, December 9, 1900, as contained in Mss. 1513", Miscellaneous Politics", OHS.

45. "Public Works", *op. cit.*, vol. 1, p. 733.

46. Letter dated September 4, 1901, found by the author, buried in the miscellaneous "Council Papers" for the year 1901, City Hall Archives.

47. *Ibid.*

48. See *Oregonian*, February 19, 20, 23, 1901.

49. *Oregon Journal*, June 19, 1910.

50. Brownell's account is supported by Governor T.T. Geer, in his *Fifty Years in Oregon*, (Portland, 1916), ch. 61.

51. Bourne Papers, *op. cit.*, letter to B.F. Mulkey, February 26, 1901. Also letter to T.A. Johnson, March 20, 1901.

52. *Evening Telegram*, February 22, 1902, S.B. #275, p.? OHS.

53. Bourne Papers, *op. cit.*, letter to T.A. Johnson, March 20, 1901.

54. See *Charter of the City of Portland, 1902*, City Hall Archives.

55. For a detailed account of the campaign, see William S. U'Ren, "The Initiative and Referendum in Oregon", *Arena*, 29(March, 1903), pp. 270-75.

56. *Oregonian*, editorial, April 22, 1902.

57. *New Age* editorial, May 10, 1902.

58. *Ibid.*, May 17, 1902.

59. "Memoirs . . . Pierce", *op. cit.*, ch. 4, p. 6.

60. For a general account of Williams' life, see: Sidney Teiser, *Almost Chief Justice:*

George H. Williams, (Portland, 1947); reprinted from *OHQ*, September, December, 1946.

61. Letter, May 4, 1870, "Letters to Deady", *op. cit.*, OHS.
62. *Ibid.*, letter, May 8, 1870.
63. "Council", *op. cit.*, vol. 20, p. 503.
64. *Ibid.*
65. "Police Board", *op. cit.*, vol. 2, p. 353.
66. See *Revised General Ordinances, City of Portland*, (1905), pp. 85-108.
67. *Ibid.*, pp. 66-77.
68. *Ibid.*, pp. 109-32.
69. Pacific Bridge Co. Papers, *op. cit.*, "Journal of the Pacific Bridge Co., 1901-1909", Box 1, "Records of the City & Suburban Railway Co".
70. See *Journal of the Senate of the Legislative Assembly of the State of Oregon, 1903 Session*, p. 30. Cited hereafter as *Senate Journal*.
71. See *Journal of the House of the Legislative Assembly of the State of Oregon, 1903 Session*, p. 154. Cited hereafter as *House Journal*.
72. *Ibid.*, p. 232.
73. *Senate Journal, op. cit.*, p. 275.
74. *Oregonian*, November 28, 1902, S.B. #38, p. 202, OHS.
75. *New Age*, February 2, 1903.
76. Letter of August 27, 1903, quoted in Scheck, "Eliot", *op. cit.*, p. 329.
77. "Miscellaneous Associations", Mss. 1551, OHS.
78. S.B. #275, OHS.
79. Pratt, *op. cit.*, p. 24.

CHAPTER X

1. Among many works, see: Virgil Smith, "Lewis, Clark Exposition . . .", *Oregonian*, June 2, 1975, p. A12; Wallace Kay Huntington, "Parks and Gardens of Western Oregon", in Thomas Vaughan and Virginia Guest Ferriday, *Space, Style and Structure, Building in Northwest America*, (Portland, 1974). vol. 2, especially pages 410-12; Gaston, op. cit., vol. 1, pp. 583-88.
2. Lewis Mumford, *The City in History*, (New York, 1961), p. 425.
3. George H. Williams, *Occasional Addresses*, (Portland, 1895), p. 146.
4. *Ibid.*, p. 147.
5. Gaston, *op. cit.*, vol. 1, p. 584.
6. Mills Papers, *op. cit.*, contain several folders of material and official records relating to the financial management.
7. Gaston, *op. cit.*, vol. 1, p. 611.
8. Appendix to the *Report of the Park Board, 1903*, City of Portland, (Portland, 1904), pp. 52-53, OHS.
9. Mel Scott, *American City Planning Since 1890*, (Berkeley, 1969), p. 45.
10. *Report . . . Park Board, 1903, op. cit.*, p. 6.
11. *Oregonian*, June 5, 1904.
12. Wilbur, *op. cit.*, p. 87.
13. *Sunday Oregonian*, July 10, 1904.
14. Mumford, *op. cit.*, pp. 425-26.
15. Mills Papers, "City & Suburban" Folder, *op. cit.*,
16. Letter, August 10, 1903, Mills to William A. White, Mills Papers, "Outgoing Correspondence", *Ibid.*
17. Letter, June 12, 1904, *ibid.*
18. Letter, May 17, 1904, *ibid.*
19. Letter, Mills to White, July 13, 1904, *ibid.*
20. Letter to White, July 14, 1904, *ibid.*
21. See *Journal of the House, op. cit.*, 1905, p. 1383; *Journal of the Senate, op. cit.*, 1905, p. 765.
22. Pacific Bridge Papers, *op. cit.*, Box 1, 1904, 1905.
23. Most of this information was culled from the Pacific Bridge Co. Papers and the Mills Papers, "City & Suburban/Portland Consolidated Folder", *op. cit.*,
24. *Oregonian*, March 16, 1904.
25. Letter, January 18, 1904, Bourne Papers, *op. cit.*,
26. *Ibid.*, January 19, 1904.
27. *Ibid.*
28. *Oregon Journal*, March 5, 1904.
29. *Ibid.*, March 7, 1904.

30. For a detailed account of this development, see Hendrick, *op. cit.,* pp. 506-7.

31. Quoted in S.B. #275, no page or date, OHS.

32. *Oregon Journal,* May 22, 1905.

33. "Miscellaneous Associations", Mss. 1551, "Portland Municipal Association", OHS. The charges were contained in a flyer, dated May 2, 1905.

34. *Oregon Journal,* May 10, 1909; also "Council," *op. cit.,* vol. 30, May 12, 1909.

35. "Minutes of the Executive Board", vol. 1, p. 342, December 4, 1903, Portland City Hall Archives.

36. *Ibid.,* p. 380, January 8, 1904.

37. *Ibid.,* vol. 2, p. 46, February 9, 1905.

38. *Ibid.,* vol. 2, p. 48, February 17, 1905.

39. *Oregonian,* editorial, September 28, 1904.

40. "Executive Board," *op. cit.,* September 4, 1903, July 8, 1904.

41. *Ibid.,* vol. 2, p. 198, June 7, 1905.

42. Puter's personal account of the Oregon timber frauds, written while in jail, is still the most thorough and accurate work on the subject. See, S.A.D. Puter, *Looters of the Public Domain,* (Portland, 1908).

43. William D. Wheelwright, "The Business Man in Politics," *Chamber of Commerce Bulletin,* 3(March, 1905), p. 4.

44. *Ibid.*

45. Steffens, "The Taming of the West," *op. cit.,* (October, 1907), pp. 592-93.

46. *Ibid.,* (September, 1907), p. 504.

47. *New York Times,* March 30, 1976.

48. Puter, *op. cit.,* p. 21.

49. As reported by Steffens, *op. cit.,* (October, 1907), p. 590.

50. Puter, *op. cit.,* p. 356.

51. *Ibid.,* pp. 378-80.

52. See *Fortune* Magazine, 9(April, 1934). Over half of the issue was devoted to the Weyerhaeuser empire and the lumber industry generally.

53. Letter to Deady, December 11, 1877, Deady Letters, *op. cit.,* letter #M-3, OHS.

54. Letter, January 3, 1905, Bourne Papers, *op. cit.,* "Incoming File".

55. *Oregonian,* January 7, 1905.

56. Letter, January 11, 1905, Bourne Papers, *op. cit.,*

57. Letter, Keady to Bourne, February 4, 1905, *ibid.*

58. The story of C.J. Reed's experience and Heney's exploits is well recounted in Steffens' two articles in the *American Magazine* already cited. Two biographies of John Reed add some additional personal flavor: Richard O'Connor, D.L. Walker, *The Lost Revolutionary,* (New York, 1967), especially pp. 20-25; Robert A. Rosenstone, *Romantic Revolutionary,* (New York, 1975), especially chapters 1-3.

59. See O'Connor, Walker, *op. cit.,* p. 7.

60. Roderick MacLeay Scrapbook, *op. cit.*

61. Rosenstone, *op. cit.,* p. 92.

62. Letter, Keady to Bourne, March 3, 1905, Bourne Papers, *op. cit.*

63. Letter, Smith to Bourne, May 20, 1905, *ibid.*

64. *Oregon Journal,* May 25, 1905.

65. *Ibid.,* May 23, 1905.

66. *Ibid.,* May 22, 1905.

67. *Oregonian,* June 4, 1905.

68. *Ibid.,* June 5, 1905.

69. See Scott's *History of the Oregon Country, op. cit.,* vol. 5, p. 88, edited by his son, Leslie Scott after his death.

70. Letter, June 30, 1905, contained in the "Mayor's correspondence" files, stored in the basement of the Civic Auditorium.

71. "Executive Board", *op. cit.,* vol. 2, p. 202.

CHAPTER XI.

1. *Sunday Oregonian,* August 21, 1914, Magazine Section, p. 4; article by Washington D.C. writer James B. Morrow.

2. *Chamber of Commerce Bulletin,* 4(March 1906), p. 7.

3. Frederick A. Marriott, "The City of Portland", *Overland Monthly,* 45(May, 1905), pp. 432-33.

4. *Ibid.,* p. 437.
5. *Ibid.,*
6. Richard M. McCann in the *Chamber of Commerce Bulletin,* 4(March 1906), p. 8.
7. Donald Macdonald, "Portland Points the Way", *Sunset,* 17(June, 1906), p. 50.
8. *Ibid.,* p. 58.
9. *Ibid.,* p. 60.
10. *Ibid.,* p. 65.
11. According to the *Chamber of Commerce Bulletin,* 4(June, 1906), p. 8.
12. *Oregon Journal,* May 1, 1909.
13. See article by Rod Paulson, *The Community Press,* July 16, 1975.
14. See O.A. Hopkins, "Black Life in Oregon, 1899-1907: A Study of the Portland *New Age,* (Reed College, B.A. Thesis), p. 21.
15. See the Standard Insurance Co. pamphlet *Fifty Years,* (Portland, 1956), p. 15.
16. *Chamber of Commerce Bulletin,* 4(June, 1906), p. 8.
17. *Ibid.*
18. Data collected from the Chester Moores Papers, *op. cit.*
19. *Ibid.*
20. H. Reed Papers, "Statistical Data", *op. cit.,*
21. "Tapes of E.B. MacNaughton", Reel 2, recorded June 23, 1960, Reed College Library.
22. *Oregonian,* June 19, 1908.
23. Cecil Tilley Barker of the *Bulletin* staff, 4(December, 1905), p. 6.
24. "Mayor's Correspondence", *op. cit.,*
25. Included in a "Memorial Address", by Senator George E. Chamberlain, from "Memorial Addresses on the Life and Character of Harry Lane", Proceedings in the Senate, September 16, 1917, Sixty-Fifth Congress, (Washington D.C., 1920), pp. 18-20.
26. "Council", *op. cit.,* vol. 23, p. 342.
27. *Oregonian,* December 31, 1906.
28. "Executive Board", *op. cit.,* vol. 2.
29. "Council", *op. cit.,* vol. 23, p. 589.
30. See Gaston, *op. cit.,* vol. 1, p. 589.
31. Mayor's correspondence, *op. cit.,* letter of December 22, 1905.
32. See S.B. #274, p. 160, OHS.
33. Gaston, *op. cit.,* vol. 1, p. 559.
34. See "Council", *op. cit.,* vol. 23, beginning on p. 690.
35. *Ibid.*
36. *Ibid.,* vol. 23, pp. 691-94.
37. *Oregon Journal,* April 28, 1907.
38. *Ibid.,* vol. 27, p. 1 ff., October 23, 1907.
39. *Ibid.,* vol. 23, p. 692.
40. As reported later in the *Oregonian,* August 21, 1914 by Morrow, *op. cit.,* p. 4.
41. "Council", vol. 23, p. 694, *op. cit.*
42. "Memorial Addresses", *op. cit.,* p. 15.
43. Morrow in the *Oregonian,* August 21, 1914, *op. cit.,* p. 4.
44. *Oregon Journal,* January 17, 1906.
45. See Holbrook, *Oregonian,* September 9, 1936, *op. cit.,*
46. Interview with Merrill, *Oregonian,* March 22, 1936, *op. cit.,* p. 6.
47. Lane, letters to City Council, August 24, 1908, Lane Papers, *op. cit.,*
48. Mills Papers Scrapbook, *op. cit.,* telegram dated November 4, 1908.
49. "Council", *op. cit.,* vol. 24, p. 189, March 15, 1906.
50. *Oregon Journal,* January 20, 1906.
51. "Council", *op. cit.,* vol. 25, p. 125; also Lane Papers, *op. cit.,*
52. *Ibid.,* vol. 41, p. 191, December 4, 1912.
53. *Ibid.,* vol. 25, p. 127. See also Lane Papers *op. cit.*
54. *Ibid.,* October 1, 1906.
55. *Ibid.,* vol. 26, July 3, 1907.
56. *Oregonian,* July 17, 23, 1906. See also, *Oregonian,* May 26, 1905.
57. *Ibid.,* June 20, 1906.
58. *Oregon Journal,* July 20, 1906.
59. *Ibid.,* July 21, 1906.
60. *Oregonian,* June 19, 20, 24, 1906.
61. *Oregonian,* October 13, 1906.
62. "Council", vol. 25, p. 612, *op. cit.*
63. White to Mills, Letter, March 9, 1907, Mills papers, *op. cit.*

64. White to Mills, Letter, March 22, 1907, *ibid.*
65. Mills to White, Letter, April 11, 1907, *ibid.*
66. "Council", vol. 25, November 7, 1906, *op. cit.*
67. This story was told many times. An account, published in the *Oregon Journal,* May 27, 1917, was found in the Lane Papers.
68. Maddux, *op. cit.,* p. 159.
69. *Oregon Journal,* November 6, 1908.
70. *Oregonian,* March 11, 15, 1907.
71. *Ibid.,* March 24, 1907.
72. *Ibid.*
73. *Oregon Journal,* May 9, 1907.
74. "Executive Board", *op. cit.,* vol. 5, p. 150, February 17, 1909.
75. *Oregonian,* April 22, May 4, 1920.
76. *Ibid.,* April 5, 1907.
77. Morrow in the *Oregonian,* August 21, 1914, *op. cit.*
78. *Oregon Journal,* June 1, 1907.
79. *Oregonian,* June 3, 1907.
80. *Ibid.,* June 4, 1907.
81. *Ibid.* See also *Arena* Magazine, 30(August, 1907), pp. 194-95.
82. White to Mills, letter, June 4, 1907, Mills Papers, *op. cit.*
83. "Council", vol. 26, July 3, 1907, p. 364, *op. cit.*

CHAPTER XII.

1. See Annual "Franchise Reports to the City Auditor", beginning in 1913, on file in "Miscellaneous" Archives, Portland City Hall.
2. See *1st Annual Report of the Railroad Commission of Oregon to the Governor,* (Salem, 1908).
3. *Arena, op. cit.,* pp. 194-95.
4. See Burrell, *op. cit.,* p. 227.
5. Mills Papers, 1907 Scrapbook, *op. cit.*
6. *Oregon Journal,* August 21, 1907; also Mills Papers, 1907 Scrapbook, *op. cit.,*
7. *Ibid.*
8. Gaston, *op. cit.,* vol. 1, p. 516.
9. White to Mills, Letter, November 11, 1907, Mills Papers, *op. cit.*
10. *Oregon Journal,* November 10, 1907.
11. Anonymous Source #1, *op. cit.*
12. Unidentified banker in *Telegram,* February 7, 1908, Mills Papers, *op. cit.*
13. *Oregon Journal,* December 26, 1907.
14. *Ibid.*
15. *Ibid.*
16. *Oregon Journal,* November 22, 1907. See also, Burrell, *op. cit.,* pp. 72-3.
17. Winch to Reed, Letter, June 8, 1893, S.G.R., *op. cit., "Letters", vol. 35.*
18. *Oregonian,* August 30, 1905; October 21, 1905.
19. *Ibid.,* October 22, 1905.
20. *Ibid.,* November 8, 1905.
21. *Ibid.,* September 23, 1906.
22. These comments were related to the author by various people who knew Ladd personally. For an eulogistic account of Ladd's life see: William L. Brewster, *William Mead Ladd,* (Portland, 1933).
23. See Ladd & Tilton Papers, "Corporate Records", vol. 1, OHS.
24. *Gaston, op. cit.,* vol. 1, pp. 527-28.
25. *Oregonian,* April 22, 1918.
26. *Ibid.*
27. Robley, *op. cit.,* p. 119.
28. "Executive Board", *op. cit.,* vol. 4, p. 668.
29. *Ibid.*
30. *Ibid.,* November 13, 1908.
31. "Council", *op. cit.,* vol. 25, p. 381, December 6, 1906.
32. *Ibid.,* vol. 29, January 9, 13, 1909.
33. *Oregonian,* April 24, 1976.
34. "Council", *op. cit.,* vol. 30, April 14, 1909.
35. *Ibid.,* pp. 379-81.

36. "Address by Col. C.E.S. Wood", *Chamber of Commerce Bulletin*, 10(February, 1909), pp. 36-39.

37. See S.B.#274, p. 168, OHS.

38. *Oregon Journal*, May 4, 1909.

39. *Ibid.*, May 1, 1909.

40. Letter, White to Mills, June 6, 1909, Mills Papers, "Gas Co. Folder", *op. cit.*

41. *Spectator*, Undated article contained in Simon Papers, *op. cit.*

42. *Oregonian*, June 8, 1909. Also see "Council", *op. cit.*, vol. 30, p. 173, April 6, 1909, the date on which the Council formally approved the measures for submission to the electorate.

43. "Council", *op. cit.*, vol. 31, October 27, 1909.

44. June 28, 1909, Simon Papers, *op. cit.*

45. Chamberlain, "Memorial Address", *op. cit.*, pp. 15-16.

CHAPTER XIII.

1. Delos F. Wilcox, *Great Cities in America, Their Problems and Their Government*, (New York, 1910, reprinted in 1974), p. 10.

2. Included in the Simon Papers, *op. cit.*

3. As quoted in Linda Jorgenson, "Portland Mayors of Days Gone By", *Old Portland Today*, May 1976, p. 6.

4. *Oregonian*, January 2, 1910.

5. *Ibid.*, June 26, 1910.

6. *Oregon Journal*, November 13, 1909.

7. *Oregonian*, January 1, 1910.

8. "Council", *op. cit.*, vol. 32, May 25, 1910.

9. *Oregonian* editorial in Simon Papers, S.B., *op. cit.*, date, May 26, 1910(?).

10. See excerpts from *Report of the Federal Commissioner of Corporations*, written by Herbert K. Smith, undated, in S.B. #50, p. 44, OHS.

11. See letter to the Editor, *Oregon Journal*, September 6, 1912, written by J.B. Ziegler, a citizen who played an active part in the promotion of the Initiative amendment.

12. *Oregon Journal*, June 14, 1910.

13. *Ibid.*, June 19, 1910.

14. *Ibid.*, June 22, 23, 1910.

15. George H. Haynes, "People's Rule", *Political Science Quarterly*, 26(September, 1911), pp. 440-41.

16. *Oregon Journal*, December 31, 1910.

17. Herbert D. Croly, "Portland, Oregon, The Transformation of the City from an Architectural and Social Viewpoint", *Architectural Record*, 31(June, 1912), pp. 591-607.

18. From H. Reed Papers, *op. cit.*, page 3 of a report compiled in 1911.

19. *Thirteenth Census of the United States, 1910, Abstract with Supplement for Oregon*, Washington D.C., 1911, p. 568-587.

20. Gaston, *op. cit.*, vol. 1, pp. 614-15.

21. *Ibid.*, p. 616.

22. Hendrick, *op. cit.*, p. 515.

23. *Ibid.*

24. *Ibid.*, p. 516.

25. *Ibid.*

26. *Ibid.*, p. 517.

27. *Ibid.*, p. 518.

28. "Council", *op. cit.*, vol. 34, p. 635, January 11, 1911.

29. Earl Riley Papers, *op. cit.*, page 6 of an undated rough manuscript prepared for a talk, possibly in 1940 during Riley's mayoralty campaign, or shortly after his election. He had been commissioner of finance.

30. Gus Tyler, "Can Anyone Run a City?", *Saturday Review*, (November 8, 1969), p. 24.

31. *Oregon Journal*, June 3, 1911, article by H.M. Esterly.

32. *Ibid.*

33. *Oregonian*, April 30, 1911.

34. *Ibid.*, May 8, 1911.

35. Haynes, *op. cit.*, p. 433.

36. "Council", *op. cit.*, vol. 36, p. 292, July 5, 1911.
37. As quoted in an article by Helen Barney, "Sporting Women", *Metropolis,* March, 1973, p. 4.
38. "Council," *op. cit.*, vol. 36, p. 612.
39. *First Report of the Vice Commission of the City of Portland,* (Portland, January 1912), p. 2, OHS. Cited hereafter as *Vice Report.*
40. *Oregon Journal,* August 20, 1912.
41. *Ibid.*
42. *Portland Daily News,* August 23, 1912.
43. *Oregon Journal,* August 23, 1912.
44. *Ibid.,* August 24, 1912.
45. *Ibid.*
46. *Oregonian,* August 24, 1912.
47. *Ibid.,* August 23, 1912.
48. *Portland Daily News,* August 24, 1912.
49. *Second Report of the Vice Commission . . . , op. cit.,* (August, 1912).
50. Holbrook, "Merrill interview", *op. cit.,* August 16, 1936.
51. *Oregon Journal,* August 26, 1912.
52. *Ibid.,* August 29, 1912.
53. *Ibid.,* September 4, 1912.
54. *Ibid.,* September 5, 1912.
55. *Ibid.,* September 1, 1912.
56. *Ibid.,* September 5, 1912.
57. *Ibid.,* September 3, 1912.
58. *Ibid.,* September 7, 1912.
59. "Council", *op. cit.,* vol. 40, October 9, 23, 1912.
60. *Portland Daily News,* November 15, 16, 18, 20, 29, 30, 1912.
61. *Oregon Journal,* December 31, 1910.
62. "Council", *op. cit.,* vol. 42, p. 2, February 20, 1913.
63. *Ibid.*
64. *Commission of Public Docks — Second Annual Report* (Portland, 1912), pp. 10-11.
65. See Barbara Word, "Can Cities be made to work?", *Ekistics,* 244(March, 1976), p. 132.
66. *Oregon Journal,* September 14, 1976.
67. See "Council", *op. cit.,* vol. 40, p. 618; *Commission of Public Docks, Third Annual Report,* (Portland, 1913), p. 7-8.
68. *Dock Commission, Second Report, op. cit.,* p. 5.
69. *Oregon Journal,* September 6, 1912.
70. *Ibid.,* August 20, 1912.
71. *The Port of Portland, Biennial Report,* 1915-1916, pp. 3-4.
72. See *Portland City Club Bulletin,* 13(August 26, 1932), for a "Report on The Port of Portland"; also Dennis Lindsay, "75 Years with the Port of Portland", *Greater Portland Commerce,* (April 1, 1966), p. 16.
73. As related to the author by C.F. Swigert's son, Ernest G. Swigert. The actual plans have been lost.
74. City Planning Commission of Portland, "The Plan-It", May, 1928.
75. William A. Bowes, speech, "Portland — A Case History of Planning", Bowes Papers, *op. cit.* No date, probably 1945.
76. For comments by Lawrence and Barbur see *The Architect & Engineer of California,* 56(March, 1919), pp. 77-101.
77. *Ibid.,* p. 77.
78. Reported in the *Oregon Journal,* August 18, 1912.
79. *The Greater Portland Plan,* ed. by Marshall N. Dana and Ellis Lawrence, (Portland, 1912), p. 34. Reprinted 1976, Portland City Planning Commission.
80. *Ibid.* The Dana edition was 46 pages in length. See also Paul Pintarich, "Portland Plan in 1912 . . . ", *Sunday Oregonian,* March 26, 1972, p. 40.
81. Quoted in the *Oregon Historical Quarterly,* 74(September, 1973), p. 212.
82. Arthur D. McVoy, "A History of City Planning in Portland", *Oregon Historical Quarterly,* 46(March, 1945), pp. 3-21.
83. *Dock Commission, Second Report, op. cit.,* p. 2.
84. Bowes Papers, "Case History . . . ", *op. cit.,* p. 2.
85. McVoy, *op. cit.,* p. 4.
86. Letter to Mills, July 5, 1912, Mills Papers, Box 3, *op. cit.*

CHAPTER XIV.

1. Quiett, *op. cit.*, p. 395.

2. *New York Times* obituary, May 16, 1976, quoted from Morison's *Oxford American History.*

3. *Organization and Business Methods of the City Government of Portland, Oregon. Report of a General Survey Made by the New York Bureau of Municipal Research,* (Portland, April 1913), p. 5. Cited hereafter as *Research Survey.*

4. W.F. Ogburn, *The Voter and The City of Portland,* Reed College Extension Course, (Portland, 1913), pp. 20-1.

5. *Oregonian,* April 20, 1913.

6. *Ibid.,* April 22, 1913.

7. *Labor Press,* April 28, 1913.

8. *Oregonian,* April 23, 24, 25, 1913.

9. *Ibid.,* May 2, 1913.

10. *Ibid.,* May 4, 1913.

11. *Ibid.,* May 7, 8, 1913.

12. *Ibid.,* May 8, 1913.

13. *Dock Commission, Third Annual Report, op. cit.,* pp. 9-10.

14. *Oregon Journal,* March 29, 1914.

15. See interview with Mische's successor, Paul Keyser, in *Metropolis,* January, 1972.

16. *Oregonian,* August 22, 1913.

17. Unidentified newspaper article dated February 17, 1914, S.B. #50, p. 54, OHS.

18. The Water Meter issue is thoroughly reported in S.B. #50, especially pp. 80-81, OHS.

19. *Oregon Journal,* March 17, 1914, as contained in S.B. #50, p. 84, OHS.

20. *Ibid.*

21. *Ibid.*

22. Maddux, *op. cit.,* pp. 160-62.

23. Barney, *op. cit.,* p. 5.

24. O'Hara, "Unemployment in Oregon", *op. cit.*

25. See unidentified newspaper article, dated March 17, 1914, S.B. #50, p. 102.

26. See the *First Annual Report of The Corporations Commissioner to the Governor of The State of Oregon,* submitted by R.A. Watson, for the year ending June 30, 1914, p. 13.

27. *Ibid.,* p. 4.

28. *Ibid.,* p. 6.

29. See the Scrapbooks of Franklin T. Griffith, S.B. #1, 1913-1917, pp. 6-7, OHS.

30. *Oregonian,* August 10, 1913.

31. *Oregon Sunday Journal,* September 28, 1913.

32. *Oregon Journal,* August 2, 1925.

CHAPTER XV.

1. Mumford, *op. cit., Oregon Journal,* July 5, 1938.

2. City Planning Commission of Portland, *The Plan-It,* June, 1927, p. 2.

3. *Oregon Journal,* December 17, 1933.

4. Chester A. Moores, Address to the National Association of Real Estate Boards, Los Angeles, October 27, 1939, Moores Papers, *op. cit.*

5. See Walter Guzzardi, Jr., "An Unscandalized View of Those 'Bribes' Abroad," *Fortune,* (July, 1976), p. 119.

6. Gaston, *op. cit.,* vol. 1, p. 637.

7. *Ibid.,* p. 640.

BIBLIOGRAPHY

Sources Cited

I. Government Documents

A. Oregon

Biennial Report of the Secretary of State of the State of Oregon, 1899-1900, 1901-1902. Salem.

First Annual Report of the Corporations Commissioner to the Governor of the State of Oregon. Salem: 1914.

First Annual Report of the Railroad Commission of Oregon to the Governor. Salem: 1908.

Journals of the House of the Legislative Assembly of the State of Oregon. Multnomah County Law Library, Portland. 1903, 1905.

Journals of the Senate of the Legislative Assembly of the State of Oregon. Multnomah County Law Library, Portland. 1903, 1905.

Report to the Oregon Committee on Seasonal Unemployment. Salem: 1914.

B. Portland

Annual Report of the Park Board of the City of Portland. Portland: 1902, 1904.

Charter of the City of Portland. Portland: 1902, 1903, 1913, City Hall Archives, Portland.

City Planning Commission of Portland, "The Plan-It," June, 1927, May, 1928.

Commission of Public Docks — Second Annual Report, Portland, 1912; *Third Annual Report,* Portland, 1913.

"Council Papers," filed by year in the City Hall Archives, Portland.

"Franchise Reports to the City Auditor," 1913-1915, "Miscellaneous" Archives, Portland.

Laws and Ordinances of the City of Portland. Portland: 1892.

"Mayor's Correspondence," filed by year, stored in the basement of the Civic Auditorium, under the supervision of the City Archivist.

Mayor's Message and Annual Report, 1885-1915, City Hall Archives, Portland.

"Minutes of the Board of Police Commissioners," 1885-1903, City Hall Archives, Portland.

"Minutes of the Board of Public Works," 1901-1903, City Hall Archives, Portland.

"Minutes of the Executive Board," 1903-1913, City Hall Archives, Portland.

"Minutes of the Proceedings of the City Council," 1851-1915, City Hall Archives, Portland. Filed by volume according to year.

"Ordinances, City of Portland," City Hall Archives, Portland.

Organization and Business Methods of the City Government of Portland, Oregon. Report of a General Survey Made by the New York Bureau of Municipal Research. Portland: April, 1913.

"Records of the Proceedings of the Water Committee of Portland," City Hall Archives, Portland.

Report of the Vice Commission of the City of Portland. Portland: 1912. Oregon Historical Society Library, Portland. First Report published January, 1912. Second Report published August, 1912.

Revised General Ordinances, City of Portland, 1905.

The Port of Portland, Biennial Report, 1915-1916. Portland: 1917.

C. U.S. Government

Thirteenth Census of the United States, 1910, Abstract with Supplement for Oregon. Washington D.C.: U.S. Government Printing Office, 1911.

II. Private Documents

"Abstract of Title," Lots 2 and 3 Block 11, Tilton's Addition, Title Guarantee & Trust Co., Portland, 1926. The Colburn Barrell property.

"Abstract of Title, Property of F.F. and B.C. Pittock," Block 115, Grover's Addition, Multnomah County, 1926. The Markle property and home.

Portland Chamber of Commerce: *Annual Reports.* Portland: Portland Public Library. (Portland Board of Trade, 1870-91).

Proceedings of the Oregon State Bar, 1908-1909, 1909-1910. Portland: 1910.

"Stock Registration for the Security Savings & Trust Co.," (1890). In custody of the First National Bank of Oregon, main branch vault.

III. Manuscripts

Albina Pioneer Society: Papers, Mss. 273, Oregon Historical Society Library, Portland.

Benson, Frank W.: Papers, Mss. 534, Oregon Historical Society Library, Portland.

Bourne, Jonathan, Jr.:Papers, A x 19, Special Collections Library, University of Oregon, Eugene.

Bowes, William A: Papers, Mss. 1372, Oregon Historical Society Library, Portland.

Branson, B.B.: *The Dayton & Sheridan Narrow Gauge Railroad, A True History.* Portland: 1884. Mss. 1506, "Railroads," Oregon Historical Society Library. Portland.

Bush, Asahel: Papers, Mss. 581, Oregon Historical Society Library, Portland.

Corbett, Henry W.: Papers, Mss. 1110, Oregon Historical Society Library, Portland.

Corbett Investment Co., The: Papers, Mss. 1021, Oregon Historical Society Library, Portland.

Couch-Glisan: Papers, Mss. 952, Oregon Historical Society Library, Portland.

Couch-Glisan: Paper, Mss. 952, Oregon Historical Society Library, Portland.

Deady, Matthew P.: "Journal," Mss. 48B, Oregon Historical Society Library, Portland. The volumes, not all numbered, are rough transcripts of the original, compiled by Malcolm Clark, Jr., They are grouped by periods of years.

Deady, Matthew P.: Letters, Mss. 48, Oregon Historical Society Library, Portland.

Dekum, Frank: Papers, Mss. 535, Oregon Historical Society Library, Portland.

Dolph, Joseph N.: Papers, Scrapbooks, CB-D698, Special Collections Library, University of Oregon, Eugene.

Failing, Henry:Papers, Mss. 650,Oregon Historical Society Library, Portland.

Griffith, F.T.: Scrapbooks, Mss. 1687SB, Oregon Historical Society Library, Portland.

Hanzen, Henry: Papers, Mss. 1019, Oregon Historical Library, Portland.

Hill, W. Lair: Papers, Mss. 1112, Oregon Historical Society Library, Portland.

Ladd & Tilton: Papers, "Corporate Records," Mss. 579, 580, Oregon Historical Society Library, Portland.

Ladd, W.S.: Papers, Mss. 579, 580, Oregon Historical Society Library, Portland.

Lane, Harry: Papers, Mss. 536, Oregon Historical Society Library, Portland.

Lewis, C.H.: Papers, Mss. 787, Oregon Historical Society Library, Portland.

Mead, Stephen: Papers, Mss. 1765, Oregon Historical Society Library, Portland.

Mills, Abbot L.: Papers, Ax191, Special Collections Library, University of Oregon, Eugene. Complete files on the Portland Consolidated Railway Co., Portland Gas Co., and the Lewis and Clark Centennial Exposition Association.

Ministerial Association of Portland: "Committee Report on Gambling Houses, Saloons," circa 1891-3, Mss. 1286 (Portland Miscellaneous File), Oregon Historical Society Library, Portland.

"Miscellaneous Associations," Mss. 1551, Oregon Historical Society Library, Portland.

"Miscellaneous Politics," Mss. 1513, Oregon Historical Society Library, Portland.

Moores, Chester A.: Papers. In the possession of Mrs. Wàyne Rogers, Portland. To be deposited with the Oregon Historical Society in 1976-77.

Oregon Railway & Navigation Co.: *Sixth Annual Report*. Boston: 1885. Mss. 1506, "Railroads," Oregon Historical Society Library, Portland.

Pacific Bridge Co.: Papers, Mss. 1769, Oregon Historical Society Library, Portland. Includes several volumes in varying condition, not well identified. Records of the City & Suburban Railway Co. and Pacific Bridge Co. are intermingled.

Pierce, Walter: "Memoirs," ed. by W. P. Bone, Mss. in preparation, Oregon Historical Society Library, Portland.

Pittock, Henry L. to George T. Myers, Letter of October 17, 1893, Mss. 1500, Oregon Historical Society Library, Portland.

Reed, Henry E.: Papers, Mss. 383, Oregon Historical Society Library, Portland.

Reed, Simeon G.: Papers, Reed College Library, Portland: "Correspondence to Reed," Vol. 31, 35.

Riley, Earl: Papers, Mss. 1123, Oregon Historical Society Library, Portland.

Simon, Joseph: Papers, Mss. 1513, 1513B, Oregon Historical Society Library, Portland.

Swigert, C.F.: Papers, Mss. 1761, Oregon Historical Society Library, Portland.

West, Oswald: Papers, Mss. 589, Oregon Historical Society Library, Portland.: "History of the Republican Party Split."

Williams, G.H.: "Speech in Support of Charles F. Beebe for Mayor," Mss. CA 1896, Special Collections Library, University of Oregon, Eugene.

IV. Scrapbooks

Oregon Historical Society Library — newspaper clippings: Nos. 26, 38, 48, 50, 53, 54, 55, 122, 253, 257, 259, 261, 274, 275.

"City Water Works Scrapbook, 1887-95."

V. Interviews

A. In Person

Ernest G. Swigert, November 25, 1975.
Mrs. Henry L. Corbett, March 29, 1975.
E. C. Sammons, April 3, 1975.
Robert Livingstone, March 28, 1975.
William L. Brewster, July 21, 1975.
Abbot L. Mills, Jr., August 1975.
Dorothy Johansen, January 26, 1976.

B. By Phone

C. F. Adams, Jr., January 27, 1976.
Henry W. Rustin, November 1975.
Alvan Markle, October 18, 1975.

VI. Correspondence to Author

Alvan Markle, Jr., September 2, 1975.
Henry W. Rustin, December 21, 1975.

VII. Autobiographies, Diaries, Memoirs, Personal Recollections

Clark, Malcolm, Jr., ed.: *Pharisee Among Philistines, The Diary of Judge Matthew P. Deady, 1871-1892,* 2 vols, Portland: Oregon Historical Society, 1975.

Corbett, Gretchen H.: Taped Interview (1967), Oregon Historical Society Library, Portland.

Geer, T.T.: *Fifty Years in Oregon.* Portland: 1916.

MacLeay, Roderick: Scrapbook, in the possession of Mrs. Richard Phillippi, Portland.

MacNaughton, E.B.: Tapes. Reel 2, recorded June 23, 1960. Reed College Library, Portland. MacNaughton recorded six tapes of his life's history, during the spring and summer of 1960.

Pratt, Lawrence: *I Remember Portland, 1899-1915.* Portland: 1965.

Puter, Stephen A.D.: *Looters of the Public Domain.* Portland: 1908.

Stout, Ray L.: "Over the Bush and Through the Trees: Surveying, 1900-1909," *Oregon Historical Quarterly,* 73 (December, 1972).

Villard, Henry: *Early Transportation in Oregon,* ed. by Oswald Garrison Villard. Monographic Studies in History, # 1. Eugene: University of Oregon, 1944.

West, Oswald: "Jefferson Street Public Levee and the Railroads," *Oregon Historical Quarterly,* 43 (June, 1962).

Wise, Stephen: *Challenging Years.* New York: G.P. Putnam's Sons, 1949.

VIII. Miscellaneous Contemporary Works:

Dana, Marshall and Lawrence, Ellis: *The Greater Portland Plan.* Portland: 1912. Reprinted by the Portland City Planning Commission, 1976.

Dunne, Finley Peter: *The Crusade Against Vice.* New York: 1902. Quotation in *Bartlett's Familiar Quotations,* Boston: Little, Brown & Co., 1968.

Gaston, Joseph: *Portland, Its History and Builders,* 3 vols. Portland: 1911.

Hawthorne, Julian: *The Story of Oregon,* 2 vols. New York: 1892.

Hines, H.K.: *An Illustrated History of the State of Oregon.* Chicago: 1893.

History of the Bench & Bar. Portland: Historical Publishing Co., 1910.

"Memorial Addresses on the Life and Character of Harry Lane," *Proceedings in the Senate,* September 16, 1917, Sixty-fifth Congress, Washington, D.C., 1920. Edited by George E. Chamberlain.

Ogburn, W.F.: *The Voter and the City of Portland.* Reed College Extension Course. Portland: 1913. Portland Public Library.

Oregon Business Directory and State Gazetteer, 1873. Portland: 1873, Lane Papers, Oregon Historical Society Library.

Portland Block Book, 2 vols. Portland: Portland Block Book Publishing Co., 1907.

Portland Blue Book, 1890. San Francisco: 1890; Portland, R.L. Polk & Co., 1895-1915.

Portland City Directories. Portland: R.L. Polk & Co., 1885-1915.

Portrait and Biographical Record, Portland and Vicinity. Portland: 1903.

Sanborn Block Maps, Oregon Historical Society Library, Portland.

Scott, Harvey W.: *History of Portland.* Portland: Mason Co., 1890.

Steffens, Lincoln, *The Shame of the Cities.* New Edition. New York: Hill & Wang, 1969.

Wilcox, Delos F.: *Great Cities in America, Their Problems and Their Government.* New York: 1910; reprinted by the Arno Press, 1974.

Williams, George H.: *Occasional Addresses.* Portland: 1895.

IX. Newspapers

Albina Weekly Courier.

American Banker, 1910.

Community Press.

Daily Journal of Commerce, Portland.

Daily News, Portland.

Labor Press, Portland.

Metropolis, Portland State University Urban Studies Program.

New Age, Portland (Albina)

New York Times.

Old Portland Today.

Oregon Journal, Portland, 1902-present.

Oregonian, Portland, 1871-present.

Portland Evening Telegram.

X. Contemporary Articles

Baker, R.S.: "The Great Northwest," *Century Magazine,* 65 (March, 1903).

Croly, Herbert D.: "Portland, Oregon, the Transformation of the City from an Architectural and Social Viewpoint," *Architectural Record,* 31(June, 1912).

Deady, Matthew P.: "Portland-on-Wallamet," *Overland Monthly,* 1 (July 1868).

"Eastside History," *Sunday Oregonian,* July 9, 1893.

Carey, Charles H.: "New Responsibilities of Citizenship," *Proceedings of the Oregon State Bar, 1908-1909, 1909-1910.*

Gilbert, J.H.: "The Development of Banking in Oregon," *University of Oregon Bulletin,* 9 (September, 1911).

Haynes, George H.: "People's Rule," *Political Science Quarterly,* 26 (September, 1911).

Hendrick, Burton J.: "Initiative and Referendum and How Oregon Got Them," *McClure's Magazine,* 37 (July, 1911).

Hendrick, Burton J.: "Statement No. 1, How the Oregon Democracy, Working Under the Direct Primary, has destroyed the political machine," *McClure's Magazine,* 37 (September, 1911).

MacDonald, Donald: "Portland Points the Way," *Sunset,* 17 (June, 1906).

Marriott, Frederick A.: "The City of Portland," *Overland Monthly,* 45 (May, 1905).

Merry, Thomas B.: "Portland, the Beautiful Metropolis of the Pacific Northwest," *The Northwest,* 3 (November, 1885).

Roberts, Edward: "The Western Portland," *Harper's Weekly Supplement, 33* (April 6, 1889).

Sawyer, Charles: "Concerning Portland's Bridges," *Portland Chamber of Commerce Bulletin,* (December 12, 1912). (No vol. #.)

Smith, Herbert K.: Excerpts from *Report of the Federal Commission of Corporations,* (undated), S.B. # 50, p. 44, Oregon Historical Society Library, Portland.

Steffens, Lincoln: "The Taming of the West," *American Magazine,* 64 (September, October, 1907).

U'Ren, W.S.: "The Initiative and Referendum in Oregon," *Arena,* 29 (March, 1903).

Wheelwright, Wiliam D.: "The Business Man in Politics," *Portland Chamber of Commerce Bulletin,* 3 (March, 1905).

Wood, C.E.S.: "Address," *Portland Chamber of Commerce Bulletin,* 10 (February, 1909).

XI. Contemporary Periodicals

The Architect & Engineer of California, 56 (March, 1919), pp. 77-101.

Northwest, The. Vol. 3, November, 1885.

Pacific Banker and Investor, Vols. 1, 2.

Portland Chamber of Commerce Bulletin, Vols. 4-12, Portland Public Library.

Spectator.

West Shore, The, Vols. 10-17. Oregon Historical Society Library, Portland. Author owns Vols. 14, 15.

XII. Secondary Works

Arlington Club and the Men Who Built It. Portland: 1967.

Burrell, O.K.: *Gold in the Woodpile — An Informal History of Banking in Oregon.* Eugene: University of Oregon Books, 1967.

Carey, Charles H.: *A General History of Oregon,* 2 Vols. Portland: Metropolitan Press, 1935.

Corning, Howard M., ed.: *Dictionary of Oregon History.* Portland: Binfords & Mort, 1956.

Groner, Alex: *American Business & Industry.* New York: American Heritage Publishing Co., 1972.

Gruen, Victor: *Centers for the Urban Environment.* New York: Van Nostrand Reinhold Co., 1973.

Lockley, Fred: *History of the Columbia River Valley,* 3 vols. Chicago: S.J. Clark Publishing Co., 1928.

Lyon, Peter: *Success Story, The Life and Times of S.S. McClure.* New York: Charles Scribner's Sons, 1963.

Maddux, Percy: *City on the Willamette.* Portland: Binfords & Mort, 1952.

Mumford, Lewis: *The City in History.* New York: Harcourt Brace & World, 1961.

Mumford, Lewis: *Interpretations and Forecasts, 1922-1972.* New York: Harcourt Brace Jovanovich, 1973.

O'Connor, R. and Walker, D.L.: *The Lost Revolutionary: A Biography of John Reed.* New York: Harcourt Brace—World, 1967.

O'Donnell, Terrence and Vaughan, Thomas: *Portland, a Historical Sketch and Guide.* Portland: Oregon Historical Society, 1976.

Oregon Bank, The: *It Seems Like Yesterday.* Portland: 1962. Oregon Historical Society Library, Portland.

Polhemus, James H.: *Oregon — Its Resources, Its People, and Its Future!* New York: Newcomen Society, 1951.

Quiett, Glenn Chesney: *They Built the West, An Epic of Rails and Cities.* New York: Apleton-Century, 1934.

Reps, John W.: *The Making of Urban America: A History of City Planning in the United States.* Princeton: Princeton University Press, 1965.

Robley, R.R.: *Portland Electric Power Co. with its Predecessor Companies, 1860-1935.* Portland: 1935, Oregon Historical Society Library, Portland.

Rosenstone, Robert A.: *Romantic Revolutionary, A Biography of John Reed,* Ch. 2. New York: Knopf, 1975.

Scheck, John F.: "Transplanting a Tradition: Thomas Lamb Eliot and the Unitarian Conscience in the Pacific Northwest, 1865-1905." Eugene: University of Oregon, Department of History, unpublished dissertation, 1969.

Scott, Leslie M.: *History of the Oregon Country,* 5 vols. Cambridge: Riverside Press, 1924.

Scott, Mel: *American City Planning Since 1890.* Berkeley: University of California Press, 1969.

Standard Insurance Co.: *Fifty Years.* Portland: 1956.

Whitesmith, Benjamin M.: "Henry Villard and the Development of Oregon." Eugene: University of Oregon, unpublished M.A. thesis, 1931.

Wilbur, Earl M.: *Thomas Lamb Eliot.* Portland: 1937.

XIII. Secondary Periodicals

Blue Flame, The; (Northwest Natural Gas Co.).

Ekistics, 39 (March, 1975).

Fortune Magazine, 1931-present.

Greater Portland Commerce

Portland City Club Bulletin. 1918-present.

Portland Magazine, (Portland Chamber of Commerce).

XIV. Secondary Articles

Barney, Helen: "Sporting Women," *Metropolis,* March, 1973.

Cochran, John S.: "Economic Importance of Early Transcontinental Railroads: Pacific Northwest," *Oregon Historical Quarterly,* 71 (March, 1970).

Gohs, Carl: "There Stood the Portland Hotel," *Sunday Oregonian, Northwest Magazine,* May 25, 1975.

Grove, Alice Wheeler: "Morrison Tie First to Span Willamette," *Oregonian,* October 27, 1963.

Hawkins, William J.: "Befriending Your Cast Iron District," *Old Portland Today,* Spring, 1975.

Holbrook, Stewart: "The Life of Fred T. Merrill," *Oregonian,* March 22, 1936.

Holbrook, Stewart: "Portland's Greatest Moral Crusade," a series of weekly articles running from August 2, 1936—September 9, 1936 in the *Sunday Oregonian.*

Johansen, Dorothy and Gill, F.B.: "A Chapter in the History of the Oregon Steam Navigation Co.," *Oregon Historical Quarterly,* 38 (March, 1937).

Jones, Michael P.: "The History of Third and Burnside is the History of the North End," *Metropolis,* January, 1975.

Jorgenson, Linda: "Portland Mayors of Days Gone By," *Old Portland Today,* May 6, 1976.

Lindsay, Dennis: "75 Years with the Port of Portland." Greater Portland Commerce, (April 1, 1966).

McVoy, Arthur D.: " A History of City Planning in Portland," *Oregon Historical Quarterly,* 46 (March, 1945).

Northwest Natural Gas Co.: "Portland Gas & Coke Co., History". (No date of issue): "Oregon, Growth and Development of the Northwest Natural Gas Co.," November 13, 1972.

Novick, Sheldon: "The Electric Power Industry," *Environment,* 17 (December, 1975).

Paulson, Rod: Various articles on Portland neighborhood history in the *Community Press,* 1976.

Pintarich, Paul: "Portland Plan in 1912 . . . ," *Sunday Oregonian,* March 26, 1972.

Portland City Club Bulletin: "Report on the Port of Portland," Vol.13, August 26, 1932. "The Negro in Portland," Vol. 26, No. 12, July 20, 1945. "The Negro in Portland: A Progress Report, 1945-1957," Vol. 37, No. 36, April 19, 1957. "Problems of Racial Justice in Portland," Vol. 49, No. 2, June 14, 1968.

Ross, Marion D.: "Architecture in Oregon," *Oregon Historical Quarterly,* 57 (1956).

Ross, Marion D.: "Portland's Architectural History," *Old Portland Today,* January 1, 1975.

Scott, Leslie M.: "History of the Narrow Gauge Railroad in the Willamette Valley," *Oregon Historical Quarterly,* 20 (June, 1919).

Sears, Marian V.: "Jonathan Bourne, Jr., Capital Market and the Portland Stock Exchange . . . 1887," *Oregon Historical Quarterly,* 69 (September, 1968).

Smith, Virgil: "Lewis, Clark Exposition . . . " *Oregonian,* June 2, 1975.

"The Flood of 1894 or Venice of the Northwest," *Old Portland Today,* 3 (March 1, 1975).

Tyler, Gus: "Can Anyone Run a City?" *Saturday Review,* (November 8, 1969).

Ward, Barbara: "Can Cities be Made to Work?", *Ekistics,* 244 (March, 1976).

XV. Useful Background Material Not Cited

Athearn, Robert G.: *Union Pacific Country.* New York: Rand McNally, 1971.

Barker, B.B.: "Early History of the First National Bank of Portland, Oregon," 1941. Oregon Historical Society Library.

Brewster, William L.: *William Mead Ladd.* Portland: 1933.

Coldwell, O.B.: "Early Days of Electricity in Portland," *Oregon Historical Quarterly,* 42 (December, 1941).

Bowen, Gwladys: "Socially Speaking," *Sunday Oregonian,* February 23, 1936. 1936.

Gutowsky, Albert R.: "History of Commercial Banking in Oregon," *Oregon Business Review,* 24 (August 1965).

Hedges, James B.: *Henry Villard and the Railways of the Northwest.* New Haven: Yale University Press, 1930.

Hinton, George: "Portland, the Optimistic, the Vigorous and Thriving City on the Pacific Coast," *Harper's Weekly,* 57 (May, 1913).

Hopkins, O.A.: "Black Life in Oregon, 1899-1907: A Study of the *Portland New Age.*" Unpublished B.A. thesis, Reed College, Portland, 1974; Oregon Historical Society Library, Portland.

Jackson, W. Turrentine: *The Enterprising Scot.* Edinburgh: University of Edinburgh Press, 1968.

Ladd & Tilton Bank: *Sixty Milestones of Progress, 1859-1919.* Portland, 1920.

"Life of Owen D. Young," *Fortune Magazine,* 3(January, 1931).

Lodge, George Cabot: *The New American Ideology.* New York: Knopf, 1975.

Lucia, Ellis: *The Saga of Ben Holladay, Giant of the Old West.* New York: Hastings House, 1959.

McFarland, C.L.: *The United States National Bank.* Portland: Binfords & Mort, 1940.

May, W.W.R., ed.: *Riley Frank Branch, Ambassador of the Pacific Northwest.* Portland: Kilham Stationery Co., 1956.

Miller, William, ed.: *Men in Business.* Cambridge: Harvard University Press, 1952.

Mills, Randall V.: "Early Electric Interurbans in Oregon," *Oregon Historical Quarterly,* 44 (March, December 1943).

Muir, Jean: "The Elegant Eighties," *Oregon Journal Sunday Magazine,* April 14, 1940.

Pike, Albert H. Jr.: "Jonathan Bourne, Jr., Progressive." Eugene: University of Oregon, Department of History, unpublished dissertation, 1957.

Prisco, Salvatore: "John Barrett and Oregon Commercial Expansion, 1889-1898," *Oregon Historical Quarterly,* 71 (June, 1970).

Roth, Frederick W.: "A Biographical Sketch of Joseph North Dolph," University of Oregon thesis, Series No. 13.

Snyder, Eugene E.: *Skidmore's Portland: His Fountain and its Sculptor.* Portland: Binford & Mort, 1973.

Staehli, Alfred: *Preservation Options for Portland Neighborhoods,* A Report on the History of Portland's Neighborhoods and Their Historic Centers, prepared for the 1974 City Options Program of The National Endowment for the Arts, in association with *The Portland Neighborhood History Project.* Portland: 1975.

Teiser, Sidney: *Almost Chief Justice: George H. Williams.* Portland: Oregon Historical Society, 1947. Reprinted from *OHQ,* September, December, 1946.

Throckmorton, Arthur L.: "The Role of the Merchant on the Oregon Frontier: The Early Business Career of Henry W. Corbett, 1851-1869," *Journal of Economic History,* 16 (1956), pp. 539-550.

Vaughan, Thomas and Ferriday, Virginia Guest: *Space, Style and Structure, Building in Northwest American,* 2 vols. Portland: Oregon Historical Society, 1974.

Wyllie, Irvin G.: *The Self-Made Man in America.* New York: Free Press, 1954.

INDEX

529

Meier & Frank Co., 51, 101

Merchants National Bank, 94, 99, 319, 358

"Merger Movement, The," 161, 164

Merrill, Fred T., 234-6, 253, 327-8, 405

Metropolitan Railway Co., 93-4, 96, 353

Metropolitan Savings Bank, 82, 91

Miller, H.B., 72

Mills, Abbot Low, character and early life, see chapter VII; 163, 165-8, 180, 230, 232. 242-7. 250-1, 254-5, 257. 266. 274-80, 286, 296, 299, 310, 320-2, 328-9, 334, 337-9, 347, 354-5, 367-8, 371, 375, 377, 395-6, 399, 401, 431

Ministerial Association of Portland, 1893 vice probe, 195-7

Minto, John, 198, 200, 212

Mische, E.T., 449-50

Mitchell, John H. (Sen.), character, 201-4; 3, 34, 40, 58, 61-3, 72, 101, 137, 144, 155, 186, 189-90, 194, 198, 200, 207-12, 215, 227, 242, 245-7, 250, 265, 280-1, 288, 294-6, 298-9, 322

Mitchell, Sidney Z., 164, 328-9

Monnastes, H.C., 97

Montague, Richard W., 316-18, 438

Montgomery, James B., 69, 127, 130, 140

Moody, Zenas (Gov.), 63

Moore, W.H., 354

Moores, Chester A., 137, 477

Moreland, J.C. (Judge), 123, 195

Morey, P.F., 158-9

Morgan, J.P., 158, 164, 175, 355

Morgan's Shooting Club, 232

Morris, W.C., 354

Morrison, Samuel Eliot, 438

Morrison Street Bridge, (1887), 80, 95, 119, 137, 145, 150-1, 153, 155-6, 200; (1904-5), 156, 275, 283 286-7

Mount Tabor District, 121, 368, 382

Mount Tabor Street Railway Co., 93, 153, 368, 400

Muir, William T., 144. 278

Muller v. Oregon (1908), 464

Multnomah Athletic Club, 176

Multnomah Street Railway Co., 82, 93, 96

Mumford, Lewis, 8-9, 175, 262, 269, 272, 476

Myers, George T., 105

New Age, The (Portland), 250, 257, 311

New England heritage, 5, 392

New York Bureau of Municipal Research Report (1913), 438-41

North American Co., 46, 158

North End District (N.W. Portland), 4, 62, 209, 213, 327-8, 345, 403-4

North Pacific Industrial Association, 81

North Pacific Lumber Co., 195, 243, 309, 327

Northern Pacific R.R., 18, 44-6, 51, 105, 164, 188, 190, 244-5, 250, 291-2, 310, 329-30, 472

Northern Pacific Terminal Co. (NPT), 11, 31, 46-7, 58, 60, 130, 151, 329, 331-2, 349, 420

Northwest Construction Co., 343

Northwest Natural Gas Co., 162

Northwest Steel Co., 343

Northwestern Loan & Trust Co., 82, 101-4

Oaks Park, 270

O'Brien, J.P., 349

Old Colony Trust Co. (Boston), 159

Olmsted, John, 137, 266, 268-9, 271-2, 321

Olmsted Plan (1904), 270-1

Oregon Banking Act (1907), 352-3, 364

Oregon & California R.R. Co. (O&C), 39-40, 43-4, 46, 70, 75, 118, 349, 387

Oregon Central R.R. of Portland (West side line), 39-40, 42, 46, 74, 330

Oregon Central R.R. of Salem (East side line), 39-40

Oregon Electric Railway Co., 168, 310, 328

Oregon Historical Society, 191, 265, 291, 321, 452

Oregon Improvement Co., 31

Oregon Iron & Steel Co., 23-4, 71, 359, 361, 363

Oregon Journal (Portland), 229, 242, 251, 256, 282-3, 301, 327, 336-7, 345, 357, 361, 374-5, 378, 383, 385-9, 400, 403-4, 408, 438, 469-70, 472, 476

Oregon Labor Commission (1906 report), 311-12

Oregon Land & Development Co., 139

Oregon Legislature, composition of (1907), 351

Oregon Lumber Co., 91

Oregon Mortgage Co., 54

Oregon National Bank, 81-2, 97, 101-3

Oregon Paving & Contracting Co., 52, 68

Oregon Railway Co., 69

Oregon Railway & Navigation Co. (OR&N), became Oregon, Washington

530

531

534